T0114585

TRANSFORMATIONAL GROWTH
AND THE BUSINESS CYCLE

This book examines the concept of Transformational Growth from a number of different historical and geographical perspectives. Transformational Growth sees the economy as an evolving system in which the market selects and finances innovations, changing the character of costs and affecting the pattern of market adjustment. This creates the possibility that markets will work differently in particular historical periods.

This book explores market adjustments in two distinct historical periods, 1870–1914 and 1945 to the present. The book focuses on six countries: the United States, the United Kingdom, Canada, Germany, Japan and Argentina. In all cases the earlier period, dominated by craft-based technologies, proves to be the one in which markets adjust through a weakly stabilizing price mechanism. By contrast, in the later period, in all cases, with the exception of Argentina, there is no evidence of such a price mechanism. In its place can be seen a multiplier–accelerator process which, arguably, reflects a change of technology to mass-production.

Edward J. Nell is the Malcolm B. Smith Professor of Economics at the New School for Social Research, New York. He is the author of *Making Sense of a Changing Economy* (Routledge, 1996).

STUDIES IN TRANSFORMATIONAL GROWTH
Edited by Edward J. Nell
Malcolm B. Smith Professor of Economics, New School for
Social Research

The fundamental insight of transformational growth is that the working of the market, in any given era, presents economic difficulties which set in motion competitively driven forces bringing about innovations designed to solve those problems. But these innovations change the character of costs and the flexibility of factor supplies, and this, in turn, if on a sufficient scale, will change the way the market system adjusts. Such changes will require adaptation by institutions – firms, households and governments – and this will react back on markets. The effect will be to bring about a new pattern in the normal working of the market, which, in turn, can be expected to present new difficulties, leading to innovations, and so, eventually, to yet another new pattern of market adjustment.

Two points follow: first, the fundamental role of markets is not bringing about the best allocation of scarce resources among competing ends – this may or may not be important. What is essential is understanding that markets drive innovation, and mobilize the resources to finance and spread investment in innovation. Second, since markets may adjust differently in different historical periods, the economic principles by which we describe and analyze the working of markets will also be different.

The Series will present a succession of studies in the application of the transformational growth framework to issues in economics and political economy, including policy questions and social problems related to economics. Most of the books will consist of closely related essays, written by a study group, although some single author monographs will be included. These essays will be primarily empirical, drawing implications for policy questions and for current debates in the literature.

TRANSFORMATIONAL GROWTH AND THE BUSINESS CYCLE

Edited by Edward J. Nell

Routledge
Taylor & Francis Group

LONDON AND NEW YORK

First published 1998
by Routledge
4 Park Square, Milton Park, Abingdon, Oxon OX14 4RN

Simultaneously published in the USA and Canada
by Routledge
605 Third Avenue, New York, NY 10017

First issued in paperback 2013

*Routledge is an imprint of the Taylor & Francis Group,
an informa business*

© 1998 Edward J. Nell

Typeset in Garamond by J&L Composition Ltd, Filey, North Yorkshire

British Library Cataloguing in Publication Data
A catalogue record for this book is available from the British Library

Library of Congress Cataloging-in-Publication Data
A catalogue record for this book has been requested

Publisher's Note
The publisher has gone to great lengths to ensure the quality of this
reprint but points out that some imperfections in the original
may be apparent

ISBN 13: 978-0-415-14855-9 (hbk)
ISBN 13: 978-0-415-86244-8 (pbk)

CONTENTS

CONTENTS

ILLUSTRATIONS

TABLES

TABLES

LIST OF CONTRIBUTORS

George Argyrous is a Senior Lecturer at the University of New South Wales. He works in the areas of evolutionary economic theory, industrial development and technological change, urban political economy, and the history and philosophy of economics, and has published in the Cambridge Journal of Economics, Journal of Economic Issues, Economics and Philosophy and History of Political Economy.

Thorsten H. Block is a Research Fellow at the Center for Economic Policy Analysis at the New School for Social Research. He received his M.A. in economics and business administration from the University of Bremen, Germany, and is currently a Ph. D candidate in the economics department at the New School. He has previously worked as a consultant for the United Nations Development Programme and the World Bank.

Enrique Delamonica has studied and taught economics at the University of Buenos Aires, the Institute for Social and Economic Development, also in Buenos Aires, and the New School for Social Research. His current research interest is in the areas of macroeconomics, technological change and industrial policy. He is currently working for the United Nations Children's Fund (UNICEF) on the financing of poverty reduction and social development policies.

David Kucera is the Assistant Director of the Center for Economic Policy Analysis in New York City, a research institute affiliated with the Graduate Faculty Economics Department at the New School for Social Research. He recently completed his Ph. D thesis in economics about differences in labor adjustment between Japan and the former West Germany. He has taught labor economics at St. Francis College in Brooklyn and is currently doing research on the relationship between globalization and social policy in Japan and Germany.

Raymond C. Majewski received his Ph. D in economics from the New School for Social Research. His dissertation was entitled 'The Elasticities to Effective Demand and the Institutions of Exchange'. His work and previous publications are in the areas of economic history, history of economic thought, and economic methodology. He has taught economics at Seton Hall University, Monmouth University and Middlesex County College, all in New Jersey.

Edward J. Nell is the Malcolm B. Smith Professor of Economics at the New School for Social Research. He has taught at Wesleyan University and the University of East Anglia and has been a Visiting Professor at the Universities of Bremen, Paris, Rome and Siena. He is the author of *Prosperity and Public Spending, Transformational Growth and Effective Demand* and the forthcoming *General Theory of Tranformational Growth*.

Helge Peukert has studied economics, philosophy, sociology and social psychology in Frankfurt, Germany, where he received a Ph. D in sociology as well as in economics. He recently finished his habilitation on the action paradigm in economic thought and is currently professor of economics in Riga, Latvia.

Thomas F. Phillips received his Ph. D in economics from the New School for Social Research, and is currently teaching economics at Trent University and Sir Sandford Fleming College in Peterborough, Ontario, Canada.

Stephanie R. Thomas is a Ph. D candidate in the economics department at the New School for Social Research. She is also a research assistant at the New School's Center for Economic Policy Analysis and teaches at CUNY. Her dissertation is an empirical investigation of the stagnationist tendencies present in the postwar United States economy.

PREFACE

This book is an empirical exploration of the idea of transformational growth. The full theory is developed elsewhere; here the focus is on a case for which enough data exists to permit careful comparisons and analyses of time series, supplemented by institutional studies. The advanced capitalist world experienced a long stretch of peaceful development in the half century prior to World War I; it experienced another following World War II. In each case the working of the system can be examined in conditions that are relatively free of the distortions introduced by wars and social upheavals. The hypothesis to be explored is that the economy adjusted in significantly different ways in the two periods – and we shall see that this is a viewpoint that has important implications both for theory and policy.

The case studies contrast the two periods for the US, the UK, Canada, Germany and Japan, with Argentina added as an example of incomplete transformational growth. In each study, however, the opportunity is taken to use the material to illuminate one or another significant economic issue or controversy.

The plan of the book developed during discussions arising out of George Argyrous's New School doctoral thesis exploring the shift from Craft to Mass Production, with special reference to the aircraft industry. I had previously formulated models of the characteristic patterns of market adjustment in the two types of economy. It seemed appropriate to develop a project exploring the stylized facts of the two cases and contrasting them empirically.

At first George was to be co-editor. Unfortunately he had to return to Australia, while the project grew far beyond its original dimension. Nevertheless, he remained an important inspiration and continued to contribute to the discussion that shaped the project.

These discussions were of exceptional importance. The group developed an ethos of its own, which gradually formed itself into a method of research: beginning from a hypothesis, or sometimes merely suggestion, derived from theory, the process would lead to working with the empirical materials – institutions and history as well as time series – after which the group would re-think the theory, refining and adapting it, then in the light of the newly revised history, returning once more to the data, and so on, allowing each to illuminate the other. The method was interactive. Theory and empirical studies each thought about developments in the other.

The interaction also extended to the group. Members found themselves able to speak easily and offer ideas freely, knowing that their words would be understood sympathetically and that criticism, however severe, would always be constructive. The empirical studies benefited from this interaction.

Some special words of thanks are due. First to George, for helping formulate the project in the first place, then to Stephanie Thomas and especially Thorsten Block for handling the many details of preparing the manuscript. Thorsten was also responsible for assembling the Bibliography. Levent Kokkessen generously provided econometric assistance, and I would also like to thank those New School students who at various times took part in our study group. We are grateful to the anonymous readers for Routledge, who provided exceptionally detailed comments. Thanks to Steve Pressman and the *Review of Political Economy* for the interview, a revised version of which appears in Chapter 12.

Finally, I owe thanks, as always, to Marsha Nell for her help and encouragement.

Part I

THE IDEA OF TRANSFORMATIONAL GROWTH

1

FROM CRAFT TO MASS PRODUCTION

The changing character of market adjustment

Edward J. Nell

Macroeconomics makes an occasional bow to history and institutions, noting their importance in understanding policy, particularly in connection with exogenous "shocks." But the models advanced in most mainstream work, as well as those in contemporary "alternative" schools of thought, tend to be perfectly general. They are not considered specific to any one historical period. Economic behavior and the working of markets are treated as universal, essentially the same, aside from "imperfections," in all times and places. Economics is grounded in rational choice, expressed most fully in general equilibrium price theory. Macroeconomics can then be derived from this by specifying any of a large number of imperfections or institutional barriers to the smooth adjustment of markets.

THEORIES AND ERAS

General equilibrium theory is abstract and non-empirical. But price theory does not have to take this form.[1] Ordinary textbook microeconomics – supply and demand – offers a strikingly detailed picture of the way markets work, from which a number of plausible empirical propositions can be derived. For example, this picture suggests that, when demand fluctuates, prices will fluctuate in the same direction, and the fluctuations will be greater the more inelastic the supply is. Movements in prices will therefore be positively correlated with movements in output. Real wages will be inversely related to employment and output. Increases in productivity will lead to lower prices. The picture has institutional implications as well: firms will grow to an optimal size and operate at that level indefinitely.

These empirical implications of ordinary price theory are seldom

3

stressed, perhaps because they do not appear to be true of today's economy. Instead, price theory tends to be developed axiomatically, and is presented as an offshoot of a more general theory of rational choice. But this is to do microeconomics a disservice. It was originally formulated as a theory of the working of markets, and it deserves to be taken seriously as just that.

Old-fashioned macroeconomics, as presented in the textbooks of the 1950s, like the simplest models today, took prices as fixed, and examined quantity adjustments. These reflected the multiplier and the accelerator, or "capital stock adjustment" principle, and provided an account of market adjustment, which could be and was examined empirically in extensive studies.[2] These models also yielded policy implications.

Macroeconomic data suggest a great difference between the working of the economy in the era in which price theory was founded and its behavior later. In the late nineteenth century, when price theory developed, production was organized largely through family firms and family farms, and steam power was used to operate processes that still reflected traditional crafts. In the Keynesian era, production came to be organized by giant modern corporations running modern technologies on electric power and internal combustion (Tylecote, 1991; Perez, 1983, 1985; Solomou, 1986). The technologies are different and so are the institutions. As a result, it will be argued, so is the way the market works.

In the earlier period the market appeared to function in some respects, as would be expected from neoclassical theory, at least in Marshallian form. In the later period aspects of its working appear to be Keynesian, and the neoclassical elements have largely disappeared. In the earlier period there is some evidence to suggest that the market and the price mechanism responded in a stabilizing manner. Financial markets and the monetary system, however, tended to be unstable. The turning points of the business cycle appear to have been endogenous. In the later period, however, the stabilizing aspects of market adjustment appear to have vanished. Indeed, market responses appear to have exacerbated fluctuations, as would be expected from Keynesian theory and from early Keynesian accounts of the business cycle. The government, however, perhaps in conjunction with the financial system, has tended to provide a stabilizing influence.

An explanation for the differences between the eras can be suggested, which is supported by the record, namely that the prevalent technology in the earlier period prevented easy adjustment of output and employment. This, in effect, imposed a form of price flexibility, which can be shown to have had a moderately stabilizing influence. But technological innovation greatly increased the adaptability of production processes, so that by the later period, output and employment could be adjusted easily, and the resulting system can be shown to have been unstable in a Keynesian sense.

TWO SYSTEMS OF TECHNOLOGY
AND GROWTH

Dynamic processes depend in part on the flexibility of production, which in turn rests on the kind of technology in use. And technology, in turn, developed as a result of learning induced by the characteristic problems encountered in operating the initial production system. An idealized contrast of early and later capitalism can be sketched: early capitalism consisted largely of family firms and family farms operating production technologies that depended on the presence and cooperation of skilled workers, working together. Such an economy tended to run at full capacity, unless seriously disrupted by business failures; product markets tended to clear through price adjustments. Employment remained fixed in the face of fluctuations in sales (short of the bankruptcy level); when output varied it was through changes in the productivity of labor. But this system created strong incentives to change the methods of production, in particular to increase the size of operations and to establish greater control over current costs, especially labor. Towards the end of the nineteenth century the methods of mass production were widely introduced, as we shall see, partly in response to pressures created by problems in the working of the earlier technology. Besides lowering costs the new methods provided a desired degree of flexibility; but their successful adoption depended on the simultaneous emergence of adequate finance and a mass market, since these new methods required large outlays of capital. The change to the new methods can be called "Transformational Growth," for, once adopted, these innovations in technology changed the way the system worked, replacing price with multiplier adjustments and full utilization with normal excess capacity.

FIXED EMPLOYMENT TECHNOLOGY
COMPARED WITH MASS PRODUCTION

The change from craft technology to scientific mass production has largely been examined from the perspective of total cost reduction (Maddison 1982). This is certainly a major factor, but the attention paid to it has perhaps led to the neglect of other dimensions. Indeed, economists have paid little attention to the actual characteristics of production technology. Output is normally considered to be a "function" of various "combinations" of the basic "factors": land, labor and capital. The variations in the qualities

5

and features of these are not considered, and neither is it explained exactly how they are "combined." The often-cited "laws of returns" do not fit coherently together (Sraffa 1926). Everything is discussed at the highest imaginable level of abstraction and, in fact, the real object of the argument is to explain the distribution of income between rents, wages and profits on the basis of marginal productivity. The analysis of costs and their relation to prices is derivative. By contrast, the input–output approach tells us something about the technical relationships, since the various inputs for each unit output are clearly set forth, but there is still no consideration of how, exactly, these inputs are combined, or what varies with what.

Yet this is just what has to be considered if we are to explore the dimensions of flexibility. Craft production has often been praised for its greater flexibility, compared with mass production, because craftsmen could often adapt product design to the customer's specifications, but this is only one aspect of flexibility, and not the most important when the survival of the firm is in question. So let us turn to an aspect of technology that has largely been overlooked, namely the extent to which the process of production permits inputs or costs (and even output itself) to be varied so as to adapt to fluctuations in the state of demand.

Fluctuations in demand, of course, are endemic both in early and in developed capitalism. They are to be distinguished from permanent changes in demand, although it often may be difficult to tell which is which. Fluctuations may be quite temporary and local, temporary and global, long-term and local or global. There are seasonal fluctuations and variations reflecting local or temporary conditions, on the one hand, and those of the general business cycle on the other. They may be foreseen, or unforeseen; if foreseen, only the direction or their direction and magnitude may be correctly anticipated. But, even if they are fully and correctly anticipated, the realization may have dawned too late for anything to be done about it; or the duration of the fluctuation may be too short to be worthwhile adapting to. This does not depend only on the ability to anticipate the market; it also depends on the technology and organization of production, for it is production which has to be adapted.

Examples will help to indicate some of the ways in which businesses may try to adapt to variations in demand. If there is no refrigeration or method of storage, the whole current supply of fish and vegetables must be offered for sale, otherwise it will spoil. If demand has fallen, supply on the market cannot be reduced, so price will be forced down. Sometimes output cannot be varied; spring planting (and the weather) determines the harvest. If demand has dropped in the meantime, output cannot be changed, although grain can be stored, so supply could be changed, but at a cost. In a traditional blacksmith's shop the forge must be lit, and the apprentices must be on hand, whether much or little work is to be done.

Energy and labor costs will be the same for quite a wide range of levels of daily output. Lighting the forge or, in steam-driven factories, building up a head of steam, is time-consuming and labor-intensive. Thus, faced with fluctuations in demand, the methods of production may or may not permit the supply offered to the market, the output produced, employment and energy costs to be varied *pari passu*. To the extent that all or any of these cannot be varied, excess or shortage of supply will exert pressure on prices. But employment is the key; if it cannot be varied then the largest part of current costs will be fixed, and output can be made variable only by changing productivity.

More precisely, if employment cannot be varied, it may not be worthwhile to vary output when demand falls; hence prices will be driven down. Yet, if employment does not change, money wages will not be much affected, so real wages will rise. Clearly, these characteristics of the technology can exercise significant influence.

However, the technological rigidities just noted do not necessarily translate in any straightforward way into corresponding economic inflexibilities, for there are at least two institutional forms that employment relations, based on craft technology, took in the past or can take nowadays (for example, in developing countries): first, there is the domestic system in which capitalists, often merchants, "put out" work, paying piece rates to craftsmen working in their own homes and using their own tools and equipment. Then there is the factory system, in which workers are assembled in central buildings, owned and equipped by the capitalist, to work under direct supervision. The latter has many significant advantages. It permits training and close supervision, with the establishment of work norms and both product and labor standards, thus providing quality control. Labor skills in general will be raised towards the level of the best-practice workers. Economies of scale will be realized, and machinery can be run off a central power source, such as steam or water. And it will eliminate the sometimes costly and bothersome travel to and fro for the delivery of materials and collection of finished work.

In each case the technology permits little adaptation to variations in demand. Current costs are the major portion of costs, and the greater part of current costs are real and fixed. But the domestic system puts this burden on the craftsmen and their households, whereas the factory system obliges the capitalist to assume it. As we shall see, the early factory operated as a (largely) fixed employment system, with little ability to run on short time or at less than normal capacity. But in the domestic system, when there was less work to be put out, the craftsmen, having to support their families and establishments, could be expected to bid for the available work, driving piece rates down and putting the least efficient workers out of business altogether. This system therefore provided early capitalism with some flexibility in response to variations in demand, thereby giving greater protection to the class of financial rentiers whose fixed-interest income depended ultimately on profit receipts.

TWO SYSTEMS OF TECHNOLOGY

To see the contrasts sharply, compare "pure" stylized cases. In a craft or fixed employment system workers control the pace of work, and drawing on their skills, using general-purpose tools, hone the usually customized product, so that the workers define the details of the final output. Under mass production the machinery determines the pace of work, and the precision is built into the equipment, which is designed specifically for the product. As an example of the first kind of system we will take an idealized economy of early factories and artisan shops, in which small family firms and farms practise traditional crafts, drawing on the traditional sources of energy, such as wind and water, animal and human effort, but also steam power. The system is capitalist, in that a (more or less uniform) rate of profit prevails and governs investment, but although workers will be gathered into factories, scientific mass production has not begun. Craft methods are practised by teams of workers following long traditions. Craft work requires the presence of the entire work team, full time, for there to be any output at all. Start-up and shut-down costs are typically large, as are storage costs. The little technical progress that takes place is unsystematic, and the few economies of scale that exist are offset by increasing risk and diseconomies. (This picture deliberately overemphasizes the fixity of employment, and neglects the flexibility provided by the 'domestic system' discussed earlier. That system was a relic of pre-capitalist industry, retained in spite of its disadvantages because of the flexibility it provided (Mantoux 1928). To understand the economic relationships of the new system of early factories, and the characteristic problems facing this economy, we must set aside this mixture and consider the pure form.)

In such an economy, in the long run prices must cover costs (including normal profits) and so will reflect distribution, but in the short run employment will be relatively stable, since work teams cannot easily be broken up, with the result that a high proportion of current costs will be fixed. Needing to cover these costs, and lacking technology for storage and preservation, when demand weakens, goods will have to be sold for whatever they will bring, so that prices will adjust to the requirements of market clearing. Employment and output will tend to be stable, with prices flexible. (Note that "putting out" effectively turns a craftsman laborer into a small business unit, so that piece wages behave like prices. The worker households have large fixed real costs and so must, in the short run, compete for whatever work there is to be had, as long as the pay for such work is more than the variable costs associated with it. Hence as piece rates vary with demand, and therefore with prices, real earnings rates will tend to remain steady, but less efficient – or less well placed – workers will find their employment varying with demand.)

Artisan production may have a well developed division of labor, and it may also be highly mechanized (Sabel 1982). (Adam Smith's pin factory has the first, and Marshall's examples of the printing and watchmaking trades exhibit the second as well.) Prior to mass production the use of machinery replaces the workers' energy; but the early machine system drives essentially the same tools, although on a much larger scale. Acceleration and deceleration will be slow and difficult; the transmission of power will be handled by belts and pulleys in a manner both cumbersome and inflexible. Such use of machinery does not affect the system's characteristic mode of operation, for neither division of labor nor mechanization will have proceeded to the point where the pace and quality of production are controlled by the machinery, as in the science-based assembly line (Howell 1993).

In the early factory/artisan economy the work team must be kept together; everyone works or no one works. In the extreme case, lay-offs will simply not be possible; the factory or shop must either operate or shut down altogether. If machinery is used it must likewise all be used. Work is skilled and workers have to coordinate their efforts; workers themselves largely set the pace of work, so that productivity depends heavily on morale. Many technical aspects of production are not (and given that craft production is customized, cannot easily be) written down, but exist in the minds and accumulated experience of the foremen and senior skilled workers (Argyrous 1991; Broehl 1959). Technological improvements thus accumulate as specific skills and specialized knowledge on the part of senior workers and foremen.

A work crew that functions well together will be highly important. Moreover, most production will be discontinuous "batch" production; a batch, once begun, must be completed. But a good work crew should not be broken up, so new batches must be started even if demand is weak. Even when early forms of continuous production have been instituted, however (especially with the use of steam power), start-up and shut-down costs will be significant, so that the firm cannot go on half time or close down for part of the week.

The inability to lay off labor has important consequences in several areas. Firms accumulate financial reserves during booms and good times which they use to tide them over hard times. Reserves are designed to smooth the cycle; they are not really available for investment. In planning production, firms will be reluctant to contract out for parts or repairs; they would rather use their own labor and facilities in slack times to do such work, and their own foremen can supervise, which may be important when designs are not fully drawn. As a result economies of specialization will be lost.

Finally, products are non-standard; they are made to order, which means that working procedures will frequently have to be reorganized. Moreover, few products can be produced to stock; storage facilities are both poor and expensive, so that losses in terms of wastage and decay will be heavy.

The system of mass production differs in every one of these respects. Products are standardized, and storage facilities climate- and pest-controlled. The pace of work is governed by the speed of the assembly line or other machinery; jobs are broken down into their simplest components, reducing the need for skill. Skills remain important but, ideally, no worker need have more than one basic skill, to be exercised repetitively, in conditions where precision equipment eliminates much of the need for judgment or timing. Tasks are regularly simplified through time and motion studies, conducted by trained engineers. Work is continually reorganized, resulting in a persistent, though variable, tendency for output per worker to rise. R&D is carried out by a staff of professional scientists, who remain in contact with universities. Very little technical knowledge will remain specific to foremen or workers, as in the craft system, although aspects of technology may still remain firm-specific. The labor force has no need to interact, so morale counts for little, and workers are dispensable and interchangeable. Finally, start-up and shut-down costs are minimal; power is provided by petroleum-based fuels and electricity. These differences in technology, energy and labor requirements make possible a very different form of market organization: the corporate industrial system of mass production (Chandler, 1990). (In practice, of course, elements of the early factory/craft system will remain, particularly in the areas of agriculture and primary production.)

Under the corporate industry form production is carried out by corporations, organized as large bureaucracies, the ownership of which is decided in the financial markets. Technical progress is regular; economies of scale are widespread. New products and new processes are frequent and innovation is one aspect of competition. The size of an operating unit in the artisan economy will be limited by difficulties of coordination, the cost of transport to distant markets, storage costs and increasing risks; in many cases, craft technologies will dictate a "natural" size for the plant, and family firms will tend to operate a single plant whose size cannot exceed the requirements of an optimal work team. In the case of mass production, however, a larger plant confers significant economies of scale, which certainly must be balanced against increasing risks and distribution costs. But plant size does not determine output capacity, since throughput can be speeded up by the redesign and reorganization of work. Still less does plant size determine firm size. (Notice that there will also be economies of scale in storage, such as canning, drying, refrigeration, grain storage and so on.)

Under mass production growth is inherent in the system, and investment is carried out as far as possible by existing firms, who will not leave it to newcomers. New entrants would threaten the arrangements in existing markets, since new equipment will normally be superior to old, providing newcomers with a competitive edge. Hence firms will do their own saving, in the form of retained earnings. Price guidelines will be set so as to earn just enough on normal operations to finance the expected required investment. Actual prices will be held close to the guidelines; fluctuations in demand will be met by adjusting production and employment.

This means, however, that any given change in demand, by causing a corresponding change in output and employment, creates a secondary change in demand in the same direction, but smaller in magnitude. This secondary change, in turn, sets up a tertiary change, and so on, until the effect is no longer noticeable. The initial variation is therefore multiplied. But this multiplier is rooted in the technology and cost structure of the system, for that is what chiefly determines the proportion of revenue that is passed along; it has nothing to do with the "psychological propensity to consume." Gross profits are "withdrawn" at each stage, since they enter business financial accounts, and households may also hold back a portion of income. "Saving," however, meaning a positive decision to accumulate assets (whether by businesses or households), is not the same thing as "withdrawal," and it is the latter that is relevant; the crucial question is what proportion of revenue continues in circulation.

Let us draw the contrasts now. The mass production system is able to maintain productivity while varying output. The artisan system, by contrast, operates with fixed-capacity utilization and variable productivity, while mass production has variable capacity utilization and fixed productivity at the margin. Hence an artisan process will have low variable and high fixed costs but the fixed costs will in large part be current costs, chiefly labor, set in real terms, rather than capital costs fixed in monetary terms. The industrial economy, on the other hand, will have much higher variable costs, and its fixed costs will be capital costs set in monetary terms. In the artisan economy, therefore, changes in demand may lead to changes in the intensity with which workers work, but not to changes in employment. If demand increases, output *per capita* may be increased, although output per unit of effort may actually decline; indeed, it normally will decline after a point, on the assumption that, with given plant, returns to additional effort diminish. Conversely, when demand declines, output *per capita* will decline, although output per unit of effort could remain constant or increase.

Under mass production a variation in demand, due to fluctuations (for example, in investment), will be amplified: the changes in investment demand will result in changes in employment, so that consumption will change in the same direction. By contrast, in the early factory/artisan economy a change in demand will result in price changes. Fundamentally such an economy has only two levels of operation: all-out or zero. To cut back output without closing down will be difficult; work must be done more slowly but, for the most part, the entire crew will still be working. Given time, work can be reorganized, so some variation in employment is possible, but given an organization of work the only way to adjust output is to vary productivity at the margin. Since this will seldom be profitable, a fall in demand will result in excess supply, pushing prices down.

This needs careful explanation. In the early factory craft economy, with employment largely fixed, worker consumption will be governed by real wages. Money wages will be set at the time of employment and, since employment tends to be relatively constant, money wages will not vary much, either. Prices, on the other hand, will reflect the need to earn as much over variable costs as demand and the competition permit. Hence, when demand is below normal, competitive price cutting will take place and, when it is above normal, prices will rise. Prices will therefore vary flexibly with demand. Hence real wages will move inversely to variations in demand. If the chief cause of variations in overall demand is investment, reflecting "the general state of business confidence," then the induced change in consumption will tend to be in the opposite direction to the initiating change in investment. Hence a decline in investment demand, so long as it is not too large (leading to bankruptcies), will lead to a rise in consumption, which is just the reverse of what happens in mass production. The system has a built-in stabilizing mechanism, so long as the fluctuations are not too large.

TWO PATTERNS OF GROWTH

No doubt artisan technology could be operated in stationary conditions but, if the economy is fully capitalist, profits will have to be invested, since the driving motivation will be to accumulate capital. But the characteristic pattern of accumulation will be through the lending of household savings to new firms, which will set up shops that replicate existing ones but serve new customers. Firms expand to an optimal size and operate at that level thereafter. However, the system's prices do not depend on growth. (In this sense an artisan economy behaves as if it were stationary.) By contrast, in an industrial economy firms retain profits and invest in expanding and improving their own facilities and set their prices to support the requirements of this growth. The reason for these differences in the pattern of accumulation lies in the different relationship of technology to competition in the two cases, and hence to differences in the nature of firms. In the first case firms are stationary, but in the second they grow regularly.

In the artisan economy success in competition comes through the development of the skills and morale of workers. The successful firm has the better product, more reliable delivery times and quicker production times (with unit costs therefore lower), and so on, all of which depend on workers' skills and their ability to function together as a team. Such characteristics are personal and intangible; improving them does not depend on rebuilding factories or re-equipping shops. Very often crucial details of the technology are never written down; they reside in the minds of the foremen and senior craftsmen. But this means the technology is unreliable; sickness or disaffection among key workers could undermine the whole year's effort.

Learning and innovation are therefore confined to work teams. An innovation may arise within a group; but keeping it secret will provide a competitive advantage. Diffusion will usually take place only as workers move from one area or company to another, or as foremen leave to set up their own companies. Diffusion and the passing along of information are difficult not only because no one tries to write such improvements down, but also because, prior to the rise of professional engineering, the standards of industrial drawing and technical writing were low and irregular, so that the competence to do so was often lacking.

In the industrial economy competitive success likewise depends on cost-cutting and improved product design, but the difference is that these are objectively grounded in the production process, rather than based on intangible personal characteristics. For the most part the technology will be written down; indeed, it will be based on science, and on a professional engineering culture centered both on universities and on private research laboratories. It is therefore reliable, but dependent on the way the technology is grounded in institutions and embodied in equipment. "Embodied" technological innovations require retooling or rebuilding plant, and this necessitates investment. Plants have to be shut down and renovated, or scrapped and rebuilt. Even "disembodied" technical change, however, requires redesigning the work flow and the organizational chain.

Regular technical change requires professional engineering. With the rise of mass production came the rise of professional standards and schools. Degrees in mechanical, electrical and chemical engineering arose; mechanical drawing developed; time and motion studies, flow and organizational charts were initiated—all in the effort to understand the process of innovation and bring it under control.

An improvement provides a competitive advantage and must therefore be matched, so there will be a need and an incentive for the economy to contain a sector which specializes in supplying the means of production, and which is large enough to meet the demand for rebuilding entire industries. Investment will be more or less continuous, and productivity will regularly rise, although not necessarily in step with demand.

The saving–investment process differs markedly between the two systems. When the artisan economy expands, household savings will be loaned to set up new firms. The system of small establishments will replicate itself; growth will not normally be undertaken by adding to the capacity of existing firms, for there are few economies of scale in traditional crafts, while adding to size increases risk. (There is a problem, however, in the traditional account of a "perfect capital market.") Industrial systems, on the other hand, do provide economies of scale, both in the design of equipment and in the organization of work. Even more important, however, technological competition between suppliers of capital goods means that new equipment is likely to be better or cheaper than old. New investors will have an edge; existing firms cannot afford to remain satisfied with their present scale of operations, leaving growth to new entrants, for new firms will be able to undercut them in their own markets.

However, existing firms do not necessarily have to scrap and rebuild every time there is a significant innovation. This would be wasteful, both socially and privately. Instead they can adopt the innovation in building new capacity to meet growing demand, carefully building just enough – at an appropriate price – to prevent newcomers from entering. The industry will then consist of a number of firms, each having both new and old plants, rather than of older firms with outdated plants and newer ones with superior equipment.

To achieve this, however, growth must take a different path from the artisan economy. To avoid competing for household savings, firms will retain their earnings and invest them directly. So long as their investments are judged to be wise, the value of their equity will rise in proportion, which means that shareholders desiring funds can obtain them by selling off an appropriate part of their holdings at the higher price (Nell 1992: ch. 21).

Industrial growth thus differs fundamentally from growth in an artisan economy. Competition requires regular investment, financed by retained earnings, with a consequent rising price of equity. Labor becomes a variable cost, and output and employment vary together in line with sales, while productivity, fixed by technology, stays constant. Capacity capable of meeting the maximum likely demand can be installed, thereby ensuring that there will be no room for newcomers, without any risk of having to meet the labor cost of that capacity when it is not in full use.

In the artisan world, growth simply replicates existing stationary relationships. But growth is built into the working of the industrial system. For example, it must occur for potential profits to be realized, but (of even more relevance here) it is part of the competitive process. If markets

14

currently clear, but there is an imbalance between the rates of growth of supply and demand, they will fall into disequilibrium in the future. If they do not clear now, but their rates of growth are in balance, they will eventually even out. Prices, moreover, are significant in relation to rates of growth: at low prices new customers can adopt a new good, so demand can expand; but low prices mean low profit margins, so little finance for construction of new capacity. This suggests that a price might be found that would just balance the rates of growth of supply and demand. Generalizing this makes it possible to work out a pattern of price determination for a corporate industrial system, showing the relation of pricing to growth (Eichner 1976; Wood 1978; Nell 1992: ch. 17).

THE PRESSURES FOR CHANGE

An early factory craft economy, in our idealized version, has a pattern of stabilizing adjustments which depend on market clearing prices. From the point of view of the system this may be good, but from the point of view of individual producers the adjustments have some undesirable properties. For example, when demand falls off, production will be run more slowly but, exceptions aside, the full labor force will still have to be on hand. From the individual owner's point of view this is an unfortunate expense, which necessitates injurious price competition. In the absence of a domestic "putting-out" system, the burden of adjustment will fall heavily on profits: when demand falls and prices are hit, if employment cannot be changed and given a mark-up of 50 per cent, a 5 per cent drop in demand means a 10 per cent fall in profits. If two-thirds of the capital were external, a 17 per cent falling off in demand could bring bankruptcy. Hence leverage must remain restricted under these conditions. Conversely, when demand is strong, the rate at which production can take place will depend on the morale of the labor force, and its willingness to put in extra effort. The capitalist does not have full or satisfactory control over the pace of work, or the level of costs.

What the capitalist needs, first, is greater control over the process of production, especially over the productivity of labor and the pace of work. Time-and-motion studies were developed to provide just this (Barnes 1956). Such methods provided greater control over labor but, since they required professional management, at the price of sacrificing family control over the firm itself. Second, firms want to be able to expand and develop with their markets, not just to reach an optimal size and stagnate, and they want greater control over output (to be able to vary production with sales). They need reserve capacity, and to be able to shut down temporarily. Third, and correlatively, firms need to be able to vary costs when sales vary, which requires being able to lay off and rehire labor

15

easily, which, in turn, depends on being able to schedule and reschedule production. To do this, start-up and shut-down costs must be minimal. Fourth, firms need to be able to store output without spoilage. If, when sales fall, output can be cut back and, along with output, costs can also be cut, and at the same time unsold inventory can be stored without significant loss or other costs, a great deal of pressure for potentially ruinous price-cutting will be lifted. Part of the problem thus can be reduced to a technical question: how can production be run at less than full blast without all workers having to be present? Alternatively, how can production be started up and shut down, easily and costlessly, so that a drop in demand can be met by running short-time?

The normal working of the system throws these questions up; the answers will help businesses to compete more effectively. Inflexible output and costs, resulting in overproduction and cut-throat price competition, is potentially ruinous. The system itself thus creates the pressures which lead to the technological developments that make labor a cost that varies with output, which in turn varies with demand. The result is an improvement in the flexibility of the firm's response to changing market conditions.

Business will attempt systematically to gain greater control over the production process, substituting mechanical power for labor power, and mechanical or electronic control for human skill, as far as possible. In general, the larger the scale on which operations take place, the better the prospects for doing this, which is an aspect of economies of scale: "the division of labor is limited by the extent of the market."

The chief method by which business can achieve these goals is to speed up throughput, and make it continuous (Chandler 1977). Processes of continuous throughput, replacing or modifying batch production, provide a steady and adjustable flow which can be matched to the level the market requires. To make this possible, it is necessary to shift from earlier and more primitive energy sources – animal power, human power, water and steam to electrical power or petroleum, especially the internal combustion engine. (The earlier energy sources all face substantial cost problems: water power is weather-dependent, often seasonal or unreliable; water and steam equipment requires substantial maintenance even when not in use; animal and human power require feeding and support even when not in use; and steam and animal power both have heavy start-up and shut-down costs.) The new methods usually reduced unit costs substantially, and this has attracted the attention of historians. But, at least equally important for the argument here, and more important in the long run for the nature of the market, was the change in the degree of adaptability of costs.

These pressures also tend to change the nature of competition. Previously it centered on prices in a comparatively simple way. But now the chief focus will become technological development, especially in relation to market share, since an increase in share can permit a larger size, which in turn will make it possible to extend the division of labor, reaping economies of scale that in turn will permit the consolidation of a lower price, and so on. Once an advantage is achieved, a "virtuous" cycle develops, enabling the successful firm to establish a leading or even dominant market position.

A "virtuous" cycle also develops for the system as a whole. In the craft economy new technical developments are seldom written down on paper and remain tied to particular workers and foremen. These may train others and the techniques will spread by word of mouth, and with the movement of labor. But the diffusion process is subjective, slow and uncertain. By contrast, once mechanization has given birth to a competitive machine-building industry, technical change is on its way to becoming endogenous, for competition in machinery and machine tools will take place chiefly in attempting to make the best improvements. The spread of these through learning and the movement of engineers between firms will begin to make technical change endogenous. As engineering becomes an established profession it will find a place in universities, together with support from government, while firms will begin to create R&D centers, further reinforcing the position of technical change as a normal aspect of industrial competition.

Yet a major hitch can arise in this: a Catch 22, in fact. It is true that mass production methods provide great advantages, but they also have costs—in particular, large capital costs which cannot be recouped unless there is, in fact, a mass market. Yet a mass market may not develop unless and until the product is widely available at a suitably low price, and without a mass market the capital costs will not be spread over enough units to lower the price sufficiently to make the new methods competitive. This creates the possibility of a bizarre dilemma: it may not be worth investing in further expansion of craft production because mass production methods are being developed, and are superior at high levels of demand. Craft investment will be wiped out as soon as mass production begins. But a mass market does not yet exist, and if any firm starts mass production at least several others will follow. There will certainly not be room for all until the mass market actually develops, and perhaps not even then. Hence it may be too dangerous to make the large investment. Consequently, nothing will be done and the economy could stagnate for lack of investment.

A mass market is essential, for the huge investment can be recouped only by long production runs. Here a further factor may intervene: as the new mass product enters into wider use, "learning by using" may occur. Aeroplanes will fly under new weather conditions, land and take off in different circumstances, and new knowledge of the strengths and weaknesses of the technical design will become manifest. Customers will

THE IDEA OF TRANSFORMATIONAL GROWTH

demand modifications, and the long production run will be lost. Frequent design changes and significant learning-by-using are incompatible with a move to mass production. These lessons will be taken up in Chapter 3 by George Argyrous, in looking at the problems of mobilizing for war.

A further problem arises in that craft work teams are not likely to want to implement a move to mass production. Even when it is clear that moving to such methods would be warranted, craft workers and foremen are likely to resist innovations that will render many of their skills obsolete. Neither will they will find it easy and natural to adapt (Hounshell 1984).

There are several ways out of these problems. Cartels may be formed and the market parcelled out, or the State may intervene, as it did in the Second World War, to plan and finance the transition. This may be a more or less straightforward matter of providing finance and assuring the market, as in shipbuilding, or it may involve far more detailed and difficult planning, extending to product design and specifications, as in aircraft. So the problem is serious. The very effectiveness of the new methods may act as a barrier to their adoption.

Nevertheless, if and when investment does begin, with competition centering on a race for improvements in technology, a shift to mass-production methods will take place (Thomson 1993). With a little massage, perhaps the preceeding could be blended into a familiar stylized picture: the famous sigmoid diffusion curve. Plot an index of diffusion (say, the percentage of firms using, or of output produced by, the new method) on the vertical axis, with time on the horizontal. Then, at first, the Catch 22 will hinder adoption and the curve will be shallow. But once a few firms have made the switch, and it is clear that a market is there, competitive pressures will compel the mass of firms to rush to make the change, and the curve will rise steeply. Finally it will flatten out, because the remaining craft producers will be those holding protected niches in the market, insulating them from competitive pressures.

One result will be that the strategic situation of firms will be fundamentally changed. Firms will no longer seek to establish their optimum size and remain there, and it will no longer be possible to permit new firms to supply the growth of the market. New firms would be able to build plants and buy equipment embodying the latest technology; they would therefore be able to establish a cost advantage and invade the markets of established firms. Hence existing firms must invest regularly, incorporating new technology into their plants, and growing enough so that, taken together, they will supply the expansion of the market. Prices will therefore have to be set with an eye to providing the profits that will finance growth. To facilitate such growth, firms will withhold profits, investing them directly, rather than distributing them to shareholders. Both the pattern of competition and the working of financial markets are altered by the move to mass-production technology and the shift from extensive to intensive growth.

TECHNOLOGY AND MARKET ADJUSTMENT

In short, when the technology of mass production becomes widespread, the system as a whole will begin to work differently. The main features of the old trade cycle are all related, directly or indirectly, to the characteristics of the technology of the period.[3] (Nell 1992: chs 16, 17; 1993) As we saw earlier, until comparatively recently technology was developed by and for small-scale operations, run largely by households or groups of households. These evolved into family firms. The first industrial revolution brought the shift from small craft operations to factories, which, however, were based on essentially the same technologies. Even though, at the end of the nineteenth century, great advances were made as steam power and steel were brought into widespread use, enabling substantial expansion in the size of plants, reaping economies of scale, the technologies still largely operated on the principles of "batch" production rather than continuous throughput. In many cases the use of steam power simply permitted a large number of work stations, each organized according to older principles, to run at the same time off a central power source. The power, in turn, ran essentially the same tools that had previously been operated by hand. Operatives had to be present at all work stations in order for any production to take place. Even where continuous throughput developed, start-up and shut-down costs were high.

These limitations had economic consequences. The economy faced continuous shocks from the outside world. Of particular importance were exogenous fluctuations in sales. Firms could not easily vary output to match changes in sales – a firm could either produce or shut down. Craft technologies were inflexible in terms of adapting output and employment (and so costs) to changes in the rate of sales. As a consequence, when demand rose/fell output could be increased/decreased only by varying productivity, i.e. work effort. The technology required team effort among workers, generally performing on a small scale, so changes in output could come only with changes in effort – or by reorganizing the work team. But neither labor nor capital was willing to change work norms, except temporarily. Hence the level of employment would have to change, but this in turn would be costly in terms of disruption, and would take place only if compensated by higher prices, at least for a time. Thus a rise in demand would drive up prices, lowering the real wage, thereby leading to an expansion of employment. Inflexibility thus can help to explain the characteristic patterns of variations in prices, output, wages and employment (Hicks 1989; Nell 1992: ch. 16)

Family firms operating craft technologies do not require extensive government oversight or intervention. A private enterprise financial system will serve this kind of economy well, except in hard times, when it will prove unstable.

By contrast, mass-production technology permits easy adaptation of employment and output to changes in sales, while leaving productivity unaffected. Variable costs will thus be constant over a wide range (Hansen 1948; Lavoie 1992). Prices will therefore tend not to vary with changes in demand. Mass-production technology also permits expansion to reap economies of scale, leading to larger firms, differently organized, and motivated to grow. Under mass production productivity will tend to grow regularly, and will be reflected in wage bargains. Rising wages for production workers will create tensions with other social groups, leading to pressure to raise their incomes, creating inflationary pressures. Large growing corporations cannot tolerate a financial system prone to crisis; mass production requires government oversight and intervention in many related dimensions. As a consequence the new trade cycle differs in every one of the above respects.[4]

How can this be reflected in elementary economic theory? First, there is a change in the way aggregate categories of expenditure vary. In the craft economy, when demand for a particular good falls – say, owing to a general decline in investment spending – the decline in employment will be comparatively small (short of a crisis, when firms are obliged to close down altogether), but prices will fall. Real wages will therefore rise, and so will household consumption. Hence *investment and consumption will tend to move inversely*. By contrast, in a mass-production economy, when investment falls, workers will be laid off, and prices will tend to fall comparatively little. Thus instead of consumption varying inversely with investment, as it did when a decline in demand led to a greater proportional fall in prices than in money wages, consumption will also decline, since the laid-off workers and their families will now have to curtail their consumption spending. The elasticity of consumption with respect to investment will now be positive.

Second, the production function has traditionally been the basic analytic tool of neoclassical theory in regard to pricing, employment and output. High theory interprets each point on the production function as representing a different choice of technique – but this was not how Marshall and Pigou understood it (Marshall 1961: 374; Pigou 1944: 51–2). For them the production function showed output as a function of current employment and the available plant and equipment. This discussion suggests that changes in technology are a primary cause of the changes in the behavior of economic variables from the old to the new trade cycle. Such a shift in technology can perhaps be represented as a change in a Marshallian production function from one with a pronounced curvature, so that the slope declines as employment increases, to one that is a straight line with a constant slope[5] (Nell 1992).

PRICE *v.* QUANTITY ADJUSTMENTS

In the earlier era markets evidently adjusted through price changes; in the later, however, prices no longer seem to be changing in relevant ways. Instead, employment and output are adjusted when demand fluctuates. These two patterns of market response are significantly different. The first is broadly stabilizing; the second, however, is not.[6]

Market adjustment in the pre-World War I era

In the earlier era, when production was carried out with an inflexible technology, a decline in autonomous components of aggregate demand – investment or net exports – would lead prices to decline. Since output could not easily be adjusted, it would have to be thrown on the market for whatever it would fetch. For similar reasons employment could not easily be cut back; hence there would be little or no downward pressure on money wages in the short run. As a consequence, when the current levels of the autonomous components of aggregate demand fall, real wages rise, in conditions in which employment remains generally unchanged. Hence – to put it compactly – when investment declines, consumption spending rises. Investment and consumption move inversely to one another.

For *relatively small* variations in autonomous demand this is a stabilizing pattern of market adjustment. For *large* – and prolonged – collapses of demand, however, the relative inflexibility of output and employment can lead to disaster. Unable to cut current costs, or unable to cut them in proportion, and facing declining prices, firms will eventually have to shut down. When prices fall to the break-even point, all their employees will be out of work. With no revenue, the firm will have to meet its fixed charges out of reserves, and when they are exhausted it will face bankruptcy. Shut-downs, of course, reduce consumption and are destabilizing.

Similarly, a rise in the autonomous components of demand leads to a bidding up of prices but not, initially, of money wage rates. Hence the real wage falls. With employment fixed, consumption declines in real terms. Again, consumption and investment spending move inversely. In addition, the fall in the real wage makes it possible for employers to absorb the costs of reorganizing work, and thus, in the longer term, to hire additional employees. But, so long as the proportional increase in employment is less than the proportional decline in the real wage, consumption will fall.

Such a fall in consumption following a rise in investment can be expected to exert a dampening influence on investment. Similarly the rise in consumption following a decline in investment activity can be expected to provide a stimulus.

These stabilizing influences are reinforced by the behavior of interest rates. When demand falls, prices fall, and interest rates follow suit. We note that according to "Gibson's paradox" interest rates are highly correlated with the wholesale price index. Hence a decline in investment will be followed by a fall in interest rates, just as consumption spending picks up. The effect will be to provide a stimulus. By contrast, in a boom, interest rates will rise, just as consumption spending turns down.

Of course, the impact of these countervailing tendencies will be reduced by bankruptcies and capacity shrinkage in the slump and by the formation of new firms and the expansion of capacity in the boom. When demand falls sharply, and closures and bankruptcies reduce the number of firms, output shrinks, and the pressure on prices may seem to be reduced. But bankruptcies and closures reduce employment and therefore consumption demand. So demand declines further, and prices continue their downward course, pulling interest rates down with them. Falling prices and low interest rates make replacement investment attractive. At some point it will be worth while shifting replacement forward in time. This could then start an upswing. In the same way, capacity expansion will tend to inhibit the rise in prices in the boom – but building new capacity itself increases demand, which will feed the pressure on prices. Interest rates will continue to rise; at some point interest and prices will be sufficiently above normal that it will seem worth while to postpone replacement. This could then prove the start of the downturn.

In short, the pattern of market adjustment provides endogenous mechanisms that could bring a boom to a close, and lead to recovery from a slump. The system is self-adjusting, and capable of generating an endogenous cycle around a normal trend. The three internal processes just described contribute to this – real wages, and therefore consumption, move countercyclically, replacement investment moves countercyclically, while the interest rate moves procyclically. These combine to exert pressure on net new investment to eventually turn against the cycle, perhaps – or probably – with a variable lag that depends on circumstances. Whether such a cycle actually manifests itself, and what its characteristics, amplitude, etc., will be, of course, will depend on the current parameters of the system, and on historical conditions.

Market adjustment in the post-World War II era

The mechanism of market adjustment in the earlier era rested on the countercyclical movement of real wages, coupled with the procyclical movement of interest rates. Neither of these patterns is observable in the post-war era. The mechanism just does not exist.[7]

In this period prices no longer vary with demand. Instead prices are driven by inflationary pressures, partly generated by the new process of transmitting productivity gains through increases in money wage rates. This tends to upset socially important income relativities. If these are restored as a result of social pressures, costs will be increased without corresponding gains in productivity, thereby leading to price rises, setting off a wage–price spiral.

But the system does respond to variations in autonomous demand. Mass-production processes can easily be adjusted to changes in the level of sales. Employment and output will vary directly with sales. Hence, when investment rises or falls, employment (including extra shifts and overtime for those already on the job) will also rise or fall, while prices and money wages remain unchanged. In the simplest case, consumption depends on the real wage and employment. As a result, consumption will vary directly, rather than inversely, with investment. This is a version of the multiplier (Nell 1992: ch. 21).

Multiplier expansions and contractions of demand, if substantial and/or prolonged, will tend to induce further variations in investment in the same direction. This is the accelerator, or capital stock adjustment principle.[8]

Early in the post-war era many Keynesian trade cycle theorists argued that the endogenous processes of the modern economy were fundamentally unstable.[9] The plausible range of values for the multiplier and accelerator seemed to imply either exponential expansion and contraction or, if a lag were introduced, anti-damped cycles. To develop a theory of the business cycle, it was necessary to postulate "floors" and "ceilings," which these movements run up against. The floor was set by gross investment; it could not fall below zero, and arguably it could not fall to zero, since existing capital had to be maintained, which required replacement. Full employment and supply bottlenecks of all kinds provided ceilings. Once the explosive movement was halted, various factors were supposed to lead to turn-arounds (which might be endogenous in the case where the multiplier–accelerator generates anti-damped movements). Thus the business cycle was seen to be made up of three parts – an unstable endogenous mechanism, which runs up against external buffers, slowing movement down or bringing it to a halt, at which point various *ad hoc* factors come into play, leading to a turn-around and unstable movement again but in the opposite direction. In short, a mixture of endogenous and exogenous.

The floors and ceilings, however, in practice have seemed too elastic to explain the turning points. Depressions could keep sinking, and full employment did not reliably stop booms.[10] Nor was it clear why, when an expansion or contraction hit a ceiling or floor, it should turn around. Even at full employment, demand in monetary terms could keep rising; even when net investment hit zero, replacements could be postponed –

23

and even when replacements had fallen off, consumption might be curtailed. Moreover, even if expansion or contraction stops, will the accelerator actually turn the movement round? The argument is more plausible for the upper turning point. But in fact, in the post-war era, most upper turning points appear to have occurred before the economy pressed against full capacity or full employment, while the economy has normally turned up before net investment settled definitively at zero. Many suggestions have been offered to account for these anomalies, yet no single explanation, or combination of accounts, has generally appeared convincing. Some authors have even contended that different cycles may rest on different factors (Duesenberry 1958). Yet, however unsatisfactory the theory as a whole may have been, the argument that the endogenous mechanism had become unstable appears to be sound.

Moreover, it has been argued that the financial system may stabilize an otherwise unstable economy. A multiplier–accelerator boom will raise incomes, increasing the transaction demand for money. Such a rise in the demand for money will increase interest rates, which, in turn, will act as a drag on investment, bringing the boom to a halt. The multiplier–accelerator then goes into reverse, throwing the economy into a downswing, but the falling level of income will bring down the transactions demand, thereby pulling interest rates down. The lower interest rates will stimulate investment, starting the upswing, setting off the multiplier–accelerator.

Recent estimates of the "multiplier" (Bryant *et al.* 1988) take these relationships into account. Most econometric models try to introduce and estimate all relevant factors (Fair 1984); hence they likewise include interest rate effects, and perhaps other factors as well.[11] This may be a mistake. Both the simple multiplier and the capital stock adjustment principle are based on solid relationships, which are structurally based and economically motivated. When spending in one sector increases, it sets off repercussions in other sectors, leading to further increases in spending. When demand increases, pushing producers against capacity, it makes economic sense for them to increase their capacity. By contrast, when income increases, while the need for a circulating medium increases, it is not at all obvious that an "increased demand for money" pushes up against a given supply, driving interest rates up. Quite the contrary, as will be argued later, in such cases credit expands, near monies arise, and/or velocity increases – all without any effect on interest rates. The chief determinant of interest rates in the post-war era appears to be central bank monetary policy. Moreover, even when interest increases, its effect on investment is unreliable. It may take a very steep rise in interest, kept in place for a long period, to bring a boom to a halt. As is evident from the early 1990s, a fall in interest rates by no means leads to expansion.

Rather than floors and ceilings, or the working of the financial system, it can be argued, politics has chiefly provided the turning points. Booms led to balance of payments crises or to inflationary wage–price spirals. Pressure from business interests would lead to an induced recession. Full employment also threatened – or was perceived to threaten – work discipline. On the other hand, slumps threatened governments at the ballot box. The actual business cycle of the post-war era has had an irregular and distinctly political character – although the ability to control the economy may well have been eroded over time.

However, the turning points do not coincide that neatly with political interests, and in several cases it is evident that policy did not produce the desired effects. Yet the cycle is still apparent, suggesting that there is room for an endogenous theory.

AGGREGATE EMPLOYMENT AND MARKET ADJUSTMENT

Let's consider the ways these different systems adjust in more detail. First, the craft economy, with its Marshallian markets, and then mass production with Keynesian adjustment.

The Marshallian production function

Even Keynes initially accepted what he called the

> first postulate òf Classical economics . . . this vital fact which the classical economists have (rightly) asserted as indefeasible. In a given state of organization, equipment and technique, the real wage earned by a unit of labour has a unique (inverse) correlation with the volume of employment . . . if employment increases, then, in the short period, the reward per unit of labour in terms of wage-goods must, in general, decline and profits increase. This is simply the obverse of the familiar proposition that industry is normally working subject to decreasing returns in the short period during which equipment etc. is assumed to be constant . . . But when we have thrown over the second postulate [that the real wage equals the marginal disutility of labor], a decline in employment, although necessarily associated with labour's receiving a (larger real) wage . . . is not necessarily due to labour's *demanding a larger quantity of wage-goods.*
>
> (1936: 17–18)

In other words, if the money wage is fixed in the short run, any change in demand will change employment in the same direction, according to a function which exhibits diminishing returns, but it will do so by changing prices, which at the same time changes the real wage in the opposite direction. Employment changes as a combined consequence of demand pressure and a fall in the real wage, itself induced by that pressure.

A. C. Pigou described the functions relating output of consumer goods and investment equipment, to labor, in conditions of given plant and equipment as follows:

> Thus when industry is in a state of moderate depression with a fair amount of idle equipment, marginal prime cost may be approximately constant over a considerable range. Obviously this will not be so when the industry is working at or near full capacity. Then marginal cost must be rising.
>
> (1944: 51–2; also see p. 9 n.)

Marshall himself held that "For short periods [we may] take the stock of appliances for production as practically fixed; and . . . are governed by . . . expectations of demand in considering how actively . . . to work those appliances" (1961: 374). Viner defined "the 'short run' . . . to be a period which is long enough to permit of any desired change of output technologically possible without altering the scale of plant, but which is not long enough to permit of any adjustment of scale of plant" (Viner 1958: 202). That is, output is a function of given plant and equipment, which remains unchanged in quantity and form, to which is applied a variable amount of labor.

J. M. Clark (1923) commented on the growing importance of large-scale fixed plant and equipment in creating overhead costs, which might apply to a variety of outputs. Not only could the level of employment and output be varied, the composition – the proportions of different products or services and thus of different kinds of labor – could also vary. Clark considered this a new development, dating from the end of the nineteenth century.

Hicks (1963) refers to the derivative of such a function as a "short-period marginal product," defined as "the additional production due to a small increase in the quantity of labour, when not only the quantity, but also the form, of the co-operating capital is supposed unchanged" (pp. 20–1). He doubts whether this conception can be given any "precise meaning" or "useful application," for a worker added to unchanged plant will produce less additional output than the "true" marginal product, which would result from optimizing the form, leaving the amount unchanged; while a worker subtracted will reduce output by more. The clear implication, nevertheless, is of diminishing returns.

Moreover, it seems that Marshall's famous example of the shepherd was of precisely this sort, as Dennis Robertson admits (1931). Robertson supports Clark's view that the "principle of variation" is the essence of marginal productivity; the marginal product is properly defined only when the "cooperating capital" changes in form, to achieve an optimal configuration, while remaining fixed in amount. But he admits that this renders the conception practically useless. By contrast, the Marshallian approach was eminently practical; the marginal principles were developed not with an eye to theoretical consistency and elegance, but as guides to understanding and policy. On the Continent it was quite otherwise; marginal productivity there was always understood to require variations in methods of production – as Hicks and Robertson also insisted.[12]

The Marshall–Pigou conception is not the modern neoclassical production function; it represents the employment of labor to operate given plant and equipment – to operate the production system – at various levels of intensity. It is what Joan Robinson later dubbed a "utilization" function, and it has no implication that technique is different at different points. Instead, different points represent lesser or greater degrees of utilization of the given plant and equipment. (But this brings up the question "Why do returns diminish?" The answer: they only diminish in a craft economy.)

If we now suppose that investment stands at its normal level, and that all and only wages are consumed, the ray from the point measuring capital costs, equal to investment spending, can be interpreted as aggregate demand. If the real wage is at its normal level, output and employment will take place at minimum average cost, and the real wage will equal the marginal product of labor.

The outputs of the two sectors can be aggregated in terms of the prices embedded in the system. Normal output and normal employment are also known; but there will be a range of possible variation above and below normal levels, provided a longer period of time is considered, during which work can be reorganized. Even below and certainly above the normal level, additional employment or increased work intensity will yield diminishing increments of output. The normal level of activity is the most efficient. Plot aggregate output on the vertical axis, and total employment on the horizontal. The origin indicates the lower limit of the range of variation. This function shows the variation in output with changes in employment or intensity of work *with given equipment and technique*.

Next, a straight line rising from the origin with the slope w/p will indicate the wage bill corresponding to each level of employment, which, by assumption, will also equal worker consumption. (State transfer payments are negligible in early capitalism.) If we neglect capitalist consumption, this will also be total consumption. (The argument is unaffected by a constant level of capitalist consumption.) Then normal investment can be designated by a point on the vertical axis, and total demand, $C + I$, will be given, for each level of employment, by a line starting from the investment point, rising parallel to the wage–consumption line. Suppose this line

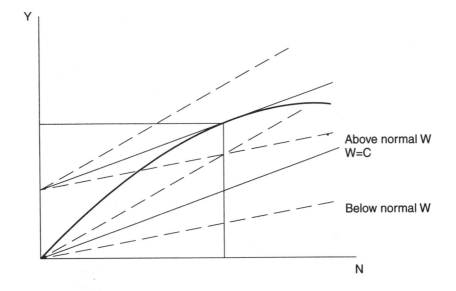

Figure 1.1 The craft economy tangency solution

lies wholly above the output curve; demand would exceed supply at every level of employment. Prices would be bid up, so the real wage would fall, until the demand line swung down so as to just touch the output curve at the level of normal employment (since we began from normal invest-ment). If the demand curve intersected the output line below normal employment, profit could be increased by cutting prices, raising real wages and employment, and so increasing output to the point at which the demand line was tangent to the output curve. Hence, at the level of normal activity, the real wage will equal the short-run marginal product of employment, in the given technical conditions.

Now consider fluctuations in the level of investment. If investment falls below its normal level, total demand will intersect the output curve below the level of normal employment; it will be possible then to raise profits by cutting prices and raising real wages and employment. Output will rise until the demand line is tangent, which will be at a point near to but below the normal level. When investment is above its normal level, total demand will be excessive, and prices will be bid up, until the real wage falls, bringing the demand line down, until it is tangent again, at a point near to but above the normal position. Changes in prices adjust the real wage, and employment as well as output, so that movements in consumption offset variations in investment.

Such a system is not without potential problems. Suppose that after a point the marginal product diminishes sharply, so that the average cost curve is markedly U-shaped. In these circumstances consider a substantial rise in investment spending, well above normal. To justify the required level of employment, the marginal product will have to fall to a negligible level; in other words, prices will rise sharply, reflecting the steep increase in average and marginal costs. With a given money wage, a sufficiently steep price increase will push the real wage below what Joan Robinson called the "inflation barrier," a conventionally defined minimum standard of living. The result will be a push for higher money wages, and a wage–price spiral.

Another possible adjustment must be considered. When the aggregate demand line lies wholly above the normal output–employment curve, pressures will build to increase the intensity of work at every level of employment, so that the normal output curve will tend to shift up – and conversely when aggregate demand lies below the normal output curve at the normal level of employment. These shifts due to changing work intensity may not be very large, but they will increase the stability of normal employment, and reduce the size of the price fluctuations required to restore equilibrium. With variable prices, then, the real wage will adjust to equal the marginal product of employment, and aggregate profit will be maximized, at a rather stable level of employment.

When money prices change relative to the money wage, changing the real wage, the most labor-intensive industries will be affected the most. For example, when the real wage falls, money prices have been bid up, and output increases, but labor productivity falls when reorganization takes place and production rises above the normal level. Similarly, when the real wage rises, output will fall below the previous norm, and productivity will

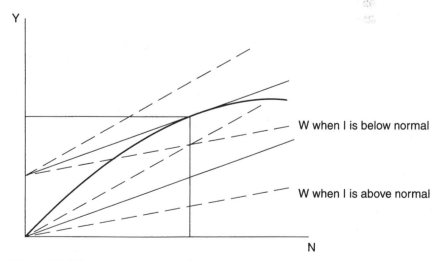

Figure 1.2 Adjusting to changing investment

increase when employment is cut back. The more labor-intensive the industry the greater the proportional change. This would seem to call for appropriate changes in relative prices.

Productivity

Starting from such a position of equilibrium, we can consider another adjustment, which will help to explain the generally downward pattern of price movements in the nineteenth century (Sylos-Labini 1989, 1993). Let there be an increase in labor productivity, due either to improved organization or to better work methods. It will shift the utilization function up over a substantial range. As a result, at the initial level of employment there will be excess output, driving down the level of prices, until the real wage line – and so the aggregate demand function – swings up enough to restore the tangency at a higher output and somewhat reduced level of employment. Since employment changes only slightly, and only after prices, the effect on money wages will be negligible. The benefits of increased productivity are passed on to consumers in the form of lower prices – but, it should be noted, increased productivity does have a small tendency to reduce employment, as representatives of the working classes have always argued.

The elasticity of consumption with respect to investment

Even though employment will not vary with changes in investment, output will, although less and with a greater lag than price. But consider the "pure" or extreme case, where the entire effect of a change in investment intially falls on price, i.e. investment demand falls by a certain percentage, and price drops by the same percentage. This means that the costs of capital inputs into consumer goods have declined by this percentage, so competition should lower the price of consumer goods in proportion. As a consequence the real wage will rise in proportion, and, on the assumption that the whole of real wage income is spent on consumer goods, consumption demand will increase in the same proportion.

Spelling this out formally, with I as investment demand, Y_k as current capital goods output, Y_c the output of consumer goods, p_k the price of capital goods, p_c the price of consumer goods, w/p_c the real wage, and C the demand for consumer goods: since $I = p_k Y_k$ in equilibrium, $dI = Y_k dp_k$ when output remains fixed; dividing both sides of the second equation by the first,

$$dI/I = dp_k/p_k$$

The relation between p_c and p_k can be written in a form used widely elsewhere, bearing in mind that these are money prices

$$p_c = RAp_k + wB$$

$$p_k = Rap_k + wb$$

where R is the gross profit rate on capital costs (capital inputs multiplied by p_k), set at the competitive rate, and w is the competitive wage rate needed to cover normal labor costs and provide labor its net earnings. When I falls, p_k will fall in proportion but will continue to cover wage costs; hence the realized rate of profit in capital goods will fall. Competition will therefore tend to push prices down similarly in consumption goods. Three effects will be felt. First, capital equipment and input costs will be lower; second, working capital will be more readily available from the banking system, at lower rates; third, resources and labor will tend to shift in, threatening to expand output. (We may assume that tools and labor's skills are easily shifted, and that many goods serve both purposes.)

On the assumption that rates of profit remain equal as prices fall, and that w remains fixed, solving each equation for R, equating, differentiating, and rearranging will give:

$$dp_k/(p_k - wb) = dp_c/(p_c - wB)$$

Suppose first that the capital–labor ratios in the two sectors are the same, e.g. in an early stage of capitalism in which the same firms make both tools and equipment and household goods. In these circumstances, when p_k falls, bringing down p_c, so that the rate of profit falls in the same proportion in both activities, since $B/a = b/A$, the above procedure yields:

$$dp_c/p_c = dp_k/p_k$$

But if the capital–labor ratios of the two sectors differ, this equality will not hold. Suppose capital goods is capital-intensive and its price falls because of a decline in I; then with an equi-proportional fall in the consumer goods price the resulting revenue would have to cover the labor-intensive wage bill, leaving a rate of profit lower than that in capital goods. However, if the current profit rate in consumer goods falls below that in capital goods, resources will no longer tend to move there, nor will working capital be offered preferentially. Once the consumer goods rate of profit has fallen to the level prevailing in capital goods the pressure on consumer prices will cease. In other words, the realized rates of profit will tend to end up the same, so the consumer goods price will not fall proportionally as much as the capital goods price, i.e. $dp_c/p_c < dp_k/p_k$. Just the reverse holds when the capital goods sector is labor-intensive; the pressure on prices in consumer goods will continue even after consumer prices have fallen proportionally as much as capital goods prices, since the rate of profit will not have fallen to the level prevailing in the capital goods sector.

When the consumer goods price changes, the real wage changes in the opposite direction.

$$d[w/p_c]/(w/p_c) = -w/p_c^2/(w/p_c) = -dp_c/p_c$$

Ex hypothesi, all real wage income is spent on consumer goods; since employment is fixed, consumer demand must rise at the same rate as that at which the real wage increases. Yet there seems to be a paradox here – the demand for and output of consumer goods are to rise while the price falls! And this in conditions in which prices are relatively flexible, compared with output and employment. But the paradox dissolves on closer inspection: capital goods demand is falling, which brings down capital goods prices and profits; this is the initiating cause. Consumer goods prices fall only because costs have fallen and competition forces them down. Consumer goods profits are reduced by the threatened or actual movement of capital out of the capital goods sector. But the resulting reduction of consumer goods prices raises real wages and therefore consumer demand. Firms and workers able to move will therefore shift from the capital goods sector, where demand is falling, to consumer goods, where demand is rising. Hence in ideal conditions,

$$d[w/p_c]/(w/p_c) = dC/C = dY_c/Y_c$$

Putting all this together, we see that

$$dI/I = -dC/C, \text{ or } [CdI/dCI] = -1$$

The elasticity of consumption with respect to investment is minus one (assuming equal capital–labor ratios). A proportional rise or fall in investment is exactly offset by the corresponding proportional fall or rise in consumption, brought about by the working of competition and the price system. This can be expressed in a simple diagram (Figure 1.3) of negative unitary elasticity.

(Note that the price mechanism does not produce a perfect Say's Law offset; that would require the constancy of $I + C$, rather than the product, $I \times C$.[13] However, the adjustment mechanism is significantly stabilizing: since $C > I$, and $dC/C = -dI/I$, $|dC| > |dI|$. So, when I falls, adjusted total income, $Y + dY = C + dC + I + dI > Y$, and, when I rises, $Y + dY < Y$. In the first case the increase will tend to stimulate investment; in the second, the decline to diminish it, thus providing a corrective in the right direction.)

(A caveat must be entered. Not all producers will be equally efficient. A

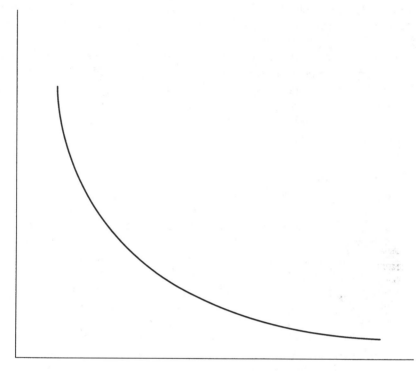

Figure 1.3 The elasticity of consumption with respect to investment

fall in price may put some high-cost producers out of business, leaving their labor force unemployed, and thus reduce consumption spending. This reduction in consumer demand may create additional bankruptcies – a bankruptcy multiplier. If the number of high-cost producers is large enough and the fall in price severe enough, the effect of bankruptcy in reducing consumption could rise to the point where it offsets the stimulating effect of the rise in real wages. The result will be a "general glut.")

The pressures of the market, leading firms to take action to reduce the fluctuations of profits, bring about changes in the technology of production, making employment and output more readily adjustable. But when these innovations have spread, this, in turn, changes the way the market adjusts. We can start with Keynes.

Adjustment in the simple case: alternative theories

Keynes developed an account of adjustment in which consumption varies in the same direction as investment. But he sought to keep his account close to the conventional approach.

On this view, income adjusts to equate savings, which varies with income, to investment, which, as a first approximation, is taken as exogenous (but later is considered to depend on income and interest rates). Investment is an addition to the stream of spending, saving is a withdrawal, and income settles at the point where they offset one another. This is definitely a demand equilibrium. But according to Keynes it is set in a context in which full employment prices and quantities are determined by supply and demand, that is, by the scarcity principle.

Keynes (1936) wrote:

> Our criticism of the accepted . . . theory . . . has consisted not so much in finding logical flaws . . . as in pointing out that its tacit assumptions are seldom or never satisfied . . . But if our . . . controls succeed in establishing an aggregate volume of output corresponding to full employment . . . the [neo-]classical theory comes into its own from this point onwards. If we suppose the volume of output to be given, i.e. to be determined by forces outside the [neo-]classical scheme of thought, then there is no objection to be raised against the [neo-]classical analysis of the manner in which private self-interest will determine what in particular is produced, in what proportions the factors will be combined to produce it, and how the value of the final product will be distributed between them.

Prices *and quantities* are therefore determined at full employment by the equilibrium of supply and demand. How is this to be reconciled with the idea of a demand equilibrium, which may occur at virtually any level of output and employment?[14]

Arguably, Keynes never provided an answer, but the conventional approach is simple and ingenious. As a matter of pure theory the only *equilibrium* is that of supply and demand at full employment. Aggregate demand may settle for longer or shorter periods at other levels – but these will be disequilibria ultimately due to wage or price rigidities. When all variables are perfectly flexible the only equilibrium position is full employment. Hence the *level of spending* must adjust – full employment supply must create the necessary demand. Below the full employment level, for example, prices must fall, raising the value of real wealth and thereby stimulating spending. Demand variables may influence the determination of the level of full employment, but the main feature is the adjustment of demand to the scarcity-determined position of full employment. However, in this approach "income" sometimes means payments to factors of production – wages plus profits—sometimes total spending – consumption plus investment—and sometimes total output – consumer goods plus capital goods. The relations between employment, productivity and output have not been clearly specified.

Consider a conventional Keynesian savings-investment diagram, with Y, "income," plotted along the horizontal axis, and S and I along the vertical (Figure 1.4). The I function rises slightly – higher Y encourages investment – and the S function rises steeply, starting from a negative value. The intersection shows the level of Y where withdrawals and injections balance. The problem here (concealed when I is taken as purely autonomous) is that Y has two different meanings, and neither can be measured on the same axis. In the S function, Y means incomes received by households, or $W + P$, wages plus profits, but in the I function Y stands for total expenditure, $C + I$, consumption plus investment. Investment rises when aggregate spending increases. Notice that this is not arbitrary; it would make no sense to think of saving as a positive function of total spending, or of investment as an increasing function of the costs of production, i.e. the incomes business is currently paying out. Since workers can save, and capitalists can consume, the two meanings of Y are not identical and need not be equal, except in equilibrium.[15]

In reality there are *three* separate and distinct ideas involved in the determination of demand equilibrium.[16] First, there is output, which, with given plant and equipment, operating a Flexible Employment technology at a constant level of productivity, will vary regularly with employment, $Y = Y(N)$. Second, there is expenditure (identically equal to revenue), $C + I$, which depends on income, $W + P$, and on expenditure itself. In the simplest case $C = W$, where W determines C, but, as we shall

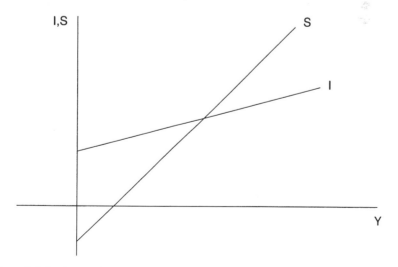

Figure 1.4 Saving and investment

see, $P = I$, and the causality runs from I to P. Income, in turn, depends on employment and on the level of the real wage, $W = wN$, and $P = Y - wN$. These relations can be plotted on a diagram (similar to that of the aggregate Marshallian system, except that here the output–employment function is a straight line): see Figure 1.5.

To clear up the ambiguities, measure employment, N, along the horizontal axis, and output, expenditure and income, expressed in monetary units, on the vertical. The first relationship above will be the line $Y(N)$. Here employment varies with output, while productivity remains constant. Output is adjusted to changing sales by varying employment rather than productivity – labor is a variable cost. The given wage rate will be the angle WON, and the wage bill will be given by the line W. Potential profit at any level of employment is therefore $Y(N) - W$. For simplicity assume that all profits are saved; if workers do not save, consumption will equal the wage bill; if they do, then it will be given by the dotted line, c_wW, where c_w is the worker propensity to consume.

Total expenditure can now be shown by marking off autonomous investment on the vertical axis and drawing from it the upward-sloping line labelled E, which represents $C + I$. If all investment is autonomous – higher levels of activity do not stimulate investment – this line will be parallel to c_wW; but, if higher activity has a positive influence on invest-

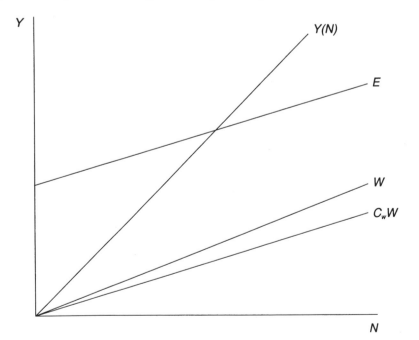

Figure 1.5 The determination of output and employment

ment, E will have a slope steeper than that of $c_w W$. Demand equilibrium is reached at the point of intersection between E and Y, where profit withdrawals just balance investment injections. The relation between Y and E is spelled out clearly and depends on employment and output. The conventional presentation was more inadequate than incorrect; it failed to show how the adjustment actually came about. Here it is clear that *employment* adjusts to equate the surplus to investment; the higher the real wage the larger the employment adjustment required for a given change in investment.

Even though Y is output and $Y(N)$ an output–employment function, this is not a conventional supply–demand equilibrium, for supply exercises no restraining force. Output and employment vary with sales, productivity at the margin remains constant. Supply thus adjusts, and the effects of such adjustment are felt as influences on demand. Supply conditions – capacity and productivity – establish boundaries, so to speak, for they define the potential profit and determine the size of the required adjustment in employment per unit change in autonomous spending. But the equilibrium point itself is a balance between influences furthering expenditure and those reducing it. There is no hint of scarcity to be found here.

Multiplier analysis of employment

Plant and equipment, then, will be designed to run at various levels with constant productivity, making it possible to adjust output to sales easily, while avoiding pressure to alter prices, which can be kept at levels appropriate for long-run development. On this view, in the long run, "normal" prices are considered determined by capital accumulation, seeking the most profitable outlets, in the light of growing markets. Given such prices, as determined in mark-up theories, variations in demand govern employment. But a central element in demand will be the real wage.

To study this we must look again at the "utilization" function, showing the degree of capacity utilized in response to demand. In conditions of inflexible employment and diminishing returns, as we have seen, changes in the real wage might well be required for changes in employment.[17]

But mass-production is designed for flexibility; start-up and shut-down costs are slight, work is designed to require minimal skills, and the pace of work is controlled by the machinery. Productivity is therefore fixed, but output can be varied in line with the rate of sales. When demand falls, production lines can be shut down or put on short time, and workers laid off; when demand recovers, workers will be recalled as production is raised. (Laid-off workers retain a connection with their firms; moreover, they still belong to the union.[18]) There is no need to reorganize work crews, or reactivate whole plants. The system is designed for flexibility. Since both output and variable costs can be adjusted easily in the short run, changes in demand need not result in price changes. With prices and money wages given, the real wage is fixed. In conjunction with the real wage, then, the level of employment determines the total wage bill. (Money wages and prices can, of course, deviate from their long-period levels during the short run, but these changes should be considered second-order modifications of the analysis.)

Since the great bulk of wages are consumed, by determining employment a substantial step is taken towards determining short-run consumption. If we further assume that profits are largely retained, and temporarily take investment as exogenous, we have the makings of a simple macro system, illustrated above, in Figure 1.5. We remember that the vertical axis measured output, the horizontal employment. We made the provisional assumption that the productivity of labor would be unaffected by changes in utilization – for the very good reason that mass-production plants are designed to ensure just that! (Barnes 1958; Nell, 1992: ch. 16) Given the real wage, the wage bill is expressed by a ray from the origin, as shown, and, on the assumption that all and only wages are consumed, this also gives us household consumption. Then adding investment, and perhaps a fixed level of consumption for managers and property owners, we get aggregate demand. Of course, worker saving will reduce the angle of the consumption function; unemployment compensation can be expressed by a line of payments inversely related to employment. But, ignoring these complications, in the basic case the multiplier depends only on the real wage and the productivity of labor, so that:

multiplier $= 1/(1 - wn)$

where w is the real wage and n is the productivity of labor. Hence assuming a closed system, and neglecting government, $Y = mI$, and $\Delta Y = m \, \Delta I$.

The multiplier requires that firms be able to adjust their current spending on wages and materials quickly and easily. Banks will find it profitable to provide funds by offering lines of credit. (For this system to work a lender of last resort will be required. The result will be to make the supply of bank money endogenous in the sense of being strictly and rapidly responsive to changes in demand (Moore 1988; Deleplace and Nell 1996; Lavoie, 1992: ch. 4.)

The multiplier and the elasticity of consumption

In à mass-production economy employment reflects the degree to which capacity is utilized. Variations in demand are met by varying utilization, keeping prices and productivity constant. When demand falls, workers are laid off, reducing their incomes and so also their consumption; when it increases they are re-employed, up to and even beyond rated capacity.[19]

38

Investment constitutes the demand for capital goods; neglecting other forms of consumer spending, wages provide the demand for consumer goods. Gross profits are withdrawn at each stage in both sectors. Given a variation in investment spending, the multiplier sequence will be:

$$\Delta C_1 = wn_k \Delta I$$

$$\Delta C_2 = wn_c \Delta C_1 = wn_k wn_c \Delta I$$

$$\Delta C_3 = wn_c \Delta C_2 = wn_k (wn_c)^2 \Delta I$$

etc.

Hence the sequence converges to:

$$\Delta C = \{(wn_k)/[1 - wn_c]\}\Delta I$$

This is the multiplier; a change in investment generates an accompanying change in the same direction in consumption. In this form the multiplier depends on the share of variable costs in revenue, and on the real wage. The psychological propensities of households are not significant (Nell 1992: chs 16, 20, esp. pp. 504–7.)

In a mass-production economy, money wages and money prices are stable or move together, so that, with fixed productivity, output is adjusted to sales. Fluctuations in investment will then lead to changes in employment as workers are either laid off or rehired or find themselves working short-time or overtime, resulting in changes in their pay and so in consumption spending. Rises and falls in investment will be accompanied by changes in the same direction in consumption. This can be illustrated on a diagram that is a simple variant of the earlier diagrams, aggregating the sectors. The output–employment function will be a straight line, since productivity is fixed by the nature of the equipment. Consumption, investment and the wage will be the same as before, and the equilibrium will be as shown on the previous diagram, with a multiplier of $1/(1 - wn)$.

To see the significance, rewrite the multiplier formula. In the aggregate integrated form it says that $I = Y(1 - wn) = P$. Business savings are withdrawn each round, until withdrawals balance the injections of investment. This is correct, but by aggregating we have lost information. In the two-sector, integrated form the formula reads:

$$Iwn_k = C(1 - wn_c)$$

This shows that the expansion takes place in the consumer goods sector, and it states the familiar result that the wage bill of the capital goods sector will be rendered equal to the gross profits of the consumer goods sector by the process of responding. This is the same relationship that has been shown to play a central role in the theory of circulation, especially in regard to the "secondary circulation" of the wage bill in the capital goods sector. In that circulation the proceeds of the sale of capital goods to the consumer goods sector moved successively through the capital goods sector, enabling the producers to pay their wages. The *spending* of those wages on consumer goods, producing the profits of the consumer goods sector, is what we see above in the multiplier formula. (In the discussion of the fixed employment systems of mercantilism and early capitalism (Nell, 1995) the spending of the wage bill of the capital goods sector returned the funds to the merchants, but with mass-production technology the spending leads to changes in employment and output. The multiplier here is the obverse of the theory of circulation, in the context of a variable employment technology.)

Finally, let the term in brackets in the two-sector multiplier formula be M, so that $\Delta C = M\Delta I$; it then follows, by integration, that $C = MI$. Dividing the former by the latter, it follows that

$$\mathrm{d}C/C = \mathrm{d}I/I, \text{ and } [I\mathrm{d}C/C\mathrm{d}I] = 1$$

A proportional change in investment generates an equiproportional change in the same direction in consumption. The elasticity of consumption with respect to investment is unity. Under mass production the market maintains the constancy of the *ratio*, I/C, rather than the product of the two, as in the fixed employment economy.

STYLIZED FACTS

Many extraneous influences affect economic variables. So it is difficult to make general claims about the economy – there will always be exceptions. Moreover few relationships in economics are fully stable; they tend to be affected by external and arguably irrelevant forces. To deal with this Kaldor suggested the use of "stylized facts."[20] These pick out central and defining features and present them with the rough edges smoothed over, highlighted, so they can be seen with clarity.

"Stylized facts" are stated in general propositions; they present observable, repeatable relationships between measurable variables. They state that two or more variables move together in some definite pattern; or that two or more variables are independent of one another, or that certain relationships, for example certain ratios, can be expressed by constants. These facts are said to be valid over some considerable range of times and places, and can be verified or supported by different bodies of data.

"Stylizing" facts means to remove noise, to remove the influence of irrelevant variables, to cut away random or extraneous factors, so as to present the central relationship in pure – and, often, in simplified – form. If the relationship is complex or awkward, it may be "rounded off," or reduced to a more manageable format. What is irrelevant, or extraneous, however, may not be obvious. It will always call for judgment; it may also be a matter of theory.

In particular, many relationships involve variations that take place in the context of a *trend*, so that the relationship cannot be seen, or seen clearly, until the trend has been removed. Detrending, however, requires identifying the trend, which may well depend on deciding which factors determine the trend and which the variations around it. Different detrending procedures are likely to result in different patterns of fluctuation around the trend (Canova 1991).

Stylized facts can be considered at two levels. There are the individual facts, each of which tells us something about a particular area of the economy, and then there is the pattern or configuration that can be seen in a group of such facts.[21] If the stylized facts encompass the main features of the economy they will give us a picture of the system as a whole. To make that judgment, of course, requires a theory that defines the main features of the economy.

A different kind of judgment is needed to determine the range of times and places for which these facts should be expected to hold. Are economic relationships timeless, that is, expected to hold always and everywhere? If they are derived from rational choice, perhaps they should. But if such a notion of rationality is unrealistic, or inconsistent with other aspects of human thought and culture, as philosophers have suggested (Hollis 1995; Hargreaves-Heap 1989; Hollis and Nell 1975), economic relationships may be *historical*, in the sense that they hold for particular periods of history and not otherwise.

This is the perspective adopted here. Fifteen general propositions have been established about the trade cycle at different times. These will be grouped under six headings, with representative sources cited. The claims will be presented separately, under the same headings, for an earlier and a later historical period. In each case, taken together, the propositions provide an approximately accurate picture over most of the period. The two pictures present a striking contrast. Moreover, the subject matter is central to economic analysis: prices, money wages, employment, productivity, expenditure, trade, investment, and money are at issue. Institutions – government and the firm – are also portrayed. Sources and brief explanations will be given, but no attempt will be made here to justify the claims in detail. Nor is it claimed that the list of proposed "facts" is complete – only that it is sufficient to suggest two different coherent pictures. The first group of propositions presents a portrait of the old trade cycle of the nineteenth century, running roughly from the Napoleonic Wars to World War I, although respectable data exist only after about 1860 – and even then much is questionable. The second covers the post-World War II era.

THE OLD TRADE CYCLE

Business units tended to be small, operating relatively inflexible methods of production, meaning that the factory or shop could be either operated or shut down, but could not easily be adjusted to variable levels of output. Prices, on the other hand, were flexible in both directions, as were money wages. The price mechanism appeared to operate. The cycle could be seen in price data.

Prices and money wages

1. The trend of prices was downwards over the whole period. By contrast, the trend of money wages was more or less flat in the first half-century, then moderately rising.[22]

Sources. Sylos-Labini (1989), esp. tables 1, 2; (1992), esp. table 1, appendix 1; Pigou (1929), esp. charts 3, 11, 14, 15, 16; Phelps Brown and Hopkins (1981), chs 7, 8. There was an upturn in prices in the 1860s, and a smaller one just before World War I, but the trend is dominant. The latter half of the nineteenth century shows a slight upward trend in money wages, more pronounced after 1900.[23]

2. Both prices and money wages changed in both directions. Changes in raw material prices (deviations from the trend) were greater in both directions than changes in manufacturing prices, which in turn were greater than changes in money wages.[24]

Sources. As above, plus Pedersen and Petersen (1938), who focus on the contrast between flexible and relatively inflexible prices. Most of their most flexible prices were those of raw materials. It is noticeable, however, that even their "inflexible" prices (prices that remain unchanged for more than one year, a number of times over the century) exhibit a downward trend (p. 222). See also Zarnowitz (1992: 150–1).

Employment, output and real wages

3. Changes in unemployment (proxy for output) were less than the changes in prices; changes in unemployment were "small." Although direct measurements of output are hard to come by, output and employment varied together, with output variations being larger. Prices and output varied together, with price fluctuations being somewhat greater than those of

output (deviations from trend). Changes in investment and net exports are often associated with opposite variations in consumption; they certainly do not lead to variations in the same direction, as the multiplier would require.

Sources. As above. Double-digit unemployment was rare, cf. Pigou (1927: charts 18, 19). Hoffmann (1959) provides an output index based on forty-three series, which Phelps Brown adapts for 1861-1913. Pigou uses unemployment as a proxy for output. Sylos-Labini (1984) compares changes in prices, wages and output. Nell and Phillips (1995, reprinted as Chapter 5 of this volume) found evidence inconsistent with a multiplier in Canadian data for 1870–1914. Block & Kucera (Chapters 8–9 of this volume) have confirmed the correlation between prices and output for Germany and Japan respectively.

4. Putting these together, it can be seen that real wages, or more particularly product wages, moved countercyclically. That is to say, real wages varied directly with unemployment.

Sources. Pigou (1927: esp. charts 16, 18, 20); Michie (1987). Michie recalculates the work of Dunlop (1938) and Tarshis (1939), and finds that product wages moved countercyclically before World War I (ch. 8). US figures are problematical, but a weak countercyclical pattern is evident in the late nineteenth century.[25] (This will be a major point of contrast with the post-war era, although Michie contends that international comparisons are so difficult that it is hard to generalize. But in the later period some patterns of procyclical movement can be detected.) Nell and Phillips (1995, Chapter 5 of this volume) find evidence tending to confirm an inverse relationship between real wages and employment in Canadian data; Block and Kucera (Chapters 8–9 of this volume), respectively, confirm the inverse relationship for Germany and Japan, as does Thomas (Chapter 6 below) for the United Kingdom.

Productivity and output

5. Output as a function of labor, both for individual plants and for the economy as a whole, was believed by virtually all contemporary – and later – economists to exhibit diminishing returns. Actual evidence, however, is weak, although, as will be explained later, a good case can be made for a version of diminishing returns. Productivity, however, is closely correlated with short-run variations in output in many industries, and positively correlated in general, and varies in both directions more than employment.
Sources. Pigou (1927: 9–10); Aftalion (1913). Calculations made from Hoffmann's data on nineteenth-century Germany show the strong correlations between productivity and output in the short run, and the greater variation of productivity compared with employment.[26]

6. Long-run productivity growth (measured in moving averages) was irregular and unpredictable, and lower than in later periods, although

significant. It was transmitted to the economy through falling prices, with stable money wages. The rise in long-run real wages is closely correlated with productivity growth.

Sources. Pigou (1927); Phelps Brown and Hopkins (1981); Sylos-Labini (1993).

Money and interest

7. The (nominal) quantity of money was correlated with both output and prices. Changes in the quantity of money appeared to affect prices. Income velocity fluctuated somewhat, but showed no trend. In some respects the system behaved as if money were fixed exogenously. This requires some explanation.

Sources. Pigou (1927: 132 *et passim*, 166–72); Snyder (1924). By mid-century the economies of Europe had shifted to the gold standard, prior to which they had operated on bimetallist principles. It is generally agreed that the gold standard behaved as if the economy relied on "outside" money, that is, on an exogenous money supply (Patinkin 1965). To be sure, bank checking deposits were beginning, and note issue by country banks was not closely bound by reserves, either in the United States or in the United Kingdom. But in a loosely organized banking system, without clearly defined policies governing the lender of last resort, prudent financial management required tightening reserves and raising the discount rate in the face of expansion and rising prices, and vice versa in times of falling prices. Central banks followed the "rules of the game" (Pigou 1927: 279; Eichengreen 1985).[27] Money may not have been strictly exogenous, but prudent management required the banking system to behave as if it were.

8. Investment booms were accompanied by over-eager financial expansion, leading to crises and crashes. These precipitated investment slumps and financial contraction. Variations in employment and prices closely matched expansions and contractions of credit.

Sources. Hicks (1989: ch. 11); Mill (1848: Book III, ch. 12); Pigou (1929); Kindleberger (1978: esp. 3, 4, 6, 8, and appendix). Interest rates and prices rose together in the upswing and fell together in the downswing. The financial crash was usually the signal for the expansion to collapse.

9. The average level of the long-term rate of interest was fairly stable from the mid-nineteenth century until World War I, and after the war continued to be moderately stable until the 1930s. Interest rates in the United States, however, fluctuated more than those of the United Kingdom, but nominal rates tended to fall as prices also fell. What Keynes termed "Gibson's paradox" held during more than a century – levels and changes of the nominal interest rate were closely correlated with levels and changes of the wholesale price index, and the long rate was more

closely correlated than the short rate. (Hence the nominal interest rate and the nominal quantity of money were correlated.) Both contrast markedly with the post-war era.

Sources. Kalecki calculates deviations from a nine-year (cycle-long) moving average of UK consols and shows that they are very small (Osiatinski 1990: 297, table 16). Kalecki considers this sufficient justification to treat the long rate as a constant in developing models of the business cycle. B. Friedman (1986: fig. 7.1) shows stable interest rates on commercial paper from 1890 to 1914. Homer and Sylla (1991: 289) show that money rates fluctuated around a declining average the decade following 1870 and then were steady the next two decades, rising after 1900 to the outbreak of the Great War. Prussian and German imperial bonds were steady from 1850 to the end of the century (Homer and Sylla 1991: 258). Keynes (1931: vol. 2) discusses "Gibson's Paradox."

Besides these strictly economic trends and relationships there are a number of important institutional facts that have changed dramatically. These, of course, are more difficult to substantiate with hard data. Nevertheless the historical record seems to support a set of generalizations – with the caveat that there may be many exceptions.

Business organization, finance and the state

10. Business was organized and operated by family firms. Firms invested to achieve an optimum size, at which they would then remain, varying their output around the least cost level.

Sources. Pigou (1927). Chandler (1977, 1989) examines the rise of large-scale corporations, beginning in the late nineteenth century. These early corporations are clearly the exception. Firms grew to their optimum size and remained at that level thereafter (Robinson 1931). Nell and Phillips, drawing on Urquhart, found marked changes in firm size and organization for Canada.

11. Once firms reached their optimum size, they did not retain earnings for investment; profits were distributed, saved (or spent) and then loaned for investment by new firms. Finance for investment was thus predominantly external, raised through issuing bonds.

Sources. As above. The bulk of investment represented borrowed savings or savings advanced by entrepreneurs, and was carried out by new firms (Clark 1895). See also Urquhart (1986) on Canada.

12. Governments tended to play a passive role in economic affairs; the "nightwatchman State" intervened little and planned less. Most intervention took the form of subsidizing development. Government spending and transfers together normally amounted to less than 10 per cent of GNP, in some cases near 5 per cent, and showed no trend until just before World War I.

Sources. Maddison (1984, 1991: esp. table 1; Hoffmann (1985); Urquhart (1986).

World trade and investment

The period of the old business cycle saw the first great global expansion of trade and investment. By 1914 the ratio of trade to GNP for Great Britain had risen to a level that was not reached again until the 1960s. Foreign investment also rose to levels comparable to those of today. But the composition and nature of that era's trade and investment differed importantly from today's.

13. Trade between advanced countries and colonies or less developed regions tended to exceed the volume of trade between advanced countries and other advanced countries. Intra-firm trade was low, and there was very little cross-border manufacturing.

Sources. Michie and Smith (1995); Nayyar (1995); Krugman and Obstfeld (1994).

14. In composition, trade in the old period was made up of primary goods, coming from the colonies and less developed regions, exchanged against final products from the central countries. The ratio of primary and final products to the total was high. The list of goods involved in trade was stable; the volume of services in trade was low in comparison with goods.

Sources. As above.

15. In 1913 the ratio of the stock of foreign direct investment to world GNP was 9 per cent; today it is 7.2 per cent. The stock of foreign investment in developing countries in 1914 was $179 billion, almost double the stock in 1980, which stood at $96 billion. In the old period 55 per cent of foreign investment went to mining and other primary sector activities, 30 per cent to transport, trade and distribution, with only 10 per cent in manufacturing, much of which was concentrated in North America and Europe.

Sources. As above, esp. Nayyar (1995).

The character of the cycle

In general, the old business cycle was long, ranging from eight to eleven years, with a long slow build-up to a rapid boom, culminating in a crisis with a sharp short fall to the bottom, followed by a slump of variable duration. Then recovery would come, gradually slowing down to a long period of normalcy, followed by another boom. The shape has been compared to a "saw-tooth." Two versions are illustrated. The cycle fluctuated around a moderate growth rate. Now consider the same categories in the post-World War II era.

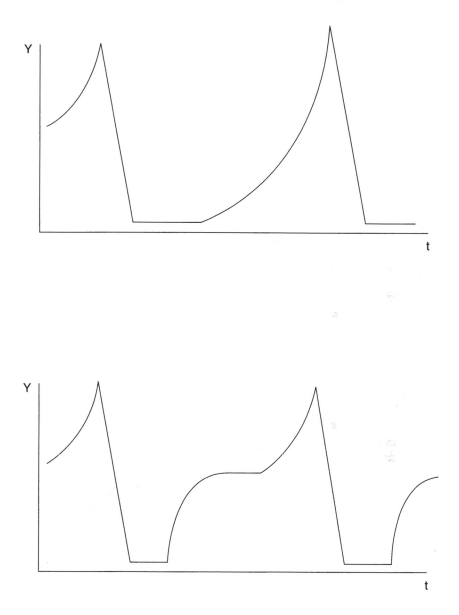

Figure 1.6 Two versions of the sawtooth

THE NEW TRADE CYCLE

The family firm has been superseded by the modern corporation, operating mass-production technology, in which it is able to lay off labor and adapt output and employment easily to changing sales.[28] The price mechanism is no longer in evidence. The cycle is more evident in relations between quantities than in price data.[29]

Prices and money wages

1. The trend of prices was upward the whole period, and the trend of money wages rose even more steeply. Neither prices nor money wages (as measured by general indices) turned down, though rates of inflation sometimes slowed in recessions.

Sources. As above. Also, for comparisons of prices and outputs with the earlier period, Taylor (1986). For wages and prices, Gordon (1986). For a brief discussion of "stylized facts" regarding wholesale and retail prices, the price level, monetary aggregates, short and long interest rates, investment, and the timing of indicators, Zarnowitz (1985, 1992).

2. Raw material prices fluctuated more than manufacturing prices, and occasionally fell, though less (in proportion) than in the old trade cycle. Money wage changes were proportionally greater than price changes. Real prices showed great stability, changing only with changes in productivity.

Sources. As above, plus Godley and Nordhaus (1987). Ochoa (1984) demonstrated the strong stability of real prices using 86 × 86 input–output tables. See also Leontief (1989).

Employment, output and real wages

3. Changes in unemployment and output were greater proportionally than changes in prices or money wages; changes in unemployment were large.[30] Output varied in both directions, while prices only rose; the correlation between the two was weak, although price rates of change – inflation – weakly correlate with output in the first half of the era. Output variations exhibit a multiplier relationship: autonomous fluctuations in investment and net exports are magnified by a factor estimated at a little less than 2.

Sources. As above, esp. Sylos-Labini (1989). Evans (1969), surveys the estimates of the value of the multiplier as of that date.

4. Changes in real wages (product wages) tended either to be mildly procyclical or not to exhibit a distinct pattern. For the United States a weak procyclical pattern has been "largely confirmed" (Blanchard and Fischer 1989: 17; Majewski Chapter 7 of this volume). See also Chapters 5, 6, 8 and 9 of this volume.

Sources. Michie (1986: chs 4–6); Blanchard and Fischer (1989: 17–19); Zarnowitz (1992: 146–50).

Productivity and output

5. Output as a function of employment tends to exhibit constant or increasing returns, according to Okun's law, supported by Kaldor's laws.
Source. Lowe (1970), esp. ch. 10.
6. Productivity growth is transmitted to households through money wages rising more rapidly than prices. It tends to move procyclically and is the major source of increasing *per capita* income. The trend over the cycle was stable until the 1970s. Its decline since then has led to stagnant real incomes.
Sources. Michie (1987); Okun (1981).

Money and interest

7. The supply of money is endogenous, responding to demand pressures. The quantity of money for transactions (M_1) is correlated with *nominal* income, but is not closely related either to output or to prices. Changes in the quantity of money appear to affect interest rates. Income velocity for M_1 shows a strong upward trend.
Sources. Moore (1988); Wray (1990); Nell (1992). "Endogenous money" has many meanings, but the point is that the money supply is not a constraint on real expansion.
8. Over time financial booms and crises became more loosely linked with the movement of prices, unemployment, and output. Real booms generated financial expansion, but financial expansion proved possible even in sluggish and slumping conditions. Credit crunches sometimes, but not always, appeared to slow inflation, and sometimes, but not always, slowed expansion. Crashes no longer led to immediate slumps.
Sources. Hicks (1989: ch. 11); Wray (1990).
9. The long-term rate of interest varied substantially in the post-war era. From the early 1950s to the early 1960s the real long-term rate rose from near zero in both the United States and Great Britain. It then fell to nearly zero – below, by some accounts – in 1975, then rose steeply to over 7.5 per cent in 1985, and fell again thereafter. Thus it fell during the inflation of the 1970s, and rose during the early 1980s, as inflation declined. But the *nominal* long-term rate closely tracked the rate of inflation, with interest close to inflation in the 1950s, lying above it in the 1960s, then falling below in the mid-1970s, and rising above again in the 1980s. The correlation is high, and the turning points match closely.
Sources. Calculated from Citibase. The long rate was calculated as a five-year moving average (the average length of the post-war cycle) from 1950

to 1990 and then plotted. The prime rate and triple A bond rates were regressed on the GNP deflator. For a similar relation between nominal short rates and inflation see Mishkin (1981, 1992).

Business organization, finance and the State

10. The modern multidivisional corporation has replaced the family firm as the organizing institution through which most of GNP is created. Growth is carried out largely by existing firms. Under conditions of mass production there are economies of scale, and technological progress accompanies investment. Firms must invest continually just to keep up. It is no longer possible to define an optimal size for firms; the question has become their optimal rate of growth.

Sources. Eichner (1976); Wood (1978); Penrose (1954, 1974); Herman (1981); Williamson (1980).

11. Finance for investment has come to be largely internal, raised through retained earnings, for expansion projects carried out by existing firms.

Sources. As above. In the 1960s the ratio of corporate debt to assets rose, then fell in the 1970s, but rose again steeply in the 1980s (Semmler and Franke 1996). Gross investment was largely financed by retained earnings, but it could be argued that a large part of net investment was financed by borrowing. Gross investment is the relevant figure for growth, however, since replacements incorporate technical innovations. Moreover, much of the growth of corporate debt in the 1980s was connected with take-overs and mergers (Caskey and Fazzari 1992).

12. Government intervention and planning became a regular feature of the post-war economic scene. Government expenditures plus transfers had risen to over a third of GNP after the war, and continued to rise as a percentage of GNP throughout the period, faltering only in the 1980s.[31]

Sources. Maddison (1982); Nell (1988).

World trade and investment

13. The volume of trade among advanced countries exceeds the trade between advanced countries and developing nations. Intra-firm trade is high, making up 40 per cent of the total of world trade, and as much as 60 per cent of US trade. Cross-border manufacturing has become extensive, with estimates suggesting that one-third of world manufacturing involves global outsourcing by transnational corporations.

Sources. Michie and Smith (1995); Nayyar (1995).

14. In trade in the post-war world the ratio of intermediate goods and capital goods to the total has been high. The list of goods traded has changed rapidly, and the ratio of services to goods in trade has been high.

Sources. As above.

15. The stock of direct foreign investment in the modern era, having fallen substantially in relation to world GNP, has now risen to a level comparable to that just before the First World War. In 1913 it was 9.0 per cent; in 1960 it was only 4.4 per cent, in 1980 4.7 per cent, but by 1991 it had risen to 7.2 per cent (Kozul-Wright, 1995: table 6.9). The flow of world FDI rose from 1.1 per cent of world gross fixed capital formation in 1960 to 2.9 per cent in 1991. However, its composition is very different from the FDI of pre-World War I. Today only 10 per cent of direct foreign investment goes to primary activities, whereas 40 per cent goes to manufacturing and 50 per cent is in services.

The character of the cycle

The new business cycle has generally been shorter, with less precipitous collapses but longer slumps and slower recoveries than the old. The boom is not so sweeping. The shape of the cycle is broadly a succession of hills and valleys, with a slow climb at the start, then up the steep slope, easing off toward the peak, turning down slowly, and then accelerating down, gradually easing off and sliding into the bottom.

The pattern of growth is significantly different. In the period of the old business cycle population growth was an important determinant of economic growth. In the new period it is less important for the United States, and population plays no role at all in the growth of the major European States. In general the cycle has tended to fluctuate around a much higher rate of growth and, in particular, a far higher rate of productivity growth. The latter has been closely associated with increases in the capital–labor ratio, and both are positively related to the level of the rate of growth. The

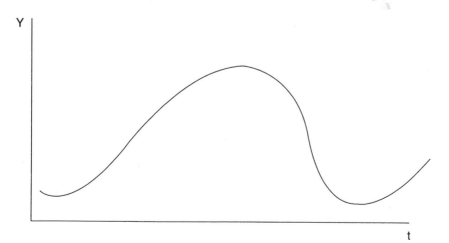

Figure 1.7 The hills and valleys of the new cycle

overall rate of growth and the average level of the general rate of profit are closely associated. (To put it another way: profits are highly correlated with investment.) The labor force participation rate is positively associated with the rate of growth.

Summary

To summarize the "stylized" differences between the two periods:

1   The agents have changed in size and character, from family firms to modern corporations.
2   Markets have changed their pattern of adjustment, from one in which prices move procyclically and real wages countercyclically to one in which prices only rise, and real wages move erratically or procyclically
3   A macroeconomy in which consumption varies inversely with investment and net exports changes to one in which the multiplier is prominent. (Variations in investment and net exports set off similar variations in consumption.)
4   The system in which productivity increases are transmitted through falling prices changes to one in which the transmission comes through rising money wages.
5   A financial system in which interest rates are procyclical changes to one in which they appear to behave erratically.
6   A money supply that is, or behaves as if it were exogenous changes to one that is endogenous.
7   And, finally, a non-intervening "Nightwatchman" State changes to an interventionist Keynesian State.

STRUCTURAL DIFFERENCES

The preceding points concern the nature of firms and the way markets work. Besides these differences there are others which describe the changes in the structure of the economy between the two eras. Two are particularly noticeable: the size relationships between sectors changed, and so did the character of costs.

All through the period of the "old trade cycle" labor flowed out of agriculture and primary products into manufacturing and services. Output in the latter two grew more rapidly. As labor moved out of the primary sector it settled in large towns and cities, which grew rapidly. In the period of the "new trade cycle" labor continued to leave agriculture, but manufacturing ceased to grow, while services changed character and became the fastest-expanding sector. Urbanization ceased, the cities stagnated and even declined. But the suburbs expanded, as did the large metropolitan areas.

Table 1.1 shows the approximate range of sizes of sectors as proportions of GDP in the two periods. The table includes government under "services." Separating it out is revealing (see Table 1.2). Labor costs have fallen in all sectors as a proportion of total costs; they were higher in the earlier era in every sector, but they have fallen as fast in agriculture as in manufacturing (see Table 1.3). In the earlier period blue-collar labor costs made up between half and two-thirds of all labor costs. In the era of mass production blue-collar work has fallen to much less than half of total labor costs.

In the earlier period plant was designed to produce a certain level of output; varying production was costly and difficult. In the later period, employment and output could be varied more easily, so that average

Table 1.1 Sectors of the world economy as a proportion of GDP (%)

Sector	Craft-based factories	Mass production
Agriculture	40–50	5–10
Services	35–50	40–60
	Mostly personal	Mostly business
	Low-tech, unproductive	Increasingly high-tech
Manufacturing	10–15	35–50
	Increasing	Stable or decreasing

Note
Because these are ranges the percentages do not add up.

Table 1.2 Government expenditure as a proportion of GDP

Craft era	Mass production
10% or less	40%–55%
Included in services	Spending on services and manufacturing; transfers; government production
Stable	Rising

Table 1.3 Labor costs as a proportion of total costs (%)

Sector	Craft era	Mass production
Agriculture	66–75	20–25
Services	75	33–66
Manufacturing	66	20–25

variable cost curves contained a long flat stretch (Hansen 1948; Mansfield 1978; Lavoie 1992: 118–28).

CONCLUSION

Real-world economies will always be a mixture; very likely no economy was ever purely a craft, fixed-employment or purely a mass-production type. But each is bound to its own mode of operation, which determines a definite way for its markets to adjust to variations in demand. In the mass-production economy, adjustment takes place through the multiplier, but in the craft economy the adjustment process works through prices and distribution – the difference resting on the different nature of costs in the two systems (Nell 1992: ch.16). But these costs, in turn, set up incentives for firms to begin the transformation from craft to mass production, and, once set in motion, the process of transformation begins to feed in a cumulative manner on itself, as we will see in the studies that follow.

This chapter has presented two distinct systems of technology – the systems of craft and mass production – arguing that they implied two distinct patterns of market adjustment, and then showing that the stylized facts for two distinct eras in the history of the developed world tended to support this conclusion. The chapters of this volume will further explore and develop these stylized facts, relating them to issues and controversies, past and present. The focus will be on the contrast between price adjustments in the earlier period and quantity adjustments in the later. The working of the monetary system and the role of financial markets – domestic and global – will have to be dealt with separately, perhaps in another volume.

NOTES

1 Indeed, it can be argued that the theory of flexible price adjustment should *not* be cast in such a mold. Neoclassical general equilibrium theory, based on rational choice, provides few, if any, empirically testable insights, while at the same time generating serious theoretical difficulties. It cannot rule out multiple equilibria, some or all of which may be unstable. It cannot find a plausible rationale for the use of money (Hahn 1973). It cannot make room for capital, earning a rate of return which competitively tends to uniformity (Garegnani 1976). A sensible price theory should give us plausible criteria for uniqueness and stability, a reasonable account of the usefulness of money, and a coherent understanding of the rate of return on capital. Early neoclassical theory, as developed by Wicksell, Walras, Clark, Marshall and Pigou, for example, aimed to supply all of these. Their constructions were defective, as later studies have shown, but the answer is surely not to abandon their goals, in order to

preserve their approach, but to adjust the approach in order to achieve the goals. Applied economics needs a plausible account of flex-price adjustment.

2 Macroeconomics is often presented as aggregate supply and demand, a sibling of microeconomic theory, expressed in the same format, with downward-sloping demand and rising supply curves. The general price *level* functions analogously to the microeconomic price variable. The analogy is flawed. Micro prices are paid and received; no one pays or receives the price *level*. Micro quantities are measurable in their own units; the macro analogues are revenues, price × quantity. Worst of all, in many formulations movements along the aggregate supply curve will cause the aggregate demand curve to shift – the two functions are not independent of one another (Nell 1992).

3 These technological changes did not just happen; they were themselves the product of market incentives and pressures, brought about by the problems and opportunities faced by firms in their everyday business. This is the subject of the theory of *Transformational Growth*, but those issues will be discussed later (Nell 1992, and in Thomson 1993).

4 For further elaboration cf Nell (1992: chs 16, 17) and Nell, in Thomson (1993) and the references cited there. Argyrous (1992) provides a case study of the aircraft industry. Howell (1993) proposes a similar classification.

5 Assuming for simplicity that all and only wages are consumed, the crucial dividing line occurs when the curvature of the production function is such as to give rise to a marginal product curve of unitary elasticity. At this point the proportional decline in the real wage is exactly offset by the proportional rise in employment. If the curvature were greater, the rise in employment would not offset the fall in the real wage – so that consumption would *decline* as a result of a rise in investment demand that led to a bidding up of prices. If the curvature were less, then a rise in investment, bidding up prices, would lead to such a large rise in employment that consumption would *increase*. This is the multiplier relationship.

6 This discussion concerns the "normal" behavior of "stylized" actual market agents, e.g. family firms or modern corporations, working-class or middle-class households. It is not concerned with the "idealized rational agents," conceived independently of social context, that populate the models of much contemporary economic theory. The normal behavior of stylized actual agents may well involve maximizing subject to constraints, and will generally be "rational" in some sense. But it is shaped and determined by context and institutions (Nell and Semmler 1991: Introduction).

7 The shift to reduced stability was remarked by Duesenberry (1958: 285): "the historical changes in the structure of the American economy which occurred during the first quarter of the twentieth century tended to reduce the stability of the system." However, Duesenberry did not offer a clear explanation. He suggested that there was a tendency for changes in investment to be offset by opposite changes in consumption in the era between the Civil War and World War I (p. 287), and he developed a multiplier–accelerator model, which, however, was defective (Pasinetti 1960). But his approach outlined a loose general framework that would apply universally, allowing for changes in parameters that would allow each cycle to be different. He did not suggest a systematic change from a stabilizing market mechanism to an essentially unstable one.

8 Evans (1969: chs 19–20) calculates a variety of multipliers, including "multipliers" with induced investment, on various assumptions, and presents numerical estimates for the post-war United States.

9 Hicks (1950) examined the plausible ranges of values of the multiplier and capital–output ratios, and concluded that, empirically, the system had either to be unstable or to generate anti-damped cycles. Matthews (1959) reviews the literature, and appears to regard models with an unstable endogenous mechanism, running up against buffers, as the most reasonable. A related school of thought argued that advanced capitalist economies had an in-built propensity to stagnate, which would have to be offset by government expenditure (Kalecki 1972; Steindl 1976), possibly abetted by various kinds of private "unproductive" expenditure (Baran and Sweezy 1966). In this case the instability is seen to hold in one direction only – or chiefly – namely downwards. But it is denied that there are any "self-correcting" adjustment mechanisms.

10 Duesenberry (1958: 278) judges that ceiling theories cannot explain the upper turning point.

11 Fair, for example, holds that the "word 'multiplier' should be interpreted in a very general way . . . [as showing] . . . how the predicted values of the endogenous variables change when one or more exogenous variables are changed" (p. 301). First the model is estimated, then the initial value(s) of the exogenous parameters are set, and the value(s) of the endogenous variables are calculated. The exogenous parameters are then changed, and the new value(s) of the endogenous variables are found. The difference between the two sets of values shows the impact of the change; if only a single parameter is changed, the value of a single endogenous variable can be divided by that change to calculate a "multiplier." The advantage of this approach is its generality; the disadvantage is that it incorporates into the same calculation of the impact of a change processes that rest on foundations that differ greatly in reliability. The "passing along" of expenditure and of costs is measurable and reliable, but the response of financial variables to other changes is less so, and the response of real variables to financial variables is notoriously unstable. Multipliers calculated by Fair's method are unlikely to be worth the trouble of estimating them. By contrast, Keynes–Kalecki expenditure multipliers are based on reliable relationships, as are the *long-run* "multipliers" calculated from input–output data. These latter, however, do not tell us anything about the effects of changes in spending.

12 The capital controversy has shown that the well-behaved neoclassical production function, in which the form of capital changes as techniques vary, is unacceptable. Of course, this critique does not affect the Marshallian function.

13 Say's law has been formulated in many ways: "supply creates its own demand" and "all savings are automatically invested" are the two most common. But as the argument between Ricardo and Malthus showed (Ricardo 1951: vol. 2; Costabile and Rowthorn 1985; Kurdas 1994) the first is best interpreted as saying that production distributes income equal to the value of output; it is a separate question whether all income is spent. The second is directed to this point; it has to mean investment will always rise to the level of *potential* (full capacity) savings, and empirically this is obviously false. Theoretically it has been hard to justify; neither interest rate mechanisms nor real balance effects have proved plausible. It is often argued that the postulate of Say's law began as a wrong but inspired guess, but has now become a part of the free-market ideology. The suggestion here is that a "Say's law" economy is a fixed employment system, in which movements in consumption and investment spending are offsetting.

14 Keynes arrived at the view that variations in investment determined output

and employment only in the spring of 1932. It was in his Easter Term lectures that he first set out this view clearly, provoking the "manifesto" by Joan and Austin Robinson and Richard Kahn, trying to clarify and sharpen his argument. The argument, however, never did get straightened out. But consider a production/utilization function with such sharply diminishing returns at the initial point that the proportional fall in the marginal product is greater than the proportional rise in employment. Expansion due to a rise in investment would thus imply a decline in the wage bill and, with a classical saving function, in consumption (Nell 1992: ch. 16). Conversely, if returns diminish only slightly, a rise in investment will lead to a proportional increase in employment that is larger than the proportional decline in the real wage. In this case, consumption will increase with investment.

15 It has sometimes been argued that sales receipts, which necessarily equal expenditure, are automatically passed along as income, so that income does always equal expenditure. This is simply wrong: income includes adjustments for inventory changes and for capital gains and losses. It is certainly not identical to, and does not necessarily even equal, sales receipts. Net income paid out, properly defined, does have to equal net output produced, but this will only equal net sales receipts if output adjusts quickly and accurately to sales. In equilibrium, of course, income, output and expenditure (sales receipts) will all be equal. But otherwise, and most of the time in reality, there will be differences. Income and output have to be equal in the final accounting, because income consists of claims to the value of output. Wages and salaries are deducted, then a portion goes to replace used-up or depreciated means of production – and whatever is left belongs to the producers, either as realized or as unrealized profits (inventory adjustments). But neither income nor output has to equal sales receipts; there is no reason to expect all output to be sold (except in a Say's Law economy). However, when output can be rapidly adjusted to sales the differences will be slight – but this is because there is a strong tendency to equilibrium.

16 Once income and expenditure are distinguished the conventional saving–investment diagram becomes hard to interpret. At a point on the horizontal axis, Y_1, for instance, conventional theory would say $I(Y) > S(Y)$, leading Y to increase. But $I(C + I) > S(W + P)$ is harder to understand; if $C + I = W + P$ at Y_1 will they still be equal at a higher level? Why? Which components will increase? What are the causal relations between expenditure and income? Analytically we have:

$$S = S(Y)$$
$$I = I(E)$$
$$S = I$$
$$Y = E$$

where $Y = W + P$ and $E = C + I$. If $I = I(Y)$ replaced the second equation, the system would make sense; $S = I$ is the balance between injection and withdrawal. But what is the rationale for $Y = E$? The familiar argument that, since income is either consumed or saved, we can write $Y = C + S$, so that whatever Y is, given $E = C + I$, $Y = E < - > S = I$, cannot be accepted. The saving function states that saving/consumption varies with *income*, $W + P$; $S = S(C + S)$ does not provide the required information, or even make sense. So what does it mean to claim $Y = E$? What kind of adjustment process is involved? How do we know such adjustments will not cause shifts in the saving or investment functions? These questions have answers, but to obtain them it is necessary to turn to the relationship between employment and output.

17 Hicks (1989) commenting on Pigou and Keynes, recently remarked, "Pigou was arguing from a fully Marshallian position, on the formation of the prices of manufactures, that in the 'short run' an increase of demand must raise their prices. So if money wages are given, an increase in 'effective demand' must lower real wages." Both Marshall and Pigou discuss short-run production functions in terms of "idle equipment" (Pigou 1944: 51-2) and consider "How actively . . . to work . . . appliances" (Marshall: 1961: 374) The conception is clearly that of a utilization function, rather than a production set from which techniques are chosen.

18 The lay-off *system* did not develop in the United States until after World War I, and did not become general until after World War II. The lay-off principle states that workers have a vested right in their jobs, implying that when laid off they have a right to be rehired in a definite order when business conditions improve. Early discussions took place in the Massachusetts state legislature in the 1890s. cf. A. Keysser, 1993.

19 A popular textbook and "newclassical" argument holds that the emergence of unemployment will bid money wages down, whereupon competition will force money prices down in proportion. Unemployment will certainly have some effect on the level of wages in new hirings, but it is difficult to see how a rise in unemployment, even over a long period of time, can affect the wages and salaries of those already in stable employment. Traditionally, the relation between wages and employment has been a long-run matter, as with other factor markets. But the discussion concerns short-term adjustments.

20 Kaldor observes that, "in the social sciences, unlike the natural sciences, it is impossible to establish facts that are precise and at the same time suggestive and intriguing in their implications, and that admit to no exceptions . . . . [w]e do not imply that any of these 'facts' are invariably true in every conceivable instance but that they are true in the broad majority of observed cases – in a sufficient number of cases to call for an explanation" (Kaldor 1985: 8–9).

21 A perhaps extreme case is the construction of "reference cycles," the method developed by Burns and Mitchell (1946) for the study of business cycles. The full cycle is divided into eight segments, and the behavior of the key variables as they move through the cycle is presented by averaging their values in these periods over a set of actual cycles.

22 Measuring trends presents notorious problems. In most of the earlier discussions variations were calculated by simple differencing. In more recent work segmented linear trends have been fitted. In the work done at the New School and in this volume many approaches have been tried; the results reported have survived different methods of detrending (Canova 1991).

23 These trends are consistent with the patterns of the previous centuries. In the latter part of the eighteenth century prices rose dramatically as a result of the French revolution and the Napoleonic Wars. From 1600 to 1775, however, prices of consumables in southern England were more or less flat, with a slight downward trend from 1650 on, broken only by sudden upturns due to wars. Builders' wages rose very moderately, staying flat for long periods, from 1600 to 1775, then rose steeply up to 1815, then went flat until the last quarter of the nineteenth century (Phelps Brown and Hopkins 1962: 170).

24 Since money wages are less flexible than money prices, it is implied that real wages are flexible. Since primary products are more flexible than manufactured goods, it is implied that the real price of primaries in terms of

manufactures changes. Other real price variations can be calculated from the data.

25 Ray Majewski has examined these figures in a dissertation, using the *Shipping and Commercial List*, and the *Aldrich Report* for pre-1890 prices, as a check on Warren and Pearson's wholesale price index. The BLS provides a historical index of wages per hour, and Angus Maddison has developed (1982) an index of real GNP, based on Gallman's (1966) study, which in turn is based on Kuznets (1961). Kuznets has been criticized by Romer (1989) and defended and revised by Balke and Gordon. Neither the Romer nor the Balke and Gordon data change the result that there is a countercyclical pattern evident in the US data. For further commentary see Chapter 7 of this volume.

26 If the relationship between output and employment were described by a well-behaved neoclassical production function, output and productivity should be related *inversely*, rather than directly. The widespread evidence of a positive relationship makes it clear that the countercyclical movement of product wages does not "confirm" traditional marginal productivity theory. Never-theless, the traditional theory appears to have been "on to something," and the object here is to find out what that was.

27 Some studies, notably Nurkse (1953), for the inter-war years, and Bloomfield (1959), for 1880–1914, have shown that central banks widely violated the rules. It is now generally recognized that central banks had considerable discretion, and that the stability of the gold standard system (which held only for the countries at the center – the periphery suffered frequent con-vertibility crises, devaluations, and internal credit crunches) reflected success-ful management (Sayers 1957), especially by the Bank of England. It was as much a sterling reserve system as a gold standard system.

28 Studies of the contrasts between the "old" and the "new" business cycle are provided in later chapters of this volume. Nell and Phillips (Chapter 5), studying Canada, find good evidence of an inverse relationship between product wages and employment in the old period, and a direct relationship in the new. They also find significant differences in the sizes and character-istics of firms, and in the nature of government between the periods. There is little evidence of a multiplier in the earlier period. Kucera, studying Japan (Chapter 9), finds similar results for product wages and output – with certain qualifications – and also a weakly negative relationship between consumption and investment in the earlier period, in contrast to a strongly positive relation-ship in the later. Block, studying Germany (Chapter 8), finds strongly con-trasting relationships between product wages and output in the two periods, as does Thomas in an examination of British data for the two periods (Chapter 6). Majewski finds similar results for the United States (Chapter 7).

29 The period from World War II to the present breaks somewhere in the early 1970s. The first part has been termed the "Golden Age" of modern capit-alism: growth rates of output and productivity were high, inflation and unemployment low, and the amplitude of the cycle was moderate. By contrast, in the later period, the growth of output and productivity became erratic and fell, inflation and unemployment became severe, and the cycle intensified. However, examining this change is not our purpose here (but see Chapters 6 and 11 in this volume). The era prior to World War I can also be subdivided into periods.

30 That is, even *with* countercyclical government intervention, the variations in employment are large in the post-war cycle. They would be far greater in the absence of such policies.

31 In addition, it should be noted that State expenditure in relation to GNP was high and rising during the period, in both military and civilian categories. It rose or remained high, in spite of explicit and politically inspired attempts to cut it back.

2

METHODS AND METHODOLOGY IN HISTORICAL MACROECONOMICS

Thorsten H. Block and Raymond C. Majewski

Everyone knows that the present will some day be history. I believe that the most important task of the social scientist is to try to comprehend it as history now, while it is still the present and while we still have the power to influence its shape and outcome.

(Paul Sweezy in the preface to *The Present as History*, 1953)

"MAKING THE CASE" FOR TRANSFORMATIONAL GROWTH

In the preceding chapter, and a series of other works, Edward Nell has sought to link fundamental changes in macroeconomic performance with changes in producer behavior. These changes in producer behavior are rooted in the "transformational growth" of capitalist economies – the growth that changes the technical and institutional structure within which producers act. In particular, Transformational Growth emphasizes the qualitative character of technical change in the shift from craft to mass-production systems in the early twentieth century. Mass-production technologies were adopted because they allowed producers to flexibly adjust output and employment to fluctuations in demand and keep prices constant at the same time. These changes in the character of production technologies in turn feed into market adjustment on the macro level. Transformational Growth is thus an attempt to ground macroeconomics on an understanding of the character of production technology: a macroeconomics based on the actual transformation of the production process in capitalist history.

This book is the first in a series designed to "make the case" for a Transformational Growth view of history. This is being done in a way that is unusual in economics. Economists as a group "delight in scientific talk, the closer to physics the better" (McCloskey 1985: 136). If you wish to persuade economists, it helps to use mathematical arguments built around physics metaphors such as equilibrium. This taste extends to empirical and historical work, where quantitative information analyzed through econometric technique is the only evidence worthy of consideration.

There is nothing wrong with quantitative analysis; Part III of this book consists of essays using quantitative methods. But we see no reason to limit our evidence to what can be counted. There is also nothing wrong with mathematical arguments. The use of mathematics has been identified as a helpful analytical tool for mainstream and non-mainstream economists alike (Dutt 1994: 7–12). Indeed, other works on Transformational Growth (Nell 1992; Nell 1997; Majewski 1996) make use of them. But we apply these techniques and metaphors as tools that complement rather than preclude other forms of analytical reasoning.

In making the case, we are trying to take history seriously, informing our theoretical work through historical study, and organizing our history with a theoretical foundation. The hope is an economics better able to understand change, an economics more relevant than purely deductive theorizing. The purpose of this chapter is to provide a link between the preceding chapter outlining the idea of Transformational Growth and the case studies which are designed to present empirical investigations informed by this perspective. In particular, we will first turn to a discussion of methodological issues in economic history with specific reference to other historical business cycle studies (pp. 62–73). We then turn to a discussion of the problems involved in using historical time series (pp. 73–76). which is followed by an introduction to some of the techniques and methods used in the country studies (pp. 76–79). We conclude by giving a brief outline of the country and case studies (pp. 79–81).

WHICH ROAD TO THE PAST?[1]

Before delving into a more detailed description of the "road to the past" adopted in this volume we will briefly present – in this and the following section – other approaches to economic history. In doing so our arguments will be organized according to two criteria (Table 2.1)[2]. First, since the birth of the "New" Economic History (which we will discuss shortly) the relationship between the role of theory and the role of narrative (facts) has been at the forefront of discussions of methodology in economic history (Field 1987). We will therefore analyze whether the different schools approach history *theory-* or *fact-driven*. In addition, one of the points of this chapter is to advocate a third, *interactive* approach in which both theory and narrative are intrinsically related in an understanding of the past. Second, economics and economic history over the last two decades have increasingly been identified with the neoclassical, marginalist paradigm as the *only* available consistent theoretical framework. At the fringes of the profession there exists, however, a small but thriving heterodox tradition which also produces historical analysis. Because of the diversity of this heterodox tradition – Marxian, neo-Marxist, post-Keynesian, institutionalist, etc. – we cannot provide an exhaustive survey here but merely attempt to highlight certain commonalities which, as we will argue, should establish heterodox economic theory as a viable alternative tool with which to investigate the past.

A good starting point in analyzing roads to the past is the "Old" narrative economic history. This history emphasized the qualitative description of a set of unique events (Stone 1981: 8). Clearly, because it does not presuppose a specific theoretical model, it stretches across the marginalist and heterodox rows of Table 2.1. There are two advantages of such a descriptive approach to economic history. First is its ability to handle uniqueness and contingency. The approach's most enduring results are in the areas where these are important, such as technical and institutional change. Second, it can result in the discovery of regularities or paradoxes that are likely to stimulate theorizing (Schabas 1995; Cairncross 1989). Field (1987: 22-3) writes in defense of narrative history that

> the contribution of such a theorist [a "New" economic historian] to the progress of economics is dependent on his or her being fed a diet of interesting and relevant puzzles or problems by those with more empirical or historical sensitivities. The belief that proficiency in axiomatic deductive reasoning can substitute for such a knowledge is a delusion. Ultimately pure theorists must look to research in economic history and other empirical fields for validation of the significance of their research, rather than vice versa.

The problems faced by the "Old" economic historian lie in the organization of the story. Facts *never* speak for themselves. Both they and the researcher arrive theory-laden. Specifying a clear analytical framework makes it possible to control for the chance of inconsistencies creeping into the analysis. It may well be that different steps in a causal chain of narrative argument are based on different theoretical models that are inconsistent with each other. A concise theoretical model has the advantage of providing a clear picture of the framework adopted and outlines the specific assumptions made to arrive at particular results. This also provides a clear-cut starting point for follow-up studies – relaxing certain assumptions, for example – or critics of the analysis who want to propose an alternative account of the same event. Since a historian's narrative is in one way or another conditioned by her experience, background and theoretical understanding, it pays to make such models explicit.

The dissatisfaction of a group of economic historians with this rather descriptive and loose qualitative nature of old-fashioned economic historians' discourse sparked a "New" economic history in the late 1950s.[3] The objective of the New Economic History was to base historical analysis on rigorous theoretical thinking as well as the application of econometric methods used in other fields of economics.[4] In short, New economic historians wanted to reintroduce economics into economic history. In general, the creation of an analytical economic history, one that is based on economic models and methods, is commendable precisely because it avoids the possibility of confusion inherent in pure narrative. The problem with this approach – as will be argued here and is implicit in the other chapters of this volume – is that it uses the marginalist or rational actor model of economics.[5]

This model can be defined as consisting of mathematical optimization exercises of individual decision-makers with given preferences, endowments and technology. Based on these core ideas, the methodological dictate of marginalist economics appears to be that all explanation of economic phenomena must be reduced to the optimizing behavior of economic agents. Applied to economic history, this view states that "voluntary exchange through incremental balancing of costs and benefits of the margin is the primary means by which individuals try to improve their lot" (Du Boff 1992: 256) or, in other words, individual maximization decisions in the realm of exchange drives economic history.[6]

Most important, the marginalist methodological dictate is supposed to be applicable universally to all phases of economic development. Or in the words of Schabas (1995: 184): "they [the New economic historians] have established a general all-purpose economic theory 'which will do for us everything we want all the time.' In short, *they have eliminated the possibility of a changing world*" (emphasis added). In terms of Table 2.1 the New economic historians clearly fall in the marginalist, theory-driven box.

This emphasis on optimization and continuity made New Economic History weak at precisely the place where the old narrative history was strong. It had little to say about the nature, formation and impact of institutions or about technical change. Attempts to address this lead to a neo-institutionalist variant of the New Economic History. Here change enters into the analysis as institutions are created to facilitate exchange and minimize transaction costs (Eggertsson 1990). In early formulations institutional change is an optimal response to relative price shifts so that institutions can be said to evolve to maintain Pareto optimality in the presence of transaction costs (North and Thomas 1973). This version of

Table 2.1 Different roads to the past

| Theory | Methodology | | |
	Theory-driven	Fact-driven	Interactive
Marginalist	Cliometrics		Real Business Cycle
Rational actors	New Classical macro		New Keynesian
Exchange relations	Real Business Cycle (Prescott)	"Old," narrative, economic history (D. Landes, P. Deane, German historical school)	Neo-institutionalist
Heterodox	Marxist history		Transformational Growth
Classes, institutions			Sylos-Labini, French regulation, NBER Business cycle (W. C. Mitchell)
Sphere of production			
Social contracts			

Notes
See text, especially pp. 62–73.

institutional history and change could, however, neither account for the differences in performance across countries and time nor explain why inferior institutional constellations persisted. The problem lies in neoclassical theory. As North puts it (1993: 159):

> There are no institutions (or if they exist they play no independent role) in the world of the neo-classical economist because the instrumental rationality postulate renders institutions superfluous. . . . The complexity of the problems humans face in interaction and the limitations of the mental models that the human mind constructs to solve those problems have produced a vastly different human history than one populated by individuals with the omniscience implied by the instrumental rationality postulate.

These difficulties have led to a complex relationship between neo-institutional and neoclassical theory. Where the problem is simple, repetitive, the information good and the motivation high neoclassical theory is useful. Outside of that other types of analysis are called for (North 1993: 161). Here ideas, ideologies, myths, rules, norms matter. They are a subject of historical inquiry. Recent neo-institutional formulations have also introduced lock-ins or virtuous/vicious circles for technologies and institutions (North 1991). These models can be developed conventionally, retaining all the assumptions of the marginalist approach. But their outcome is a historical contingency. Because of the independent roles of ideas, norms, etc., and the introduction of path dependence the neo-institutionalist model fits into the interactive category.

We now turn more specifically to the analysis of business cycles. There exists a literature on the historical analysis of business cycles[7] so that we should perhaps explain why the studies collected in this volume contribute to a further understanding of economic fluctuations. Or, in other words, what have other people done and why can't we use their results to substantiate our claims? Some of the relevant theoretical literature is reviewed in Chapter 1. Here we focus on some selected empirical studies of historical business cycles. Again, we don't attempt to provide an exhaustive survey here but merely mention a few studies in order to highlight the methodological problems involved.

In short, the answer to the above question is that we can only partly use other empirical work because these studies are generally geared to substantiating a specific theoretical model. A good example are the NBER business cycle studies of the 1950s, 1960s and 1970s, which are largely based on the Keynesian synthesis framework.[8] A key proposition of the models and indeed the usual finding in empirical studies is the positive dampening effect of macro-policies on business cycle fluctuations (Zarnovitz 1992). Consequently, much of the research design focused on the volatility of individual series and how that diminished over time. In addition, different measures of business cycle length and intensity were developed. One of the claims of the economists working in this tradition in the late 1960s was that the post-war business cycle was better characterized as a growth cycle because upturns were generally longer than downturns (Tichy 1994). This was then supported by different indicators measuring the length of different phases of the business cycle. The emphasis was on nominal variables such as prices and money wages, owing to their crucial role in the neoclassical synthesis theoretical framework. Therefore, although this branch of business cycle analysis provided a great deal of insight into the changing nature of business cycles, its use for investigating the propositions of Transformational Growth is limited. In terms of its methodological approach to history this school clearly thrived on the dialogue between business cycle empirics and theory exemplified by a constant reformulation and broadening of the NBER business cycle chronology.

There is now a vast empirical literature within the Real Business Cycle (RBC) school.[9] While not explicitly a theory of economic history it shares the basic marginalist model with the New economic historians and has produced a series of business cycle studies encompassing nineteenth-century developments (Backus/Kehoe 1993 is a good example). The RBC methodology is to search for regularities or stylized facts in economic variables and build small general equilibrium models that are then evaluated on their ability to simulate the facts. This methodology has been termed *quantitative theory* (Danthine and Donaldson 1993). While the evaluation of theoretical models on the basis of their ability to represent observable business cycle patterns is certainly a positive development within mainstream macroeconomics, there are none the less problems with this kind of methodology. The search for stylized facts as a measure of model performance seems to imply that RBC analysts believe in the existence of objective facts. But there is no such thing as an objective fact or truth – as we have seen when discussing the old view of economic history. The way we see the world we live in is necessarily dependent on the model underlying our perception, and economists are certainly no exception. Therefore, the collection of stylized facts as well as their replication in equilibrium models cannot be undertaken without making certain judgments.

In fact, Prescott (1986: 21), one of the foremost proponents of RBC analysis, admits as much by demanding the use of more theory in collecting appropriate data:

> An important part of this deviation [of the model estimation from "reality"] could very well disappear if the economic variables were measured more in conformity with theory. That is why I argue that theory is now ahead of business cycle measurement and theory should be used to obtain better measures of the key economic time series.

Of course, this request stems from the problems RBC models have in replicating observable facts, in particular the low measured labor elasticity of output (the relationship Prescott believes is measured wrongly), which is much lower than assumed in the models. One can't help but wonder whether RBC modelers because of their problems in replicating business cycle facts have to resort to "blaming the facts." Or, in other words, Prescott's claim seems to indicate that data or facts should be collected according to their particular model of the economy, which happens to be of the standard neoclassical general equilibrium variety. But how could these generated facts be an objective standard for evaluating models? Danthine and Donaldson's (1993: 3) prognosis that "the RBC methodology is by nature ideologically neutral in the sense that it prefers the model or set of models that is (are) best able to replicate the stylized facts independent of the hypotheses underlying it (them)" seems to be overly optimistic and overestimates the ability of mainstream economics for change. Here the similarities between the New Economic History and RBC traditions become clear. Schabas (1995: 186), criticizing New economic historians for their search for the optimal counterfactual, notes that the New economic historians "may be uneasy with the prospect that some judgments must remain subjective. A main feature of their search for an objective history is to let the facts speak for themselves, whatever that might mean." There obviously exists a considerable confusion – for RBC modelers and New economic historians alike – about the methodological implications of their respective research agendas.

Furthermore, according to Tichy (1994), the different lists of stylized facts representing relevant business patterns are rather *ad hoc* and give the impression that facts are collected according to the ability of the different calibrated models to replicate them. Once again, judgments made by the researcher clearly influence the analysis (and therefore the results) simply by selecting facts that supposedly represent the relevant portion of reality. From the perspective of Transformational Growth, for example, the omission of nominal variables from their lists should be emphasized. Price fluctuations and the resulting distributional consequences can play no role in the *real* analysis of equilibrium business cycle theory. In fact Kydland and Prescott (1986: 1) assert: "business cycles can be explained almost entirely by just real quantities". One of the key differences between the OBC and the NBC stipulated by Transformational Growth is the change in the price-setting behavior of firms. The resulting changes in the cyclical variation of real product wages and thus in the distribution of income in turn feed into the character of macro-adjustment. Hence the cyclical behavior of prices and real product wages will be a major focus of the country studies in Part III.

Others still have adopted a different way out of the theoretical *impasse*, namely to include non-Walrasian elements in their list of assumptions.[10] These models come close to the New Keynesian business cycle models, which impose certain imperfections on otherwise perfectly functioning markets to generate cycles in output and employment.[11] However, the introduction of imperfections is rather arbitrary and does not always fit the actual institutional development of capitalist societies. It seems that mainstream economists are not yet ready to abandon the straitjacket of marginalism altogether but rather accommodate change by appealing to the imperfect functioning of markets.[12] It is therefore quite difficult to fit these different RBC approaches into our theory/methodology matrix. All share the basic assumptions of the marginalist model, including the New Keynesians. In terms of methodology the differentiation is less obvious. On the one hand, Prescott's dogmatic approach falls certainly in the theory-driven column. Neoclassical theory should serve as the guide not only to constructing computable models but also to collecting appropriate data. On the other hand, a lot of the latest RBC models are willing to substantially modify their theoretical models based on new stylized facts. Danthine and Donaldson (1993: 3), for example, go so far as to say that "[T]he best RBC model may thus ultimately be a demand-driven money model with substantial non-Walrasian features." We have voiced our concerns earlier about this supposedly theoretically neutral approach of the RBC school but they are certainly willing to "stretch" standard neoclassical theory and are thus filed in the interactive column.[13]

HISTORY WITHOUT MARGINALISM

The road to the past adopted by the theory of Transformational Growth abandons this straitjacket of marginalism and adopts an interactive approach to economic history. With interactive we mean a constant dialogue between historical observations and theoretical conceptualizing. Economic history means

> to make theory the servant of historical analysis rather than a substitute for it. A general theoretical "vision" provides us with a basis for asking certain questions of history. Historical analysis provides us with the knowledge required to make relevant theoretical abstractions or to modify our adherence to abstractions previously held . . .
>
> (Lazonick 1991: 305)

Theory has to guide empirical work and vice versa.

Like other heterodox approaches Transformational Growth is also interactive in a different way. Common to most of these theories is its predisposition for change. Capitalism is constantly changing and the economic theorist has to constantly keep abreast of new historical developments because these may present a break with the past, thus making part of the prevailing wisdom obsolete. History is thus not merely the passing of time but the process of change. The Present *is* History not just because we *can* change it (see the Sweezy quotation at the beginning) but because it *will* change.

Hence Nell's work is part of a tradition in economics, originating in classical authors such as Smith, Marx and Mill, that emphasizes historical discontinuities in economic behavior. Since neoclassical economics became dominant, this tradition has been largely relegated to the left and is currently found among Marxists, institutionalists and post-Keynesians.[14] These traditions present a broad spectrum of economic thought and disagree on many things but they share some common differences vis-à-vis the marginalist school. First, instead of the neoclassical preoccupation with optimal exchange arrangements through markets the focus is on the sphere of production. The key to understanding markets and growth is the analysis of the creation of surplus and how it is distributed. Second, while neoclassicals base their models on the choices of individuals, heterodox schools start from the analysis of classes or income groups and attempt to understand how their behavior is conditioned by their role in society. Third, economic relations are understood to be embedded in other social relations. Social contracts in the form of wage or price setting, for example, play an important role in understanding economic processes.

A good example of work on the historical characteristics of business cycles incorporating all three virtues of heterodox thought are the contributions by Paolo Sylos-Labini (1984, 1993). His work on the changing nature of business cycles is similar in spirit to our analysis and covers much of the same ground. He is not constrained by the methodological dictates of marginalism and recognizes the importance of historical time. His empirical analysis is, however, very limited in scope and methods used. Most of his work deals with the historical experience of the United States and the United Kingdom. Some evidence from Italy is also presented. Similar to the Keynesian research design described above, his analysis is focused on the changing behavior of prices and money wages. One of his key findings is the downward flexibility of prices in the nineteenth century as compared with the constant inflation after World War II. Again this focus is explained by his particular theoretical model. Sylos-Labini is interested in studying business cycle fluctuations in connection with the process of growth. He argues that the growth process in the nineteenth century was characterized by the transmission of productivity growth through falling prices. This was possible because the market institutions during that period allowed prices to fall. With the oligopolization and unionization of large parts of the economy, however, prices and wages became inflexible downward and the fruits of productivity growth were disseminated via steady money wage growth. In short, Sylos-Labini's theoretical concepts and his findings are certainly compatible with the ideas put forth in this book but leave out part of the story which is relevant for investigating the claims of Transformational Growth.

Similar to the perspective of Transformational Growth the French regulation school attempts to understand history as a succession of changing patterns through time. This school has produced a vast empirical and theoretical literature over the last two decades. The task here is not to review this literature or criticize it but to point out methodological similarities with the ideas advanced in this book.[15] Although based on Marxian concepts the regulation school moves away from an understanding of capitalism merely in the form of a single set of laws of motion that remains unchanged from its inception until its eventual supersession.[16] Instead, it is argued that the specific combination of regimes of accumulation and modes of regulation gives rise to a distinctive mode of development. These modes of development bear within them contradictions resulting from the constraints imposed by the already existing mode of regulation upon the regime of accumulation. These contradictions will eventually lead to structural crisis, the collapse of the old and the subsequent birth of a new mode of development (Brenner and Glick 1991: 48).

Boyer (1988), one of its most prominent proponents, defines the regulation approach on methodological grounds as an attempt to create links between economic history and theory. He (1988: 69-70) criticizes economic theorists for implicitly using historical facts "to fit a given general theory, already available" and sees the solution in constructing "intermediate notions and models in order finally to organize an appropriate and careful comparison with observed facts." More precisely, he demands "a new theoretical framework which would combine a critique of Marxian orthodoxy, and an extension of Kaleckian and Keynesian macroeconomic ideas, in order to rejuvenate a variant of earlier institutional or historical theory" (1988: 70). Furthermore, the regulation school favors detailed, comparative country studies of the various forms of institutions and social reproduction in present and history (Boyer 1990).

The similarities with our interactive approach are evident and the results of the school's vast empirical work are a valuable reference point. However, the regulation school focuses on the process of accumulation and neglects business cycle fluctuations in its empirical study. Moreover, it neglects the changes in the process and pattern of market adjustment and how these changes interact with technological development. Again, as with Sylos-Labini's contribution, the work of the regulation school is similar in spirit to our framework but of limited use with respect to our specific goal of studying changes in the business cycle.

As argued in Chapter 1, the purpose of this volume can best be described as trying "to make a case" for a historical approach to macroeconomics. The studies collected in this volume are a first step in order to gather evidence for the claims of Transformational Growth. The qualitative nature of the methods of production is at the core of the market mechanism and at the core of Transformational Growth. In the first part of Chapter 1 we are introduced to two systems of technologies and growth, craft and mass production. The history of advanced capitalist economies can be characterized by a period in which craft production dominates, followed by a period when mass production dominates. This technological and institutional narrative is subsequently enriched by a set of stylized facts representative of the two periods.

Nell's stylized history and stylized facts are drawn largely from British and American sources, but lack specifics of time and place. As a mode of argument this has advantages. One can concentrate on the logic of each period, making relationships clear and understandable. One can simplify, assuming away some of the complexity of history. This offers the possibility of modeling in a style that economists have become accustomed to. In these stark outlines the characteristics and differences in the two systems of technology can be clarified. It is a historically informed theorizing.

But "history is above all a discipline of context" (Stone 1981: 31). It deals with specifics of time and place where prior experience matters. If we are to be truly historical, i.e. interactive, in our approach context cannot be ignored. We must move beyond stylized history and confront the historical record in a more concrete and rigorous way. This is done not out of an abstract historicism. Economic policy always takes place within a context. A successful policy analysis requires an appreciation of the context (Hawke 1993: 80). If the aim is to provide a theory of prescriptive value, rigorous historical analysis is a prerequisite (Lazonick 1991: 304).

Ironically, this approach is similar to the one used by one of the originators of marginalist economics, Alfred Marshall. As Joan Robinson (1980: 53–4, quoted in Du Boff 1992: 252) observed: "he was studying a recognizable economy in a particular phase of its historical development, in which recognizable classes of the community interact with each other in a particular framework of law and accepted conventions."[17] Hence implicit in Marshall's analysis was the attempt to develop a historical view of the economy, an analysis that identifies the institutions and technology of a specific historical period and their effect on market adjustment.

One way of developing this kind of historical view is with the help of industrial history (case studies) found in Part II of this book. The questions here are inspired by the stylized history of craft and mass-production technology. George Argyrous provides us with case studies of the American aircraft industry during the Second World War. Helge Peukert in Chapter 4 looks at the merger movement in the United States prior to World War I. He shows how this movement is related to mass production, and how it might affect the fluctuations of prices and wages. They use the methods of a theoretically informed narrative history to examine the characteristics of craft and mass production for a specific time, place and industry. The narrative style offers at least two advantages. First, it allows the use of many types of historical evidence, including contemporary accounts, government studies and managerial literature. Some of this evidence is both persuasive and not easily summed up through quantitative methods. Second, the narrative style is especially useful in capturing processes where contingency and path dependence matter (Rockoff and Walton 1991: 256–7). Indeed, contingency is a central theme in Argyrous's and Peukert's work.

The chapters in Part III of the book use a third approach, that of quantitative macroeconomics. Aspects of the history of six countries, the United States, Germany, Japan, Great Britain, Canada and Argentina, are examined. The specific histories of the countries matter but the focus is on common patterns of business cycle adjustments as laid out in the stylized facts of Chapter 1. The next two sections deal with the methods and data requirements for this undertaking and the problems involved.

In summary, Transformational Growth is seen as a dynamic process that requires institutional and technological change in order to occur.[18] The focus is on the character of the methods of production and how their change over time influences macroeconomic outcomes. Transformational Growth is therefore similar in spirit to what Calomiris and Hanes (1994) call historical macroeconomics:

> macroeconomic history offers more than long strings of data and special examples. It suggests a historical definition of the macro-economy, . . . Historical macroeconomics is not the application of standard macroeconomics to data from the distant past, or the selective exploration of the past to discover interesting experi-ments; it is "thinking historically" about macroeconomic change – an alternative approach to analyzing data both from the recent and distant past.

We believe that Transformational Growth represents a first step towards Du Boff's (1992: 254) request for a "frame of reference that borrows as needed from the post-Keynesians, Marxian and Institutionalist traditions [and] shows the way toward a genuinely new economic history, based on the study of cumulative and irreversible changes that flows primarily from production technologies."[19]

HISTORICAL TIME SERIES

Among economists it is good practice to critically examine the data being used. Among historians such a view is considered essential. Indeed, many of the professional practices of historians are designed to expose evidence to critical comment (Stone 1981: 33). For the data used in macroeco-nomics this is difficult. The series are constructed in complex ways from large sets of underlying data. Sources and construction methods are often very far from clear.[20] But knowing this and understanding the problems of the data are vital to understanding both the strength and the limitation of one's argument.

For historical work two issues are of particular importance, the quality and the comparability of the data. Quality can be assessed in three dimensions: validity, extent and reliability. Validity is the correspondence of a variable to the theoretical concept being investigated. Is the variable measuring the right thing and does it do so in an unbiased way? Extent considers the data underlying a series. How were they gathered? How many industries, firms, or individuals were they gathered from? How often were they collected? Reliability asks, if we could take the sample again how would it compare with the set we are looking at (Griliches 1986)?

Comparability is an "apples and oranges" question. When we are comparing a variable from two different times (or places) we have to ask whether these series are similar enough to be compared. We want our results to be products of economic behavior, not differences in data collection or series construction. Ideally we would compare series "constructed in similar ways from similar data" (Hanes 1993: 269).

These questions need to be asked specifically about each series used in our empirical investigation. But there are a few generalizations that can be made. Sometimes economists work with data collected by economists for purposes similar to the way they are being used. More often economists work with found data, data collected for other purposes. Many of the data for the new business cycle are of the first class, especially the national income, wage and price data. As such their extent and validity are easily assessed and their quality is better than that of most of the data economists work with.

For the OBC we are often forced to rely on found data. The extent of such data is limited and some useful data are totally missing. For example, in the United States there is little data on retail prices before World War I and almost none before 1890. In other cases data available may vary considerably from one year to the next. US data on wages and prices are much more extensive for census years than for the years in between. Even where data exist they may be hard to assess in quality. A useful source of wholesale price data in the United States before 1890 is a newspaper, *Shipping News and New York Prices Current*. We have prices for over 100 goods collected twice a week for several decades. But we don't know how the information was gathered.

When the evidence is collected by economists we may still have problems. American wage data for the period after 1885 are thanks to Carol Wright and colleagues at the Bureau of Labor Statistics. For their time the collection and tabulation procedures were state-of-the-art. But by modern standards the sample is small, extending to only a small number of industries, occupations and locations.

We encounter some of our most serious quality problems in constructing valid series that fit our theoretical concepts but lack sufficiently extensive underlying data. Consider the American GNP series. When Simon Kuznets attempted to construct this series for the period before World War I he ran into a problem. Before 1911, when the income tax Act was passed, income data are scarce and GNP cannot be calculated from the income side. The manufacturing census allowed him to do output-side calculation once a decade. Less extensive data could be used to connect these census year calculations. But there was yet another problem, in that the available data outputs were priced at wholesale rather than consumer or final prices. This meant that the output of a number of important service industries, such as retailing, was missing. Kuznets got round this problem in an ingenious way, but it has been argued that his method led to excess cyclical volatility in the series (Romer 1989). There are now two competing series (Romer 1989; Balke and Gordon 1989) that represent improvements but are not without validity problems either. So the quality of OBC data will in general be below that of the NBC and has to be viewed with particular caution.[21]

This brings us to the second issue, comparability. Because so many of our data are found, limited in extent or simply missing, it will be rare to have truly comparable series between the OBC and NBC. Indeed, many of the series are not comparable within each period. American GNP series are based on different sources before and after 1890. Most pre-World War I wage series are actually four different series, from different sources linked (Hanes 1993). This problem is not limited to the OBC. Data collection has evolved considerably during the post-World War II years. For example, the goods basket underlying the producer price index of 1955 is different from the one used nowadays.

Does this make comparisons between (or even within) periods invalid? Some differences in series reflect differences in the economies under consideration, they are done to ensure the validity of the series. In an economy undergoing Transformational Growth new products, industries and occupations are the norm. Consequently, time series can rarely be strictly comparable in Hanes's sense over longer periods of time. Our samples, procedures and series must change to reflect this. In fact, since the process of (qualitative) change is implicit in time series data, attempts to construct strictly comparable wholesale price series (Hanes 1995) eliminate that aspect of change and introduce a bias of a different kind.

The availability of data should itself be seen within the context of Transformational Growth. In a craft economy, of small firms, there is limited private interest in economic data. Typically firms produce in a single location for a single industry, using local labor. They may be buying inputs or selling product in markets outside their own community. This is likely to be done through middlemen. These producers and middlemen are likely to have an interest in wholesale prices in these markets. Furthermore, one of the points of Transformational Growth is that the OBC is better reflected in price than in quantity series. It is therefore no surprise that the best data we have for the period are wholesale prices.

Most of the other data used were produced by governments either as a by-product of administrative activities or collected specifically for public purposes. The limited managerial capabilities in the craft economy applied to government too. This helped restrict its administrative range and the data produced. Data will be collected for public purposes when demand is sufficient to cover the cost (Kuznets 1972). Improved managerial, computational and communicative techniques that accompanied mass production tended to lower the cost of data collection. The larger role of the "visible hand" increased the interest in information of this kind.

The growth of government data collection tends roughly to parallel the development of mass production. With some limited exceptions, mostly population censuses, systematic collection begins in the last third of the nineteenth century. In Germany the Imperial Statistics Office (1872) systematizes the efforts of the various state offices, and adds to them output data, particularly in the mining and engineering industries. In the United States we see the birth of "The Bureaus": Department of Agriculture (1866), Bureau of Statistics (Treasury Department) (1866), Bureau of Labor Statistics (1884), Geological Survey (1879), the Interstate Commerce Commission (1882), a permanent Bureau of the Census (1901) (Lacey 1993).[22] The Province of Canada establishes statistical bureaus in the Finance Department (1863) and Agriculture Department (1866) (Godfrey 1918). Japan's Imperial Bureau of Statistics dates from 1881, though it is very limited in its activities till after the First World War (Imperial Bureau 1919). These efforts are expanded in most countries in the years around World War I and approach modern levels after the Second World War (Kuznets 1972).

This brief section has attempted to interpret the evolution of data-gathering as part of the process of Transformational Growth. On the one hand, it is a supply-driven evolution as a result of the development of technologies and the availability of resources allowing better information management and larger samples. On the other hand, the process is demand-driven because a greater role for government in social insurance and fiscal or monetary policy requires more detailed information about economic indicators. Clearly, by their very nature facts are historically conditioned.

IDENTIFYING BUSINESS CYCLE PATTERNS

The link between the transformation of capitalist economies from craft to mass production and the changing nature of business cycle patterns is a rather complex relationship and difficult to test. To identify the connection we use historical narrative as in the case studies of Part II of the book or provide accounts of the different country experiences, using simple quantitative methods. The focus of this section is on business cycle patterns and how to identify them. This is generally done by concentrating on key relationships between variables like product wages and industrial wholesale prices and how they change over time. One exception is Chapter 8, on Germany, which in order to allow comparison with RBC studies attempts to identify broader, more comprehensive patterns.

Students of the business cycle should be aware of the fact that the choice of a particular research design will influence the results. A recent survey of the cyclical behavior of real wages, for example, concludes that empirical results are dependent on the choice of detrending procedure, cyclical indicator, wages and deflator, time periods and data frequency: Another reminder of the non-value-free nature of economic facts. In the following these key choices are discussed with respect to their implications for the study at hand.

1   *Detrending.* Choosing the proper trend is important. Econometrics is full of results that have to do more with detrending than with the data themselves. Trends come in two varieties, deterministic and stochastic. Intuitively, a deterministic trend is one that changes little through time. If a trend is deterministic, knowing the trend from say 1950 to 1960 will allow you to predict pretty well what it will be from 1960 to 1970. A neoclassical growth model with steady rates of population growth and technical change would theoretically yield such an effect. Stochastic trends change, they have a drift to them, but knowing the trend in one period doesn't help much predicting the next. Testing for this is a simple procedure. All of the series used in our country studies have a stochastic trend.

   Recent advances in time-series econometrics have not succeeded in identifying a superior detrending technique which solves the problem of separating business cycle fluctuations from slowly evolving secular trends. The trend–cycle decompositions are therefore still *ad hoc* and rather mechanical in the sense that the method is only required to produce business cycle fluctuations which are stationary to allow further econometric use.[23] Examples of techniques in common use are (1) application of two-sided moving averages; (2) first-differencing; (3) removal of a linear or quadratic time trend; and (4) application of the Hodrick–Prescott filter (Baxter and King 1994). The case studies in this volume mainly use first-differencing to extract business cycle fluctuations. This seems to be justified by the fact that the procedure is used in most historical business cycle studies. Moreover, the choice of detrending method can also be explained on the basis of our theoretical observations. In the Transformational Growth perspective it does matter, for example, whether prices fall, i.e. whether there is deflation. In addition, we cannot *a priori* decide on a specific data frequency that we would like to extract from the time series. The first-difference filter, for example, emphasizes higher frequencies while down-weighting lower frequencies. If one stipulates, as Transformational Growth does, that there exists an automatic stabilizer in the OBC it may be advisable to look at exactly these high-frequency fluctuations and see whether there are patterns to be detected rather than noise.

Chapters 8 and 9 both use the Hodrick–Prescott filter in addition to first-differencing in order to allow comparisons with the results of RBC-type empirical studies. The resulting business cycle patterns are largely the same, and there is no reason to doubt that such would also be the case for the other countries. Our results, therefore, don't seem to be dependent on the detrending method used.

2 *Cyclical indicator.* Throughout the book both industrial production and GDP are used if available. However, manufacturing data would be preferable, since Transformational Growth identifies the manufacturing sector as a dynamic sector in which transformation from craft to mass production is most apparent. However, the wage and price data that are available for the nineteenth century also cover the industrial sector rather than manufacturing, so that using industrial output as the cyclical indicator ensures comparability in that respect. Once again, our choice is motivated by the underlying theory but constrained by the lack of appropriate historical data.

3 *Time periods.* Chapter 1 broadly defined the OBC as the period between the middle of the nineteenth century and the beginning of World War I. Lack of reliable data for the early period, however, usually necessitates starting the analysis somewhat later, in the 1870s and 1880s. The exact periodization, of course, depends on the specific country situation. Sometimes, as in the case of Germany, periods can be neatly divided into self-contained phases on the basis of political developments. The OBC starts in 1871 with the founding of the German Reich and ends with World War I. The NBC period begins with the creation of the Federal Republic and ends with reunification. The New Business Cycle in all studies begins after World War II and lasts to the present. The inter-war period is generally regarded as a transition phase in which elements of both craft and mass production are still in place and mass production is not yet the dominant method of production. The exception is Japan as a late industrializer, where the transition to mass production occurs somewhat later and in a shorter time span (see Chapter 9). For the case of the United Kingdom, in Chapter 6, Thomas experimented with different timings of structural change and found the best fit with 1913 and 1945 as breaking points. In short, we derive the periodization from a careful analysis of the specific country situation and relate it to the framework set by the perspective of Transformational Growth.

4 *Data frequency.* Another crucial issue in business cycle analysis is the frequency of the data used. Quarterly data are generally preferred, especially in order to determine turning points and the length of upturns and downturns. Unfortunately, historical series only are available in annual frequency, so that all our studies are based on annual data for both periods to ensure comparability. However, this choice

can also be justified by our specific research interest, namely the identification of business cycle patterns and their comparison between two historical periods. Hence we are interested in the covariation of variables. Granger (1977) argues that low-frequency data are better at finding statistical relationships between variables, since such data are less likely to be noisy.[24]

Measures of volatility are a less contested subject in business cycle analysis. We use either the standard deviation of the deviation from the trend or the coefficient of variation. Another aspect taken up in most of the country studies is the significance of structural change between the OBC and NBC. Here we use a simple dummy variable technique that has been used before for the analysis of the cyclical variability of money wages (Hanes 1993). When regressing a specific variable like prices or product wages on the cyclical indicator the inclusion of a dummy variable allows the coefficient on this cyclical indicator to change at a pre-specified point in time. These simple regressions obviously don't present fully specified structural models of wage or price behavior but simply measure the correlation with a cyclical indicator.

In conclusion, detecting business cycle patterns is a difficult procedure where the results are likely to be dependent on the techniques and data used. Our strategy throughout this book is to make the reader aware of the choices made. Whenever possible we try to test for robustness by using a different data series or detrending technique to see how sensitive our results are. In fact, by including different countries in our empirical study, thus adopting a comparative framework, we implicitly test our results for robustness.

OVERVIEW OF CASE STUDIES

The individual chapters attempt to collect evidence to establish the existence of different market adjustment mechanisms over two historical periods across a sample of countries. We try to detect whether similar patterns of change occur in spite of the fact that each country has its own historical and institutional characteristics. At this point a few words about the evolution of this book and the individual studies in it may serve to clarify the characteristics of our interactive approach to economic history. The project was initiated by a Nell working paper presenting an outline of the theory of Transformational Growth and including tentative stylized facts (mostly for the United States and United Kingdom) extracted from the literature. On this basis preliminary country and case studies were designed in order to provide a broader empirical basis of analysis. Considerable effort was invested in identifying appropriate historical time series data. Initially the data were prepared in the form of graphs and simply visually inspected. The results of this exercise led to the extension, revision and refocusing of the initial theoretical statements and accompanying stylized facts. In the next step our results were related to the relevant literature and methods of analysis. The data analysis was extended to other countries, different data sets and more sophisticated quantitative tools. Constant interaction between the authors during this period led to the standardization of the country studies but the authors were also encouraged to write a narrative of the relevant transformations in their respective countries to complement the data analysis. This reformulation of the case studies and the patterns emerging from it was taken as an ongoing challenge to the theoretical concepts underlying the project. This is what we mean by taking history seriously.

In addition, the history/theory dialectic was found to be useful in responding to the relevant discussions and confusions in the literature. The country studies should thus be regarded not only as empirical evaluations of Transformational Growth but also as responses to different themes in the relevant literature. In general, the discussions are informed by the attempt to suggest the necessity of a historical foundation of macroeconomics. In this sense, we use the Transformational Growth perspective as a methodological tool to reiterate and clarify issues raised in theoretical debates by adding the historical dimension. Chapter 7, for example, has to be seen as a response to the issues raised by the volatility debates. Similarly, Chapter 8 evaluates RBC analysis and compares it with the Transformational Growth perspective, taking the case of Germany. In the following we will briefly outline the themes of the individual case studies.

Chapter 4 focuses on a group of newly oligopolized industries at the turn of the century in America. This period saw the first great merger movement in the United States. It was largely due to the development of mass production in those industries. The chapter investigates the connection between oligopolization and price stability. It finds that mass production and growing concentration did not automatically lead to price stability. Rather it required the active intervention of innovative economic agents to achieve.

Chapter 3 is about the interaction of craft and mass production in the US aircraft industry during the Second World War. Mass-production industries create standardized products with specialized equipment. This makes flexibility valuable in capital goods industries, especially machine tools. Craft production provides the ability to vary the characteristics of output at the cost of the ability to vary the volume of output. Wartime conditions place the interaction between these industries in sharp relief. But their relationship is a structural property of the production system with dynamics of enduring interest.

Chapter 6, on the United Kingdom, provides a new perspective on the pricing debates of the 1930s and 1940s (several papers in the *American Economic Review*) which centered on the exact nature of the pricing mechanism. The chapter argues that the participants in the debate failed to take into account the changing nature of competition resulting from the evolution of the business firm. The perspective of Transformational Growth can shed new light on this debate because it adopts a historical perspective on the development of pricing behavior and macroeconomic adjustment.

Chapter 7 takes up two discussions in the literature for the case of the United States. First, it emphasizes the data issues brought forth by the so-called volatility debates and reinterprets their conclusions from a Transformational Growth perspective. Second, it identifies a lesser-known analysis in Keynes's *General Theory* and discusses its relevance to different adjustment mechanisms in the OBC and NBC.

Chapter 9 deals with some specific issues of the transformation from craft to mass production for the late industrializer Japan. Transformational Growth can be seen in the development of the institutions of mass marketing. The chapter thus extends Chandler's analysis of the corporation to the Japanese *zaibatsu/keiretsu* by linking it with the perspective of Transformational Growth. The main point of this chapter is that the broad patterns of a change in business cycle patterns can also be observed in Japan in spite of the many institutional differences from the Western world.

Chapter 8, on Germany, takes aim at recent developments in RBC empirics. It argues that RBC studies fail to recognize changes in the patterns of business cycle adjustment. Hence their claim that business cycles are all alike cannot be maintained. Instead, the chapter suggests, short-run adjustment was dominated by prices in the OBC but by quantities in the NBC. The modeling of business cycles therefore requires a historical dimension which cannot be accommodated by RBC models and their focus on real quantities.

Chapter 10 is a study of a less developed country, Argentina. The structural change that brings about a mass-production economy does not fully take place here. The industrial structure that results contributes to the instability of the post-World War II period. After 1945 the economy shows the price instability of the OBC, with the output instability of the NBC.

CONCLUSION
HISTORICAL FOUNDATIONS OF MACROECONOMICS

The analysis of historical data requires economic, statistical and historical judgment. Judgment is a good word, it has a legal ring to it. And the legal metaphor is worth considering. In making the case for Transformational Growth, theory and stylized history are paired with the narrative account of the sector or country history, complemented by using quantitative tools. When uncertain of a time series's "testimony" we seek corroboration. We look at series constructed in different ways. We compare results among countries. And we look at other evidence. Are our results consistent with institutional evidence? With contemporary observation? The narrative history allows us to mobilize some of this evidence. Further, the evidence may not be simply true or false. When there are problems we may be able to say something about their nature and modify our belief accordingly.

Given the kinds of data problem we often find within OBC data, and the comparability problems of OBC and NBC data, the possibility that the results are artifacts of data collections and construction can never be fully dismissed. But investigations of Transformational Growth do not rely upon a single technique or type of evidence. The theory, institutional reasoning of stylized history, the evidence of case study (historical narrative) and data study are all used. From the evidence collected in this manner we hope to "present our case" convincingly and let the reader be the judge or juror.

We hope that this volume is a first step in the direction of a new analytical macroeconomic history.[25] Textbooks are a good source for the prevailing research paradigms of the discipline. On this basis neoclassical macroeconomists are increasingly preoccupied with bringing macroeconomics into closer touch with microeconomics (see, for example, Dornbusch and Fischer 1990). This chapter has attempted to outline some of the limitations of this agenda. In contrast, we would argue for bringing macroeconomics into closer touch with history in order to truly understand the present as history.

NOTES

1 This metaphor is borrowed from Fogel and Elton (1983), a collection of essays that address similar questions raised in the following two sections.
2 Sometimes these two criteria seem to be rather crude when associating theories with a specific box in Table 2.1. Obviously, this cannot do justice to the variety of work within the specific traditions. Some New economic historians, for example, acknowledge the danger of purely scientific, theory-driven history (see, for example, Field 1987). It seems, however, reasonable to make these judgments in order to highlight certain differences between the approaches.
3 New Economic History still coexists with the old-fashioned descriptive, narrative history. This is especially the case in Europe, where the New Economic "revolution" has not been nearly as successful as in the United States (see Dumke 1992).
4 For a survey of New Economic History studies see Crafts (1987), Dumke (1992) and Romer (1994). The work on historical macroeconomics in this tradition is reviewed in James (1984) and Thomas (1987).

5 We therefore vehemently disagree with Christina Romer's announcement of the end of economic history: "My view of recent developments in economic history is that the war is over and the good guys have won. More, concretely, the field of economic history is no longer a separate, and perhaps marginal subfield of economics, but rather, is an integral part of the entire discipline" (1994: 49). Economic history should be an integral part of economic theory but not solely on marginalist terms. In fact, one hallmark of heterodox approaches to economics such as Marxism, post-Keynesianism and institutionalism has always been the explicit recognition of economics as a historical (and social) science.

6 Arguably the most famous and controversial example of this view of economic history is Fogel and Engerman (1974), which characterizes the slave economy of the ante-bellum south as a viable exchange relationship between the rational actors slave and slave owner.

7 See, for example, the contributions in Gordon (1986) and the collected works of Zarnovitz (1992).

8 See, for example, Bronfenbrenner (1969), Mitchell (1951) or Burns's (1954) collected articles.

9 See Chapter 8 in this volume, and the literature cited therein.

10 Danthine and Donaldson (1995) and Rotemberg and Woodford (1995) are good recent examples. The former develops two models with labor contracting (fixed labor supply) and efficiency wages (a favorite feature among new Keynesians as well) as the imperfections of choice.

11 See, for example, Mankiw and Romer (1991).

12 This obviously brings up the question of whether the RBC/new Keynesian scientific research programs are still *scientifically progressive* in Lakatos's sense or whether they are *degenerating* because of the constant addition of *ad hoc* imperfections to accommodate the new stylized facts. A discussion of this question is, however, beyond the scope of this chapter.

13 The best example of the willingness of RBC theorists to stretch neoclassical theory in the face of "strong" stylized facts is their reinterpretation of standard marginal productivity theory – implying countercyclical real wages – based on the observation of procyclical real wages. Whether their solution to this problem based on the introduction of technology shocks into a general equilibrium growth model is satisfying is discussed in Chapter 8 below.

14 Among neoclassical economists W. W. Rostow is unusual and interesting in his considerations of historical discontinuities.

15 The following is largely based on Boyer (1988, 1990) and the survey by Brenner and Glick (1991). All these are excellent introductions to the work of the regulation school, to which the interested reader is referred. We should also mention that the Social Structures of Accumulation (SSA) approach developed by Gordon and others in the United States shares many features of the regulation school (Kotz *et al.* 1994 presents a concise comparison). Our criticism (positive as well as negative), therefore, also applies to the SSA framework.

16 We should point out that the preoccupation of Marxian economics with laws of motion universally applicable to capitalist social formations justifies its filing in the theory-driven, heterodox box. Similarly, history is somewhat predetermined by the succession from feudalism to capitalism to socialism.

17 It is perhaps even more ironical that, by relying on the microeconomic postulates first developed by Marshall, neoclassical theory inevitably imposes features of craft production on modern macroeconomics.

18 In that respect the Transformational Growth perspective is similar to the view of the early development economists such as Kuznets, Hirschman or Chenery, just to name a few. They emphasized the character of development as a process of structural, qualitative change as opposed to the unidimensional concept of economic growth.

19 The example of such a new analytical economic history that Du Boff is referring to is the work of Alfred Eichner, in particular his *The Emergence of Oligopoly* (1969). As the perspective of Transformational Growth Eichner identifies the early twentieth century as a crucial period of change. The nature of new technologies involving heavy fixed costs necessitates for corporations to get control over prices. In short, Eichner presents a theory of the development of mark-up pricing, a hallmark of post-Keynesianism. Instead of looking at the heavy fixed costs of new technologies Transformational Growth emphasizes the flexibility the new mass-production technology brings with it.

20 Stone's critique of cliometrics places considerable weight on this point. He feels that too often this lack of transparency in the data violates the canons of good historical practice (Stone 1981).

21 Lawrence Stone (1981) notes that most data from before the mid-twentieth century are found data. He suggests that history journals reject papers that use such data and report results beyond two decimal places. The data are not good enough to support results of that kind. There is much to Stone's point, though we have not followed his suggestion here.

22 Prior to 1901 each census was run by a temporary agency that was closed upon its completion.

23 Canova (1991) and Enders (1995: 166-85) provide good, readable introductions to the subject.

24 We should note that other studies using quarterly data for the post-war period generally confirm our NBC patterns of, for example, acyclical/countercyclical prices and procyclical wages. See Danthine and Donaldson (1993) for a study of eleven countries.

25 Our goal is thus complementary to Dutt's (1994) call for a new analytical political economy.

Part II

INDUSTRIAL HISTORY

3

THE US ECONOMY DURING
WORLD WAR II

George Argyrous

Transformational Growth is the process by which an economy comes to be dominated by mass production technology, replacing the old craft technology. However, this transformation only comes about through an incremental and cumulative process. Specifically, the transformation does not occur across all industries simultaneously. Rather, the division of labor and the application of mass production in one industry is affected by and in turn affects the same process occurring in other industries. Three sets of transfers across industries are crucial to this cumulative spread of mass-production technology: transfers of organizational ability; transfers of technological capacity; and transfers of demand. The US economy during World War II provides a unique example which enables us to observe the relations between these various transfers. The economy did not simply use old methods of production to produce more output – a radical transformation occurred. The volume of output needed to fight the war necessitated the adoption of mass-production technology in industries which previously had used craft systems. However, given that Transformational Growth is based on the interplay of these mutually dependent factors, the spread of mass-production technology can be limited by problems in any one of the transfer processes.

This was most clearly illustrated in the changes that occurred in the aircraft industry. The aircraft industry did revolutionize its method of production, so that many features of mass production were evident by 1944. Problems on the demand side, however, due to the inherently discretionary nature of the demand for aircraft, caused immense problems for the automobile industry's ability to transfer its organizational expertise to aircraft production. Similarly, the rapid increase in the demand for machine tools from all sectors created a bottleneck in the machine tool industry which threatened to undermine the entire war production program. The result was that the shift to mass production was mediated by the State, which had to intervene on both the supply and demand sides in order to buttress the effects that the demand expansion had on the Transformational Growth process.

THE TRANSFORMATION OF AIRCRAFT PRODUCTION

The US aircraft industry undertook a transformation in its production system in a period of four years which under "normal" circumstances would require decades. All the components of the cumulative causation model of Young and Kaldor were evident: increases in output leading to increases in productivity through the division of labor, leading to falls in unit prices and an increase in the size of the market. The production statistics tell a very bold – but in themselves superficial – story. The aircraft industry went from being the forty-fourth ranked industry by size in the United States in 1939 to the largest industry in the world by 1944. In 1939, the United States produced 5,865 planes at a value of $279.5 million. In 1944 the industry produced 96,369 planes valued at $16.7 billion (Nelson 1949: 238), and a total of nearly 300,000 military planes, 802,161 engines, and 807,424 propellers, in the four years from January 1940 (Craven and Cate 1955: 331).

This increase in output was matched by an increase in productivity. Average monthly weight output per employee increased from twenty-eight pounds in 1941 to 125 pounds in August 1944[1] (AIAA 1946: 89). The Aircraft Industries Association of America attributed this productivity growth to the introduction of specialized tools, jigs, dies, and fixtures which required less skill to operate, and to the redesign of plane parts for speedier fabrication and assembly through simplification and standardization. These changes freed aircraft production from the constraints of skilled labor, leading to an influx of unskilled workers. The work force rose from 63,200 in 1939 to 347,100 in 1941 and to 2.1 million in November 1943 (Modley and Cawley 1956: 17). Firms adopted radically different recruitment policies in their search for large pools of unskilled labor. Lockheed, for example, apart from the massive influx of women into its plants, employed the handicapped, the elderly, and disabled veterans. Blind workers with seeing eye dogs moved around the shop floor, along with over 4,000 high school boys working four hour shifts after school (Rae 1968).

Most important, labor productivity increased at a faster rate than output. The Aircraft War Production Council produced the figures in Table 3.1, which reflect the increasing returns achieved as the production run of a typical fighter plane increased.

According to the Aircraft War Production Council, every doubling in the total number of fighters built resulted in a cut of almost 75 per cent in

Table 3.1 Productivity gains of larger output

Plane	Model	Man hours
First	A	157,000
Tenth	A	59,000
Hundredth	C	26,500
Thousandth	C–F	7,800

Source: Cleveland and Graham (1945: 78–9).

man hours required per plane. These increases in productivity brought corresponding falls in the real price of planes:

> By the end of the war the cost of a long-range, four-engine bomber fell from $15.18 per pound to $4.82, which shaved over $500,000 off the price of each plane. The cost of a single seater fighter plane dropped from $7.41 per pound to $5.37, a saving of more than $20,000 on each plane.
>
> (Nelson 1949: 238)[2]

CHANGES IN THE STRUCTURE OF PRODUCTION

These achievements in raising output and productivity were due to changes in industrial structure that took the aircraft industry down the path to mass production. The changes were captured in a study of the aircraft industry by a team from Harvard Business School, conducted in 1940 and 1944 (Lilley *et al.* 1946). The Harvard study argued that the aircraft industry had moved to an intermediate position between its craft origins and true mass production, which it labelled "line production". Line production involved

> a controlled flow of the product through work areas in which balanced operations have been laid out in a progressive sequence. By 1944, all major airframe and engine companies were applying these basic principles . . . [so that] special purpose, multi-station machines and arrangements of other equipment to form short production lines for parts were characteristic of engine production in 1944.
>
> (Lilley *et al.* 1946: 40)

For example, in 1940 North American installed overhead monorail conveyors on which components were moved by hand to consecutive work

89

stations. Similarly, the Downey plant of Consolidated-Vultee introduced the first powered assembly line in the industry, which was an overhead track that carried fuselage frames in cradles through twenty-five assembly stations. This change alone cut assembly time by 75 per cent and costs by 40 per cent (Rae 1968: 127). Assembly plants became long, slender buildings to accommodate these progressive assembly lines, although production was not truly continuous and still exhibited the back-tracking evident in the job shop.

This sequential arrangement of operations differed sharply from the pre-war job shop method of production in batches, with the newer plants occupying substantially more space than the older ones. For example, the Chicago plant of Chrysler's Dodge Division, which constructed Wright engines, was the biggest facility constructed for the aircraft program. It occupied 6.5 million square feet, equal to the floor space of the entire aircraft engine industry in early 1942. Production floor space increased from 13 million square feet on January 1, 1940, to 167 million in December, 1944. "The average company had expanded its production twenty-fold in a period of three years" (Bollinger and Lilley 1943: 17).

Despite the increase in the size of the production unit, each facility actually produced fewer types of aircraft, reflecting the economies of scale inherent in mass-production technology.[3] For example, Pratt & Whitney's pre-war East Hartford plant continued to produce a diverse group of models whereas its two new factories with larger peak outputs specialized in the production of only one or two models. The newest Pratt & Whitney plant, at Kansas City, was completed in May 1944. While its output was rated at 3 million h.p. per month, the plant manufactured only the model 2800-C 2100 h.p. radial-power unit (Cleveland and Graham 1945: 81). Similarly, in 1944 Republic devoted the entire production facilities of its Farmingdale and Evansville plants to the production of 6,986 P-47 fighters alone (Eaton 1948: 86).

VERTICAL SPECIALIZATION OF AIRCRAFT PRODUCTION

The foundation of these production achievements was the vertical splintering of the production process into distinct layers of firms, each producing the inputs for the next stage. By the war's end, at the assembly stage, there were a small number of large producers making increasingly similar, or even identical, planes, while at earlier stages of production there emerged a multitude of smaller firms operating as feeder plants into the larger operators.

These changes were dependent on the degree of standardization achieved in the industry. The integration of the plans of various producers requires a high degree of coordination in their activities, and this is possible only where the detailed knowledge of the production process can be shared between them. It is not possible where knowledge of the production process resides in the heads of the skilled workers. The craft system of producing aircraft, where the foreman would draw rough sketches as to how assembly fixtures would be erected, for example, did not encourage the distribution of the production process to centers where he could not supervise what was happening. There are problems of communicating manufacturing information, maintaining adequate quality control, and problems of transportation when subassemblies need to be cross-hauled between various subcontractors, and between the subcontractors and primary producer. For production to be decentralized, in other words, industrial knowledge must be codified, with sufficient detail on paper and communicated to licensees and subcontractors. An important step in this process was the establishment of the National Aircraft War Production Council by the major producers. Through this body the major producers were able to share technical information and coordinate production efforts to achieve the necessary economies of scale across the industry (AIAA 1946).

Two particular practices allowed this specialization of production: licensing between the major producers, and subcontracting.[4] The extensive use of licensing arrangements meant that by the end of the war no major producer turned out just its own planes. The Tulsa plant of Douglas, for example, produced an airplane designed by Consolidated but whose parts were fabricated by Ford (Day, 1956: 23). Seven of the thirteen plants producing engines for combat planes were licensees and accounted for 47 per cent of the 1940–44 total horsepower output (Lilley et al. 1946: 67). The extent to which major producers produced each other's products is reflected in Table 3.2, which shows how the production of the various aircraft and engine types was distributed between firms.

The licensing process resulted in an increase in the number of firms operating in the industry, but it also established the dominance of the larger producers who held the licenses. The largest five operators produced over 60 per cent of wartime output (Craven and Cate 1955: 355), generating a level of industrial concentration that was unheard of in the pre-war period. The smaller firms either became increasingly tied to larger firms, or else maintained some independence by finding niches in the aircraft markets where small-scale craft production was still viable, such as in the production of gliders and training aircraft.

The subcontracting system paralleled the development of licensing. With the breakdown of the production process into its component parts and the decline in importance of skilled labor, it was no longer necessary for an aircraft to be built almost entirely within the same plant. This was certainly not the case in 1939, where only about 10 per cent of production

Table 3.2 Producers of major airframes and engines

Aircraft model	Producers
B-29	Boeing, Bell, Martin
B-17	Boeing, Douglas, Lockheed
B-24	Consolidated-Vultee, Douglas, Ford, North American
Corsair	Vought, Brewster, Goodyear
Wildcat	Grumman, General Motors
Avenger	Grumman, General Motors
Helldiver	Curtiss, Fairchild (Canada), Canadian Car & Foundry
P-38	Lockheed, Consolidated-Vultee
Pratt & Whitney Engines	Pratt & Whitney, Nash-Kelvinator, Buick, Chevrolet, Ford, Continental, Jacobs, Packard
Wright Engines	Wright, Dodge, Studebaker, Continental
Hamilton Propellers	Hamilton Standard, Frigidaire, Nash-Kelvinator, Remington-Rand

Source: AIAA (1946: 91).

was subcontracted (Cunningham 1951: 183). By the latter part of the war, however, 30–8 per cent of airframe construction was subcontracted (Day 1956: 16).

The factor which allowed the growth of subcontracting was the sub-assembly system. The assembly of the final product was broken down into a number of component processes, which became assembly points in themselves. For example, an engine can be broken down into a number of parts and processes such as crankshafts, crankcases, pistons and rocker arms, propeller shafts, master and articulated connecting rods, gear-making, cylinder making, and magnesium casting. The production of these individual subassemblies was then treated as a separate production process to which mass-production techniques were applied to a greater or lesser degree. Once the production of aircraft had been broken down into its component subassemblies, it was discovered that only three activities – experimental engineering, final assemblies, and flight testing – necessarily had to be performed by the prime contractors. The other steps could be turned over to firms with little or no experience in aircraft manufacture (Cleveland and Graham 1945: 85). It was then possible for smaller manufacturers, who had previously been involved in the mass production of a variety of products from elevators to furniture to concentrate their efforts on producing aircraft subassemblies for the larger assembly plants (Day, 1956: 22).

The overall effects of these licensing and subcontracting arrangements is summarized in the following comments by Cleveland and Graham:

The factories best equipped to do a particular job did an increasing share of the whole industry's work along those lines, and accordingly reaped the efficiency of ever-greater production. And non-aviation contractors who had hesitantly accepted small orders of aviation parts when the war began confidently expanded in their new line. Once assured of a high, steady demand for the product (usually a subassembly) which they themselves had learned to make efficiently, they became in effect one big department of the prime contractor who took their output. Moreover, new subcontractors . . . shifted from making many items (some for aviation companies, others non-aviation material) to manufacturing a single unit or several units, thus increasing their efficiency tremendously. In short, the subcontractors as a body did the work of those prime contractors' small departments which had been dispossessed when the final big plant expansion was completed . . . The second impact of this new and close teamwork fell largely on prime contractors, the powerful 'big-name' plane producers. Before the war each of their plants was an independent unit, capable of turning raw materials into finished products. Today the firms retain their identity . . . but none is an airplane builder, or even an engine, propeller, or instrument producer in the strict prewar sense of the word. They are primarily designers and assemblers of these products. Their development departments perform almost all engineering functions – experimental and production – for all their subcontractors. These vendors, in turn, serve as the manufacturing departments for the prime contractors . . . For every worker [in 1944] under the prime contractor's direction there are another two, nominally under other management, actually making his product by his methods.

LIMITS TO TRANSFORMATIONAL GROWTH: PROBLEMS OF DEMAND

While these changes in the production system indicate a successful transformation in the manufacture of aircraft, they in fact mask some major problems that confronted the industry. The source of the problem was the nature of demand, which was not compatible with the line production methods that were being adopted. As a result the transformations we have just described were introduced only under considerable duress and with substantial government intervention. The ability of firms already engaging in the mass production of other commodities, most notably automobiles, to transfer their organizational and technical know-how to the production of aircraft was hampered by *the discretionary nature of the demand for aircraft*.

Although the machines and equipment used in the automobile industry *could* be used to produce aircraft, in a strict technical sense, the structure of demand for aircraft did not make it economically feasible. Mass production requires mass markets, and the existence of a mass market for aircraft was not immediately present – the total size of the aircraft market took on mass proportions but this demand remained largely discretionary, so in effect the aircraft industry was in the worst of two worlds. It had to produce a large volume of output, but it could not do this on the basis of a completely standardized design fixed for a sufficient length of time.

The discretionary demand for aircraft is due to the fact that a learning-by-using process between the commodity producer and the final consumer of airplanes is a normal feature of the development of aircraft (Mowery and Rosenberg 1982). This consumer-producer feedback can create problems because it results in a market that is not homogeneous and stable enough to allow the degree of mechanization necessary for mass production. Mowery and Rosenberg argue that this is a normal feature of "complex products with elaborately differentiated, interdependent components" (1982: 165), so that "the interaction of these complex systems is crucial to the performance of an aircraft design, yet extremely difficult to predict from design and engineering data . . . Performance in many cases cannot be predicted definitively before the initial flight" (1982: 164). The rapid pace of technological change in the industry during the war is a testimony to this constant adaptation of plane design to the learning process. As a result, the demand for aircraft was constantly adjusted to take account of what the final user had discovered about its operation – information from the fighting front was used by the military services to push the case for changes in the designs of aircraft. In 1940 the Office of Production Management, the precursor to the War Production Board, found no fewer than fifty-five different plane types on order (Janeway 1951: 212). And, as the range of environments in which aircraft were used increased, the need for frequent and more complex design changes increased as well. The military services wanted to have the best of both worlds: quantity production and constant variation in the type of product.

This created problems for the aircraft producers, who wanted long production runs in order to recoup very high development costs. The producers pointed to the gestation period for producing aircraft as an indication of the development costs which they had to incur. During the war the fastest program required nineteen months from go-ahead to the production of 1000 airframes. Most programs required between two and three years, with a median of thirty-one months for one- and two-engine aircraft, and thirty-three months for four-engine bombers (Craven and Cate 1955: 357). These long lead times put aircraft producers in a vulnerable position if demand for aircraft changed and costs could not be recouped on the outdated models. The cost implications of such changes is described by the Aircraft Industry Association of America (1946: 91):

> One type of radial-powered fighter plane had reached the model series 'N' and was undergoing constant refinement even as its quantity production continued on schedule at the time of surrender. The first production model of this plane cost 260,000 engineering man-hours. It has since undergone 189 master changes and 3,000 minor engineering changes at an engineering man-hour cost of nearly three times that expended to bring the first model to its production stage
>
> (1946: 91)

The Senate Special Committee to Investigate the National Defense Program (the Truman Committee) investigated the dilemma between the need for long, stable production runs, and the need for constant design changes. The performance of aircraft could be substantially improved by paying attention to the information coming back from the military services as planes were put to the test. And, given the costs of not having technical superiority over the enemy in wartime conditions, this information had to be incorporated into the production process. Yet the economic implications for the actual producers of aircraft, if they were to adopt mass-production methods, could not be ignored. The result was a constant tension between the military's demand for frequent design changes and the producers' need for standardization: a tension which was never fully worked out to everyone's satisfaction, and which continued to hamper production.

In the end, the Truman Committee urged two changes to the structure of demand. First was the standardization of plane designs, and the second was to "lock in" the standard design for at least two or three years. Indeed, the military themselves slowly realized the importance of reducing design changes and expanding production runs if they were to get the quality of aircraft they required in the numbers they also wanted. Thus, General Arnold ordered in mid-1940 a first priority on "the continuous production of current types of airplanes" (cited in Craven and Cate 1955: 229). In 1941 the Secretary of War established what was to become the Joint Aircraft Committee to coordinate American and other Allied purchases and to "consider and decide all matters pertaining to aircraft standardization and aircraft delivery schedules" (cited in Craven and Cate 1955: 273). This committee enforced a degree of standardization between the Navy and the Army Air Force, and between America and the British, on many parts such as nuts, bolts and pipe fittings, as well as on equipment such as propellers and communication equipment. In July 1942 the Air Materiel Planning Council was established to coordinate changing tactical and strategic requirements of aircraft with production requirements. As a result of these efforts the number of new types of both airframes and engines was reduced, so that only two types of airframes on which design work had begun after June 1940 were used extensively during the war: the Republic P-47 and Grumman F6F. The only new engine models were the Pratt & Whitney R-4360 and the experimental jet engines, none of which was used in combat to a significant degree (Lilley et al. 1946: 17).

However, these changes to the structure of demand were far short of creating a truly mass, homogeneous market for aircraft. Even though a basic range of aircraft types was settled upon early in the war, they all underwent major models changes over the following years. For example, the development of the turbosupercharger in the early stages of the war by Sanford Moss made high-altitude operation of aircraft possible. The use of aircraft in hitherto untested environments led to further modifications in practically every aspect of plane design as operation under these new conditions led to information feedback. In total, there were eight major types of engines used during the war and nineteen major types of airframes, each undergoing various modifications in design. In total the industry introduced into the production line a total of 150 separate types of military aircraft, and of these basic types more than 417 separate and distinct models and additional thousands of detailed engineering changes (AIAA 1946: 90). A similar story exists for the production of engines. For example, the production of the Pratt & Whitney R-1830 engine went through six major and eighteen minor variations, for a total of twenty-four models, none of which were completely interchangeable.

The story of the P-47 illustrates this point. Originally designed in 1940 with a liquid-cooled engine, the design was then redrawn for the P-47B to incorporate a newly developed air-cooled engine. The experimental model did not fly until May 1941, and the first production units were not accepted until December. However, problems integrating a new supercharger continued to hamper production plans. The first combat group using the P-47 was not equipped until November 1942, and it was not until March 1943 that difficulties with the engine and communications equipment were sorted out. It was not until the model D in 1943 that large-scale production began. By the time the model N was produced the weight had increased by 3,000 pounds over the D model, and fuel capacity had grown from 300 gallons to 1,266 gallons through the addition of belly and wing tanks (Craven and Cate 1955: 216–17). Similarly, most major aircraft types had to be adjusted according to the theater of war to which they were applied: a plane used in the Aleutian Islands performed differently than the same plane used in Europe. The interaction of the various complex systems that comprise an aircraft varied according to such factors as climate,[5] average flying speed and altitude, and the extent to which the plane was pushed to its speed and weight limits – factors which could not be fully anticipated in the design stages of production.

Since the government could achieve only *limited* standardization of aircraft demand it also intervened on the supply side, in order to cushion the cost implications of high-volume production. The most dramatic way was for the government to simply pick up the cost of capacity expansion. In total the US government spent over $20 billion on privately operated manufacturing establishments during World War II (Gordon 1969), of which $3.3 billion was spent on aircraft production facilities (Argyrous 1990: 49), the second largest amount behind the construction of ordnance facilities. The other major way in which the structure of supply was altered to fit the needs of long production runs was through the government's development of "modification centers". In total the State sponsored the construction of twenty-one modification centers at a cost of over $100 million, out of a total of twenty-eight centers for the whole industry. These modification centers were separate from the main production lines and retained a largely craft-based system of operation (Hotchkiss 1943; Nash 1990: 72–3). At their peak in June 1944 modification centers employed over 43,000 workers (Rae 1968: 149). The aircraft industry thereby was split between the large assembly plants that followed line production methods, and the modification centers that still utilized craft techniques. Through this arrangement major producers could concentrate on producing basic models of airplanes, and leave it to the modification centers to adjust these models to the specific needs of the military as they arose. These centers in a sense "quarantined" variations in production designs from the bulk of the production process, thereby allowing both quantity production and variety in "tastes" for aircraft. The important point is that the changes were made *after* the planes came off the production line so that tooling and plant layout did not have to be rearranged in the large fabrication and assembly plants.[6]

THE TRANSFER OF ORGANIZATIONAL KNOWLEDGE: AUTOMOBILE FIRMS AND AIRCRAFT PRODUCTION

The development of line production techniques in aircraft manufacture, we have argued, was based on the licensing and subcontracting systems. These systems allowed production to be divided into specialized stages and also allowed firms engaged in mass production of other commodities to enter horizontally into the aircraft industry. However, often aircraft manufacturers used subcontractors and licensees only under duress from the government, which wanted to see more small producers benefiting from wartime prosperity and wanted the productive capacities of other industries mobilized for the war effort. With the aircraft industry only just becoming familiar with the problems of large organization, subcontracting often placed incredible strains on the still evolving management systems. In March 1943, in fact, the chairman of the Aircraft Production Board attributed the existing lag in production to ongoing management problems. Scheduling inputs at the required rates and amounts, maintaining quality control, and coordinating transportation and cross-hauling of parts and subassemblies were problems which often limited the benefits which the prime contractors derived from subcontracting (Craven and Cate 1955: 338–9).

The most obvious manifestation of the problem of the horizontal spread of mass production was in the attempt to bring the large automobile firms into the aircraft industry. Part of the difficulty was the difference in the respective complexities of aircraft and automobiles. For example, an average automobile had around 5,000 parts, whereas a B-25 bomber had some 165,000, not including engines, instruments, propellers or 150,000 rivets (Rae 1968: 152–3). The 18 ft nose of the B-29 plane alone had over 50,000 rivets and 8,000 kinds of parts (Simonson 1968: 119). However, the difficulties faced by car manufacturers in moving into aircraft production were more than just a technological matter. Automobile producers were already locked into production for mass markets, a process which generates rigid inflexibility as a consequence of specialization. The aircraft producers, on the other hand, even with the efforts of the government, required much more flexible methods of production. The auto industry was already too far down the road to mass production for it to retrace its steps; the advance of the plane producers from their modest starting point down this same path was necessarily limited.

In 1939 the management structure of aircraft producers reflected their craft production methods. Many producers could still be described as one-man companies in the sense that they were identified with a single person who made most of the decisions which seriously affected output. Operations were kept at a small enough level where such key individuals could supervise production on the basis of informal relationships that could adapt to the specific task at hand. Even in the "larger" firms, where there was some form of management hierarchy, the senior managers were still closely tied to the shop floor. As the Harvard study commented:

> the vice-president in charge of manufacturing was usually a master mechanic who had risen to that position because of his knowledge of how to make airplanes. He would participate in the day-to-day decisions on the factory floor and would often

make the final decision on such details as modifying an assembly jig to conform to a design change.

(Lilley *et al.* 1946: 61)

Within the structure of the small job-shop the role of the foreman was especially important. Foremen handled such key matters as planning, tooling and production control, usually on the shop floor as the specific needs of the particular job became evident. Obviously in such a situation the scale of operation was limited to the capacities of these key individuals.

The informal nature and "flatness" of the management system meant that systematic information about the production process was not extensively recorded. Design standards, parts specifications, information about the sequence of operations involved in assembling aircraft, and detailed time standards were not written down because these factors varied from job to job:

> Procedures were based on such low volume of production that informal methods of control were sufficient. The focal point in building the airplane was the shop foreman. Engineers collaborated very closely with the foreman and frequently resorted to informal sketches in working out a change in design. In other cases, the foreman worked directly from dimensioned drawings and sketches, making up his own templates and tools as required, with practically no paperwork involved. The engineers maintained such close contact with conditions in the shop and quantities were so small that no effort was made to keep accurate, complete, or up-to-date drawings on file in the engineering department.
>
> (Lilley *et al.* 1946: 48)

The Harvard study went on to estimate that typically only around 80 per cent of an aircraft was covered by drawings of any kind in spring 1941.

While such a management system is ideal for craft production, mass production cannot function on such a basis. The production of thousands of units of identical, interchangeable parts across a vast number of operations requires *coordination* and easily transferable, detailed information. In late 1938, when the Air Corps stated a requirement for 12,000 combat and 2,000 trainer planes in the first six months after M-day, the manufacturers were unable to provide the detailed information to achieve this and requested that the Air Corps finance plant studies to gather the data. Without such codified information, subcontractors and licensees were hampered by the poor quality of the drawings and specifications provided by the aircraft makers, as the following comment indicates:

Alcoa representatives pointed out that aircraft manufacturers were guilty of long delays in providing drawings for the parts ordered. Merely placing an order was not enough. Detailed drawings and specifications had to accompany an order. Without these it was impossible to begin work on the construction of forging dies. If, as was often the case in 1940, aircraft manufacturers were trying to put models into production directly from the drawing board, it is not surprising that all too frequently the necessary detailed drawings were not available when orders for parts went out to suppliers. Even when drawings were sent with initial orders, it sometimes happened that subsequent design changes were introduced and the partially finished dies had to be reworked.

(Holley 1964: 251)

It was no longer possible to maintain the informal relationships characteristic of the job-shop. Whole departments had to be established to take over the functions that previously were the responsibility of the individual foreman or supervisor. Concerns such as purchasing, materials control, industrial relations and tool engineering became critical to the maintenance of the flow of production, whereas they were rarely an issue under the craft process.

The evolution of the required management systems by established aircraft producers proved to be a slow and difficult process, as is illustrated in the story of Curtiss-Wright. The strains placed on the as yet undeveloped management structure became so bad at Curtiss-Wright's Cincinnati engine plant that the Truman Committee held extensive inquiries after complaints from the services regarding the quality of output from the plant (*Hearings* Part 20; *Report* Part 10). The engine producer had adopted a policy of one hundred per cent interchangeability of engine parts to meet the surge in demand, but this objective required much finer tolerances and finish of parts. Therefore Curtiss-Wright employed an inspection service of 2,400 people, yet, even with such a large team, management found it difficult to ensure that the higher standards were reached. The Army rejected many of the engines which came off the line, with a resulting slow-down in production. One of the major problems was excessive oil flow which led to overheating – a problem which derived from a poor fit between the crankshaft and the bearings. In its defense Curtiss-Wright argued that it would have been better for the government not to have expanded capacity as much as it did, and instead should have allowed management to increase productivity, at smaller capacity, through a learning-by-doing process, giving management the time to evolve appropriate practices. In the end the company abandoned its hopes of 100 per cent interchangeability. With management unable to take over the function of quality control, part of this function reverted back to the shop floor through the adoption of selective assembly of certain parts.

Thus the decision to bring automobile firms into aircraft production was due as much to the need to exploit their existing management systems as it was to exploit their existing production facilities. For example, most pre-war aircraft operators used locally designed, non-standard business forms, whereas firms in the automobile industry had already moved to punch-card business machines. However, the variability in the demand for aircraft did not make the transfer an easy one. As Charles Sorenson, a leading Ford executive, stated:

> The most annoying feature of our bomber operation was changes in design during production. We would agree on freezing a design, then be ready to go ahead. Back from the fighting fronts would come complaints or suggestions regarding certain features; and the plane designers came through with alterations in design with no consideration for the production program.
>
> (Sorenson 1956: 298)

The limited extent to which auto firms had already entered the aircraft industry prior to the war indicates the importance of mass markets in creating the possibility for the horizontal spread of mass production. For example, GM's aircraft operations were related to the prospect of mass markets for small craft. According to Alfred Sloan, GM bought into Bendix and Fokker because "there was in the late 1920s a great deal of talk about developing a 'flivver' plane – that is, *a small plane for everyday family use* . . . as one aviation miracle succeeded another, our conviction grew that the flivver plane was at least a possibility" (1972: 424, emphasis added). Although this anticipation may seem unrealistic today, the prospect of a mass market for cheap aircraft to match that for automobiles enticed GM to maintain some connection with the aviation industry. But until such a mass market developed, this connection was actually restricted to those aspects of aircraft production where long production runs were feasible: the production of engines through its Allison Division, and the production of the AT-6 trainer by North American. After the war, when the prospects for the flivver plane seemed remote at best, GM abandoned most of its connections with airframe production: "it became increasingly clear that General Motors could not employ its mass production techniques effectively in the airframe industry. We decided, therefore, that it would be in the best interests of both General Motors and North American to dispose of our holdings in the company" (Sloan 1972: 437).

The whole problem of applying mass-production technology in advance of the development of mass markets was crystallized around Ford's construction of the huge assembly plant at Willow Run, or, as it came to be called, 'Will-it-Run.' Despite Henry Ford's pronouncement that his company could produce one thousand planes of standard design a day, the necessary level of standardization and freezing of designs did not materialize. In fact the Ford executives quickly came to realize that in 1940 the auto and aircraft industries stood on opposite sides of the divide between craft and mass production systems, and this would be the major stumbling block:

> The work of putting together a four-engine bomber was many times more complicated than assembling a four-cylinder automobile, but what I saw reminded me of nearly thirty-five years previously when we were making Model N Fords at the Piquette Avenue plant . . . The nearer the B-24 came to its final assembly the fewer principles of mass production there were as we at Ford had developed and applied over the years. Here was custom-made planes, put together as a tailor would cut and fit a suit of clothes.
> (Sorenson, in Rae 1968: 136)

The gap between the two industries was vast. In 1937, ninety-two aircraft establishments employed just over 24,100 people, while 131 automobile firms employed over 194,000. These ninety-two aircraft firms produced 3,100 units worth nearly $107 million, whereas the 131 automobile firms produced nearly 5 million units valued at over $3 billion. In other words, the auto makers produced over 1,500 times more units but with a workforce only eight times larger (Holley 1964: 26–7). The relative importance of fixed capital in auto production is evident in the fact that Chevrolet's investment per worker in plant and equipment was $2,600, whereas Martin, a comparable firm in aircraft production, invested around $800 per worker (Bryant Woods 1946: 4). Some authors, in fact, compared the aircraft industry in 1939 with the automobile industry in 1910–11 (Craven and Cate 1955: 187).

Ford tried to overcome this gap in one step: it obstinately built its assembly line on the principles used to make autos, refusing to incorporate "several hundred modifications" into the production process (Truman Committee *Report* 10 Part 10: 348). As a result, the services refused to put a B-24 produced at Willow Run into combat – until early 1943 they were used only for training.

The aircraft manufacturers, on the other hand, were not prepared to adopt mass-production techniques so readily, given the nature of demand for aircraft by the military. As Jansen, the factory manager of the Curtiss Aeroplane Division of Curtiss-Wright stated,

> As far as adapting automobile plants or any other mass production industry to build airplanes in large quantities at a very early

date – that is definitely an impossibility . . . airplane design simply is not "frozen" to the point of so-called mass production based on two or three year plans.

(Quoted in Day 1956: 20)

Consolidated-Vultee, Ford's partner in the Willow Run project, refused to accept the need for drastically new production methods to achieve an increase in output. This led to continuing engineering problems which slowed down the production effort. For example, aircraft engineers usually worked from fairly general blueprints and designs, since they could count on the skilled labor on the shop floor to interpret them and modify the designs as necessary. The mature mass production system of the auto industry, on the other hand, required far more detailed specification of the production process, since discretion on the part of labor could not be permitted if parts were to remain interchangeable.

> When Ford was licensed to produce the Consolidated B-24, it was necessary to break down the assembly process into approximately 20,000 drawings before an assembly line could be set up at Willow Run. Only then could there be sufficient specialization so that aircraft could be produced by the lesser skilled personnel on whom the industry was forced to rely for the rapid production expansion.
>
> (Simonson 1968: 119)

The situation at Willow Run became so bad that in September 1943 the Materiel Command of the AAF seriously suggested that the government take over the project. In the end an intermediate position prevailed. Ford reduced the proportion of work it had originally planned to do at Willow Run, in favor of subcontracting work to more flexible smaller producers to allow the incorporation of desired modifications into the plane design. The Willow Run factory was the aircraft industry's most advanced move into mass-production technology. By 1944 it was producing more than any other plant and nearly 10 per cent of industry output (Lilley et al. 1946: 36). But even these achievements did not meet the expectations of the project – Willow Run never produced at its peak. It produced a total of 6,791 planes, 5,476 during 1944–45. At its highest rate of output Willow Run only produced at two-thirds of its monthly capacity, and the obsolescence of the B-24 by 1945 made the whole plant redundant (Rae 1968: 160).

The relationship between the auto and aircraft industries indicates that the spread of Transformational Growth is not a smooth or rapid process, but rather a cumulative and incremental process involving a number of technical and organizational problems which cannot be seen in advance.

THE TRANSFER OF TECHNOLOGICAL KNOWLEDGE: THE MACHINE TOOL INDUSTRY

The rapid expansion in the demand for aircraft, without a corresponding standardization of the demand for planes, hampered the ability of auto firms to introduce their organizational know-how of mass-production technology. It similarly hampered the machine tool industry's ability to provide the actual hardware upon which mass production is built. In fact, the main structural and technological problem which faced policy-makers during the war was how to realign the pattern of relationships between final goods producers and capital goods producers to meet the needs of wartime production.

The machine tool industry is pivotal in the transfer of technology from an existing mass-production industry to an emerging one. Tools and equipment in craft firms are relatively unsophisticated and the product of in-house craftsmen such as blacksmiths. But under mass production precision and durability of machines become paramount in an environment where high volumes of standardized products and interchangeable parts are the order of the day. Thus, in aircraft production during World War II special-purpose tools began to replace wood, rubber and plaster constructions in order to produce interchangeable parts in the quantities required.

> Temporary assembly jigs were broken down into smaller sections, strengthened through the use of heavy steel members, simplified by the removal of unnecessary portions of the template detail, and rendered more suitable for higher production through better location of control points and greater accessibility. These changes were, however, variations to meet the needs of increased volume.
>
> (Lilley *et al.* 1946: 38)

Similarly, the higher volumes of aircraft production required the introduction of more durable and specialized cast-steel tools and dies. Although the first machine had been patented in 1849 (for the casting of type), and die-casting had been used commercially in the production of phonographs and cash registers in the 1890s, it was not until the turn of the century and the mass-production of bearings for automobile connecting rods that die-casting gained pre-eminence over earlier casting methods. Die-casting relies on permanent metal dies which can produce thousands of identical castings, whereas sand-casting requires a new mold for each casting or gate of castings, but requires only a small investment in the die itself and associated patterns, jigs and fixtures for machining. Although they had much finer tolerances and were not "disposable", steel dies could take several months to produce and were much more expensive.

The result was that the aircraft industry devolved machine tool production to the specialist machine tool producers, rather than making the necessary equipment in-house, as it had done in the past. This generated an immense increase in the demand for tools from the aircraft industry. The machine-cutting industry built over one million machine tools during the war, more than the total number of machine tools produced by the industry in the forty years before 1939 (DiFilippo 1986: 30), and about one-third of the total number of tools produced during the war were consumed by the aircraft industry (Wagoner 1968: 274). The total number of tools in place in the aircraft industry increased from 8,780 in 1940 to 276,466 in 1945 (DiFilippo 1986: 29; Stoughton 1949: 81).

The intrinsically craft-like nature of machine tool production acts as a brake on the cumulative process of expansion. In fact, the very processes which allow machine-using industries to eliminate craft production in their own operation reinforces craft production in the machine-producing industry itself. This inherently craft-like nature of the machine tool industry was reflected in the fact that in 1940 only about half of the 400 plants were specializing solely in the production of machine tools, while the other 200 made other products as well. Similarly, there was a large proportion of shops whose output was insignificant in relation to the industry as a whole: around 200 of the shops produced only 5 per cent of the output. Similarly, the industry could hardly be said to be highly concentrated: the largest thirty companies carried only 62 per cent of the dollar volume of production (Stoughton 1949: 7).

The dominance of craft methods in the bulk of shops limited the ability of the industry to respond to the need for increased output, and led to the most important production bottleneck of the war program. The physical constraints upon expanded output that are a feature of craft operations manifested themselves along a number of dimensions. The first was a constraint imposed by labor supply. Relying on skilled labor acting in work teams meant that increases in output came more from an extension of the average working week rather than through the use of multiple shifts. Under craft conditions firms cannot easily draw labor in as demand fluctuates, since labor of the necessary type and skill to put on extra shifts may be difficult to find in an industry where it can take over four years to train a skilled machinist (Broehl 1959: 168–73). Broehl, in his study of three machine tool shops in Springfield, Vermont, found that "the twelve hour shift . . . was the basic day for all three shops by early 1942, giving an average work week of between 60 and 72 hours, depending on the days off in the particular week" (1959: 171). For the industry as a whole, by the end of 1941 the average work week of two-thirds of machine tool firms was between fifty-five and sixty-five hours. Although

all firms were also running second shifts, the number of machine operators on this shift was about half that on the first (Wagoner 1968: 254).

This practice was criticized as not making full use of the capacity of the
machine tool industry, thereby setting back the entire war effort. However, machine tool builders and the Machine Tools Section of the War
Production Board were reluctant to make extensive use of the multiple
shift system, as was the case

> in plants mass producing war equipment and supplies [since]
> much more supervisory and instructional time was required in
> machine tool plants and supervisors could not be spread too
> thinly over a large number of untrained and inexperienced
> workers.
>
> (Wagoner 1968: 256)

This was particularly the case where special machine tools were being
made.

> Some major parts required more than one shift to complete and
> the skilled machinist, unlike the machine "operator" in mass
> production, would not tolerate a division of work with a worker
> on a succeeding shift. In such cases the work remained in the
> machine until completed even though this took several days.
>
> (Wagoner 1968: 257)

The second dimension along which the output of the machine tool
industry was constrained was financial, so that machine tool firms found
it difficult to expand without government financial assistance. The craft-
like nature of machine tool production meant that it was closely tied to
the ebbs and flows of the trade cycle, and would often have to accumulate
financial resources during boom periods to cover losses during the just as
frequent slack periods. This limited the ability of firms to raise the finance
for major expansions externally. The retained earnings of many machine
shops were insufficient to finance large-scale investment, however,
because they were needed as a reserve fund to cover losses and pay for
working capital during slack periods.

To overcome this problem, the government financed the construction
of thirty-five new machine tool plants and added machinery to another
131 (White 1980: 75–6). New facilities for producing machine tools cost a
total of over $160 million, out of which the Defense Plants Corporation
paid $70 million and $90 million was privately financed. A part of the
latter total, however, was financed by advances from the DPC on pool
orders, which will be discussed below (Wagoner 1968: 271). The result

was that one-third of America's machine tools in 1945 were government-owned (Wagoner 1968: 318).

The third dimension along which the machine tool industry was limited in expanding its output was due to its own needs for machine tools. Since machine tools are needed to expand the capacity of the machine tool industry, during the period of its own expansion the industry became a net "importer" of tools, thereby setting back the expansions in other critical industries. This meant that the government was reluctant to expand capacity too far in this industry, and led to a directive by Eberstadt, the executive director of the Army–Navy Munitions Board, in January 1942 that no further general facilities expansions be approved for the machine tool industry. As a result, the total increase in the level of capacity in the tool industry was not as great as in other industries. By mid-1941 capacity had expanded by about 10 per cent. Yet in the year between August 1940 and August 1941 output had grown from just under $41 million to over $64 million (Wagoner 1968: 249–50), and in 1942 the industry turned out over 307,000 machines valued at $1.3 billion (Broehl 1959: 183).

The need to overcome these constraints forced the government to intervene, such as the financing of new facilities just discussed. In order to buffer the machine tool industry from the massive increase in demand emanating from the aircraft (and other) industry, the government inserted itself between the final user of the tools and the producer, and thereby absorbed the costs of constant fluctuations in demand which would otherwise have been borne by the tool firms. The specific policy for this was the government's pool order system.

Pool ordering meant that the government acted as a central purchasing agency, placing orders on the basis of *anticipated* needs. The Defense Plant Corporation placed pool orders in advance of the prime contractors on the basis of expected demand, and the prime contractor would then purchase the tools from the DPC when they were needed. This was the principle of "too much, too soon", whereby "machine-tool builders were given pool orders for about 50 per cent more equipment than called for by manufacturing schedules" (Stoughton 1949: 68). The contract between the tool producer and the DPC provided for an advance amounting to 30 per cent of the list price. When the tools were produced the machines were shipped direct to customers who had by that time placed an order on the pool. The 30 per cent advance was refunded to the DPC at the time the customer was billed. Where orders from aircraft builders or other manufacturers had not materialized, the DPC was notified that the tools were completed, and the tool builder was instructed to ship to storage. The DPC was then billed for the remaining 70 per cent of the agreed cost. The extent of pool ordering in relation to total machine tool output during the war is reflected in Table 3.3.

This purchasing system eased the pressure on craft producers in the

Table 3.3 Machine tool pool shipments, 1941–45, (millions of dollars)

	Shipments of DPC tools	*Total machine tool production*
1939		200
1940		440
1941	221	775
1942	530	1,320
1943	807	1,180
1944	109	502
1945	32	407
TOTAL	1,699	4,184

Source: Truman Committee (*Hearings* Part 1: 102); White (1980: 83).

industry by ensuring continuity and stability in demand and by guaranteeing firm orders, i.e. orders which were not subject to cancellation. The guarantee of such orders is crucial for craft producers where the recoupment of production costs depends on the sale of the individual job lot rather than a mass of output. In a craft system where there is a significant lag in the placement of an order and its fulfillment, an order poses a major risk if there is no guarantee that payment will be made upon delivery. Therefore if orders are cancelled prior to purchase of the goods, producers are stuck with the costs of that job which cannot be recouped without cutting prices. "The pool-order device eliminated the fear of cancellation of orders, so that tool builders were able to get out the maximum possible production without being in constant fear of the whole program's collapsing on their shoulders" (Stoughton 1949: 65).

Guaranteed advance ordering relieved pressure on machine tools builders in other ways. The 30 per cent advance provided essential working capital when it was needed most – at the start of production. In fact the industry was so starved of working capital that the chief of the OPM Tool Branch, in December 1941, ordered all tool builders to insist on an advance payment of 30 per cent from all tool purchasers, not just those related to the pool ordering scheme. Moreover, by scheduling supply in advance of demand, pool ordering ensured that the lag between the placement of the order and delivery of the goods did not slow down the rest of the production effort: many specialized tools could take over six months to be delivered once an order was placed. By having the government order in advance of requirements, when plane producers needed certain pieces of equipment they would already be available:

> Take one component – magnetos – as an example. They would be required in tremendous volume for the large number of airplanes being planned. Many specialized machine tools would be needed to produce magnetos, but, ordinarily, orders for such machines

would not reach the machine tool builders until the contracts were let for the planes, subcontracts for the engines, and finally, subcontracts for the magnetos. Thanks to pool orders, machine tool builders were building the machines magneto makers would need long before the magneto contracts were placed.

(Stoughton 1949: 65)

The pool ordering system not only smoothed out demand for tools by enabling orders to be placed in advance of needs, and mitigated the effects of continued demand changes, it also served to homogenize the demand for certain types of tools. By acting as a single purchasing agent the government reduced the variety of tools that could perform the same tasks. The government was also able to concentrate the production of certain types of machines at certain producers, and to impose standardization of specifications where feasible. Stoughton (1949: 66) argues that these initiatives helped tool producers in the following ways:

1 Decrease in inspection, machining, and assembling time,
2 More routine and, consequently, more rapid, operations, with help more easily trained,
3 Ease in the procurement of parts, materials, and components from suppliers.

This allowed the machine tool industry to reap some of the benefits of economies of scale and standardization. Stoughton gives the example of forging line equipment, where the government insisted that such equipment be interchangeable. An agreement was established between the press companies so that they would all use the one design, and the company whose design was chosen was paid a special royalty. The pool orders were placed with the press companies, who then decided among themselves how the total order was to be met (Stoughton 1949: 70).

CONCLUSION

This analysis raises some general issues about the role of the state in industrial development. It indicates that there are specific junctures at which the process of cumulative causation may break down and government intervention may be required if the process is to start again. It essentially draws attention to the need for governments to transform the structure of demand rather than focus exclusively on its aggregate expansion. This structure has many aspects. First is the need to ensure the expansion of mass markets for products previously made under craft conditions. No better way of doing this exists than to ensure that the great bulk of the working population have secure employment and improving life styles. This can facilitate the transfer of labor out of domestic production and its replacement with "domestic labor-saving" devices. Indeed, this was probably the most enduring, if unintended, consequence of World War II. The massive redistribution of income which took place, the transfer of poor farm workers, especially African Americans, out of rural poverty and into the cities, where they received a modicum of training, the creation of new urban centers in the west, and the guaranteed income support of nearly 15 million veterans through the GI Bill of Rights, buttressed the expansion of markets in such a way that America embarked on a long period of prosperity rather than a return to depression. These forces were arguably more influential in establishing the cumulative character of growth and expansion during the post-war period than the traditional measures of Keynesian macro management to which the long boom is usually ascribed.

The government can also establish the conditions for a virtuous cycle of growth through its own purchasing system. As a major consumer of a variety of manufactured articles – everything from office furniture to automobile fleets – it can ensure the homogenization of demand which we have seen is crucial for the spread of mass production techniques. It can also essentially subsidize the transformation from craft to mass-production by purchasing in the initial stages of the transformation when productivity gains have not been realized and relative prices have yet to fall.

The other major conclusion that emerges from the discussion of wartime production is the need for government policy to ensure that elasticity of supply in the machine tool industry keeps pace with the expansion of markets. Too rapid an acceleration of the growth rate in the short term may actually have damaging long-term implications, possibly even turning a virtuous cycle of growth into a vicious one of recession. The more rapidly demand is expanding the more dramatic government intervention may have to be to ensure that a critical bottleneck does not develop in the machine tool sector.

NOTES

1 Although a standard measure of productivity in the industry, this simple quantitative measure does not reflect the substantial improvements in quality brought about by the introduction of mass-production techniques into aircraft production (US Senate (Truman Committee) Report 480 Part 5: 56–63).
2 See Elberton Smith (1959: 292), for a survey of the reductions in unit costs which occurred for a variety of planes, engines and propellers during the course of the war.
3 Robinson (1958: 19) calls this the Integration of Process: "the large firm often

differs from the small firm in having fewer rather than more processes of manufacture." See also Stigler (1951).

4 Subcontracting involves passing on the production of individual parts or subassemblies to other producers, whereas licensing involves the outside company producing the entire airframe or engine.

5 This was sometimes called "winterizing" and "summerizing" a plane according to the climate in which it would be used.

6 Craven and Cate (1955: 334–5) also point out that AAF depots in the various theaters of war turned to modification work, along with regular maintenance and repair, in order to take advantage of the learning-by-using process. Existing so close to where the learning took place, these maintenance depots were important centers of technological change whose role in this process, unfortunately, has not been adequately recorded.

4

TRANSFORMATIONAL GROWTH AND THE MERGER MOVEMENT FROM 1895 TO 1904

Some theoretical, empirical and historical evidence

Helge Peukert

THE QUESTION

According to Transformational Growth, the function of the market is to generate competitive pressures to innovate. Two ideal type periods are distinguished: the period of craft technology, where declining demand leads to a decline in prices, and the following period of mass production, in which batch production is replaced by continuous throughput and the ability to vary employment and output with demand. The general trend of prices is downward in the old system, generating productivity growth. In the new system, (both) prices (and money wages) have the tendency to be sticky or to rise.

The question which will be discussed in this chapter refers to the proposition of Transformational Growth that in the new system "money prices either rise or stay steady; they seldom, if ever, fall" (Nell and Phillips 1995: p. 129). The fact that the general price level hardly falls in times of mass production does not exactly prove this assertion, because it is conceivable that all prices fluctuate violently, and 50 per cent of them fall and the other 50 per cent rise. The result will be a stable aggregate price level, although prices may vary in every industry or firm. The fact that according to Nell adaptive variation of output can be undertaken in the new system does not exclude the use of prices and their change as a further decision variable. In Nell (1992: chapter 17) a model on the micro level is developed, which links demand, benchmark pricing and growth. The model presupposes "a market for a well defined product," "firms must know how the market will react to changes in prices" and "the long-term normal 'benchmark' price is the one which . . . will be generally known," etc. (Nell 1992: 393). His post-Keynesian analysis – linking pricing and investment – is therefore concentrated on markets, where innovations have already been established and where expectations about the demand/price relationship are possible on the level of the firm to plan the adequate price/output/profit/growth relationship, which influences the aggregate movement of money wages, etc.

However, "there are two cases where the traditional story holds . . . In a new market, the growth of demand is often likely to be both substantial and erratic . . . The second case concerns a stagnant or declining market" (Nell 1995: 23). Both exceptional conditions hold true for the first great merger movement (new markets due to innovations and the following depression). It will be shown that even in a short-run supply/demand framework strong reasons for the stickiness of prices can be found, although at first sight it may seem more plausible that in technologically induced concentrated industries changes in prices will follow changes in demand (as Cournot taught us long ago in the case of monopoly). When there are several firms in the market and demand declines there is a strong motive to enter into a price war: because of the probably high fixed costs in mass production firms have to sell what the market will bear to get these fixed costs paid, regardless of what the profit per unit of output will be. (When high fixed costs and constant variable costs are assumed, a price cut does not necessarily lead to a decline in profits because total average costs per unit go down; but if competitors follow suit and expand to their limit, who shall buy the products?)

Accordingly, at first sight the thesis of fixed prices in a mass-production regime seems to be counterintuitive. Two possible proofs of the presumption of a necessary connection between mass production and sticky/rising prices are historical investigations and price theoretical arguments on the firm level. Historically, the transition from craft to mass production in certain industries began in the 1870s and led to the first great merger movement in the American economy, between 1895 and 1904, which transformed the American economy in essential ways. It will therefore be asked if the link between mass production and sticky/rising prices can be established in this most important transitional period of the US economy.

The analysis takes place in a historical, short-run, profit-maximizing framework, whereas Nell's analysis is more structural and long-run, using post-Keynesian models. The reasons for these differences are due to the period under consideration here. The historical perspective which asks if, why and how innovative agents ensure price stability through active endeavors is adequate because the great merger movement at first produced the structural setting on which Nell's structural theory is concentrated. Price stability, like vertical/horizontal integration, the M-form firm, cost accounting, listing of manufacturing firms on the stock exchange and other characteristics of American mass production did not emerge spontaneously or fully formed with the Bonsack cigarette machine. They were innovations that allowed the realization of the potential within the engineering techniques of mass production. They take place in specific time, place, and ways.

In the time period under consideration, in ten to fifteen years, almost all firm strategies, markets and the so-called data changed completely, so that for this period a long-run perspective seems not appropriate. The assumption of profit maximization is used because the methods of internal finance, which are of major importance for post-Keynesian theories, were not applicable during the transition period.

The following arguments are only part of the story. R. Majewski convinced me that besides the emergence of dominant firm oligopolies sticky prices are too general a phenomenon to be explained by sticky prices only. The change from flexible to sticky prices was probably due to five effects: the Nell effect (technical flexibility), the Sylos-Labini effect (oligopoly), the Hicks effect (changing location of inventories), the Okun effect (customer markets), and the Gardiner Means effect (price tags). All of these are results of mass production and mass marketing. The following arguments put forward some estimates about the importance of some of these effects and their interrelationship. It is surely only part of the whole story. In brief, the subject of this chapter is the emergence of sticky prices, Nell's model refers to the – form an *ex post* perspective – probably more interesting question, what happened when these changes led to mature industries? The former refers to dynamics and history – growth takes place in the long run. The latter is more theoretical in so far as in the long period all theoretically implied adjustments which are conceivable have taken place.

INTERLUDE
THE ADMINISTRATIVE PRICE DEBATE

The hypothesis of a fundamental break in the functioning of market economies seems to find profound evidence in a certain body of the theoretical literature. Taking the pattern from Veblen (1964 [1923]), Berle and Means (1932, see the overview in Lee and Samuels 1992) published their well known book *The Modern Corporation and Private Property*, which provoked a heated debate about corporate control structures. It delineated the administered price hypothesis, stating that, in opposition to market prices, manufacturing and other branches are ruled by prices which are set by administrative decision-making (of a trust, conglomerate, etc.) and held constant over a period of time.

Their thesis of a revolutionary new regime of administered prices beyond the market includes five statements:

1   There is, in point of fact, a tendency for most prices to change either relatively frequently or infrequently: "We are dealing with two quite different types of prices."
2   There is a direct relationship between frequency of change and amplitude of change: "The items which changed frequently in price showed a large drop during the depression while those having a low frequency of change tended to drop little in price."
3   There is an inverse relationship between price and production declines: "for industries in which prices dropped most during the depression, production tended to drop least, while for those in which prices were maintained, the change in production was usually greatest."
4   "Price rigidity is due principally to concentration in the market." (Blair 1972: 421-422; the citations are drawn from Means's writings.)
5   A control of output can be pursued, which allows the firms to engage in an autonomous price policy, i.e. a predetermined price can be maintained by restricting output (exemplified at the steel industry in Means 1962, where political implications for public policy are also discussed; in Means 1975 statistical evidence is given for the combination of concentration, market power and sticky/rising prices, which led to the new type of administered inflation).

The administered price hypothesis and Nell's Transformational Growth have the important theoretical device in common that there is a structural break concerning the functioning of markets and the operation of the price mechanism, but the similarities go even further. Blair has developed a "short-run target return model", which explains in detail why prices tend to rise/be sticky only in the new regime and the objectives of firms change too.

> Unlike competitive markets, a producer in a concentrated industry is not restricted to the price that equates marginal revenue with marginal costs; rather, he can elect one of a number of alternative prices. It is submitted, that the price elected will usually be governed by the considerations developed in studies of full-cost pricing . . . The thesis set forth here is that the company will seek to attain its target objective not simply over the long run, with good and bad years averaging out around the target, but in each year. Hence the term, 'short-run target return model'.
>
> (Blair 1975: 56-7)

If material costs per unit of output and wage costs are assumed to remain constant up to a high level of output, prices will rise in the model when (1) bottlenecks will be felt by an expansion of output and (2) demand decreases and the fixed costs have to be brought in by fewer products to assure the return with less than standard volume output.

This could be the end of the story, Nell's Transformational Growth and old institutionalism closing ranks, and the administered price theory could be adopted as the microfoundation of the macroeconomic reasoning of Transformational Growth. But, unfortunately, the administered price hypothesis has some severe shortcomings, which impede direct adoption in Transformational Growth. First, it reduces pricing behavior to an adaptation to short- or longer-run price conditions in the firm or industry, and Blair does not question the profit motive as the single motive of the firm's planning. In the last thirty years or so a vast body of literature has emerged which shows that in general there are many factors influencing pricing behavior. Besides the conventional price theory (Ott 1979), there are the full cost theory (Andrews 1949), the viability theory (Alchian 1950), the industrial organization theory (Bain 1968), rate of return maximization (Jennihsen 1967), sales revenue maximization (Baumol 1958), the trade position theory (Knauth 1956), sales growth maximization (Baumol 1962), output maximization (Lynn 1968), growth maximization (Marris 1963), the entrepreneurial utility theory (Olsen 1973), the behavioral theory (Cyert and March 1963), the homeostasis theory (Boulding 1952) and the managerial discretion theory (Williamson 1964; see the study of marginal pricing by Diamantopoulos and Mathews 1995). Without specifying the firms' and industries' historical development and actual environment no general statement seems possible.

Second, it is not made clear why concentration occurs at a certain time and place. Although Means often mentions technological and organizational changes which happened around the turn of the century, his remarks remain rather vague. Transformational Growth, for example, states in a more clear-cut way that ownership becomes a form of finance – it leads to a change in the character of capital markets.

Third, it is not clear what market power (to administer prices) really means. Long ago, Boehm-Bawerk (1975 [1914]) accepted the fact of power in economics but remarked that power can be exerted only through economic "laws" or tendencies. His own explanation failed (Peukert 1996: 294-315), but his methodological principle should be upheld. In fact even the monopolist has, according to Cournot again, only a definable margin of freedom; he can, e.g., not exert power over the demand side, oligopolists have to face the reactions of rivals, etc. A critical discussion between the market power school and the more orthodox mainstream never took place, so that the economic validity of the market power school is not evident.

Fourth, the thesis can be debated that corporate size and greater dispersion of stock ownership lead to a separation of ownership from control, and to a revolutionary shift in the aims of the now ruling managerial class (from profit to growth).

> Although Berle and Means described with drama and insight the growth in the overall importance of large firms and, especially, the separation of ownership and control in the large corporation, they had almost nothing to say about the effects of these changes on market concentration and market power.
>
> (Herman 1981: 6)

(Herman himself belongs to this school in a broad sense; for a more profound discussion of the administered price theory see his chapter 1.) The general and underlying problem in the discussion of the relationship between mass production, industrial organization, economic performance, the pricing behavior of the firm, etc., lies on the one hand in the fact that even the most advanced theoretical reflections about oligopoly and even the most formal and sometimes unrealistic models in game theory have not led to a concluding answer to the question of how oligopolies should behave rationally (see the broad-minded discussion in Tirole 1988). On the other hand, the historical-empirical study of the relationship between mass production, economic structure and performance (e.g. pricing strategies) seems to face even more difficult problems. Although a general trend of concentration can be detected in all economies over the last 100 years, it cannot be asserted that the narrow oligopoly, which is at the core of the administered price hypothesis, is due to technological necessities. This would coincide with a narrow interpretation of Nell's presupposition that there is a causality from technology over industrial structure to pricing behavior (sticky/rising prices). Bain has shown in his influential study, testing twenty industries with the engineering approach, that

> in a preponderance of cases, plant scale curves tend to be at least moderately flat (and sometimes very flat), so that plants of half-optimal scale would experience no more than a 2 or 3 per cent elevation in unit costs and plants of quarter-optimal scale no more than a 5 or 6 per cent elevation . . . 1. Two industries had "very important" plant scale economies, in the sense that minimum optimal plant scale exceeded 10 per cent of total market capacity, and that unit costs would be elevated by 5 per cent or more at half-optimal plant scale. (These industries produced automobiles and typewriters.) 2. Five industries had "moderately important" plant scale economies, in the sense that minimum optimal plant scale was in the neighborhood of 4 to 6 per cent of total market capacity, and that unit costs would be elevated by at least

5 per cent at half-optimal plant scale. (These industries produced cement, farm machinery, tractors, rayon, and steel.) 3. Nine industries had unimportant plant scale economies, either because the minimum optimal scale was small, or because the plant scale curves were quite flat back to rather small scales, or for both reasons. (These industries produced cigarettes, liquor, petroleum products, soap, rubber tires, shoes, flour, meat, and canned goods.) 4. Four industries were not classified.

(Bain 1968: 192–3, see also Bain 1956)

The actual concentration in an industry diverges distinctly from that required for efficiency.

1. In six industries, the average size of the first four firms was such that each could control from nine to twenty-four plants of minimum optimal scale. 2. In nine industries, the average size of the first four firms was such as to allow each from three to eight plants of minimum optimal scale. 3. In five industries, the average size of the first four firms was such that each could control from one to two plants of minimum optimal scale.

(Bain 1968: 197–8)

According to Bain, the reasons for concentration can be found in the desire to restrict competition, the advantages of large-scale promotion, the advantages of barriers to entry, legal and financial considerations, etc.

Scherer argues, like Bain that the long-run cost curve of firms is more flat than the U form with an evident lowest-cost point and "that, at least in the American economy, production and physical distribution scale economies seldom require very high seller concentration . . . that in many and perhaps most American industries high concentration is not a technological, marketing, or financial imperative" (Scherer 1971: 103; for a critique of newer industrial organization approaches see Shepherd 1989). If the flat cost curve is typical for mass production, it could be argued that Transformational Growth gets clear-cut corroboration: output can be varied in the relevant part of the curve (the flat region) without changing the price, whereas in the earlier period of craft production the cost curve was U-shaped, so that under competitive conditions prices had to vary accordingly. But, against this simple version of a deterministic cost/price relationship, an approach seems appropriate which takes into account that the restriction of output faces a basic difficulty: the spread of high fixed costs which will become apparent in the next section of this chapter.

The result of this section is that the basic stipulation of the administered price approach, that concentration in industries is an indisputable necessity, does not hold and that the explication of firm/industry structures and their pricing behavior needs a more refined, decomposite approach. The most interesting period of this transformation is the change from small enterprises operating in local markets before the American Civil War to the gradual structural change into large-size firms operating on a national market until World War I (which takes cumulative causations into account).

ON THE EVE OF MASS PRODUCTION IN THE UNITED STATES

The manufacturing sector underwent its most dramatic change between 1895 and 1904, when an avalanche of mergers took place, signalling the transition from a craft economy where the central price strategy to maintain prices consisted in product differentiation to earn profits on high margins instead of volume expansion and technological improvements. Near the end of the nineteenth century a fundamental change of strategy occurred, which depended on three characteristic environmental changes. These changes will not be analyzed in detail; only the implicit logic of the story according to Lamoreaux will be dealt with (1985, see the reviews of Cain 1986 and Davis 1986). (1) Transportation and communications led to national markets and extended competition. (2) A rising *per capita* income expanded the market even further. (3) A series of innovations took place; events which were often narrated for different industries (Chandler 1977, Baron 1962, Fell 1979, Eastman 1968). A number of innovations

> made it possible to exploit that market: the refrigerated car, which permitted the shipment of perishable goods over long distances; the Bessemer process for large-scale conversion of pig iron to steel; continuous-process rolling mills that made cheap steel rods for wire production; wood-pulp based paper for mass-circulation newspapers; the Bonsack machine for manufacturing cigarettes; new products such as glucose, barbed wire, the bicycle; new raw-material discoveries such as Pennsylvania petroleum and Western copper, lead, silver, and gold.
>
> (Lamoreaux 1985: 28-9)

The entrepreneurs focused on volume instead of price management, i.e.

> earning profits on volume of output rather than on a high margin per unit. Firms that adopted this strategy of mass production had essentially the same goals as those that differentiated their products: to defend the firm against competitors and withstand

119

fluctuations in business conditions. However, the means they used to achieve these goals differed significantly. By producing large quantities of homogeneous goods, they intended to exploit the efficiencies of volume production, reduce unit costs to the minimum, and protect themselves against price cutting by rivals . . . The general effect of these developments was to stimulate the growth of large, capital-intensive, often vertically integrated firms – a trend that is apparent even in the aggregate statistics. Between 1880 and 1900, the average amount of capital invested per manufacturing establishment increased 75 percent, from $11,000 to $19,200 while the capital–output ratio for the manufacturing sector as a whole rose 44 percent, from 0.52 to 0.75 year.

(Lamoraux 1985: 28-29)

Between the small differentiated firms and the emerging large massproducing enterprises some profound differences showed up, because firms have no longer a fixed optimal size compared to one that grows and changes. This is an organizational transformation, but it also implies a new strategic posture and new thinking on the part of the business unit. According to Transformational Growth, corporations do not have a definable optimal size but retain earnings and grow *pari passu* with their markets. In order to grow, they must develop long-run pricing policies in conjunction with their investment plans. Pricing policies are part of their sales management; investments must be planned in concert with the anticipated – and manipulated – development of the market.

For theoretical reasons, the most important short-term change is the higher capital intensity of production processes, so that the fixed portion of costs corresponds to a higher percentage of total costs. From a Transformational Growth perspective, there are two distinctions which are often confused in the literature here dealt with: fixed *u* variable and capital *u* current costs. In the craft economy, fixed costs – according to Nell's research – were very high, as a percentage of total costs, but capital costs were low, sometimes very low. Current costs, therefore, were high. As the factory system developed – at first on a craft basis, drawing on water and steam power – capital costs rose at the expense of current costs which still remained largely fixed. With the development of continuous throughput, replacing batch systems, and with assembly line methods, based on electric energy, and internal combustion, start-up and shut-down costs fell, and current costs became variable. Labour could be laid off, or put on short time. Energy costs also became more flexible. But this required still further increases in capital costs. Unsually these distinctions are not made in mainstream theorizing. Conventional cost curves do not capture them. But they do – and that is the reason why they are used here – express the idea that there is an optimal size for the firm, and an optimal level at which to operate a firm of a given size. In the following the comparison is between two stages with different relative amounts of fixed capital costs, other things being equal (*ceteris paribus*), i.e. energy systems and the flexibility of labour input. What changed was the transition from batch systems to assembly line methods which is reponsible for the higher fixed capital costs.

> In the paper industry, for example, the capital–output ratio for the industry as a whole rose from 0.71 year in 1870 to 1.32 years in 1900. This meant that if a firm had to set aside each year the equivalent of 10 percent of its capital investment to meet interest and depreciation charges, the proportion of each dollar of sales needed to pay these expenses increased 86 percent between 1870 and 1900.
>
> (Lamoreaux 1985: 30–1)

The same tendency holds true for many other industries, (see e.g. Eichner 1969 on sugar refining). Besides the higher share of fixed costs, Chandler emphasized the process of vertical integration to realize "economies of speed" (1977: 281–3). Both led to the fundamental shift in the priorities of entrepreneurs from price maintenance to output considerations, more precisely to produce at full capacity. This strategy does not coincide with two presuppositions of Transformational Growth because the former strategy does not include fixed prices and a fine-tuning of output in response to business cycles. The strategy predicts instead a maximization of the volume of output to gain a greater share of the market and to spread the fixed costs over a maximum of products (which contradicts the Transformational Growth assumption of easy output variations and fixed prices).

The market structure at that time (around the 1870s and 1880s) was generally not characterized by a few giant firms or one dominant firm, with the exception of the steel industry, where Andrew Carnegie (see Livesay 1975) undercut prices to outdistance competitors by continuously introducing cost-saving technologies, integrating backward to coal and forward into transport, besides using tactics to establish barriers of entry, which is proper for a supposed robber baron. (But his strategy of increased output/lower prices does not fit into the picture of Transformational Growth either, because it included lower prices.) The ideal type industry/market structure of that time contrasts with the small differentiated firms market structure and can be described as wide oligopoly, i.e. firms could influence or set the price of their (mostly non-differentiated, homogeneous) products and their price/output decision influenced the market situation of their competitors. The problem of oligopolistic price interdependence could not easily be resolved by the price leadership of a technologically leading firm because there existed large firms almost equal in technology and size so that no obvious asymmetry existed. Nevertheless, the problem of rational pricing did not trouble the economic agents that much in the period of general expansion in the 1870s and 1880s.

The overall growth of markets procured a niche for many new firms. The example of the paper industry, where the Fourdrinier machine was perfected in the early 1880s, may be cited as an example of the general state of industrial arts at that time.

> The substitution of wood pulp for rags had reduced the cost of newsprint by the 1880s and greatly stimulated consumption, attracting new investment to the industry. This influx grew especially heavy during the boom of the late 1880s and early 1890s, when most of the important mills of the next decade were built. It was in this period, for example, that construction began on the plants of three of the eight largest firms in the industry, and at least four of the remaining five firms made substantial additions to their works. A number of smaller, though still important, enterprises also entered the industry in this period. According to the *Boston Advertiser*, in the summer of 1891 there were forty-two paper mills (chiefly newsprint and book paper) under construction, and *Paper World* reported that in 1891 alone production of newsprint and book paper increased 20 percent.
>
> (Lamoreaux 1985: 41–2)

The aforementioned tendency to produce at full capacity and lowered prices seems to be a bad start for Transformational Growth at first sight, because the emergence of mass production seems to contradict its basic presuppositions.

THE RATIONALE OF CUT THROAT COMPETITION
THE LOGIC OF THE NEW SYSTEM AND THE NEED TO LEARN

But, alas, when the time looked bright, the recession of the 1890s was just around the corner. The policy of firms to reduce prices and run at full capacity, and to expand whenever possible, could not be maintained. First, firms tried to continue the now old rule to run at maximum capacity whatever the price in the short run, which fostered severe price wars in the depression. But the general decline in demand taught them that this was a bad and non-sustainable strategy: low sales and low prices combined

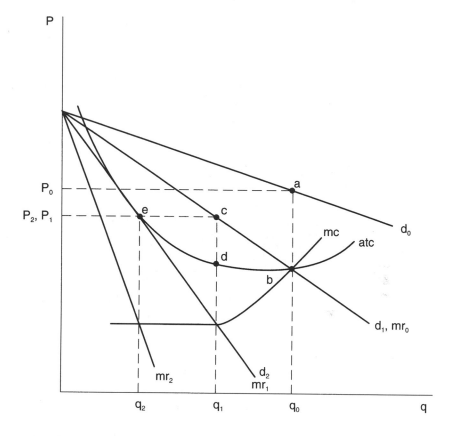

Figure 4.1 Cost and revenue curves for the firm. *Source*: Based on Patinkin (1947) and reproduced here from Lamoreaux (1985: 48), by courtesy of Cambridge University Press.

with overproduction. It seems to be completely irrational behavior if it is looked at through the lenses of traditional microeconomic cost curve models. Figures 4.1–5 all argue in a short-run perspective. The rationale is that in the long run, to paraphrase Keynes, these firm structures and very often the firm as independent units were all dead.

Figures 4.1–2 describe an industry with a small number of firms, with identical technologies, and without barriers to entry; the firms realize the interdependence of their decisions. Figure 4.1 refers to the industry's demand curve d_0 and the least-cost level of production q_0. Figure 4.2 contains the total industrial output and price (Q_0 and P_0). After an influx of new firms the supply/demand equilibrium will be at a demand of d_2/mr_1 without profits and incentives for new firms to join the party. (Figure 4.2 demonstrates the same process for the industry as a whole.) In this

123

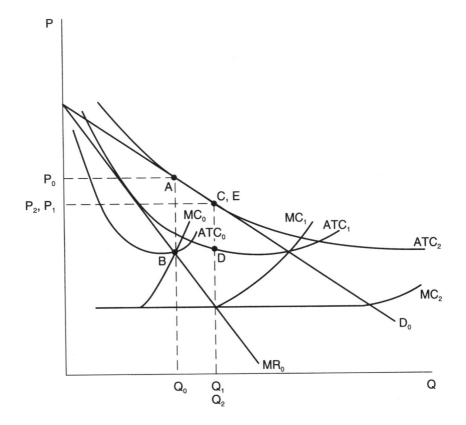

Figure 4.2 Cost and revenue curves for the industry. *Source*: Based on Patinkin
(1947) and reproduced here from Lamoreaux (1985: 49), by courtesy
of Cambridge University Press.

picture, the world is ordered and the invisible hand does its job: no cut-
throat price competition and overproduction occur. But this description,
which may be characteristic of certain aspects of the old business cycle,
does not take the fact into consideration that a change in technology was
under way (viz. mass production) with higher fixed costs, whereupon the
most interesting explanation of the seemingly irrational behavior is based
(see e.g. Scherer 1971 and Eichner 1969: 93–119).

   Although Jones concludes, "it appears that the factors that tend to
make railroad competition ruinous are not present to anything like the
same degree in the case of manufacturing enterprises" (1920: 518), Bell's
(1918) early statistical and theoretical evidence and arguments gave some
good reasons for a contrary conclusion. His evidence can be highlighted
by Figure 4.3. The enigma which has to be explained is why in the late
nineteenth century increasing capital intensity led firms to undercut the

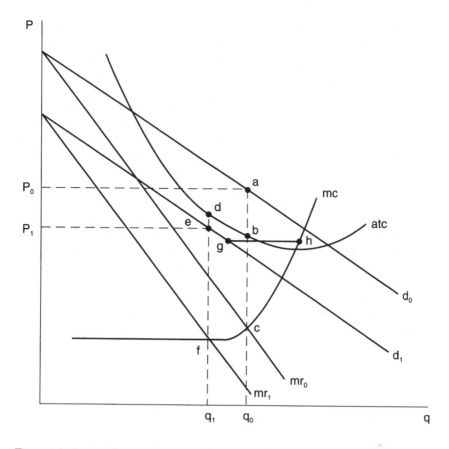

Figure 4.3 Cost and revenue curves for a firm with high fixed costs. *Source:* Based on Scherer (1971) and Eichner (1969: ch. 1), reproduced from Lamoreaux (1985: 51), by courtesy of Cambridge University Press.

prices of their rivals when demand declined. With demand d_0 in Figure 4.3, the output will be q_0 and the price P_0 (where marginal cost and revenue are equal) and the profit per unit of output will be *ab*. The depression leads to a reduction in demand (d_1); according to the profit maximization hypothesis this results in the q_1/P_1 combination. The firm will realize a loss of *de* because of the shapes of the *atc* and *mc* curves; the fixed costs weigh heavily on the remaining units of output. Now the profit-maximization position is combined with a loss, the cost of fixed investments cannot be met. This may work for a while, but

as pressures mount to meet interest (and, as well, dividend) payments, or to replace obsolete and worn-out equipment, the incentive to adopt another pricing strategy will grow. Realizing that by increasing output it can reduce unit costs, the firm will be tempted to cut prices in order to increase its share of the market. By moving off its original (constant-share-of-the-market) demand curve along some line such as *gh*, it can reduce or possibly even eliminate its losses.

(Lamoreaux 1985: 51–2)

The fixed-cost hypothesis has been criticized for many reasons, the most intriguing being that rational agents would foresee that a strategy of mutual price cutting can only make the situation worse. At this point Lamoreaux introduces a principle of overdetermination or cumulative causation. She combines the fast-changing and new situation in a technologically and otherwise uncertain environment with the fixed-cost theory, whose validity she restricts to the specific circumstances in the 1880s and 1890s, when uncertainty, the bounded rationality of the actors and their inexperience with the new situation caused a specific behavioral pattern.

One would expect the type of behavior predicted by the fixed-cost hypothesis to have occurred with great frequency in industries (such as tinplate and newsprint) in which the great majority of firms were new. In such industries the existence of a large potential market, and an innovation, discovery, or change in the tariff that made it possible to exploit that market, created an opportunity for profit . . . the long gestation period that elapsed before the product reached the market meant that price changes lagged seriously behind the decision to enter and sent misleading signals to potential investors . . . New firms were continually entering the market, and prices were already in a state of flux. The equilibrium market shares of the firms had not yet been determined.

(Lamoreaux 1985: 59, 61)

THE NEW ECONOMIC POLICY OF FIRMS
PRICE STABILITY AND OUTPUT
MANAGEMENT

There were three merger movements in the US economy: 1897–1905, 1925–26 and 1960–69 (see Bain 1968; Blair 1972; Scherer 1971; Nelson 1959). The first wave consisted mainly in horizontal concentration; its importance "in shaping our present-day industrial structures can hardly be exaggerated. Not only did the consolidations put together during a short span of about 10 years transform competitive industries into oligopolistic structures, they determined the form of the oligopoly itself" (Blair 1972: 257). It was a reaction to the tremendously changing legal, technological, transportational, etc., conditions in the second half of the nineteenth century. Scherer describes some facts of this restructuring process.

It involved at least 15 per cent of all plants and employees occupied in manufacturing at the turn of the century. Its outstanding characteristic was the simultaneous consolidation of numerous producers into firms dominating the markets they supplied. Nelson found that the pioneer in the market-dominance-by-merger game was the Standard Oil Company. Incorporated in 1870, it brought together 20 of the 25 existing Cleveland area petroleum refiners in early 1872 . . . The pinnacle of the 1887–1904 merger wave was reached with the formation in 1901 of the United States Steel Corporation, combining an estimated 785 plants into the first American industrial corporation with a capitalization exceeding $1 billion . . . During the late 1890s, a series of mergers consolidated more than 200 formerly independent iron and steel makers into 20 much larger rival entities.

(Scherer 1971: 105)

The next step is to consider why this consolidation movement occurred and how it changed economic behavior. Besides the explanation that fluctuations in stock market prices and the volume of trade were responsible (Nelson 1959), or that efficiency gains should be secured, either in the capital markets (Davis 1966) or raw-material supplies (Chandler 1977), a fixed-cost explanation is put forward here. Lamoreaux provides case studies of three industries (the wire-nail, the tin-plate and the newsprint industries) and gives a second type of evidence for this hypothesis with an econometric study based on R. Nelson's data on consolidations, which reveals the importance of fixed costs and the rate of growth in their explanation (see Lamoreaux 1985: ch. 4, which contains her logit regression analysis).

This explanation means not that mass production is directly responsible for oligopolistic market structures because of technological efficiency gains, but that it was a historically unique response of business to the restructuring problems of pricing in high-fixed-cost industries. Other chapters in this volume show that although this can be called the American solution, similar solutions were found in Germany, Japan and other countries producing under mass production. It would seem the problem is inherent in mass production and the solution is contingent on law, custom, accident and history. A first explanatory hint can be found by comparing the price-cutting in the 1890s with the behavioral changes during the second great depression in 1907 for steel and newsprint manufacturers, where in 1893 the attempts to stop the price war had failed.

> after the Panic of 1907, manufacturers successfully prevented outbreaks of price competition from recurring, and with only a minimum of organization . . . Until January 1908, for example, manufacturers held the price of common-grade tinplate steady at its predepression level of $3.90 per box. Then, in response to the decline in demand, US Steel announced a reduction to $3.70 per box, and this price was maintained without apparent difficulty for the rest of the year. Similarly, despite the Panic, the price of wire nails held at $2.23 per keg until US Steel reduced it to $2.13 in April 1908. Manufacturers were able to maintain this price for a full year, again with little or no apparent difficulty . . . In the newsprint branch of the paper industry the situation was much the same. Although the demand for paper fell sharply in 1907 and 1908, papermakers did not cut prices as they had fourteen years before. Instead, led by the International Paper Company, they uniformly restricted production so as to maintain prices at pre-depression levels.
>
> (Lamoreaux 1985: 118–19)

The new behavioral pattern (whose consequences from an antitrust and consumer standpoint are not discussed here) which emerged after the consolidation as a result of the learning process after the catastrophe of 1893 coincides exactly with the thesis of Transformational Growth: mass production with specific cost structures enforced a learning process, which restructured industrial relations to enable the firms in an industry to hold prices at least sticky and to allow output adaptations to market conditions and business cycles. Theoretically, this capability can be explained by the application of the dominant-firm strategy, analyzed by Scherer (1971: 165; Stigler 1968 finds some evidence that US Steel adopted this strategy successfully in the first decades of the century). See Figure 4.4.

As a result of consolidations, an industry is characterized by one giant multi-plant firm and many smaller independent firms which are not capable of influencing the price and which are endowed with similar technologies. When the combine makes a quantity/price-decision, the independent firms behave as price takers, adopting the dominant firm's price as given, and having no incentive to reduce prices because this would diminish their output. DD' equals total demand, $S'S$ the demand of the competing small firms; at a price less than S' the price leader has the market for himself and between S' and G competitive firms get a

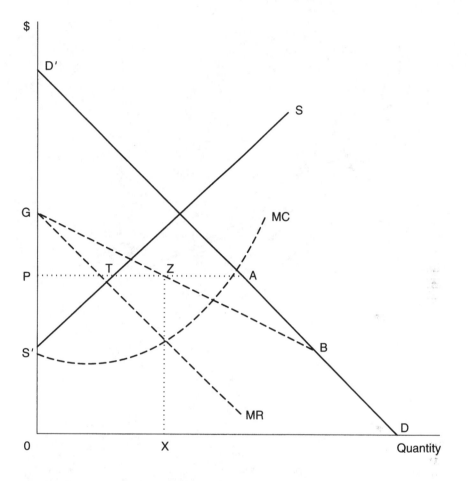

Figure 4.4 Equilibrium under dominant-firm price leadership.

share. The derived effective demand for the dominant firm is *GBD*, it sells
Z at price *P* and quantity *OX*, the small firms sell *ZA*. Because of rising
marginal costs (a reasonable assumption in the short run, whereas a flat
curve seems to be more realistic in the longer run), a reduction of prices
by independent firms will reduce their output (see figure 5.2 in Lamoreaux 1985, p. 122). When demand declines in a slump, a sharp cut of
prices is not likely in this model (see Figure 4.5).

Suppose demand is initially at D_0. On the basis of residual-
demand curve DR_0, the consolidation's profit-maximizing price
is P_0. The limit price, as before, is P_2; so the consolidation is likely
to charge a price greater than or equal to P_2, but less than or

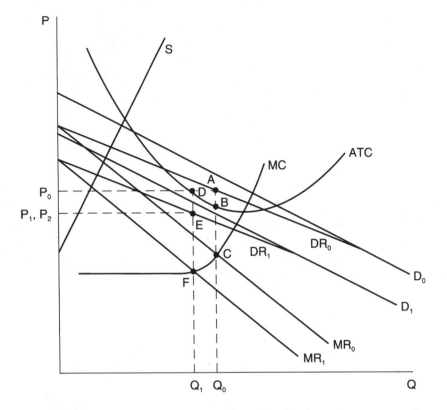

Figure 4.5 Effect of a decline in demand on the dominant-firm strategy. *Source* Lamoreaux (1985: 125), by courtesy of Cambridge University Press.

equal to P_0 (as this particular case is drawn, the consolidation is no more efficient than the independent firms, and so it will likely charge a price above P_2). Now suppose that depression reduces the demand for the industry's product to D_I. The combine's residual-demand curve falls to DR_I. Its profit-maximizing price approaches and . . . may even fall below the limit price. In the event of a downward shift in demand, therefore, the consolidation is likely to cut prices.

This move will not trigger a price war. So long as the consolidation follows the dominant-firm strategy . . . competitors have no incentive to initiate price cuts.

(Lamoreaux 1985: 124–5)

Thus the dominant firm strategy generates a determinate solution, but in a dynamic perspective it is not a stable one because it presupposes *inter alia* that it knows the supply and demand functions of the competitors, that it has (in Scherer's model) a technological or other cost advantage over the competitors, that no new firms with a newer technology are attracted by stable and high prices, and that the dominant firm does not follow a strategy of cutting prices in order to ruin competitors and to enhance its market share.

As Lamoreaux points out (1985: 126), all these challenges became apparent in the newsprint and other industries and the darker face of "cooperation" in business loomed, like the controlling of ore deposits through vertical integration by US Steel or inducing retailers not to carry rivals' output. The potential and real dangers of the dominant firm strategy initiated a new stage in the restructuring of industrial relations to ensure (or change?) high prices and flexible output management (e.g. by collusive price leadership). "Were these consolidations able to maintain their dominant position? . . . What was the political response of a nation long distrustful of large-scale economic power? . . . How much of her analysis is applicable to the current merger movement?" (Cain 1986: 134).

Many questions emerge which will not be pursued further at this point. Although sticky/rising prices may be the basic characteristic of the mass-production system, this brief discussion of the first merger movement shows that innovative economic agents have to ensure price stability through active endeavor.

There are many and complex interconnected factors that led to the dominant firm strategy with sticky/rising prices and fluctuating output: high fixed costs, technological innovations, the rapid growth of a larger number of capital-intensive industries in the years after 1887, the depression from 1893 to 1896, the uncertain retaliation against price under-cutting, the process of learning, the devastating consequences of these price cuts, and the institutional rearrangement (consolidations, whose logic and shortcomings can be explained by economic analysis).This proves the usefulness of the methodological principle of cumulative causation (including theoretical, technical, institutional and behavioral factors in their respective historical-dynamic setting) and the basic presuppositions of Transformational Growth concerning price, quantity (wage, rent), etc., movements in different stages of (pre)capitalist development. For the first and probably the most important merger movement at the turn of the century – which is here understood in the last instance as a consequence of a new method of production, viz technology – the substantial and methodological theses of Transformational Growth hold true, whose analytical force sets in when market shares are settled and firms move to a lay-off/variable labor cost system (see Nell 1992).

Part III

STUDIES OF STYLIZED FACTS

5

TRANSFORMATIONAL GROWTH AND THE BUSINESS CYCLE

Edward J. Nell and Thomas F. Phillips

The recent stagnation of many industrialized economies has revived research on the business cycle and on the effectiveness of measures to control it. Part of this literature has examined various historical measurements of output in order to study the relative volatility of the business cycle in different periods (Altman 1992; Backus and Kehoe 1992; Balke and Gordon 1989; Sheffrin 1989; Romer 1986, 1989). A dominant issue in recent work has been the effectiveness of Keynesian stabilization policy: it is claimed that if stabilization policy has been effective, evidence should show that the volatility of the business cycle has decreased since World War II, compared to earlier periods. One side maintains that there is little evidence of a decrease in volatility; the other, for the most part examining the same data over the same time period, claims that the cycle has been damped.

Implicit in this argument is the view that the only relevant differences between the economy of the late nineteenth and early twentieth centuries, compared with the economy after World War II, is the role of government as a stabilizer of the economy. The question of business-cycle volatility across wide historical periods is not, however, so simple. Not only do the two periods differ structurally, but evidence shows that different economic mechanisms are at work in the economies; that is, the market systems both generate different internal dynamics and adjust differently to external shocks, so that different explanatory principles apply in the two periods.

TRANSFORMATIONAL GROWTH: AN ALTERNATIVE FRAMEWORK

Altman (1992) re-examined volatility measures for several industrialized countries for the periods 1870 to 1928 and 1947 to 1986, and employed new estimates of Canadian GNP to measure the severity of Canadian business cycles. Altman concludes, "The hypothesis that business cycles were prone to much less stability before the Great Depression than after World War II is strongly supported by the volatility estimates for Canada, the US and Angus Maddison's twelve country sample" (1992: 270). Admittedly, this conclusion is debatable with respect to the method of measurement of volatility. Moreover, for the purposes of a thorough historical analysis of the business cycle, Altman properly recognizes that his evidence "can in no way serve to prove the validity of the Keynesian claim that increased government macroeconomic intervention since World War II contributed towards increased cyclical stability" (ibid.: 271). The reason is indicated, if only obliquely, when he points out that "The extent to which such intervention actually did affect cyclical volatility, as opposed to other factors which might have affected this outcome such as the changing structure of the economy, remains a matter for further empirical research" (ibid.).

Transformational Growth provides an alternative framework for examining the changing nature of the business cycle, including changes in the role of government. It focuses on changes in the mechanisms that govern the working of the economy, as well as the explanatory principles that describe it. For example, in regard to the Canadian economy during the periods pre-World War I, post-World War II and between the two wars, strong evidence suggests that the focus of recent business-cycle research has been myopic, neglecting critically important historical changes in the nature of business cycles. In particular, cycles in the earlier period were primarily manifested in prices and money wages, and only secondarily in output and employment, whereas in the later period the cycle has become primarily a pattern of fluctuation in output and employment, with prices and money wages relegated to a distinctly secondary role. The business cycle thus changed in *character*, as well as in volatility, and these changes, we suggest, may also help to account for the altered size and roles of government.

THE TRADITIONAL APPROACH

Underlying the recent debate has been the politically charged question of the efficacy of Keynesian-style governmental intervention. It has been claimed that if demand management policies worked the business cycle should be less pronounced in the post-World War II era. Historical evidence of the volatility of the business cycle in what we will call the periods of the "old business cycle" (OBC) and the "new business cycle" (NBC) has presented a mixed picture.

Some studies show little discernible improvement in the volatility of output (Romer 1986, 1989) while others show a marked reduction (Altman 1992; Balke and Gordon 1989). Although these studies make historical comparisons of the business cycle, they do not address, or even seem aware of, the important differences in the economic mechanisms, and therefore in the explanatory principles applicable to the two periods. However, this is not unusual in modern economic analysis.

Traditionally, Neoclassical economics has treated intertemporal comparisons of economic behavior without regard to possible historical changes in the underlying market mechanisms and, therefore, explanatory principles. Its fundamental belief in the global optimizing behavior of abstractly defined consumers and firms does not lend itself to treating historical periods differently. In most contemporary business-cycle analysis, the market, with its "optimizing agents", is taken as given in both the OBC and the NBC periods – that is, the nature of the market is assumed to be the same in both. Neoclassical theory determines equilibrium on the basis of given endowments, preferences and technology; equilibria, in turn, are shown to be optimal, at least in a limited sense. Hence government policy interventions tend to be seen as interfering with the efficient operation of freely working markets, and therefore attempts to stabilize the economy may be judged misguided. Markets are understood to perform the function of allocating resources to their best uses. The New Classical approach, for example, stresses the ineffectiveness and suboptimality of government policy intervention.

On the other hand, where markets are imperfect, or when other institutions, in the course of serving legitimate functions, prevent markets from working freely, government aciton may be called for. This is the perspective of "New Keynesian" analysis, which sees three different ways in which market "imperfections" may open the door for effective policies to improve welfare. Nominal or real rigidities may exist which prevent markets from adjusting or from adjusting rapidly enough. "Coordination failures," due to asymmetric information and/or risk aversion, or to confusion caused by the existence of multiple equilibria, may exist which prevent firms from adjusting. Finally, agents may make decisions in terms of "near rationality," rather than full rationality, on the grounds that it is too expensive to recalculate all the time. Any or all of these may interact with the market structure in such a way that small deviations from perfect adjustment are magnified, leading to large welfare losses (Mankiw and Romer 1991).

Unfortunately this approach also assumes that the function of markets, always and everywhere, is to allocate scarce resources efficiently, through "the price mechanism." The problems arise when something *prevents* full market functioning. Hence this approach fails to see that *different* economic mechanisms operate in the OBC and in the NBC, even though its adherents see an important role for government in the economy.

In short, traditional economic analysis does not recognize, let alone explain, the differences in the explanatory principles describing the different way markets work in the OBC and NBC. By contrast, the theory of Transformational Growth does. Here we first sketch that theory, and then present a case for the reconsideration of the analytical foundations of recent business cycle research by providing some stylized evidence of the fundamentally different economic mechanisms at work in the OBC and NBC, which call for models based on different explanatory principles.

TRANSFORMATIONAL GROWTH

At the heart of Transformational Growth is the claim that the function of the market is to generate competitive pressures to innovate and to assemble the financial resources to invest in innovations. Allocation of existing resources is of secondary importance; moreover, in practice, competition often generates waste, offsetting allocative efficiency. To make a huge generalization – in the manner of textbooks – one could argue that innovation, driven by competition, is what distinguishes the capitalist West since the Renaissance – broadly, Europe and North America – from all other economic systems, past and present. Such a sweeping claim needs many qualifications – but no more than the equally sweeping claim that markets, always and everywhere, allocate scarce resources efficiently. And it has the additional advantage of being nearer the truth!

Technology, both directly and indirectly, affects the structure of an economy in ways that influence the working of markets. In the OBC, the nature of technology led to the development of small firms, typically craft-based family firms, that were relatively inflexible in terms of adapting output and employment to changes in demand. Firms grew to an optimal size – the size at which a production team could most efficiently work. Fluctuations in demand were accommodated, on the one hand, by varying the intensity of the production team's effort and, on the other, through price changes dictated by the marketplace.[1] In the first case, output was varied by varying productivity, a solution that could not be satisfactory to either employers or employees. Employers would not wish the slower pace of hard times to become a norm; employees would not wish to be held to the faster pace of booming times. In the second case, output would be maintained, but with fixed supply and weaker demand, for example, prices would be driven down. Again this could not be satisfactory; firms would take losses on their inventory, and the market might become "spoiled".

With craft technology varying output in line with the market was not easy. In some cases, the nature of the production process, for example, water or steam power, required full operation or none at all. Some processes simply could not be operated at half speed, or lower intensity.

Further, in many cases, all hands had to be present for the process to be operated at all. Employment was thus fixed by the size of the production team, apart from clean-up jobs, and the like, so that output could be changed only through varying the intensity of the inputs – the same labor force would have to work harder and faster when demand was strong, but could take it easy in slack times. Growth in demand was accommodated by adding new firms of optimal size – not through the expansion of existing firms. The fixed nature of the production process did not allow many economies of scale; when these were exhausted, limits to effective size would be reached rapidly, although the optimal size from the point of view of production might not be the same as the best size from the marketing or financial perspective (Robinson 1931). Once its optimal size was achieved, however, there was no economic motive for a firm to expand.

Moderate changes in demand would be met by changes in the utilization of factors and through changes in price. A sharp fall in demand would result in falling prices, which, if substantial and sustained, might force many of the small production establishments out of business. Similarly, large increases in demand would be associated with rising prices and the opening of additional, optimally sized, production establishments, employing the same technology as existing firms. (A single firm might operate several establishments, of course, but the family's managerial resources could not be stretched far.) Moderate declines in investment or net exports, for example, would be met with falling prices but relatively stable employment and output – there was little or nothing in the way of Keynesian multiplier effects. Quite the reverse: the lower prices implied a higher real wage, so, with stable employment, the effect would be higher consumption spending, an induced change in the *opposite* direction. Drastic declines in demand, however, would lead to a sharp collapse in prices, resulting in bankruptcies that would or could have successive rounds of repercussions, but the multiplier, in these circumstances, would be a bankruptcy multiplier – not the traditional Keynesian spending multiplier.[2]

The adaptability of prices to changes in demand within an environment of stable output, employment and money wages suggests a more complex view of the volatility of the OBC. As suggested above, if an increase in demand drives up prices, real wages fall. Since working-class households in the OBC have few assets against which to borrow to sustain consumption, their consumption is governed by their real earnings. Consequently, the initial increase in exogenous demand would be offset by a subsequent induced fall in the level of consumption. The same offsetting effect would come into play if exogenous demand fell and brought declining prices. Lower prices with fixed money wages imply higher real wages and, hence, increased household consumption. Therefore, the explanatory principle describing adjustment in the OBC portrays an inherent, though limited, *stabilizing* mechanism that is inextricably associated with the nature of the technology of that era (Nell 1992: ch. 16). (The financial system in this period appears to have destabilizing propensities – but that is another story.)

In the NBC, technology dictates that firms produce in a mass-production mode. Production is performed not so much by teams but through integrated tasks. Batch production is replaced by continuous throughput (Chandler 1990). Both output and employment can be varied with demand – output more nearly in exact proportion than employment, since some labor is overhead – while the overall expansion of production is accomplished through increasing the size of the production establishment. Expansion reaps the benefits of economies of scale, which in turn leads to larger firms, differently organized than small production teams, and motivated to grow.

The ability of mass-production systems to vary employment and output with demand has led to two very important characteristics distinguishing the NBC from the OBC: prices could be more stable, predictable and controllable, while varying employment and output in response to changes in demand have resulted in typical Keynesian multiplier chains of respending. The price adjustment mechanism evident in the OBC is not found in the NBC. But the characteristic output and employment adjustments tend to be destabilizing. A strong expansion – or contraction – in output can lead to adjustments in the capital stock, with further multiplier implications for output. Prominent features of the NBC, the multiplier and capital stock adjustment, are evidently mechanisms that tend to display a degree of inherent instability, in contrast to the OBC.

In the OBC the general trend of prices relative to money wages is downward, reflecting productivity growth. By contrast, in the NBC both prices and money wages tend to rise, with the latter rising faster. The benefits of productivity growth are transmitted to the economy through higher money wages, rather than lower money prices. One consequence of this change is persistent inflationary pressure, arising from the pressure by groups, whose productivity has not risen to maintain traditional relativities. In the NBC money prices either rise or stay steady; they seldom, if ever, fall.

A stabilizing factor in the NBC, however, is provided by the government, playing a role that did not exist in the OBC, when government's activities were generally supposed to be limited to the duties of a "night watchman."[3] The greater role that government plays in the NBC is characterized both by its considerable and growing size, and by the steady nature of the activities it undertakes. Both of these characteristics act to dampen the inherent volatility of the NBC. Therefore, when comparing the relative volatility of the OBC and NBC, the different inherent stabilizers in the two periods must be considered.

The period between the OBC and NBC can give us a great deal of insight into how the economy was transformed from the craft-based OBC to the mass-production NBC. In Canada the beginning of the move to mass production took place early in the twentieth century. By the end of World War II mass production prevailed. In the period of transformation, the inherent volatility of the mass-production system without the off-setting stability of a large government sector is observed. Only with the emergence of the expanded role for government during and after World War II did the fully developed NBC present itself.

EVIDENCE OF TRANSFORMATIONAL GROWTH, WITH SPECIAL REFERENCE TO CANADA

In its preoccupation with rational maximizing agents, Neoclassical economics may have lost sight of the historical nature of social change. Yet various writers have recognized the differences in the adjustment patterns in the two periods described above. To take an author with views similar to our own: Sylos-Labini (1989, 1992) clearly contrasts the market mechanisms operating in the business cycles of the nineteenth century in the United Kingdom and the United States with those of the twentieth century. He discusses differences in the "wage and price mechanisms over historical time," showing how changes in the way markets adjust affect the ability of the economy to grow through improved levels of productivity, for they result in differences in the " . . . mechanism for distributing the fruits of technical progress . . . " But Sylos-Labini finds that it is only in the period after World War II that wages and prices both consistently rise, with wages rising faster than prices. Prior to World War I money wages held steady (or rose very slowly), while prices fell; productivity increases were transmitted to the economy at large in the form of lower prices. Either way, of course, real wages rise; but the monetary mechanisms are different.

Other writers, further from our concerns, have also found historical differences in the behavior of market variables. Bordo (1981), for example, describes differences in the pre-World War I and post-World War II periods in terms of output and prices. For the United Kingdom and United States, Bordo concludes that prices and output in the short run were more variable before World War I than after World War II. However, as a monetarist, he ties these differences to the presumed changing volatility of the money stock. Rich (1988) finds evidence to support Bordo's conclusion in the Canadian case. Altman (1992) also finds evidence of more volatility, using several different volatility measures, in the pre-Depression period than in the period after World War II for Canada.

But monetarists, like Bordo, treat the differences as reflecting the exogenous volatility of a single variable, the money stock, which is held responsible for causing differences in business-cycle volatility. Why presumably exogenous money should be more volatile in the era of the gold standard than in the time of Bretton Woods is not explained. The possibility that money might be endogenous, or that the system may have shifted from the former to the latter, is not considered.

By contrast, Keynesians consider cyclical volatility to be caused by changes in investment and exports that are passed on through the economy by the mulitplier/accelerator mechanism. But they do not clearly distinguish between the price volatility of the earlier period and the quantity fluctuations of the later. Sylos-Labini, however, does, and attributes the changing volatility of the business cycle to the changing organization of production. It is unlikely that historical differences in the business cycle can adequately be described by one of these approaches alone; rather, it is likely to be the combined effect of changing industrial structure, market relationships and institutions, reflecting changes in the nature of production, that has altered the mechanisms behind the business cycle.

To illustrate, we present some reflections on the Canadian economy, concentrating on the 1890–1914 period (OBC) and the 1945–72 period (NBC). The behavior of several economic variables is considered in the context of identifying general characteristics, or "stylized facts," for the two periods. The interpretation of these stylized facts is meant to identify those areas in which considerably different behavior is observed in the two historical periods. The point is not to measure the degree of difference in the variables but to identify differences in general economic behavior. These stylized facts for the Canadian economy are offered as examples of evidence in support of the theory of Transformational Growth, along with the results that Sylos-Labini and others have compiled with regard to the pre-World War I and post-World War II periods. But they are not meant to explain the underlying forces determining the changes.

CAPITAL AND THE ORGANIZATION
OF BUSINESS

A Transformational Growth perspective leads one to suspect that the movement from the craft-based economies of the late twentieth century to the mass-production economies of the mid-twentieth century began in Canada around the turn of the century. The Canadian data show evidence of the differences in firm size between the two periods. Table 5.1 reveals

Table 5.1 Canadian manufacturing

Year	No. of establishments	No. of employees	Employees per establishment
1870	38,898	181,679	4.7
1890	69,716	351,139	5.0
1905	15,197	382,702	25.2
1951	37,021	1,258,375	34.0
1961	33,357	1,352,535	40.5
1971	31,908	1,628,404	51.0

Sources: Urquhart (1965: 463); Leacy (1983: Series R795–825).

that a substantial rise in average firm size occurred between 1890 and 1905, with further increases after World War II.

Although the changes in the number of establishments are striking, differences exist in the collection of data between 1890 and 1905. In 1905 only establishments with four or more employees were included. Nevertheless, evidence of growth taking place through increasing the size rather than the number of establishments is still clear. Since the 15,197 largest establishments in 1905 averaged more than twenty-five employees, there would have had to have been 150,000 small establishments employing an average of three apiece to bring the average over all establishments in 1905 down to the level[4] of about five per establishment that prevailed for all establishments in the 1870 to 1890 period.[5] Evidence suggests no such massive growth in the numbers of small manufacturing establishments; on the contrary, it suggests that production was becoming concentrated, causing much concern among writers in economics and law at the turn of the century.

In the *Journal of Political Economy* in 1906 W. W. Edger wrote that "the formation of associations of employers according to their trades has developed greatly in Canada in recent years – a tendency which has been likewise manifest in the United States, England, and other countries" (1906: 433). As an indication of the extent of these new "associations," Edger observes, "there are at present [in 1906] 220 employers' associations, of which no less than 84 were formed during the past five years" (ibid.). It seems safe to say, given the later increases in the concentration of manufacturing, that at the turn of the century in Canada the organization of production was in the early stages of changing from a system in which many small manufacturers dominated to one in which larger-scale producers dominated, especially in manufacturing – consistent with moving from a craft-based economy to a mass-production economy.[6]

If Canada's earliest stage of movement toward mass production did occur around the turn of the century, capital formation that is needed to underwrite mass-production processes must have risen. In 1904 the level of capital formation as a proportion of GNP was higher than in any year from 1870 to 1903. Prior to 1904 the proportion of capital formation to GNP had remained relatively constant, but from 1904 to the beginning of World War I the tendency was clearly upward, with a high of 34.1 per cent in 1912. The beginning of the concentration of production seems to have preceded the period of intensive capital formation. This is not unlikely, given the development of "associations" that first brought several craft-based producers together and then developed new integrated mass-production processes. This growth in capital formation and the concentration of production strongly indicated the emergence of methods of mass production around the turn of the century in Canada (Urquhart 1986: 33, table 2.11).

In the OBC the typically small firm employed relatively few supervisory and office staff; in craft systems of production management was direct and personal, and bureaucracy limited. For example, in 1905, 15,107 manufacturing establishments employed 382,702 workers, divided into 347,672 production workers and 35,030 supervisory and office workers, a ratio of ten to one, rising to almost eleven to one by 1910. By 1959 the ratio had fallen to three to one – 997,907 production workers against 306,049 supervisory and office workers (Urquhart 1986: 463). Not only did size increase, but the internal organization of the firm changed (Nell 1993: ch. 17, 1992b).

Prior to the turn of the century market patterns appear to be broadly consistent with the Marshallian picture. Producers in the OBC grew to their optimal size, after which any further expansion occurred through an increase in the number, rather than size, of establishments. As a result of factors not examined here – a shift to new energy sources, permitting new technologies in production and leading to a profound reorganization of manufacturing – the economy moved into a new stage, the NBC. In this new phase, characterized by oligopoly and Keynesian processes of adjustment, expansion predominantly occurred through increasing the size of the already existing producers. Such a view is consistent with M. C. Urquhart's judgment that "the Canadian economy developed in a fundamentally different way after 1900 than it had before" (1986: 60). Business organization is differently structured in the OBC and the NBC.

THE CHANGING STRUCTURE OF INDUSTRY

Chandler (1990) provides substantial evidence of the importance of technological and organizational change in the development of industrial economies in this century. When considering the development of the United States, the United Kingdom and Germany, Chandler concludes that "industrial activities played the central role of transforming an agrarian commercial economy into a modern industrial economy" (1990: 3). The same can be said of Canada. He also identifies the importance of the infrastructure necessary for an industrial economy to develop.

> As a result of the regularity, increased volume, and greater speed of the flows of goods and materials made possible by the new transportation and communications systems, new and improved processes of production developed that for the first time in history enjoyed substantial economies of scale and scope.
>
> (Ibid: 8)

In terms of the organizational nature of industrial economies, Chandler sees the emergence of new production processes leading to the need for changes in the way industry was organized and managed. Therefore, with the emergence of mass-production economies, the types of jobs people performed changed. Production moved to industry from agriculture, the role for government grew, as did the need for the services to support technologically and organizationally sophisticated production processes.

The changing structure of employment exhibits these substantial differences between the OBC and NBC. This is shown in Table 5.2. The striking movement is from agriculture to services – including government. Although, in both agriculture and natural resources, the proportion of employment declined, owing to technological improvement, the levels of output grew enormously. Technology has been a substantial force in expanding the productivity of both agriculture and manufacturing, but along with this came the growth of services to support the mass-production economy. Not only did technology play a key role in the structure of the economy, but the impact that government had in the NBC was reflective of the new role that government was called on to play

Table 5.2 Canadian employment (%)

Industry	1891	1971
Agriculture	46.5	5.6
Resources	3.7	2.8
Manufacturing	27.9	33.0
(Strictly manufacturing)	(15.0)	(19.8)
Services	22.0	42.5
Government[a]	–	8.2
Unspecified	–	7.9

(a) Government included in other categories in 1891.

Sources: Urquhart (1965: 59); Leacy (1983: Series D8–85).

Table 5.3 Structure of the Canadian economy: OBC and NBC, selected years

Components of the Canadian real GNP

OBC	1881		1891		1901		1911	
	$ thousands	% of total	$ thousands	% of total	$ thousands	% of total	$ thousands	% of total
Manufacturing	120,651	28.00	172,503	31.30	206,353	25.90	418,651	28.20
Railroad	14,337	3.32	28,647	5.20	64,317	8.07	195,689	13.20
Mining	4,855	1.12	14,971	2.72	48,766	6.12	61,343	4.14
Construction	21,240	4.92	32,796	5.95	41,486	5.21	131,149	8.85
Forestry	10,374	2.40	11,796	2.14	14,542	1.83	16,390	1.11
Fishing	9,546	2.21	9,149	1.66	12,340	1.55	11,530	0.78
Agriculture	175,912	40.80	170,881	31.00	246,703	31.00	348,753	23.50
Wholesale and retail	33,385	7.73	50,349	9.14	72,726	9.13	171,314	11.60
output								
Commerce, business, personal services	41,310	9.57	59,779	10.90	89,431	11.20	127,589	8.61
Total	431,610	100.00	550,871	100.00	796,664	100.00	1,482,408	100.00

GDP at factor cost, by industry

NBC	1945		1955		1965		1975	
	$ million	% of total	$ million	% of total	$ million	% of total	$ million	% of total
Manufacturing	2,954	27.50	7,301	28.50	12,751	26.10	32,035	21.30
Transportation	874	8.13	1,903	7.42	3,078	6.30	8,023	5.32
Mining	323	3.01	1,080	4.21	2,067	4.23	6,157	4.08
Construction	310	2.88	1,519	5.93	3,124	6.39	11,729	7.78
Forestry	208	1.94	486	1.90	499	1.02	1,092	0.72
Fishing	77	0.72	64	0.25	105	0.21	198	0.13
Agriculture	1,144	10.60	1,648	6.43	2,258	4.62	6,147	4.08
Wholesale and retail trade	1,169	10.90	3,207	12.50	5,923	12.10	18,191	12.10
Commerce, business, personal services	924	8.60	2,776	10.80	7,512	15.40	29,973	19.90
Storage	31	0.29	73	0.28	116	0.24	352	0.23
Communications	152	1.41	533	2.08	1,265	2.59	3,738	2.48
Electricity, gas and water utilities	216	2.01	597	2.33	1,357	2.78	4,071	2.70
Financial, insurance, real estate	755	7.02	2,819	11.00	5,606	11.50	17,313	11.50
Public administration	1,611	15.00	1,624	6.34	3,233	6.61	11,707	7.77
Total	10,748	100.00	25,630	100.00	48,894	100.00	150,726	100.00

Sources: Altman (1992); Leacy (1983: table F55–75).

in the era of mass production. Transformational Growth argues that government was required to be more active in the economy owing to the nature of mass-production technology and organization. This will be examined shortly.

First, however, let's look at the changing components of Canadian real GNP in Table 5.3. During the OBC, from 1881 to 1911, manufacturing output stayed constant, but railroads, mining and construction rose, while forestry, fishing and especially agriculture fell, and service output presented a mixed picture. During the NBC, on the other hand, services of various kinds, and utilities, rose substantially, except for public administration, while agriculture, forestry and fishing continued their decline, and manufacturing, mining, transportation, which had risen in the OBC, now began to decrease. The patterns are obviously different.

Altman (1987) shows that around the turn of the century the structure of Canadian manufacturing started to develop in new directions. In addition to changes in its relation to the rest of the economy, the manufacturing sector itself changed internally. The process began with a wheat boom that stimulated economic growth, but, as the theory of Transformational growth suggests, this led to technologically more sophisticated manufacturing, operating on a larger scale. Using constant dollar measures of value added, Altman calculates that iron and steel, and transportation equipment, grew more quickly relative to other manufacturing sectors and, therefore, assumed greater importance in Canadian manufacturing (Altman 1987: 105). Given that these sectors require technologically sophisticated production processes, it is reasonable to suspect that a shift to mass production had begun. These sectors could not expand as craft-based processes, especially given the need to be competitive with contemporary developments in the United States. It should be emphasized that these were only the first steps – the Canadian economy had a long way to go before it became the sophisticated mass-production economy that it was at the end of World War II.

THE BEHAVIOR OF PRICES, WAGES, OUTPUT AND EMPLOYMENT

The Canadian economy had many of the characteristics in both the OBC and the NBC that Sylos-Labini (1989) identified for similar periods in the United Kingdom and the United States. Throughout the OBC it was more common for manufacturing prices to fall than for wages to fall. Both fluctuated in both directions, however, but prices declined more. The rates of growth of wages and manufacturing prices displayed no consistent trend – wages were certainly not consistently growing faster than prices. Over the whole period prices remained stable or declined. Productivity

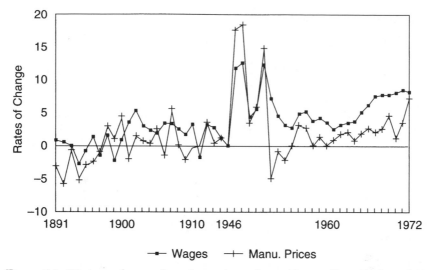

Figure. 5.1 Wages and manufacturing prices. *Source Eastern Economic Journal* 21, 2(1995): 136, by courtesy of the University of Connecticut, Storrs, Conn.

growth was therefore transmitted through lower prices, with given money wages.

The NBC reveals a very different story. At no time over this period did wages ever fall, and from 1950 on both wages and prices rose, with wages consistently growing faster than prices (see Figure 5.1). This implies, as Sylos-Labini (1989) points out, that the benefits of productivity increases were transmitted to the economy through rising wages rather than falling prices.

These points can be illustrated in the following sets of summary statistics, analyzing the rates of change in the two periods of the relevant variables: output, implicit prices, real wages, money wages, and manufacturing prices. It is convenient to compare these in two groups of three, for each period. First, consider output, implicit prices and real wages in the OBC and NBC in Table 5.4.

Price variability, as measured by the coefficient of variation, is greater than output variability in both periods, but in the first period prices were 2.5 times more volatile than output, and only 1.7 times in the NBC. Prices and outputs showed both rises and declines in the OBC – making bankruptcy more significant in the OBC;[7] by contrast, in the NBC prices and outputs normally only rise (six declines in the OBC, one in the NBC.) Real wages were more volatile than output in the OBC, and inspection of the evidence shows that in nine years real wages fall, which we do not find in the NBC. Real wages remained relatively stable in the OBC, but rose fairly steadily in the NBC. (There is some indication of an inverse relationship between real wages and output in the older period, whereas in 1946–56 and 1967–72

Table 5.4 Implicit prices and real wages

Variable	Mean	Standard deviation	Coefficient of variation
OBC (1890–1914)			
Output	4.560	5.140	1.127
Implicit prices	0.947	2.976	3.113
Real wage	0.364	2.431	6.687
NBC (1945–75)			
Output	4.915	2.475	0.504
Implicit prices	4.471	3.831	0.857
Real wage[a]	2.449	1.195	0.488

Source: Calculated from *Historical Statistics of Canada*, various series.

Note (a) 1945–72.

Table 5.5 Money wages and manufacturing prices: rates of change

Variable	Mean	Standard deviation	Coefficient of variation
OBC			
Money wage	1.274	2.251	1.767
Manufacturing prices	−0.007	2.751	−0.393
NBC			
Money wage	6.156	2.928	0.476
Manufacturing prices	4.749	6.325	1.332

changes in real wages corresponded to changes in the same direction in output – see below.)

Next consider rates of change of money wages and manufacturing prices in Table 5.5. In the OBC manufacturing prices have a slight downward drift; they fluctuate in both directions quite strongly. The mean and standard deviation of rates of change of money wages in the OBC are less than the corresponding measures for output, and fairly close to those for implicit prices. Both money wages and prices show larger average changes and larger standard deviations in the NBC, and both only increase. The coefficients of variation for both wages and prices are smaller in the NBC than in the OBC. The average increases are larger for money wages than for manufacturing or for implicit prices – from 1952 on they are consistently higher – indicating that real wages are rising.

The Canadian evidence, like that of the United Kingdom, is thus consistent with the Transformational Growth understanding of the different nature of market relationships in the OBC and NBC. This has important further implications. If output and employment in the OBC were relatively fixed and inflexible, then the manner in which the market's activity levels would adapt to changes in demand would be more in keeping with the Marshallian story. A rise in demand would bid up prices, but leave money wages unaffected; the fall in the real wage would first lead to an offsetting movement in household consumption; then, if the demand increase appeared stable, it would lead to a reorganization of production with increased employment. The converse is true for a decline. By contrast, in the NBC, production (and employment) could vary with changes in demand. Therefore, there should be evidence of different aggregate output reactions to autonomous increases in demand in the two periods. If the nature of production does not allow production to vary with changes in demand, then there should not be evidence of a Keynesian multiplier in the OBC. Only in an era when production can effectively change with changes in demand will there be evidence of a Keynesian multiplier (Nell 1992: ch. 16).

Considering year-to-year differences in exports and absorption (the aggregation of consumption, investment and government expenditures) reveals no consistent relationship in the OBC but a very consistent and proportional relationship in the NBC. This provides some evidence of the existence of a multiplier effect in the NBC that did not exist in the OBC (see Figures 5.2 and 5.3) and thus gives credence to the Keynesian depiction of the NBC. On the other hand, it also suggests that, given the differences in the nature of production, a Keynesian (short-run, demand-driven) multiplier relationship may not have existed in the OBC.[8]

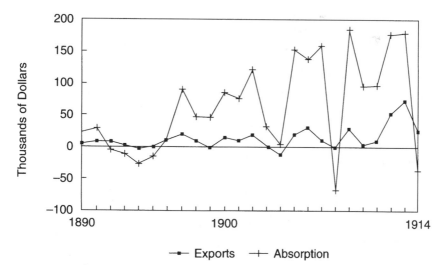

Figure. 5.2 Year-to-year differences in exports and absorption: OBC. *Source Eastern Economic Journal* 21, 2(1995): 139, by courtesy of the University of Connecticut, Storrs, Conn.

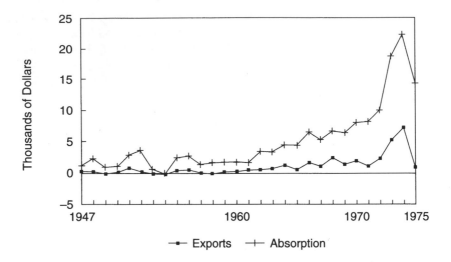

Figure. 5.3 Year-to-year differences in exports and absorption: NBC. *Source Eastern Economic Journal* 21, 2(1995): 139, by courtesy of the University of Connecticut, Storrs, Conn.

Comparing the rates of change in real output and the real wage also reveals an important difference between the OBC and NBC. In the NBC from 1945 to 1956 and 1967 to 1972 the rates of change in real wages and real output consistently varied together. In the intervening period the rates of change in real output were consistently greater than the rates of change in real wages, but the rates did not vary consistently. Therefore, in the periods in which the rates of change in real output and the real wage varied together, an increase in employment (as indicated by an increase in real output) was matched by increases in the real wage – the real wage and employment varied together.

In the OBC no extended period existed similar to those in the NBC in which real output (and employment) and the real wage varied together. More important, for twelve years in the period from 1890 to 1914, the rates of change in real output and the real wage varied inversely. Therefore in the OBC an inverse relationship between real wages and real output (or a positive relationship between unemployment and the real wage) was far more common than in the NBC (see Figure 5.4). This points to the existence of the Marshallian stabilizing market mechanism in that era.

The changing nature of the relationship between real output and the real wage is consistent with the Transformational Growth approach to the changing structures in the OBC and NBC. As a reaction to an increase in demand, increases in real output in the OBC, in which production, employment and wages were relatively fixed, would increase the intensity of labor use and thereby increase output. But with the increase in demand

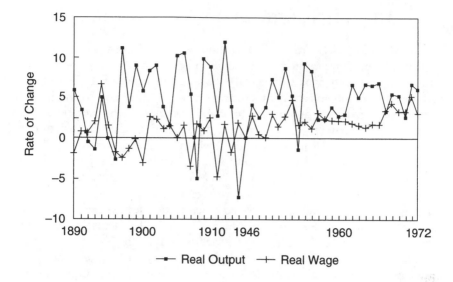

Figure. 5.4 Real output and real wage: OBC and NBC rate of change. *Source Eastern Economic Journal* 21, 2(1995): 139, by courtesy of the University of Connecticut, Storrs, Conn.

came a rise in prices and therefore a fall in the real wage and a subsequent fall in consumption. Therefore, in a relatively fixed production environment, it is not surprising to find an inverse relation between the rates of change in real output and the real wage, or, in other words, a positive relation between unemployment and the real wage. This characteristic reveals the inherent stability of the OBC, in that demand changes were moderated by the offsetting effects of consumption but, if strong and persistent, led to permanent changes in employment. This is in keeping with the Marshallian description of market behavior.

In the NBC, where mass production can easily be varied with demand, an increase in the real wage will increase demand and output and more labor will be required to increase the level of production. More demand for output increases production and greater demand for labor tends to drive up the real wage. Thus real wages and real output (and employment) will rise together. Also, a rise in employment will tend to be associated with economies of scale in the NBC and therefore with a rise in productivity, which therefore tends to increase the real wage yet again. The overall relationship is one in which the rates of change in real output and the real wage vary together – unemployment and the real wage are inversely related. This is a much more Keynesian story than that of the OBC.[9]

THE CHANGING ROLE OF GOVERNMENT

The OBC and NBC are thus described by very different explanatory principles, which are related to the technology of production in the two periods. But the changes between the two periods are not limited to the technology and organization of production. The changes also imply different roles for government in the two periods. In the newer period government is required to do more than simply stabilize the economy; it must also provide support for the system of mass production. Mass production requires greater theoretical and technical skills and a higher proportion of office and staff workers. Moreover, the skills required are constantly changing, since technical progress and innovation are continuous, rather than sporadic. The system therefore requires levels of education too sophisticated for the producers to provide themselves. In the craft economy skilled workers could be trained in the family – fathers passing on skills to sons – or through apprenticeships. Even engineers could be trained on the job. Not so in the modern era. Government support is required to provide professionally managed education to ensure the supply of adequately trained personnel.

The size and concentration of production also call for government involvement, and not only to prevent excessive concentration. Increased urbanization brought with it the centralization of production in modern facilities, requiring the provision of the urban infrastructures and services to support producers and the people that work for them. Streets, and street lighting, traffic control, police, sewage and water systems, waste disposal and public health all become significant issues, in ways they were not in the earlier era. Transport and communication systems become a necessity of a modern mass-production economy that also require the support of government. The change in government's role in the economy, as more than just a stabilizer, is substantial and should be accounted for in any comparisons of the OBC and NBC.

This puts the characteristics of economies at different historical times in a new perspective. If the rates of change in real output and implicit prices in the Canadian economy for the OBC, NBC and in the intervening period are considered, the changes in volatility fit very closely to the Transformational Growth explanation. In the period between the OBC and NBC both real output and implicit prices varied more in either the OBC or NBC. That is, the standard deviation of the annual rates of change in both real output and implicit prices was greater in this period than in either the OBC or the NBC (Altman 1992). This is consistent with Bordo's (1981: 13–16) observations in the United Kingdom and United States and Rich's (1988: 27–8) in Canada: more volatility in prices and output existed in the period between the OBC and NBC than in the periods themselves.[10] This too is consistent with the theory of Transfor-

Table 5.6 Total Canadian government expenditure as a percentage of GNP

Year	%
1889	3.6
1900	3.6
1914	5.8
1946	15.2
1960	18.7
1975	20.2

Sources: Urquhart (1986: table 2.1); Leacy (1983: Series F14–32, 1983).

mational Growth. This period of transformation is when the Canadian economy was maturing as a mass-production economy but the role for government as a counter-force to the natural volatility of the mass-production economy had not yet fully developed. Therefore the instability of the period of transformation can be explained through the inherent characteristics of the emerging mass-production system and the lack of any stabilizing force to compensate for its natural volatility. By the time World War II had ended, the governmental structures promoting greater stability were in place and the inherent instability of the mass-production economy had been largely suppressed (although it has partially re-emerged in the past decade and a half).

As *prima facie* evidence of the different role of government in the two periods we ran a regression that considered the influence of the rates of change in government spending, private sector capital formation (private sector investment) and net exports on the rate of change of GDP. These were calculated for the OBC and the NBC respectively and are reported in Table 5.7.

Clearly the rate of change in government spending had little influence on the rate of change of GDP in the OBC, but, by contrast, it had significant effects in the NBC. Not surprisingly, private capital formation played a considerable role in both periods, although net exports were important only in the earlier period.[11]

Only in the NBC, then, is there a close relationship between the rates of change of government expenditure and the rates of change in GDP. Although many other factors ought to be considered, this is, nevertheless, an indication that in the later period the activities of government and the activities of the economy as a whole were tied more closely. The fact that government has both become so much larger and come to be systematically linked to the economy does not, however, explain *why* government's role as an active player in the economy changed so dramatically. Rather than it reflecting a change in people's "tastes" for government involvement in the economy, Transformational Growth sees the altered

Table 5.7 Effects of government, investment and trade on output

Variable	OBC	NBC
Rate of change in:		
Constant	1.237	3.046[b]
	(1.099)	(3.812)
Government spending	−0.002	0.219[b]
	(−0.042)	(4.928)
Private capital formation	0.293[b]	0.341[b]
	(6.023)	(8.884)
Net exports	0.295[a]	0.0002
	(2.599)	(0.222)
RR^2 squared	0.737	0.800
Adjusted R squared	0.700	0.776
F statistic	19.662[b]	33.289[b]

Notes
(a) Significant at the 5 per cent level.
(b) Significant at the 1 per cent level. t statistics appear in parentheses.

role of government as a necessary and inherent consequence of the mass-production economy of the NBC.

Traditional approaches to the growth of government spending see such things as the growth of *per capita* income and the income elasticity of demand for public goods, the political acceptance of new "tax thresholds"[12] or issues of political change and new social values leading to more government involvement in the economy. Technological changes, they also claim, lead to new public infrastructure demands on government. But these traditional approaches rarely see the growth of government as necessary to support the age of mass production. All too often the expansion of the role of government in this century is thought to be the result of socially and economically misguided political ideologies. Transformational Growth argues that it is from within the nature of a mass-production economy itself that an expanded role for government arises. Indeed, it may be the foundation upon which modern, technologically advanced economies have been built.

CONCLUSIONS

The theory of Transformational Growth proposes that there are different explanatory principles in different historical epochs. In the light of the evidence provided here, the explanatory principles operative in the OBC appear to be substantially different than those of the NBC. Many factors must be considered in describing these differences.

To understand the contrasting natures of the OBC and NBC it is necessary to begin from, but also go beyond, the structure of the economy. There are fundamental differences in the nature and technology of production, and in the way it is organized by firms. These lead to differences in the market relationships between wages and prices and between output or employment and real wages. There is also evidence that the multiplier works differently in the OBC and NBC. Undoubtedly, the role of government had radically changed over these periods, a change that includes, but is much greater than, government's new role as a stabilizer of the modern industrial economy.

These stylized facts provide a sketch of the differences in the Canadian economy over three different historical periods. Other authors observe greater instability in the OBC than in the NBC and even greater instability in the period between the OBC and NBC (to 1928) in Canada. Their evidence also supports our contention that the market mechanisms at work are different, calling for the application of different explanatory principles in each period. The theory of Transformational Growth provides an arguably more sophisticated foundation on which to compare business cycles than can be had from traditional theory and, in the case at hand, reveals some of the forces acting on the Canadian economy, from the late nineteenth century through most of the twentieth century, that have resulted in changes in the market mechanisms.

Neoclassical theory and Keynesian theory both incorrectly assume that the same explanatory principles apply to both the OBC and the NBC. By contrast, the theory of Transformational Growth provides a theoretical framework for the historical comparison of business cycles: different epochs are typically characterized by different mechanisms of market adjustment, setting up different patterns of competitive pressures for technological and institutional development. Historical analyses of the business cycle would do well to abandon their inhibiting assumptions and widen their focus to include critical differences in the explanatory principles applying to the business cycle in different epochs of economic development.

APPENDIX 5.1

This chapter has used some of the stylized facts of the Canadian economy to distinguish the Transformational Growth approach to the changing nature of the business cycle. There are other stylized facts concerning Canadian economic development that provide some insights into the propositions put forward by Transformational Growth with respect to its description of the OBC and NBC.

More rigorous tests have been performed to determine the characteristics of the OBC and NBC in Canada more precisely. Although the surveys of other industrialized countries indicate greater price than output volatility in the OBC, as Transformational Growth would predict, there is mixed evidence for the Canadian economy. Although the coefficients of variation show greater price than output variability in the OBC, tests on the variances of the rates of change in the real output and implicit prices give contrary results. Also, using the Hodrick–Prescott filter on level data to isolate cyclical behaviour reveals that there was greater volatility in output than in price. This may be due to the considerable differences in, for example, the Canadian and US economies pre-World War I.

For the period 1889–1914 the Canadian economy was still predominantly agriculturally based. From 1896 the Wheat Boom had had a very strong positive impact on the economy, and had set in place the foundation for the transition from the OBC to the NBC. Although farms in Canada's OBC were certainly craft-based family businesses, the technologically determined forces that made output relatively fixed in craft-based manufacturing were quite different in agriculture. The levels of output were determined not so much by the nature of technology as by nature itself. Output, under these circumstances, was volatile, but employment remained constant, since craft-based methods were used. With the theory of Transformational Growth being primarily built on craft-based manufacturing, the recognition of differences in the explanatory principles in an agriculturally based economy suggests that the theory must be broadened to reflect this.

Taking the inherent volatility found in the Canadian OBC reveals interesting differences in the underlying forces moving the economy of the OBC and NBC. In the OBC, because of the impact of such factors as weather on output, there were considerable exogenous forces acting on the economy – forces beyond the control of any, or all, producers. In contrast, the primary forces acting on output in the NBC were endogenously determined – factors that made producers able to voluntarily vary output. There is also another perspective that can be taken on this important distinction between the OBC and NBC: the source of factors most influencing agricultural output were found in the nature of supply, whereas such factors were from the nature of demand in the NBC. Given these perspectives on the OBC and NBC, the roots of output volatility in both the OBC and NBC can be more generally determined as supply shocks in the OBC and demand shocks in the NBC. The nature of the supply shocks in agriculture makes output more volatile since they were significantly influenced by exogenous factors rather than shocks in craft-based manufacturing that primarily came from the restrictive technological methods of production.

The more rigorous tests also revealed something interesting about the NBC. In the periods from 1945 to 1952 and after 1972 in Canada, prices (implicit, raw material, and manufacturing) showed considerable volatility, but in the 1952 to 1972 period they were very stable. Many of the tests did not conclusively support the theory of Transformational Growth for the whole NBC (1945–1975), but clearly supported it in the 1952 to 1972 period. Therefore, the preliminary evidence suggests that the explanatory principles outlined by Transformational Growth are verified for this period of time. In effect, this indicates that the NBC in Canada existed from 1952 to 1972.

Along with the many significant differences that have been found between the OBC and NBC there is evidence of a change in returns regimes. For instance, in the OBC large increases in demand were satisfied by increasing the number (not the size) of firms, but in the NBC large increases in demand were met by increasing the size of existing firms. Overall, the oligopolistic nature of the NBC meant fewer firms producing more as the economy grew. The shift in returns regimes is from a diminishing returns regime in the OBC, especially in agriculture, and an increasing returns regime in the NBC – especially in manufacturing. This distinction is fundamentally important in how economies under different returns regimes can be described theoretically.

Neoclassical theory requires that diminishing returns exist if a unique, optimal, equilibrium is to be reached. When increasing returns dominate, it is possible to have multiple equilibria and there is no means by which a preferred position can be selected. Therefore, Neoclassical analysis cannot describe the functioning of an economy when increasing returns exist.

The difference in returns regimes helps establish the role of Neoclassical analysis for Transformational Growth. In the OBC, where diminishing returns dominate, Neoclassical analysis can be used to describe the behaviour of producers in that it sets prescriptive rules that lead to an efficiently run operation. At the macro level, the economy shows signs of acting like the aggregation of its micro units. For instance, prices tend to both rise and fall, and real wages tend to fall when the economy is growing and vice versa. This is very consistent with the Marshallian description of how an economy may work. In the NBC, the role of neoclassical analysis is much smaller. At the micro level, the prescriptive theory still applies in setting rules by which producers can run efficiently, but at the macro level the economy is not an aggregation of its micro units. The cumulative forces that come from increasing returns makes the cumulative economy significantly different from the aggregate economy. That is, the overall economy cannot be adequately described by the extrapolation of micro behaviour to the macro economy – the fallacy of composition applies.

The shift in returns regimes from the OBC to the NBC suggests that Neoclassical theory can be used as both a prescriptive and a descriptive theory of the OBC, but can be only a prescriptive theory in the NBC. The descriptive theory of the NBC must take into account the cumulative forces generated by economies that are dominated by increasing returns. Therefore, accounting for cumulative forces may be seen as a necessary distinction that can be made between the micro-economy and the macro-economy much like that made by Keynes. In fact Transformational Growth argues that the economy of NBC is a Keynesian economy where the multiplier plays an integral role, but the OBC is a Marshallian economy without strong multiplier effects. In the NBC, where cumulative effects are strong, the aggregation of micro behaviour cannot adequately describe the economy because it mistakenly treats the aggregate economy as the cumulative economy. Neoclassical theory maintains its prescriptive role in the NBC but cannot be appealed to in forming an accurate description of the period.

NOTES

1 Marshall's production function should be understood as a kind of utilization function. When demand drove up prices, money wages remained relatively unaffected, since employment was difficult to change. Real wages therefore fell, making it worth while to undertake the disruptive process of adding to the work teams – disruptive because new working patterns had to be developed. Note that this rests on *local* optimizing in historically specific conditions.

2 The difference is that, in the case of the Keynesian or macroeconomic multiplier, the funds withdrawn from circulation each round are known as a precise fraction of the level of expenditure. Such funds are saved by businesses or households, and the saving propensity is assumed known and fixed. Hence the impact in each round is determinate. In the case of bankruptcy, however, the withdrawal is involuntary, and neither the amount withdrawn nor the moment of its occurrence can be known reliably in advance. Nor will it be clear exactly what the impact will be on the next round – a decline in expenditure due to bankruptcies may lead to price reductions and increased sales, or to price reductions followed by further bankruptcies, or to a mixture of both.

3 In actual fact in the second half of the nineteenth century governments played a considerably larger role than the expression suggests. Think of eminent domain and the building of the railroads, or the canals, to say nothing of managing, or mismanaging, the currency. But, even so, the size of government in relation to GNP, for most advanced nations, tended to lie between 5 per cent and 10 per cent right up to the years before World War I.

4 Concentration of production was initially accomplished through the development of "associations" that coordinated production for collective ends. This quickly led to the formation of large incorporated associations, an important step toward the modern oligopolistic economy that exists today.

5 Altman (1987: 104) offers a parenthetical comment that also makes this observation – "(if one assumes that the percentage of manufacturing output produced by small firms collapsed after 1900)".

6 Chandler considers the growth in productivity in the expansion of new industrial enterprises was due in part to "placing the several intermediary processes employed in making a final product into a single works" (1990: 22).

7 Bankruptcy liabilities as a percentage of nominal GNP are much larger in the OBC than in the NBC, as one might expect, given that prices are downwardly flexible, while output and employment are more difficult to adjust. (In the NBC variations in output and employment tend to be *voluntary*, in the sense that firms *choose*, for example, when sales are sluggish to lay workers off in an orderly manner. By contrast, in the OBC a higher proportion of variations in output and employment is *involuntary*, in that they occur because firms have been forced to shut down and liquidate.) In the OBC a regression of real GNP on commercial failures reveals a negative relationship that is significant at the 1 per cent level, although the R^2 is only 0.27. It may be too much to say that 27 per cent of the decreases in GNP is the result of increases in bankruptcies, but it is interesting to note that no such relationship is significant at all in the NBC.

8 In any economy that can be described by a fixed coefficient input–output system a matrix multiplier can be defined showing the additional direct and indirect inputs and labor that will be required by an increase in final output, or in any component of final output. But such a calculation, by itself, implies nothing about the pattern of market adjustment to changes in demand pressures, The Kahn–Keynes–Kalecki multiplier states that a change in spending, in the short run, will induce additional changes in spending in the same direction, so that the total change is a multiple of the original, and the spending changes will be reflected in changes in output and employment. By contrast, in a Marshallian system, the spending changes will initially and chiefly affect prices, with only small effects on output and employment, and, as a consequence, there will be no additonal *induced* effects operating in the same direction. To the contrary, there will likely be induced effects in the *opposite direction* (Nell 1992: ch. 16).

9 Recent studies at the New School have yielded further evidence supporting this picture of systematic differences between the OBC and the NBC for various countries. Ray Majewski has developed some of the contrasts for prices, money wages and output in the United States; Thorsten Block has found significant structural changes between the OBC and the NBC in the behavior of product wages in the relation between and in relation to employ-ment and output, consumption and non-consumption (investment, net exports) for Germany, while David Kucera has found the same for Japan (see other country studies in this volume).

10 Altman (1992) shows that volatility was greater in the period 1908–28 than in 1870–1902, but then fell again in the post-war period. This is what we would expect on the basis of a Transformational Growth approach. Thanks to Will Milberg for calling our attention to Altman's article, and relating it to Trans-formational Growth.

11 As a further check, government expenditure on public capital projects was added to the model. Nothing essential changed. Public capital formation was not significant, and all other variables performed as before.

Variable rate of change in	OBC	NBC
Constant	1.059	2.866[b]
	(0.872)	(3.412)
Government spending	−0.022	0.216[b]
	(−0.353)	(4.781)
Public K formation	0.021	0.043
	(0.450)	(0.760)

Variable rate of change in	OBC	NBC
Private K formation	0.288[b]	0.316[b]
	(5.780)	(6.271)
Net exports	0.312[a]	0.0003
	(2.564)	(0.317)
R^2	0.737	0.804
Adjusted R^2	0.688	0.772
F statistic	14.237[b]	24.689[b]

(a) Significant at the 5 per cent level. (b) Significant at the 1 per cent level. t statistics appear in parentheses.

12 Peacock and Wiseman (1961) argued that a threshold was reached by the end of World War II, when the tax revenues that once went to the war effort were redirected to expanded social programs, since the economy was now able to cope with higher tax levels.

ACKNOWLEDGMENT

First published in the *Eastern Economic Journal* 21, 2 (spring 1995): 125–46.

6

UK BUSINESS CYCLES

Stylized facts and the marginal cost/marginal productivity debate

Stephanie R. Thomas

There is usually some element in the prices ruling at any time which can only be explained in the light of the history of the industry.

(Hall and Hitch 1939)

During the 1930s and 1940s an important debate developed regarding the validity of marginal theory for solving real world economic problems, particularly in the production sphere. The point of contention was whether or not firms, in making their everyday output and employment decisions, were using marginal principles. One group of economists maintained that pricing, employment and output decisions were executed on the basis of wage bills and the marginal productivity of labor. Another faction argued that firm decisions were more institutionalized. They maintained that the intricate marginalist calculations were based on information that was not readily available in a form that could be easily used to execute these decisions. Many papers appeared in the *American Economic Review* over a span of that decade or so, arguing as to the exact nature of pricing, output and employment decision-making mechanisms.

This chapter takes the position that both sides of this debate missed the point in that their analyses were inherently ahistorical; each argument was based on an incomplete picture of how the economy works *over time*. No common historical decision-making process for prices could be agreed upon because *no common process existed*. It is unrealistic to expect that economic processes will remain uniform over different historical epochs. The Transformational Growth approach recognizes this fact and provides an account of these macroeconomic processes based on era specificity. Prior to the 1930s, what Transformational Growth terms the old business cycle (OBC), one set of production techniques and associated macroeconomic adjustment processes were in operation. After 1945 mass-production techniques became dominant, with a different set

163

of macroeconomic adjustment processes. During the OBC adjustments to changes in demand were made through changes in prices. Prices were flexible both upward and downward. Because of the new production arrangements, and the institutional implications brought about by mass production, a fundamentally different set of adjustment processes were in place after the 1930s. Specifically, output and employment fluctuated with changes in demand.

Therefore we see that the reason why no common solution to the pricing debate could be attained was because the two groups failed to recognize that the organization of production had shifted, or, in some cases, was in the process of shifting. They were looking at two different time slices of economic history, in which significantly different production schemes and adjustment mechanisms were at work, as if they were one continuous period. Examination of economic history in this manner is inaccurate; distinctions need to be made on the basis of production systems and techniques in use at the time. An inherently historical analysis is required.

The theory of Transformational Growth explains the timing of these marginalst debates rather nicely. We argue that during the inter-war period there was a fundamental shift taking place in technology affecting production structures. There was a movement from craft production and adjustments through the price mechanism to systems of mass production, incorporating adjustments through output and employment changes. By the end of World War II mass production was firmly established as dominant within the economy, and family firms had been superseded by the modern corporation. Thus the placement of the Transformational Growth structural shift and the outbreak of these debates coincide perfectly. Because we are talking about essentially two different economies in these debates, we cannot have one pricing policy. The set of stylized facts Nell has developed explains the two sets of processes in the two different time periods.

In addition to responding to the marginalist debates of the 1930s and 1940s, I will also perform some econometric verification of the stylized facts set forth by Nell in Chapter 1. The empirical analysis in the present chapter will focus on testing the UK business cycles for structural breaks and an examination of the cyclicality of prices and product wages.

THE MARGINAL COST/MARGINAL PRODUCTIVITY DEBATE AND THE CYCLICALITY OF PRICES AND WAGES

Throughout the history of economic thought, price and wage cyclicality has been a staple research topic; the marginalist debates of the 1930s and

1940s do not mark the first appearance of this question. The beginning of the analysis can be traced back to Keynes's *General Theory*, where he assumed that prices were set equal to marginal cost and hypothesized that wage rates would move countercyclically to product prices: "an increase in employment can only occur to the accompaniment of a decline in the rate of real wages."[1]

As Hanes points out, some of the first empirical studies of real wage behavior were consistent with Keynes's prediction. He states that Lorie Tarshis (1939) found that changes in real hourly wages are in general opposite in direction from changes in labor hours. However, the patterns exhibited after the Second World War show different results, varying somewhat with the use of different measures of the price level. But most find real wages to be acyclical or procyclical (a recent example is Solon *et al.* 1994). These studies are offered both as a refutation of Keynesian theory and as support for real business cycle (RBC) theories (for example, Christiano and Eichenbaum 1989: 430). However, no sweeping generalizations can be made regarding the cyclicality of wages and prices for all times and all places. Before arguing for or against counter-cyclical real wages, one must specify what historical period one is speaking about, whether the country is industrialized or developing, etc. What these studies fail to recognize is that, prior to the Second World War, a different economic system was in place. After 1945 a mass-production economy was in effect; prior to 1914 the economy was characterized by craft production. Thus the differences in cyclicality patterns exhibited do not imply that one theory is correct and the other incorrect; each may be correct for the specific period of economic history from which it came. This point has been largely overlooked in the literature.

Although many studies support our hypothesis that there are in fact two distinct periods, I have found the explanation of the existence of the split between the two periods to be somewhat lacking in other work. This volume is unique in explaining the *causes* of the structural shifts in behavior patterns. For example, Hanes writes that a number of studies have looked at the cyclical "flexibility" of nominal wages and prices over the twentieth century. The general conclusion is that the amount of change in the rate of inflation is associated with sharp changes in output and employment. Many studies found wages and prices to be less flexible since World War II than in the interwar period or the decades just before World War I. The most common explanations of these changes relied on the *deus ex machina* of government intervention.[2]

It is agreed that wages and prices have been found to be less flexible in the NBC than during the OBC, but there is more to the story than just the expansion of government intervention. Although the stance of the government is significant, it is not the only relevant variable in explaining the shift of the exhibited behavior of macroeconomic variables. This volume makes the argument that the *structure of production itself* is the main cause of this shift over time, and this aspect has been largely overlooked in works on this subject. Historically we know that the OBC and the NBC are characterized by two fundamentally different production structures, accompanied by two different patterns of labor organization. In the OBC craft production was in operation. The small scale of operation and small size of the business unit meant that relatively inflexible methods of production were in use. Thus production was not easily adapted to changes in output. The firm was essentially confronted with two choices: produce or shut down. Output variation was simply not an option. Work teams were essential for production and temporary lay-offs, reduction in hours worked, etc., were not easily accommodated by the organization of production. Thus, rather than changes in output and employment, we see changes in prices, wages and productivity.

However, the NBC is characterized by mass production. As Nell points out, the family firm has been superseded by the modern corporation, operating mass-production technology. Under this production arrangement, output and employment are easily adapted to changes in sales. Layoffs and reductions in hours worked are commonplace and are the preferred means of adjustment. These dramatic differences in production techniques are the fundamental causes of the shift in wage, price and output movements across time. Unlike the OBC, productivity changes in the NBC are usually only positive and come about as a result of learning by doing, investments in human capital, technological advances that allow workers to labor smarter, etc. During the OBC, however, productivity was flexible in both directions. Because production was organized around the work team, during slow times people would work less productively rather than being laid off. Similarly, in prosperous times, rather than hiring additional laborers, work would be intensified and the existing workers would work harder.

As stated above in the introductory section, there were a series of debates in the *American Economic Review* regarding the validity of marginal analysis in the actual business decisions taken by firms, particularly pricing decisions. Athough these debates did not explicitly discuss production processes and adjustment mechanisms, they are most certainly implied in the discourse.[3] The *American Economic Review* discussions can perhaps best be showcased by the ongoing exchange between Richard Lester and Fritz Machlup. Lester puts the argument for institutionalized pricing policies, whereas Machlup is a defender of marginalist principles. In his March 1946 article Lester provides results from an industry survey he conducted, and shows how those results refute conventional theories of employment according to marginal productivity theory. For example, he states that businessmen expressed the view that operation of their equipment requires "just so many men" and that 'during peacetime, employment is more or less permanent . . ..' It is clear from numerous interviews that most business executives do not think of 'labor as a function of wage rates but as a function of output' . . . Businessmen do not think of deliberate curtailment of operations and labor as an adjustment to increases in wage rates, partly because some plants and operations require a fixed crew under existing techniques of production and partly because businessmen believe that variable cost per unit of production increases as production and labor are curtailed.[4]

From this passage we see that Lester is making an argument against labor and output as the dominant adjustment mechanism. This is really to be expected, since his study was conducted during the OBC; his conclusion is exactly what Transformational Growth would hypothesize. Lester poses serious objections to the marginal cost and marginal productivity of labor approach to the determination of employment and output decisions. If output and employment policies are based on assumptions of decreasing marginal variable costs up to full-capacity operations, then much of the economic reasoning on employment adjustments to increases or decreases in wage rates is invalid. Thus a new theory of the wage–employment relationship for the industrial firm is required. Any attempt to analyze normal entrepreneurial behavior in the short run in terms of marginal curves is undermined by the empirical result Lester obtains.[5] Lester's results also make it impossible to assume that wages in the short run will bear any close relation to the marginal product or marginal revenue of the labor employed.[6] Lester follows this initial result by remarking that employment decisions are based more on current and prospective demand for products and the full-crew requirements of the existing facilities rather than on the current level of wage rates.

This point leads into his discussion of how production techniques affect employment decisions. Lester's argument fits nicely with Transformational Growth's account of craft production techniques. The following comment seems to have been written specifically for the OBC:

> Certain techniques of production, allowing little variation in the use of labor, may be the only practical means of manufacturing the product. Under such circumstances the management does not and cannot think in terms of positive or negative increments of labor except perhaps where it is a question of expanding plant and equipment, changing equipment, or a redesigning of the plant. The flexibility of many plants is, however, extremely limited. From much of the literature the reader receives the impression that methods of manufacture readily adjust to changes in

relative costs of production factors. But the decision to shift a manufacturing plant to a method of production requiring more or less labor per unit of output because of a variation in wage rates is not one that management would make frequently or lightly.[7]

From this we can conclude that switches in production methods are not likely to arise from changes in wage rates, and that basically production techniques are sticky.

Note also that Lester cites a 1930s Temporary National Economic Commission study of wage rates, labor costs and technical change at two shoe companies, two paper companies, two mills of a textile company, and plants of the International Harvester Company. The results indicate that increases in the wage rate were not the most significant factor, and might in fact have no influence, in the determination and timing of technological change. Little evidence was found of a causal relationship between increased labor costs and the introduction of capital improvements. Additionally, Eiteman (1945) illustrates the "hopeless complexity" involved in attempting to apply marginal calculus to these decisions. Lester argues that Eiteman's demonstration "leaves no doubt" that it would be highly impractical for the manager of a multi-process plant[8] to vary the amount of labor hired so as to constantly equate marginal costs and marginal returns for each factor of production.

From Lester's arguments and his supporting evidence from Dean and Ytena, Eitemann, etc., we see the argument being made that, because employment is relatively inflexible owing to the organization of production, labor inputs cannot be changed very much at the margin. Therefore it is inappropriate (and incorrect) to assume that pricing decisions are made on the basis of marginal calculus.

Opposed to Richard Lester is Fritz Machlup, who supports marginalist propositions. Machlup addresses the "general misunderstanding of marginalist principles" as applied to pricing policy. He states that to use marginal cost as a pricing factor need not mean that price will be set at the marginal cost level. Indeed, this will never be done. In the exceptional case of pure competition, price cannot be "set" at all but is "given" to the firm and beyond its control. In the normal case of monopolistic competition, the firm will never charge a price as low as marginal cost. Rather, the firm will set the price where marginal revenue is equal to marginal cost. (As we learned in our principles course, this is precisely where the firm should set price in order to maximize its profits.) Additionally, marginal cost will be equal to price not because of any price policy but only because of adjustment in the firm's production volume.[9] This is exactly the macroeconomic adjustment process Transformational Growth hypothesizes for the NBC: prices are more or less inflexible, and adjustment comes through changes in output and employment.

In his discussion of technology Machlup argues that marginal productivity theory is broad enough to cover all sorts of technological possibilities as well as supply and demand conditions. In thinking about demand and supply in marginal terms, we see that changes in the supply conditions of a factor can cause shifts in the marginal productivity schedule of that factor.

> The cost of the factor itself is not a part of its marginal net productivity but, instead, is the counterpart with which a balance is sought. Marginal factor cost . . . is the total increase in payment for the particular type of productive service: it consists of (1) the price (wage) paid to the additionally employed, and (2) the price increase (wage increase) paid for the amount of services employed before the addition.[10]

Thus his argument leads into his hypothesis regarding firm behavior: in considering hiring more workers, a firm will ask whether the additional labor will pay for itself. Machlup believes that this decision is executed in an intuitive manner:

> The businessman who equates marginal net revenue productivity and marginal factor cost when he decides how many to employ need not engage in higher mathematics; he would simply rely on his sense or his "feel" of the situation. There is nothing very exact about this sort of estimate. [A] businessman would "just know," in a vague and rough way, whether or not it would pay him to hire more men.[11]

However, this discussion which Machlup states is about technology, really does not discuss technology at all. I would argue that Machlup, and Lester as well, appears to have a misinformed concept of technology and no understanding at all of technology as a system. Marginal analysis allows us to write production functions and equations expressing the marginal products of factors employed. But production functions and such are tools used for understanding factor prices and *distribution*, not the actual physical production process making use of the technology as a system existing in the economy. This is where the theory of Transformational Growth as a methodological framework has an advantage over marginal analysis; the story of Transformational Growth is built around systems of technology in which technology is conceived of as production processes. In the OBC a particular type of technology existed, and production processes took the form of craft production as a consequence of the technological conditions and the available degree of labor specialization according to that ruling technology. The NBC is characterized by a different system of technology which makes a greater division and specialization of labor possible, and hence we see production processes taking the form of mass production. Mass production is associated with continuous throughput and lower start-up and shut-down costs because of the type of technology embodied within this system. Note that the shift from one production scheme to another is driven by a change of technology *as a system*. The transition from craft to mass production is not driven by technological change taking the form of shifting marginal productivity curves; there is a fundamental shift in the organization of production, labor, etc., and technology as a system that has a deeper nature than shifting marginal productivity functions.

Machlup also addresses various structures of competition, although rather inadequately. He argues that a monopolistic or monopsonistic market does not invalidate the proposition that firms in these market structures will equate marginal productivity and marginal cost of input. He notes that marginal net revenue productivity reflects the degree of monopoly in the market, and any degree of monopsony is fully reflected in marginal factor cost. Again, however, he is really talking about distributional effects rather than the physical methods employed in production, and he avoids the issue of *why* these different levels of market imperfection arise. Transformational Growth argues that the degree of market imperfection can be linked directly with the prevailing technological system at the time. Changes in technology regimes will cause changes in the level of competitiveness of the market. For example, large corporations operating mass production in the NBC are more likely to be able to control their market than the small family firms in the OBC using craft production techniques.[12] The NBC is more appropriately characterized by oligopoly as a direct result of mass production. Because of economies of scale, extensive outlay on fixed plant and equipment, etc., it makes sense for an industry organized around mass-production technology to be monopolistically competitive. It makes sense that a few large firms should come to dominate the market and exert some control over the market conditions. However, craft production is organized around a set of scattered family firms whose size and importance limit their control over the market. Thus this type of production will tend naturally to a more competitive environment than mass production. Hence we see the connection between technology and competitive structure.

Of cyclical variation, Machlup states that average cost and revenue calculations must be computed to take into consideration these variations over time, and such calculations are not inconsistent with marginal cost and revenue principles.

> [I]f increases in output are under consideration, the marginal
> changes of revenue and cost as functions of output will have to

comprise any changes over time that will affect revenue or cost. That the firm figures with these averages over time does not mean that it makes decisions concerning price policies on the basis of an average-cost rule rather than the maximum-rule principle.[13]

It is precisely these average calculations that cause prices to be inflexible, failing to be an adjustment variable. Of inflexible prices based on average calculations in mass-production technology Machlup has the following to say:

> a change in the market situation may make it wise and profitable to change the selling price, but that price has been anchored to an average-cost calculation which it is now difficult to disavow . . . [The firm has] to put up with relatively inflexible prices which . . . might be as much against their own interests as against those of the consumers.[14]

Again, this is completely consistent with the Transformational Growth characterization of the mass-production era.

Machlup also addresses average cost in relation to demand elasticity, stating that average cost may be the most important datum for the estimate of demand elasticity. In order to estimate how much market share will be lost owing to an increase in price, the firm will consider whether existing or potential competitors can supply substitute products at the particular price. The supply from competing sources will depend on their actual or potential cost of production. Assuming that competitors have the same access to production factors, materials and technology, their production cost cannot be much different from that of the producer considering a price increase.[15] This scenario provides support for the Transformational Growth hypothesis that during the NBC firms are less likely, owing to identical average cost structures across producers in the same industry, to enact adjustments through price changes. Therefore adjustments in employment, rather than in the price mechanism, are the more likely outcome.

Lester wrote a refutation of Machlup, asserting that variations in the total volume of employment are primarily the result of actual and anticipated changes in the volume of sales or orders for the products of the plant. Employers do not think or act in the labor market in terms of equating marginal net revenue productivity and marginal labor cost. Lester adds that:

> If businessmen think that their unit variable cost (to say nothing of their overhead costs per unit) change in that fashion, I submit that it is extremely difficult to explain both the wide variations

171

that occur in the scale of plant operations and the size of the average deviation from 100 percent plant capacity that occurs over say a decade (especially in plants producing articles not carrying the producer's brand names) on the assumption that businessmen adjust their rate of operations according to the principle of maximizing money profits by equating "marginal net revenue productivity" and "marginal factor cost" over the long or short run.[16]

As may be expected, no reconciliation was ever reached between these two conflicting viewpoints. Both sides were correct in that each found empirical evidence to confirm its own position and refute that of the other. But both sides were also wrong in that they failed to recognize that the evidence was being drawn from two completely different historical eras operating two different types of production technology. Had one side or the other seen the different institutional arrangements of the two bodies of data, perhaps the debate would not have raged on, and this volume would not be so contradictory of generally accepted economic constructs.

As can be seen from the above discussion, there are direct implications from this debate for our hypotheses being investigated here. The crucial question to be gleaned from the *American Economic Review* debates is whether the economy operates under a Say's law process or a multiplier–accelerator process. Thus we are in effect considering whether the economy adjusts by a price mechanism (OBC) or through changes in output and employment (NBC). Perhaps the easiest way to examine this is to ask what will happen given a change in demand. We know that a change in demand will be followed by either a change in price or a change in employment. If an increase in demand is followed by an increase in the price level relative to the wage rate, with no corresponding change in output, the real wage will decline. Constant output is taken to mean a constant level of employment and a constant wage rate. A decrease in demand forces every firm in the industry to face a demand problem. If shut-downs and lay-offs are costly, all firms will lower the price of the goods, continue production on the same scale, and sell as much as possible at the reduced price. Production may not be scaled back because firms may find that they are able to sell as much or more at the reduced prices, thereby making up for the loss from the lower price. Thus, given a decline in demand, output, employment and the wage rate will all remain unchanged; the only effect will be a decrease in price until the shutdown price is reached. So we see an increasing real wage when price declines relative to the given wage rate.

Note that the above examples assume inflexible production structures with high start-up and lay-off and shutdown costs. If production is sufficiently flexible, changes in output and employment are easily accommodated and a different adjustment mechanism occurs. If output rather than price changes in response to a change in demand, the following mechanism is actuated. Given an increase in demand, production will expand, increasing output. The expansion of production will require a proportional increase in labor employed at the given wage rate. Thus we see an increase in demand accompanied by a constant real wage and an increase in employment. Note that the same process holds in reverse for a decline in demand.

The flexibility of the production structure can be analyzed in a number of ways, one of which is by average costs. For the purposes of our discussion we will assume that production structures are either inflexible or flexible, and that the average cost curve can take one of two shapes: it will be very steep or very shallow and flat.

A very steep AC curve is indicative of rigid production systems; in the extreme case, the average cost curve is completely closed, making production possible at only one point. Under such circumstances a change in demand leads to a change in price, since there are substantial costs to changing the scale of production and adjusting the quantity of labor employed. However, if the average cost curve is flat, a range of production points is possible, and the scale of production is easily changed. Labor can easily be added or removed, whereas price changes are not as likley to occur. Under this system, additional labor will be employed whose productivity equals its product wage, and labor that does not pay in terms of its product wage will be dismissed.

In general, then, we can say that under one set of production circumstances, characterized by inflexible production such as that found during the OBC, the variable cost curve is fairly steep, making the relevant range of production possibilities fairly small. Therefore price adjustments, rather than adjustments in the scale of production, take place. Because of the changes in price at the given wage rate, the real wage becomes countercyclical. In contrast, if production is sufficiently flexible, and the variable cost curve is relatively flat, a range of relevant production points exist and changes in output and employment, rather than changes in prices, take place. Hence we see a procyclical – or, more likely, acyclical – real wage.

In conclusion, the debates in the *American Economic Review* during the 1930s and 1940s have a direct bearing on the study of Transformational Growth; the debate really centers on the shape of the average cost curves; Lester is arguing for steep curves, such as those characterizing the OBC, and Machlup is arguing for flatter curves, such as those found during the NBC. Lester's position clearly represents the OBC; during the OBC, Transformational Growth hypothesizes a countercyclical real wage, based on the argument that a price mechanism is in effect. Note also that, during this period, technological advances and gains in productivity are passed along as a decrease in price. Lester's argument reflects craft production methods and the OBC rather than mass-production techniques and the NBC. Hence it is not surprising to see Lester making the argument that the level of employment is not a function of the wage rate. This means that labor employed is not a function of its marginal productivity relative to its cost. Labor employed is an institutionally determined variable, owing to the organization of production. Lester makes this point explicitly when he speaks of inflexible work teams, etc., and therefore cost factors really have no role in determining the level of employment.

Machlup's argument based on marginalist principles tends to support the structure of mass production found during the NBC. We see from Nell that a mildly procyclical or acyclical real wage is hypothesized during the NBC. This is inherent in the point of view expressed by Machlup, who argues that labor employed is a function of the wage rate based on marginal calculations undertaken by firms. Under mass production, adjustments take place through changes in employment rather than through a price mechanism. This is possible owing to the high degree of division and specialization of labor; assembly lines have replaced the traditional work teams. Lay-offs are easier to carry out than changes in wage rates. Wages are downward rigid, owing to institutional arrangements such as unions, minimum wage requirements, etc. For example, given a decline in anticipated demand, output will be reduced. Therefore either a drop in wage rates to employ the same number of workers or a decline in the number of persons employed at the same wage rate is required, owing to revenue constraints. Since the wage rate is somewhat institutionally fixed, and rigid at the least, a reduction in labor hired is the option selected.

If we make the marginalist assumption that marginal variable costs per unit of output decline as output is expanded up to full capacity, an increase in output leads to a decrease in variable costs per unit of output. Therefore, in an attempt to maintain their marginal calculations, firms will either increase the amount of labor employed or increase the wage rate. If the decrease in marginal variable costs per unit of output is due strictly to the fact that the firm is producing at a higher level, it is most likely that the number employed will increase. If, however, we see the decrease in cost arising from an increase in productivity due to technological factors, the wage rate will rise. Regarding productivity gains, note that in the NBC productivity gains are passed on as a rise in wage rates, whereas during the OBC they are passed on as a reduction in prices. However, in either case the end result will be an increase in the real wage. I would hypothesize that, in general, both effects will take place: when costs per unit of output decline, part of the decrease can be attributed merely to the increase in the scale of operations, while another part comes from productivity gain, e.g. the institution of new technology, learning by doing, etc. Thus we have a mildly procyclical (in the case of productivity advances) or acyclical real wage (in the case of increasing the scale of production).

In conclusion, then, the Transformational Growth hypothesis fits into the pricing debates of the 1930s and 1940s as follows. The OBC was characterized by craft production under which marginal calculations were not performed by firms. The owners of the family firms "just knew," as Lester says, what the appropriate production conditions were. Operations were small enough where elaborate calculations and a large amount of managerial time devoted to cost analysis was not required. These conditions generated a countercyclical real wage (product wage) which was a stabilizing force in the macroeconomy. In contrast, with the high degree of mechanization and specialization of production in the NBC, operations were expanded and the family firm was replaced by the modern corporation, which *does* undertake the marginalist calculations and devote a good share of its time and financial resources to managerial functions. Thus we see marginalism affecting the behavior of employment and the real wage (product wage), generating adjustments through employment and a mildly procyclical or acyclical real wage. The great failure of these debates is that both sides were missing the fact that they were speaking about two different historical periods giving rise to two completely different sets of macroeconomic behavior.

Therefore we see the reconciliation Transformational Growth can provide to this debate. We now turn to an empirical verification of the cyclicality of real wages just elaborated above. Empirical data for the United Kingdom will be used for the hypothesis testing. The case of the United Kingdom is particularly relevant to studying the existence of the two production regimes, since it was one of the first nations to undertake this development from craft into mass production.

DISCUSSION AND VERIFICATION OF THE STYLIZED FACTS OF THE OBC AND THE NBC IN THE UNITED KINGDOM

The case of the United Kingdom is slightly different from some of the others considered in this volume in that the industrialization process began slightly earlier. Thus the shift to full-scale mass-production techniques may have occurred prior to the shifts in the other nations under consideration. However, this should not greatly affect dating the two business cycles. Certainly we can argue that the period of 1945 to 1987 is characterized by mass-production techniques. Additionally, although the transition from craft to mass production was clearly in process by the onset of World War I, it is still appropriate to characterize the period from 1850 to 1913 as generally a craft production one. The classification of

OBC/NBC is based on the decomposition provided by Nell in Chapter 1 of this volume and is organized around his set of stylized facts describing the relative movements and covariations in prices, wages, employment and output. The use of Nell's stylized facts permits the construction of the following hypotheses which can be examined using standard econometric techniques:

1   With regard to cyclicality, in the OBC we expect product wages to be countercyclical. This countercyclicality will be reflected in negative coefficients with high significance in regression results where prices and wages are the dependent variables. In contrast, during the NBC we expect to see mildly procyclical or, more likely, acyclical behavior of product wages. This will be reflected in positive coefficients or, more likely, insignificant coefficients in regression results.
2   Regarding wholesale prices, we expect to see a strong positive relationship with output during the OBC, but a weaker relationship during the NBC. This will show itself empirically in statistically significant positive coefficients for the OBC, and statistically insignificant coefficients for the NBC, perhaps with a negative sign. However, the decline in significance alone is enough to support this hypothesis.
3   Based on our decomposition of the aggregate time period into two subperiods, we would expect to find statistically significant structural breaks in the relationships at the inter-war period.

As pointed out in Chapter 8, the econometric specifications are not designed to provide a model of wage, price and output behavior. We are only testing for the existence of a structural break in an attempt to support the main hypothesis that the time periods in question exhibit different adjustment mechanisms. Obviously our regression equations are highly underspecified, specifically so to illustrate the points we are trying to make. Expanded specification would be required for estimating the behavioral relationships. Before we turn to estimation, however, a word needs to be said about data and data problems.

A NOTE ON DATA AND PROBLEMS SPECIFIC TO THE UNITED KINGDOM

The examination of macroeconomic patterns over an extended period of time is inherently problematic, owing to data difficulties; this issue is discussed at length elsewhere in this volume. The case of the United Kingdom is slightly preferable to that of the other countries considered in this volume in that the existing data for the United Kingdom are of somewhat better quality than those of others (for instance, see Chapter

7 for a discussion of US data), but they are still subject to some problems and should be approached with caution. For example, between 1919 and 1920 a change in almost all data series collected for the United Kingdom took place. Prior to 1920, southern Ireland was included in the series collected, whereas after 1920 it is excluded. As Hanes (1993) points out the construction of a series affects behavior exhibited, and therefore it is critical that the series be constructed in the same manner across time:

> Within any period, business-cycle movements in wages and prices and output vary across goods, industries and even geographic regions. The cyclical behavior of an aggregate series may be sensitive to small changes in the way the series is constructed. To compare cyclical patterns across time, one must have series describing the same (or arguably similar) sectors in the same way. Otherwise one cannot be sure that differences between period on series behavior reflect changes over time rather than differences between sectors at a point in time.[17]

As stated elsewhere in this volume, imperfect data do not prevent us from drawing meaningful conclusions from them; the conclusions should just be judged with the quality of the data in mind and viewed with caution. The exclusion of southern Ireland after 1920 is not an issue that will prevent us from performing statistical analyses, as there is not an insurmountable break in variable values between 1919 and 1920. None the less, it should be noted that this change in data collection does exist, and it is possible that it could affect results generated from testing, particularly the significance of the coefficients of structural change. Feinstein provides two statistics for 1920: one including southern Ireland and one that does not. The difference between the two is very small, and therefore I expect that it will not disrupt the analysis of cyclicality and structural breaks.

The empirical testing of our hypothesis regarding the cyclicality of prices and product wages essentially requires three series: some measure of output, a price index and a money wage. Since the hypotheses set out above pertain specifically to the manufacturing sector, data specific to this sector are preferable. Our measure of output is the index of total production for the manufacturing sector. The data are taken from Feinstein (1972: table 51, column 3).[18] The price index used in this study warrants a comment. Wholesale price index data for 1850 to 1988 are taken from Mitchell (1976, 1992). However, Mitchell notes that after 1955 the wholesale price index was no longer compiled by the United Kingdom in its complete and comprehensive form. For the period 1956 to 1988 he provides a weighted average of the components of the wholesale price index in an attempt to replicate this series. I have simply reproduced his constructed series here for this period, as Mitchell's work is viewed as highly reliable and essentially is seen as the definitive source. The wholesale price series was used since a price index for manufactured outputs could not be obtained in a reliable and comprehensive form for the period as a whole. From the mid-1960s on, this series is available in the International Monetary Fund *International Financial Statistics Yearbook*. Obviously the index of manufactured outputs is the index that would be preferable to use for both the OBC and the NBC periods. However, there is limited information on this series prior to 1960 for the NBC; additionally the IMF did not collect these data for the OBC period, and I have been unsuccessful in locating any such series. Most of the price series available for this early period are highly aggregative, or deal with the prices of primary products purchased by the manufacturing sector as inputs.[19] However, for the purposes of the analysis at hand, input prices are less preferable than the prices of manufacturing output, and therefore the wholesale price index was selected for the OBC.

The money wage series used is taken directly from Mitchell (1992). Again, owing to data problems, I have not been able to locate an ideal wage index, specific to the manufacturing sector. All of the available series include other sectors. For example, Mitchell's series from 1850 to 1874 is based on G. H. Wood's index for workers of unchanged grade in full work, including farm work. From 1874 to 1914 the basis is the average wage of all laborers in building, engineering, mining, textiles and agriculture. From 1945 to 1946 the weekly wages of all laborers in industry and service are used. From 1947 on, the index is based on the weekly wages of adult males in manufacturing as measured in October. Average weekly earnings include bonus and overtime payments before any deductions for one week in October. Prior to 1983 the figures include certain other industries (mining and quarrying, building, transport, public utilities, government industrial establishments, laundries and dry cleaning, and railways). For the years 1970 to 1980 the series was for adult (over eighteen) male full-time manual workers; railways were excluded. Industries are classified according to the 1968 Standard Industrial Classification until 1982. From 1983 industries are classified according to the 1980 SIC. Finally, from 1983 the series is for full-time male manual workers on adult rates in manufacturing industries.

As can be seen, none of the series, aside from the index of manufacturing output, is precisely the data required, uncontaminated by sectors other than manufacturing, and none is precisely the exact measure that we are looking for. This is just one of the many difficulties of doing economic historical work, and, frustrating as the problem is, it must be dealt with and we must seek the best possible data available for the specific research question at hand. Although this data set is not the ideal set, it still allows us to say something about the questions at hand and can be used effectively to explore our hypotheses.

Table 6.1 Results of augmented Dickey–Fuller tests

Variable	Uproot 1 lag	MacKinnon criticals	
		1%	5%
Manuf	−5.9323	−2.5813	−1.9424
Price	−4.3560	−2.5813	−1.9424
ProdW	−7.3260	−2.5813	−1.9424

Note that all variables are expressed as growth rates for the purposes of analysis; growth rates were generated (to be consistent with the series in other chapters of this volume) by taking the first difference of the natural logarithm of the initial series. Generation of growth rates, in most cases, effectively detrends the series. Once the series has been detrended, one can perform the econometric tests without the worry that the series is non-stationary.[20] Note that stationarity is an issue because, if the series are non-stationary, spurious regression results can occur and the conclusions drawn from the results can be completely inaccurate.

In order to test formally for stationarity, one needs to test for the existence of a unit root. This is most easily accomplished with the Augmented Dickey–Fuller test.[21] The ADF was used to determine whether the series employed here are stationary. As can be seen from Table 6.1, the statistics obtained from the ADF are very large and negative, lying to the left of the appropriate critical value, indicating that the series are in fact stationary in their growth rate form.

ECONOMETRIC METHODOLOGY AND TESTING RESULTS

Given that our series are stationary and adequately detrended, we are now ready to begin the empirical verification of the hypotheses set out earlier. The stylized facts of the OBC and NBC regarding cyclical variability tell us that, in the early period, product wages moved countercyclically, whereas in the later period product wages tended to be either mildly procyclical or acyclical. Additionally, we expect to see a strong relationship between wholesale prices and output during the OBC, with the strength of this relationship declining as we move through the inter-war years into the NBC.

The econometric technique used to analyze the cyclical movements and relationships hypothesized regarding the various time periods is slightly different from that used throughout this volume. Like other chapters of this volume, I have tested for cyclicality through the use of the dummy variable technique, with one slight modification. I have included a dummy intercept term in the regression. The addition of a dummy intercept term allows the two periods to take both different slopes and different intercept terms. In essence, this technique estimates a spline function. Note that this form allows us to express the model as a single equation in which the variance of the error term is assumed to be constant over the two periods.[22] Thus the equation takes the following form:

$$X_t = b_0 + b_1 Y_t + b_2 Y_{t-1} + b_3 \text{ Dummy} + b_4 \text{ Dummy} * Y_t + b_5 \text{ Dummy} * Y_{t-1}$$

We now turn to an examination of the empirical results obtained. The first set of results shown are for the price index and manufacturing output, given in Table 6.2. The dummy variable method results are shown first, including both the current period and one-period lagged values of manufacturing output. Note that, because the one-period lag coefficients were not significant, the regression was re-estimated using only current-period values. As can be seen from the results, our hypothesis of a strong procyclical price in the old period and a weakened acyclical or counter-cyclical relationship in the new cycle is confirmed by the highly significant positive coefficient of manufacturing output and the highly significant

Table 6.2 Testing results of the price/output relationship using dummy variables. Hypothesis: $b_1, b_2 > 0$, $b_4, b_5 < 0$. Mitchell price data and Feinstein manufacturing output data

$\text{Price}_t = b_0 + b_1 \text{ Manuf}_t + b_2 \text{ Manuf}_{t-1} + b_3 \text{ Dummy} + b_4 \text{ Dummy}*\text{Manuf}_t + b_5 \text{ Dummy}*\text{Manuf}_{t-1}$

Variable	Coefficient	Std error	T stat.	One-tail sig.
C	−0.0120	0.0156	−0.7767	0.2197
Manuf	0.360	0.1874	2.0602	0.0211
Manuf(−1)	0.0414	0.1874	0.2210	0.4128
Dummy	0.0704	0.0239	2.9407	0.0020
DManuf	−0.3115	0.2261	−1.3584	0.0889
DManuf(−1)	0.0008	0.2261	0.0036	0.4986
r	0.3804	0.1004	3.7875	0.0002

R squared 0.3243. Adjusted R squared 0.2802.
Durbin–Watson statistic 2.0030. Probability(F statistic) 0.00002

Variable	Coefficient	Std error	T stat.	One-tail sig.
C	−0.0100	0.0145	−0.6895	0.2461
Manuf	0.3793	0.1825	2.0780	0.0202
Dummy	0.0703	0.0221	3.1750	0.0010
DManuf	−0.315	0.2172	−1.4531	0.0748
r	0.3737	0.0980	3.8126	0.0002

R squared 0.3206. Adjusted R squared 0.2920.
Durbin–Watson statistic 2.0570. Probability(F statistic) 0.0000.

negative coefficient of structural change. Note that the equations have been corrected for autocorrelation through the use of the Cochrane–Orcutt iterative procedure.[23]

Based on the results shown in Table 6.2, we have strong evidence of a structural shift in the behavior of prices between the two periods, with a very high level of statistical significance. This result is additionally reinforced by the fact that the series are contiguous throughout the shift period. The splice in the series does not take place until 1969–1970, and we can conclude that the series construction does not artificially impose a break point. For the price and output relationships, our hypotheses are therefore confirmed.

We now turn to an examination of the product wage and output relationship. We hypothesize that this relation will be countercyclical, indicated by a negative coeffcient, for the OBC and mildly procyclical or acyclical for the NBC, as evidenced by positive coefficients and/or statistically insignificant coefficients. The results obtained are given in Table 6.3. As can be seen, these results are not as strong as those obtained for the price relationship. We see that the only coefficient that is highly significant is b_5, which we hypothesized would be positive and insignificant. However, the results should not lead to a complete dismissal of the Transformational Growth approach. As was noted in the discussion of the data and data problems, the wage series is not exactly a precise fit to the argument we are trying to make; perhaps wage data specific to the manufacturing sector would yield better results. The empirical results may not be as strong as we had hoped, since the wage data contain other elements from the agriuclture sector, etc. Nevertheless, the price mechanism is the driving force in the product wage relationship, and, as

Table 6.3 Testing results of the product wage/output relationship, using dummy variables. Hypothesis: b_1, $b_2 < 0$, b_4, $b_5 > 0$. Mitchell wage and price data and Feinstein manufacturing output data

$\text{ProdW}_t = b_0 + b_1 \text{Manuf}_t + b_2 \text{Manuf}_{t-1} + b_3 \text{Dummy} + b_4 \text{Dummy}*\text{Manuf}_t + b_5 \text{Dummy}*\text{Manuf}_{t-1}$

Variable	Coefficient	Std error	T stat.	One-tail sig.
C	0.0139	0.0112	1.2500	0.1073
Manuf	−0.2053	0.2054	−0.996	0.1601
Manuf(−1)	0.1011	0.2041	0.4954	0.3108
Dummy	0.0141	0.1762	0.8001	0.2129
DManuf	−0.0319	0.3615	−0.0385	0.4847
DManuf(−1)	−0.7068	0.3551	−1.9903	0.0248

R squared 0.0779. Adjusted R squared 0.0267.
Durbin–Watson statistic 1.7978. Probability(F statistic) 0.1911.

we saw above, the price–manufacturing output relationship is strongly confirmed.

CONCLUSION

As can be seen, the marginal cost/marginal productivity debates of the 1930s and 1940s tie into the theory of Transformational Growth; additionally, it was shown how Transformational Growth can reconcile the two sides of the argument. Because each side of the debate held different assumptions regarding the nature of the average and marginal variable cost curves, two different outcomes were arrived at; one side, represented here by Lester, held average variable costs constant and therefore rejected the notion that employment decisions were based on the marginal productivity and marginal revenue of labor. The conflicting position, expressed by Machlup, held that average costs decline with increases in output, and therefore found a basis for using marginal calculations in employment decisions.

The assumptions regarding average and marginal variable costs have implications for the behavior of wages and prices; if constant average cost is assumed, the real wage takes on a countercyclical behavior, acting as a stabilizer by making adjustments through the price mechanism. However, if we assume declining average costs with increases in output, real wages take on an acyclical behavior. Thus the cyclicality of the real wage is, at least for the purposes of this discussion, directly dependent upon the assumptions made regarding the nature of average variable costs.

In looking at this debate in a historical context, we see that each side was really looking at a different time in economic history; Lester's findings are consistent with craft production and small-scale operations, whereas Machlup's argument makes the most sense when placed within the context of mass-production technology. Thus, the debate ties in with Transformational Growth in that our hypotheses can accommodate the conflict regarding the nature of average variable cost: during the OBC average variable cost is constant, and during the NBC average variable cost is declining with increases in output. Therefore, based on our assumptions regarding how average variable cost determines the cyclicality of real wages, we hypothesize a countercyclical real wage during the OBC and an acyclical real wage during the NBC. This is, in fact, exactly what we find empirically, in a collectively robust form, thereby showing support for the Transformational Growth hypotheses.

APPENDIX 6.1

The post-war empirics of the United States and the United Kingdom

One of the main hypotheses being explored in this volume is that the economic experiences prior to 1913 are fundamentally different than those experiences after 1945. We argue that there are several differences between the OBC and the NBC, and because of the differences we must treat these two subperiods of time differently in our analysis. It would be inappropriate to conceive of the OBC in mass-production terms, and equally inappropriate to attempt to force the NBC into a Marshallian framework. Our account of these differences, how they arise, and their significance are contained in the other chapters. But an additional word should be said about the homogeneity of the NBC.

If we look at the NBC as a whole with respect to the rate of growth and the real rate of interest, an interesting dichotomy can be seen. The aggregate period divides itself into two subperiods, roughly twenty-five years in length. During the first subperiod we see very strong rates of growth coupled with low or even negative real interest rates, and in general we can make the assertion that the rate of growth lies above the real rate of interest. The two rates seem to track one another fairly well through the early 1970s. But the onset of the 1970s brings with it a change in the relationship between these two rates, and by the end of the decade the pattern has reversed itself – the (real) rate of interest now exceeds the rate of growth.

The United States is not the only country to exhibit this relationship between the rate of growth and the real rate of interest. Phillips (Chapter 11) finds similar results for Canada, and, as can be seen from Figure 6.2, the same behavior can be found in the United Kingdom. The same basic features are found in the post-war UK data as were present in the US data. Looking at the plot of the UK relationship, we see that, in general, the rate of growth lies persistently above the real interest rate throughout the first subperiod, and generally lies below it during the second subperiod. This is consistent with the relative movements found in the Canadian, American, and German data, and I would expect a similar experience for all industrialized nations.

The relative movements of the rates of growth and interest are more than a mere *curiosum*. Associated with these relative movements are policy implications for expansion and stagnation. If the rate of growth exceeds the (real) rate of interest, the mass-production economy's tendency is to expand. Conversely, if the rate of growth lies below the rate of interest, the natural tendency is toward stagnation. Inappropriate policy, such as setting an interest rate too high in times of low growth and low inflation,

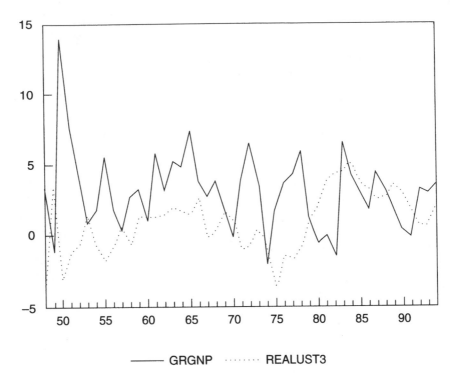

Figure 6.1 Real rate of growth and the real rate of return on three-month US Treasury securities, 1948–94.

can tend to reinforce these inherent tendencies and tend to prolong the stagnationary experience. I am still pursuing research into the expansionist and stagnationist tendencies of the mass-production economy, but it appears at this stage that these tendencies are inextricably linked with the sign of the discrepancy between the rate of growth and the real rate of interest. The relative movements of the rates of growth and (real) interest and of the differential between them also have some distributional implications. Additionally, preliminary evidence indicates that there is a connection between the rate of growth–rate of interest relationship and the components of the money supply, namely that different components of the money supply exhibit different behaviors as a result of changes in the rates of growth and interest. I am currently in the process of exploring this connection in more detail.

It would appear from this set of post-war US data that the relative movements of the real rates of growth and interest seem to behave according to some systematic pattern. Although it is difficult to form a general conclusion from the preliminary data, there does seem to be some suggestive evidence that some systematic forces may be at work. Cur-

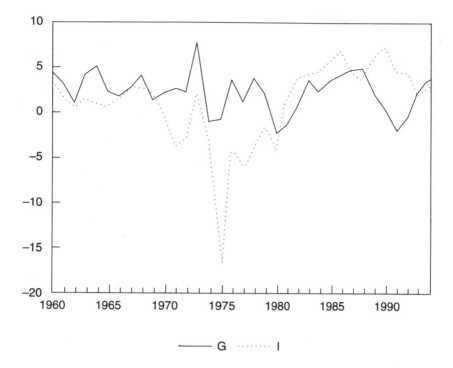

Figure 6.2 Real rate of growth and the real rate of return on UK Treasury bills, 1960–94.

rently we are in the midst of a complete exploration of what those forces are. Our ongoing research indicates that globalization may have a large part in explaining the differences between the two halves of the post-war period. One preliminary hypothesis regarding globalization emphasizes risk: higher globalization increases the risk in the system as a whole, and as a result we see an upward trend in real interest rates to offset the risk. Because of changes in borrowing costs, potential exchange rate and terms of trade problems, and possible currency difficulties, we hypothesize that the level of imports (at least from developing nations, if not at the aggregate level) will fall. This is essentially a reduction in (advanced nations') demand, which acts as a drag on output and therefore growth.

Another preliminary hypothesis concerns competition; the nation with the highest real interest rate will attract short-term funds. These capital movements will act to destabilize exchange rates. Once the exchange rate structure (regardless of type of exchange rate regime) begins to be destabilized, all countries will be driven to match the highest real interest rate. Similarly, the nation with the lowest real wage, adjusted for productivity, will attract a higher level of "detachable production processes," that is, aspects of production and assembly which can easily be separated and placed abroad. This tends to drive productivity-adjusted real wages down globally; downward pressure on the real wage will in turn tend to slow the rate of growth. Thus, through the tendency for real interest rates to rise globally and for the real wage to fall, dragging the rate of growth down, we hypothesize that higher levels of globalization will reinforce, and perhaps even create, a stagnationary regime.

Our hypothesis is only a working hypothesis, and serves only as a departure point. Clearly there are other factors involved in explaining the dichotomy of the post-war era – we happen to think globalization is one of the leading factors. We are exploring the effects of globalization on the rate of capital accumulation, employment levels, inflation rates, and nominal interest rates. Although we have only preliminary evidence at this stage, we have found that increasing globalization is at least a contributing factor that warrants further study.

NOTES

1 Keynes (1936: 17).
2 Hanes(1993: 733).
3 Note that the shape of the average cost curve was one of the critical points in these debates.
4 Lester (1946: 67).
5 Note, however, that Lester received only forty-six completed surveys of the 520 he sent out.
6 Ibid., p. 71. See also Hall and Hitch (1939: 32).
7 Lester (1946: 73).
8 A plant in which there is more than one type of process taking place and which, therefore, has more than one cost center.
9 Machlup (1946: 541).
10 Ibid.
11 Machlup (1946: 535).
12 Note that one of the main ways though which firms exercise greater control over their markets is though advertising. With mass production came mass marketing. For a fuller discusson of mass marketing see Chapter 9.
13 Machlup (1946: 539).
14 Machlup (1946: 541).
15 Machlup (1946: 543–4).
16 Lester (1947: 137–8).
17 Hanes (1993: 733).
18 Note that this series was extended to 1987 based on Feinstein's cited sources and the work of Liesner, who cites the following sources for these series: *Annual Abstract of Statistics*, Central Statistical Office, HMSO, London; *Economic Trends*, September 1984, Central Statistical Office, HMSO, London; *Economic Trends*, Annual Supplement 1989, Central Statistical Office, HMSO, London;

B.R. Mitchell, *European Historical Statistics 1750–1975* second edition, Macmillan, London, 1980.
19 One such index is the Rousseaux price index, provided by Mitchell for the period 1850 to 1913.
20 See Canova (1992) for a detailed examination of detrending.
21 For an explanation of the Augmented Dickey–Fuller stationarity test see Pindyck and Rubinfeld (1991).
22 For further details on spline functions and dummy variable techniques see Pindyck and Rubinfeld (1991: 104–9) or Kennedy (1992: ch. 14).
23 For a discussion of the Cochrane–Orcutt iterative procedure to correct for serial correlation see Pindyck and Rubinfeld (1991).

7

PRODUCT WAGES AND THE ELASTICITIES OF EFFECTIVE DEMAND IN THE UNITED STATES DURING THE OLD AND NEW BUSINESS CYCLE

Raymond Majewski

Transformational Growth, like other Post Keynesian approaches sees the cycle as caused primarily by changes in the level of effective demand. To this it adds three propositions. First, there is a difference in the way the economy responds to effective demand changes between the old and new business cycles. In the OBC the dominant effect is an increase in prices relative to money wages. At its extreme this is the kind of effect exhibited in the Cambridge growth models of the 1950s. In the NBC output responses dominate and prices move little compared to money wages. Once again at its extreme this is exhibited in a Keynesian cross or simple Kaleckian model. The second assertion is that this response in the nineteenth century tends to dampen the business cycle, in the sense of reducing fluctuations in output and employment, while the twentieth century response does not.[1] Once again, a simple Cambridge model shows an extreme version of this. That is, autonomous changes in effective demand are met by offsetting changes in real consumption, with no net effect on output. A simple Kaleckian model shows another extreme, with consumption and autonomous demand moving in the same direction, with prices (relative to wages) unchanged. Third, the cause of the difference is a shift from an economy dominated by craft production to one dominated by mass production.

This chapter attempts to establish the first of these propositions for the US economy, by looking at the cyclical responses of wages relative to prices in two periods, in a pre World War I OBC and a post World War II NBC.

The microfoundation of this is based on firm–product market behavior rather than on worker–labor market behavior. (Nell 1992, and Chapter 1 above; Majewski 1996). This product market and the Keynesian orientation suggest two ways of looking at the phenomena. The first is looking at the cyclical movement of product wages. Product wages are money wages deflated by a producer price or wholesale price index. They are commonly used for looking at the wage from the producers' point of view rather than the workers'. In the OBC product wages should be clearly counter-cyclical, prices rising relative to wages in an expanding economy and falling in a contracting one. In the NBC this movement should be weaker, non-existent or perhaps even pro-cyclical.

The second approach is to look at the Keynesian price elasticity of effective demand. Keynes in his theory of the price level (chapters 20–1 of the *General Theory*) argues that the price level's response to changes in effective demand depends on the response of money wages, and the response of output. He sums up these responses in two elasticities, e_p and e_x, namely the price and output elasticities of effective demand.

While there are several ways of deriving these elasticities, I will follow the simple method used by Keynes himself.[2] Starting with real GNP X, the price level P and nominal GNP Y

$$Y = PX$$

dividing through by the wage unit w

$$Y = PX$$

where Y = nominal GNP in wage units, or Y/w and P = the price level in wage units, or P/w.
Therefore

$$dY = dPX + dXP$$

Through some simple manipulations

$$1 = (dP/dY)(Y/P) + (dX/dY)(Y/X)$$

or

$$1 = e_p + e_x$$

where $e_p = (dP/dY)(Y/P)$ and $e_x = (dX/dY)(Y/X)$ In a simple Cambridge model $e_p = 1$ $e_x = 0$ and in the Keynesian cross or simple Kaleckian model $e_p = e_x = 1$. Keynes himself expected both elasticities to be positive. From the transformational growth point of view we expect a difference between the two periods with $e_p$obc > $e_p$nbc, the price elasticity for the OBC being greater than the price elasticity of the NBC.

Having established the nature of the differences, we will attempt to estimate these relationships, starting with the product wage.

PRODUCT WAGES

To look at the cyclical nature of product wages we will need a cyclical indicator, money wage series and producer price series. For cyclical indicators I've chosen real GNP and an index of material production, for money wages, manufacturing wages, and for producer prices, broad wholesale price and producer price indices. The series used are the product of a number of compromises, involving extent, validity and comparability of data.[3] These will be discussed in the final section of the chapter.[4] Because of these problems multiple series were used for the OBC, to assure us that the results are not the product of a specific series construction. All series used were logged annual series. Dating of the OBC and NBC is at this point very rough and ready.[5] However looking at the years 1869–1907 for the old and 1947–82 for the new should give us a good idea of behavior in each period.

Simple inspection of the data shows powerful trends in the series. We are interested in the cyclical relationship between the two series. Hence it is necessary to separate the cycle from the trend in each series. Based on recent studies, there are good reasons to suspect that the real GNP, total material product and product wage series will be difference–stationary (see Nelson and Plosser 1982). To confirm the suspicion, Pierce's (1975) procedure was used. In several cases the results were inconclusive. This is not surprising, given the short length of the series. To deal with this Schwert's (1987) procedure was used. All series were difference–stationary. They were stationary after first differencing.

To test for difference between the two periods a simple regression was run:

$$V \log w/p = a + b \, V \log(\text{cyc}) + c \, V \log \text{D(cyc)} + u$$

where V is the difference operator, D is a dummy variable equal to 0 for the OBC and 1 for the new and cyc is a cyclical indicator. A difference between the two periods would be indicated by the c coefficient being significant. The relationship between product wages and real income that we are interested in is indicated for the OBC by the b coefficients. In the new business cycle they can be found by calculating:

$$g = b + c$$

Table 7.1 Cyclicality of product wages

DEP. VAR.	w/p Douglas	w/p Douglas	w/p Douglas	w/p Hanes	w/p Hanes	w/p Hanes
Constant	0.006	0.007	0.007	0.007	0.006	0.007
	(2.054)	(2.205)	(3.152)	(2.508)	(1.966)	(3.10)
GNP	0.052			−0.065		
Gordon	(0.343)			(−0.432)		
GNP		−0.018			0.012	
Romer		(−0.104)			(0.071)	
TMP			−0.046			−0.057
Frickey			(−0.674)			(−0.08)
dum * GNP	0.099	0.109		0.106	0.094	
	(4.215)	(4.137)		(4.511)	(3.551)	
dum * TMP			0.129			0.119
			(9.309)			(8.59)
r²	0.81	0.81	0.81	0.77	0.77	0.77
DW	1.809	1.833	1.88	1.89	1.86	1.92
NEW CYCLE	0.151	0.091	0.082	0.040	0.106	0.061

On the basis of the Transformational Growth hypothesis we would expect b to be less than zero and c to be greater than zero. While the sign of g is ambiguous, we would expect $c < g$.

The regressions have some common results. In all cases the c coefficients are significant. This indicates a difference in the behavior of product wages between the OBC and NBC. The c coefficients are all positive, which is consistent with the expectation that the NBC will be less countercyclical than the OBC. Indeed the g coefficients indicate that product wages are procyclical in the NBC. The b coefficients of output in the OBC are the problem in these results. While they are negative in most cases, in all cases they are not statistically significant. The predicted countercyclicality of product wages during the OBC cannot be established. We can conclude that product wages move differently in the two periods and are less procyclical in the OBC than in the NBC. These results are robust. They are found not only for alternative series, but also for alternative specifications of the regression (Majewski 1996).

However, there are some problems with the data that must be addressed before we can have confidence in this conclusion. These are considered in the final section of the chapter.

ESTIMATING THE PRICE ELASTICITY OF EFFECTIVE DEMAND

To estimate the price elasticity of effective demand money wage, nominal GNP and price level series were used.[6] Once again multiple series were used for the OBC. Econometric procedures were similar to those above. It was determined that the series were difference stationary and that first-differencing was required. The following equation was estimated:

$$V \log P = \alpha + \beta \, V \log Y + \gamma \, V \log DY + u$$

remembering that P and Y are the price level and GNP in wage units.
  The coefficient β is the partial derivative:

$$\frac{\delta \ln \bar{V} P}{\delta \ln \bar{V} Y}$$

Since it is the derivative of logs it is roughly the price elasticity of the OBC. As in the previous section, differences in price elasticities between the OBC and NBC will be indicated by the significance of the γ. The NBC's price elasticity can be calculated:

$$\Phi = \beta + \gamma$$

It is expected that $\beta < \Phi$. Results are reported in Table 7.2.

Table 7.2 Price elasticity of effective demand

DEP. VAR	P GORDON DOUGLAS	P ROMER DOUGLAS	P GORDON HANES	P ROMER HANES
CONSTANT	−0.008 (−9.257)	−0.009 (−8.305)	−0.008 (−7.818)	−0.009 (−8.011)
Y GORDON DOUGLAS	0.261 (5.74)			
Y ROMER DOUGLAS		0.379 (6.028)		
Y GORDON HANES			0.238 (4.517)	
Y ROMER HANES				0.405 (6.320)
DUM * Y	−0.130 (−23.914)	−0.142 (−26.375)	−0.130 (−23.941)	−0.136 (−21.783)
r²	0.94	0.94	0.93	0.92
DW	1.61	1.91	1.85	1.79
NEW CYCLE	0.107	0.141	0.237	0.269

Looking at the results, all of the γ coefficients are significant. This shows that there is a difference in the price elasticities of effective demand between the two periods. If we look at the β and Φ coefficients, the price elasticities are positive for both periods, but the elasticity of the NBC is lower than that of the OBC ($\Phi < \beta$). Roughly this implies that a 1 per cent increase in effective demand (here nominal GNP in wage units) is associated with a 0.26 per cent to 0.40 per cent increase in prices (relative to wages) in the OBC and an 0.13 per cent to 0.27 per cent increase in prices in the new.[7] This means that output adjustments are more important in the NBC than in the old. Such a difference is consistent with the Transformational Growth hypotheses.

INTERPRETING THE RESULTS

So far the analysis supports the theoretical expectation. But in any empirical work it is necessary to assess the quality and comparability of the data being used. This is especially true for historical studies. In assessing quality we are looking at the validity, extent and reliability of data. In assessing comparability we want to be sure that series are constructed in similar ways, from similar sources of data. (see Chapter 2 above) Unfortunately, there are significant quality problems with the old business cycle data, related mostly to extent but also to validity. Further, there are significant problems of comparability within the OBC series and between them and their NBC equivalents. This will make the interpretation of results complex.

We will examine the evidence in more detail, beginning with GNP. There are three nineteenth-century GNP series in common use, that of Kuznets (1961), which was refined by Gallman (1966), Romer's (1989) series, and Balke and Gordon's (1989) series. Of these Kuznets–Gallman is the original and the foundation of the others.

Before 1913, when income tax records became available, calculating GNP in the usual manner from the income side is impossible. Most pre-1919 and all pre-1909 estimates are based on outputs.[8] The manufacturing census conducted by the US government every ten years offered reasonably detailed information on the size and composition of output. Kuznets used this information to construct benchmarks. As representative of trend these figures are as good as we are likely to get.[9]

To create the annual series, "the components of these benchmark figures were interpolated for intercensal years on changes index drawn up from less comprehensive data" (Gallman 1966: 25). In constructing this index Kuznets is using a commodity output series that does a good job representing mining, agriculture and parts of manufacturing. Because he has no adequate series of consumer prices, output is valued at producer prices. This means that value added from distribution and transportation activities is unrepresented, as are other service activities. There was no way to fill this in using available data. Kuznets assumed that a relationship he observed between the commodity index and GNP for 1919–38, when he had income-based GNP estimates, held for previous years. In other words, because the data were not extensive enough, Kuznets was forced to construct a series in a different way from later GNP series.

Few have questioned the validity of this series for issues involving growth, but Romer (1986, 1989) has questioned its validity for studying the cycle. She argues the use of data from the Great Depression leads to excessive volatility in the pre World War I series. She attempts to correct this using Kuznet's method, but excluding the years of the Great Depression and including post-World War II data. From the Transformational Growth point of view this is unattractive, since we expect differences in economic behavior in the post-war years. Balke and Gordon (1989) offer a third GNP series, constructed using somewhat different methods from roughly the same years as Kuznets. It is the most attractive of the three series. I have chosen to use both Romer and Balke and Gordon. It is clear that they are different from the Commerce Department series used for the NBC. But it does not appear that the difference should systematically affect our results.

The same is not true of the nominal GNP or implicit price deflator series. Their construction seems to overstate OBC nominal GNP and price level movements. The culprit here is once again the lack of consumer price and income data. In contemporary GNP series nominal GNP can be estimated either from income data or from production data at final prices. To get real GNP the production version is deflated using price indices of which the CPI and the PPI are the most important. The implicit price deflator is the average of these price indices weighted by the composition of GNP in the current period.

In the OBC production data at producer prices are the starting point. Deflated and corrected to get real GNP and than inflated to get nominal GNP. Limited consumer price information is used in this process, but on the whole producer prices are used much more extensively than in the contemporary series (Romer 1989). Since producer prices are more volatile than consumer prices (in the OBC too) this would overstate price level movement and the movement of nominal relative to real GNP.

To deal with some of the weaknesses in the GNP series an alternative cyclical indicator was used for the product wage tests. It was a linked version of the Frickey (1947) and FRB (1986) indices of material production. Both of these indices are based on physical output measures. The Frickey index covers the OBC. During this period few data points were collected on consumer and other finished goods. The series is based on the output of materials, like paper, lumber, zinc, that go on for further processing. Final products are mostly transport vehicles and goods subject to excise tax such as cigarettes and liquor. Hence it is more like a materials production series than an industrial production series (Romer 1986). The Fed's material production index contains no final products, but is close enough to be used for comparison. As a cyclical indicator there is a problem. The FRB materials production index is more volatile, than its industrial production index. It therefore may overstate cyclical movements. This is usually attributed to the pro-cyclical nature of material inventories (FRB 1986; Romer 1986). Whether this is also true for the OBC is a matter of speculation. Wholesale prices are the best data available for the OBC. The most commonly used price series for this period is the wholesale price series of Warren and Pearson (1932). In actuality it is not a single series but two. Warren and Pearson's own nineteenth-century series was designed to correspond with and was linked with the wholesale price series of the Bureau of Labor Statistics that starts in 1890. The BLS series covers a wider variety of commodities and we know much more about the underlying sources of its data. Warren and Pearson do not describe how their prices were observed (Hanes 1992: 273). The series are less extensive in terms of both commodities and locations covered than the NBC producer price index. Because we know less about collection methods, we are uncertain whether we are seeing list or transaction prices. Examination of some of the underlying sources such as the Aldrich Report (Aldrich 1892) and *Shipping and Commercial Lists and New York Prices Current* suggest that we are seeing both. The major reason to suspect a systematic problem is the overrepresentation of primary goods. This may lead to excess volatility in the series.

Money wages are more of a problem. Collection here is more sporadic than with wholesale prices. There are several major changes in sources, methods and the extent of the data within the OBC series. The data are dramatically less extensive than the modern BLS series, particularly outside of census years. Since they are concentrated in manufacturing, I've chosen to compare them with the contemporary BLS manufacturing wage series. Systematic problems are unclear, but the data are so limited that it has been suggested that the results are biased by the specific characteristics of the industries involved. Douglas (1930) and Long (1960) are linked versions of commonly used manufacturing series. Hanes (1992) is a series constructed from the same industries and occupations for its whole length, but it is very narrow.

This gives us two specific problems and one general one for the interpretation of results. The specific problems are in the OBC's implicit price deflator's overstatement of price level movements and the Frickey/ FRB material production indices' overstatement of cyclical movement. The general problem is comparability. All our OBC series are constructed differently from the NBC series. This may impact upon our results but in unknown ways.

The specific problems are easier to deal with. For the problem of the implicit price deflator, consider the results found in Table 7.2 especially the *b* coefficient, which is the price elasticity to effective demand for the OBC. Romer's series, whose construction de-emphasizes the difference between the OBC and NBC, has a higher price elasticity than Balke and Gordon's series. It provides stronger support for the Transformational Growth hypothesis than the other series. We still have a problem with the implicit price deflator, but we do not need to throw our results away on the basis of it.

For the materials production index, compare the results in Tables 7.1 and 7.2. For the issues under consideration here the different cyclical indicators produce similar results. Unless the Romer GNP series is also excessively volatile, it is not likely that excess volatility is the source of the favorable results.

The general problem is more troublesome. The problem of comparability is most severe in the case of the money wage series. Examination of the *b* and *e* coefficients in Table 7.2 shows that changing the wage series has relatively little effect on elasticities to effective demand. The effect on the coefficients of the cyclical wage tests (Table 7.1 and 7.2) are somewhat larger, but still not very important. Changing the GNP series or the cyclical indicator affects the coefficients more dramatically. But the key point is that series constructed in different ways still yield results consistent with the Transformational Growth hypothesis.

Yet the comparability problem has not been eliminated. Even so the agreement of multiple tests suggest it is not the sole source of our results.

CONCLUSION

This chapter began with the idea that there was a difference in the way the economy responds to changes in effective demand between the OBC and NBC. In the OBC price changes (relative to money wages) play a larger role than in the NBC. The implication is that output (and perhaps employment) changes are more important in the NBC.

The results support this. They are also supportive of the Post-Keynesian perspective more generally. The OBC elasticity is what one would expect from a reading of the *General Theory*. Keynes's aggregate supply and demand model would be quite consistent with what is found here. Later post-Keynesians have tended to de-emphasize these price movements. For the post-war American economy this de-emphasis seems to be well taken.

NOTES

1 This assertion does not mean that the OBC is less severe than the NBC. In the twentieth century large government and changes in the financial system acted as stabilizing mechanisms especially in the period after World War II. In the OBC the financial system was de-stabilizing, especially in the American case.

2 Paul Wells (1960) derives these elasticities from the Keynes' aggregate supply function. His model produces results consistent with the OBC. Sidney Weintraub (1971) provides an alternative Post Keynesian treatment. The elasticities are estimated for the 1949–70 period. These two approaches are adapted to Transformational Growth and the OBC and NBC explicitly modeled in Majewski (1996).

3 For the OBC Romer's (1989), Balke and Gordon's (1989) GNP series and Frickey's (1947) material production series were used as cyclical indicators. Hanes's, (1992) and a linked version of Douglas (1930) and Long's (1960) money wage series deflated by Warren and Pearson's wholesale price series were used for product wages. For the NBC the Commerce Department's (1983) GNP and the Federal Reserve Board's (1986) materials production index were used for cyclical indicators. Hanes's (1995) and the BLS's (1991) hourly earnings in manufacturing series deflated by the BLS (1991) producer price index were used for product wages. To study both periods the various series were linked: Romer to Commerce Department, Balke and Gordon to Commerce Department, Frickey to FRB, Douglas and Long to BLS, wholesale price index to producer price index. The Hanes series is continuous for both periods. The linked series are referred to by their old business cycle component.

4 The microfoundations of Transformational Growth focus on the manufacturing sector of the economy. It is asserted that the production characteristics of mass production are the source of a change in product wage movements between the two periods. It is here, rather than in services or agriculture, that mass production is most important. It is also asserted that these and other changes should lead to changes beyond that manufacturing sector. Hence it is possible to test the hypothesis by looking at the manufacturing sector in isolation or the aggregate economy. I've chosen the latter approach largely because of the limitations in producer price data from the nineteenth century.

5 The story of craft and mass production is not a simple matter of one type of production process replacing the other. Since the second third of the nineteenth century they have coexisted. Sometimes the techniques are competitive, mass-produced cigarettes replacing craft-produced ones. Sometimes they are complementary, as in the relationship between a mass production automotive industry and a craft machine tool industry. In some cases the two techniques coexist within segments of the same industry, such as mass produced textiles and a specialized craft produced fine textile segment. The point is that they are difficult to pick out from aggregate data. Establishing their relative proportions will require some rather fine work, perhaps using the manufacturing census, that has not yet been done. Without this it is difficult to date NBC and OBC properly.

6 For the OBC, Romer's and Balke and Gordon's nominal GNP series and implicit price deflator series were used. They were deflated by the Douglas and Long and Hanes money wage series. In the NBC the Commerce Department's nominal GNP and price deflator series were deflated by the Hanes and BLS hourly earnings in manufacturing series. As above combined series are referred to by their OBC components. For citations see note 3.

7 Since $1 - e_p = e_x$ this implies an output elasticity of between 0.7 and 0.58 for the OBC and 0.83 and 72 for the NBC.

8 The Sixteenth Amendment, which allowed the federal income tax, was not ratified until February 1913. Pre-1919 income data is spotty. Kuznets generates estimates of GNP from the income side for the period 1909–19 but he considers these estimates unreliable and inferior to output-based GNP series. Balke and Gordon concur in this view, but Romer includes these estimates in her series.

9 Even the trend is not without its problems. The quality of the 1869 manufacturing census is somewhat in doubt, leading to the possibility of an overstatement of trend in the 1870s. See Friedman and Schwartz (1982: 99).

8

PRICE *v.* OUTPUT ADJUSTMENTS

The changing nature of the business cycle in Germany, 1871–1989

Thorsten H. Block

> I wish to propose for the reader's favourable consideration a doctrine which may, I fear, appear wildly paradoxical and subversive. The doctrine in question is this: that it is undesirable to believe a proposition when there is no ground whatever for supposing it true.
>
> (Bertrand Russell)

INTRODUCTION
TECHNOLOGY, SHOCKS AND FLUCTUATIONS

Economic growth over the last 125 years has been accompanied by vast changes in the institutional framework of market relationships. These changes range from the structure of the macroeconomy and the role of the state to the characteristics of technology and the organization of business. Conventional approaches to economic organization and the allocation of resources, however, are fundamentally based on the choices of utility-maximizing individuals and disregard the role of market institutions. Following the theory of Transformational Growth it will be argued in this chapter that institutional and technological change is pivotal for understanding macroeconomic behavior. For the case of Germany it will be shown that business cycle adjustments are indeed fundamentally different if one compares the post-World War II period with the last half of the nineteenth century.

Recent developments in equilibrium business cycle theory provide a good example of the lack of institutional grounding of mainstream economic theory. Real Business Cycle (RBC) theory is a variant of equilibrium business cycle theory in which cycles are the result of exogenous shocks.[1] These shocks shift production functions up or down and thereby drive the cycle. The impact of shocks on output is amplified by intertemporal substitution of leisure – a rise in productivity raises the cost of leisure, causing employment to increase. However, models based on these core propositions are not able to replicate the behavior of certain key variables. First, the model overpredicts the correlation between productivity and output. This is due to the fact that RBC models have to assume a high volatility in productivity (shocks) in order to generate sufficient volatility in output. In other words, RBC models are calibrated in such a way as to replicate the cyclical behavior of output but have to assume a productivity series that is not at all what is observed in reality. In fact, productivity tends to be only mildly procyclical or to exhibit no cyclicality at all (Stadler 1994). Second, the model underpredicts the variability of employment measured in hours worked. The dilemma is that micro-studies usually find the elasticity of labor supply to be too weak to generate the employment volatility observed in advanced economies. With elasticities being weak, productivity shocks should be largely reflected in strong real wage procyclicality but real wages tend to be only mildly procyclical. It is therefore not surprising that "while Real Business Cycle models can generate cycles, these are, as a general rule, not like the cycles observed" (Stadler 1994: 1751).

One of the problems with the RBC approach is its underlying concept of technology. In equilibrium cycle models – and indeed in most neo-classical models – technology is exogenous and represented by a production function. A technology shock is simply an upward or downward shift of this function. There are several problems with this conception of technology in explaining business cycles. Calomiris and Hanes (1994) show that in a historical perspective this view of technology is untenable as an explanation of recessions. The RBC school is, for example, unable to explain a phenomenon like the Great Depression because "[T]echnological regress does not appear to correspond to any event in Western economic history since the fall of the Roman Empire" (p. 21). Furthermore, a closer look at the history of technological innovations reveals the diffusion process is too slow to generate sufficiently large short-run productivity shifts needed in RBC models in order to explain the cycle.[2]

In addition, there is no reason to assume that technology shocks changed in nature or magnitude to account for changes in business cycle behavior. Finally, and especially relevant to our analysis, this approach is unable to provide an explanation for changes in business cycle patterns because cyclical fluctuations are derived from the representative agent's optimizing behavior, which is assumed to be universal across historical periods.

For the purpose of studying the behavior of macroeconomic variables over the business cycle it seems to be more fruitful to adopt a theoretical framework with a historical and institutional grounding than one that stretches marginal productivity theory to explain macroeconomic fluctuations and thereby has to rely on arbitrary external shocks. The theory of Transformational Growth states that the evolution of technology and institutions changes the structure of the economy in ways that influence the working of markets, particularly macroeconomic adjustment over the business cycle (Nell 1992).[3] In this framework decision-making on the micro-level is not based on marginal productivity theory (Nell 1992). Firms are still optimizing and profit-seeking but it is emphasized that they act within specific constraints set by the character of technology. Decisions are made within a complex business environment and cannot be adequately understood within a representative agent/firm approach. A similar critique of neoclassical microfoundations as a basis of macroeconomic analysis is made by Taylor (1991: 10-11):

> Agents may well behave sensibly or with rational intent within their particular bottles – or bottlenecks – of feasible choice, but the first thing to get clear is just how much freedom they deploy. . . . the neoclassical focus is always on dynamic optimizations subject to given constraints (budget constraints, production function), rather than historical analysis of how the constraints affect macro equilibrium subject to plausible closure assumptions, as they themselves change over time.

The Transformational Growth perspective rejects a "black box" characterization of technology and instead adopts the broader view of technology as an institutional system. Technological change is not simply a sudden shift in an abstract function but the slow qualitative change in the process of production as it relates to production techniques and the organization of business. From this perspective incremental quantitative changes can eventually translate into an economy-wide regime shift. This shift from craft and to mass production cannot adequately be described as the change from batch to assembly production but needs to be understood as an endogenously driven transformation of the institutions of capitalism, with implications for micro-decisions as well as macro-outcomes (see Chapter 1 of this volume). It tries to show how business strategy is shaped by technological options and constraints and how this in turn affects the workings of markets and the macroeconomy.

According to the theory of Transformational Growth the key constraint firms face in the pre-World War I period, the old business cycle (OBC), is the inflexibility of the craft production system, so that output and employment can be adjusted only in a very limited way to changes in aggregate demand. Therefore prices have to be varied to clear the market. In contrast, mass production technology in the post-war period, the new business cycle (NBC), is designed to vary output/employment with sales. Hence prices can be set with a view to long-term strategic considerations and kept stable thereafter.

Preliminary studies of the UK and the US economies have found supportive evidence for the hypothesized change in the behavior of prices, output and employment over time (Sylos-Labini 1993). The purpose of this chapter is to provide an analysis of the changing characteristics of the business cycle for the case of Germany in order to investigate further the claims of the theory of Transformational Growth. This will entail a critical evaluation of and comparison with the RBC school, especially as regards its inability to account for changes in the cyclical behavior of output, employment and productivity.

The analysis will be presented in the following way. First, we will outline the main transformations of the German economy as they relate to technology and the business enterprise. At the center of the analysis will be the shift to a mass-production economy that has taken place in the inter-war years. Second, stylized facts for the periods of the OBC and the NBC will be presented, with the emphasis on volatility and covariation. This section also contains a brief description of the German data and the sources used. Third, the hypothesized structural changes in the cyclical behavior of prices and real product wages will be formally tested, using simple econometric techniques. Fourth, some implications for the construction of (historical) macroeconomic models are put forth, together with preliminary empirical results analyzing the change in the relationship between consumption and investment. In the last section our findings are summarized and some implications for further research will be suggested.

TRANSFORMATIONS OF THE GERMAN ECONOMY

The purpose of this section is to sketch the transition of the German economy from a craft to a mass-production system. In particular, the focus will be on the interaction between the evolution of technology and the organization of business. The founding of the German Reich in 1871 is the starting point of most historical accounts of Germany's rapid ascent to the rank of the foremost industrial power on the European continent. Stolper (1967) notes that, though industrialization and a certain growth dynamic started earlier (in Prussia), unification created a large area free of trade barriers, and brought with it the emergence of a unified State with a single currency. In the subsequent years other institutions of modern market economies like a central bank (the Reichsbank in 1875) and a system of technical education were created. Furthermore, a unified legal framework was established, as was a modern banking sector.

In the 1880s the evolution of the multi-divisional firm from small craft shops begins but is largely confined to the so-called "Great Industries" – chemicals, metals and machinery including electrical machinery (Chandler 1990). Fischer (1976), however, notes that small-scale craft production maintained a considerable share of output and employment (see also Ritter and Tenfelde 1992: 276). Table 8.1 gives an indication of the change in the size of establishments for the years in which surveys are available. The data show that there is indeed a shift towards larger production units in the period between 1882 and 1925. The share of employees in establishments of more than fifty increases two and a half times to just over 54 per cent of total employment. However, small-scale manufacturing in establishments with fewer than five employees retains a share of 31 per cent and 22 per cent of total employment in 1907 and 1925 respectively. Establishments with fewer than fifty employees thus still account for almost two-thirds of employment just before World War I and 45 per cent in 1925. The size of businesses can give only an indication of the adoption of mass-production technologies. Craft methods might still be dominant even in larger production units at the same time as small companies with fifty workers restructure the work process from batch to continuous flow production. In general, the adoption of mass-production methods, however, requires larger units to reap economies of scale. It is not before the late 1920s that oligopolistic market structures emerge in most sectors and that mass production dominates on the national level.[4]

In Germany unique organizational arrangements emerged to deal with

Table 8.1 Size of business in German industry, 1882–1925

| Year | No. of employees | | | | | |
| | 1–5 | | 6–50 | | >50 | |
	No of establishments in % of total	No of employees in % of total	No of establishments in % of total	No of employees in % of total	No of establishments in % of total	No of employees in % of total
1882	95.9	59.8	3.7	17.4	0.4	22.8
1895	92.8	41.8	6.5	24.7	0.8	33.5
1907	89.8	31.2	8.9	26.4	1.3	42.4
1925	87.1	22.3	11.1	22.9	1.8	54.8

Source: Fischer (1976).

the uncertainty and volatility of capitalist production in this period. Contrary to the United States, cartels were not only legal but even encouraged by the government. The growing cartelization in German industry is in some sense an outgrowth of the cyclical pattern of growth. Stolper (1967: 47) writes that "whenever prices tended to drop below costs, cartels were organized in order to keep businesses 'in the black'."[5] This is also supported by Maschke's (1969: 235) finding that "where cartels had been formed during cyclical depressions as 'children of bad times', entrepreneurs not infrequently reverted to free competition during the upswing." It is apparent from the above statements that the downward flexibility of prices seems to have been a major problem for companies during this phase of industrialization and that cartels were formed to stabilize returns (Chandler 1990: 501).

The State had already played an important role during this period, especially as compared with its role in Britain and the United States. One characteristic of the State's role has been the increasing public ownership of railroads. While only slightly less than half of the German railroad system was state-owned in 1875, it was almost entirely nationalized by 1912 (Borchardt 1976: 144). Similarly, the rise of a Welfare State was initiated early, mainly as a response to the increasing strength of the Social Democratic Party (the largest socialist party in the world at the time). Different laws covering health, accident, old age and disability insurance were enacted during the 1880s. However, state expenditure as a percentage of total product remained low compared with post-war levels. Andic and Veverka (1963/4), for example, estimate the share of government expenditure in GNP at 10 per cent in 1882, rising to 17.7 per cent in 1913. Despite state efforts in the area of social insurance, state expenditure in that area amounted to only 0.3 per cent of GNP in 1885, increasing to a still relatively low share of 1.8 per cent in 1913. In fact the nature of the State in this phase of capitalist development in Germany is best described as "developmental". The State protected and nurtured infant industries and invested heavily in infrastructure. However, the State did not exhibit "Keynesian" features – consistent macroeconomic management through fiscal and monetary policies – before the post-war period.

The growing organization of business and labor is another feature of German development in the pre-war period, eventually transforming labor market mechanisms. We have mentioned earlier that cartels increased in number and scope to become a characteristic element of German industrial organization in response to the uncertainties of capitalist production. At the same time labor unions struggled to increase membership and political influence in spite of the anti-socialist laws which lasted until 1890. However, the negotiating strength of the trade unions did not affect money wages until the end of the century (Borchardt 1991).[6] This is confirmed by the observation that until around 1900 wages were simply set by the employers every week or month and then posted on the factory bulletin board (Ritter and Tenfelde 1992: 355). The unions had no more than 330,000 members in 1891, and until 1895 their freedom of industrial action was severely constrained, owing to persecution by the government and to the attitude of employers. Up to 1913 the number of trade union members increased to over 3 million, or about 11 per cent of the work force and 30 per cent of all industrial workers. By that time the Social Democratic Party, which was associated with the Free Unions, the most influential union organization (2.5 million members in 1913), had become a major political force.

As mentioned earlier, the transition to a modern mass-production economy accelerated in the inter-war period and especially during the late 1920s. This period has often been described as that of the great rationalization movement in German industry (Brady 1933; National Industry Conference Board 1931).[7] After the war many German businesses were struggling to recover from wartime destruction and the loss of foreign markets. Furthermore, the hyperinflation of the early 1920s created enormous uncertainty and volatility. The immediate response was to create IGs (communities of interest) or *Konzerne* (National Industry Conference Board 1931). These forms of cooperation had the advantage of being less costly, less permanent and more flexible than mergers. Only after the economy had stabilized in the mid-1920s did mergers become the dominant form of reorganization (Chandler 1990: 512). All of these forms of concentration, however, had the purpose of strengthening the competitive position by enhancing specialization of plant and machinery and by encouraging diversification into related markets.

Concentration and the introduction of mass-production technologies are related processes. The processes are accompanied by increasing efforts to standardize products and production processes. Specialization and routinization are essential prerequisites for the introduction of assembly production. The smooth functioning of mechanically regulated mass-production methods would otherwise not be possible. The move towards standardization in Germany, while present even before World War I, accelerated only after the war. Starting in 1917, several commissions (like the Deutscher Normenausschuss) were founded and thousands of basic and industry standards established (Brady 1933).[8]

The process of electrification plays a crucial role in the adoption of scientific mass production and provides an interesting case study of the relationship between technical change and the organization of production. The availability of alternating current and the rapid innovations in electrical machinery played an important role in the introduction of flow production. Experiments in the early 1890s had proven that alternating current could be transmitted over long distances without significant voltage drop. This sparked innovative activity in the electrical equipment sector, in particular in the improvement of adjustable alternating current motors (Grabas 1992: 225). However, these innovations did not transform production processes before the war. Around the turn of the century less flexible gas and steam engines still dominated in the factories. Only after 1910 did electrical machinery driven by alternating current start to replace other forms of energy – a development that was accelerated by the war and the subsequent rationalization movement. Investment in electrical machinery increased by 21.3 per cent annually in the five years before World War I and the use of alternating current in factories quadrupled in the period 1907–13 (Grabas 1992: 250–7). This account of the slow adoption of electric power serves to confirm the superior characterization of technology in Transformational Growth compared with RBC models discussed above. Any one improvement in the process of electrification would have been insufficient to cause productivity surges of the type that drive RBC models. However, over time this specific type of technological change had a profound impact on the efficiency and organization of production.

Several authors have pointed to the increased flexibility of the production process due to the introduction of electricity and electrical machinery. Brady (1933: 225) describes the advantages of electric power in the following way: "The efficiency requirement of smooth, uninterrupted, and continuous flow of materials, parts, and processes, and of perfect adaptability of volumetric change at any point with volumetric change at all other points is met in the ideal form by electric energy." In addition, Landes (1969: 282) emphasizes the possibility of adjusting cost to output: "The user can also draw precisely the amount of power needed, large or small, and can change it when necessary without time-consuming adjustments or sacrifice of efficiency. And he pays for what he uses." Finally, Hughes (1983), in his excellent analysis of the electrification of Germany, concludes: "Rationalization was much discussed in the 1920s . . . As applied to industry in general, the concept was decidedly influenced by developments in electric supply" (p. 368). Interestingly, the electrical equipment industry is a good example of an oligopolistic sector slowly adopting mass-production organization. Within the individual plants flow production was introduced in nearly all manufacturing operations of a repetitive, automatic or semi-automatic, and standardized character. Describing this process for the case of ELMO works – a producer of electric motors and part of Siemens – Brady (1933: 176) writes:

> All machine tools and apparatus are arranged as required by the natural progress of manufacture, all work-places are connected by suitable transport devices, as, for instance, an endless conveyor with hooks and buckets running through three stories for a

distance of 500 yards. The semi-finished parts are assembled on a long bench the platform of which moves forward at definite intervals from one operative to the next, after which the completed machines pass through the testing station, are painted, pass through a 33 ft. drying stove and are finally delivered either to the packers or the stores.

In summary, innovations in electrical supply combined with improvements in electrical machinery provided a crucial prerequisite for the introduction of mass-production technology in the inter-war period. Transformational Growth focuses on the advantage of mass-production technology in flexibly adjusting to fluctuations in sales. This brief analysis has supported the claim with specific reference to the nature of electric power.

It should be noted, however, that the reorganization of the production process was by no means uniform across industries. In the engineering industry, for example, the prevalence of customized production and smaller production units slowed the adoption of serial or flow production as well as the introduction of scientific management practices (Brady 1933: 155–62). The situation is similar in Chandler's (1990: 514–19) "Lesser Industries," including textiles and branded, packaged products. The most dynamic sectors, however, had fully adopted modern technologies and forms of organization by the mid-1930s, transforming the functioning and indeed the character of the entire system. To quote Brady (1933: 305): "A drop in output in any one stage tends to ramify immediately and in proportion throughout the entire system . . . . The system tends to move in a unit, instead of by pieces." And he concludes (p. 321)

> The period under review has been essentially transitional in character. In many branches the old competitive and unregulated capitalistic order has been definitely left behind, or so seriously modified in outline and in principle that it is fair to say that the Smithian system has been clearly abandoned.

Brady thus clearly recognizes the impact of the technological and organizational transformation of the system as a whole. Instead of the Smithian system of price competition the modern economy is characterized by multiplier adjustment processes made possible by the flexibility of output and employment on the level of the individual firm.

By 1945 economic life in Germany seemed to have come to a complete halt as a result of the devastation of World War II. During the 1950s, however, in the period of the so-called *Wirtschaftswunder*, economic growth rates in the Federal Republic were spectacular, among the highest in the world at some 8 per cent per annum. By 1960 unemployment had been

207

reduced to less than 1 per cent, inflation was low, the current account showed a continuous surplus and the country's share in world exports of manufactures nearly trebled.

The economic doctrine and policy during the 1950s and 1960s became known as a "social market economy," which is a mixture of liberal *laissez-faire*, on the one hand, and of state intervention to correct income inequalities through various tax measures and social policies, on the other. However, as Braun (1990) has pointed out, in reality economic policies very much resembled Keynesian anticyclical demand management.[9] The upswing of 1950, for example, was not only due to growing exports associated with the outbreak of the Korean War but also the result of economic policy measures, namely an employment and housing program. Downswings were also related to restrictive policy measures, as in 1961, when the revaluation of the Deutschmark and the curtailment of public building orders had contractive effects. Thus Keynesian policies were used well before the "Act to promote Economic Stability and Growth" (*Stabilitätsgesetz*) was passed in 1967. This law thus merely represented the retroactive legal codification of federal economic and financial policy-making and provided the government with additional tools to stabilize the economy. The increased role of the State is also reflected in the high state share of GDP throughout the post-war period. It rose from 33 per cent in 1960 to 46 per cent in 1990 and peaked at almost half of total output (49 per cent) in 1980 and was thus substantially larger than in the period up to World War I. Transfer payments and welfare expenditure now constitute a substantial portion of total expenditure.

With respect to the labor market, labor unions and collective bargaining are now fully legally and politically acknowledged. In fact, labor relations in the early post-war period were relatively peaceful, considering the strength of the union movement (almost half the labor force was unionized). There was a social consensus for a productivity-oriented wage policy that allowed real wages to rise in accordance with productivity advances. Furthermore, the structure of industry after the war was similar to the one that had emerged in the inter-war period. Although the Allied powers dismantled most of the big conglomerates, the oligopolistic nature of German industry was still essentially the same. In the chemical industry, for example, the large IG Farben was broken up but its dominant players, Hoechst, BASF and Bayer, re-emerged as the leading companies after the war, capturing a large share of the domestic market and becoming strong competitors internationally. In addition, the automobile industry – the quintessential mass-producer – joined the other "Great Industries" as the most dynamic sectors of the German economy in much the same way as it had done in the inter-war years in the United States.

The point of this section was to establish differences in the institutions and structural features of the German economy between two historical periods. In particular, we have focused on the transformation of Germany into a mass-production economy in the inter-war years as it relates to the process of technical change and the evolution of the firm. The response of the German industrial system to volatile prices and returns in the period before and shortly after World War I is different from the institutional response in the United States. German industrialists – supported by the government – preferred cartel arrangements in order to stabilize prices. Only after the economy had stabilized in the mid-1920s did mergers become the dominant form of restructuring, as was the case in the United States. It is only with this rationalization movement that the system as a whole is transformed into a mass-production system. The change was accompanied by the growth of the role of the State in terms of absorption of total product as well as increasing macroeconomic management. The system of collective bargaining and the multi-divisional firm that emerged in the early twentieth century have become dominant features of the post-war economy.

STYLIZED FACTS FOR THE GERMAN BUSINESS CYCLE

This section attempts to contribute a detailed empirical investigation of the changing nature of the business cycle. In particular, we will analyze the hypothesis that the period of the OBC was indeed characterized by macroeconomic adjustment through the price mechanism as compared with output adjustments in the NBC. In addition, our results will be used to evaluate the propositions of RBC theory.

The collection of stylized facts has become a common practice in business cycle analysis in order to provide a benchmark model against which different theories of the business cycle can be tested.[10] There is, however, no agreement on what constitutes an appropriate list of stylized facts. In fact it seems that researchers depending on the theoretical background construct their own "personal" set of stylized facts. This practice is of course subject to the criticism that empirical evidence is collected to fit the theoretical model in question (Tichy 1994). The approach adopted here is to direct attention to the validity of stylized facts for a particular historical period for a major capitalist country with an emphasis on the manufacturing sector.[11]

The two different historical periods are defined as follows. The period of the OBC extends from the founding of the German Reich in 1871 to 1913, the year before the beginning of World War I. The period of the NBC begins in 1950, one year after the creation of the Federal Republic of Germany, and ends with the fall of the Berlin Wall in 1989. Although boundaries and political systems are quite different between the two periods, there is relatively little change within the periods. Note, however, that the Federal Republic of Germany's population and territory are, of course, much smaller than those of the German Reich at the onset of World War I. Since our analysis is focusing on fluctuations at business cycle frequency it is justifiable to assume that the periods are appropriately defined for comparative purposes. The inter-war years are excluded for two reasons: (1) the reliability of data for that period is highly questionable as a result of the two wars and the hyperinflation in the early 1920s and (2) the period was identified earlier as the transitional phase to mass production, so that no clear patterns in terms of price and output movements can be expected.[12] Second, the focus of analysis is on the industrial sector as the most dynamic sector during both periods. Technical change has been pervasive in all three sectors of the economy but the transition from craft to mass production is most clearly associated with the industrial sector. Third, previous analyses of business cycle behavior in Germany have been very limited owing to the lack of appropriate data (see, for example, Kehoe and Backus 1992). One of the contributions of this work is thus also to provide a data set for nineteenth-century Germany that is comparable with the data available for the post-war period.

The collection of historical data for business cycle analysis is inherently difficult (see Chapter 2). Before the end of World War II there was no systematic and comprehensive collection of data in Germany. A comparative study of international business cycles concludes that German data for the nineteenth century are likely to be less reliable than US, UK or Swedish data (Backus and Kehoe 1992). Backus and Kehoe's German data, however, are based on data compendia and not on local sources. Most of the series used in this chapter are from German sources like the excellent and comprehensive work of W. G. Hoffmann and his collaborators, whose work was published in 1965.[13] This leads us to believe that our data are indeed superior to those used previously. For example, industrial output and employment series are both taken from Hoffmann *et al.* (1965). In order to ensure comparability across periods, only industrial activities are included. It should be noted, however, that the series used here are not perfectly compatible for the nineteenth century because the wage and price series include both construction and mining while the Hoffmann data exclude mining.

It was especially difficult to derive a producer price series that is compatible with the output and employment series. Furthermore, such a series should also be somewhat comparable with the producer price index for manufacturing and mining that was used for the post-war period. The problem is that wholesale price series for the nineteenth century are heavily weighted toward primary goods. In order to alleviate this problem we used the Jacobs–Richter wholesale price index and extracted only the data on industrial goods. The resulting series is still based largely on semi-manufactures rather than final manufactured products but excludes agricultural goods as well as other raw materials. Comparison with Hoffmann's index of investment goods, which is not reported here, showed that the cyclical character of both series is similar, in particular with respect to volatilities.

To test for the robustness of our findings two money wage series constructed by Bry and Desai were used, but Desai's series seems to be preferable, owing to its greater industry coverage, starting in 1887. Owing to the unavailability of hourly series for employment and wages in the OBC these had to be constructed, using Schröder's (1980) series of average hours worked per week. Schröder's study is a careful analysis of the development of work time until 1913 and allows us to account for the downward trend in the average work week. Moreover, it adds volatility to the employment and wage series, because the downward trend in work time is by no means uniform and was sometimes reversed in the early phases of the German Reich. All hourly series should, however, be regarded with caution. In what follows money and real wages are presented as hourly series, whereas employment and productivity are measured per worker as well as per hour.

In order to analyze business cycle fluctuations it is necessary to be able to differentiate between the cyclical and the trend components of a variable. In a study of the cyclical behavior of US GNP, Canova (1991) finds that different methods of detrending do indeed extract different business cycle components of time series. This result is confirmed in the excellent survey by Baxter and King (1994). Since these results show that there is no superior detrending method, this chapter will employ two different methods to test for the robustness of our results. On the one hand, first-differencing is used because of its ease of application as well as its widespread use in historical business cycle analysis. The Hodrick–Prescott filter, on the other hand, is frequently used in the empirical RBC literature and is selected here to allow us to compare our results directly with those studies.[14]

In the following the stylized facts presented in Chapter 1 will be taken as a guideline to analyze changes in the character of the business cycle in Germany. We will look at trends in both periods but pay particular attention to relative volatilities and cross-correlations among the key variables. The analysis is limited to the labor and product markets. In the OBC prices – producer prices as well as the cost-of-living index – exhibit virtually no trend over the whole period (Table 8.2). A closer look at the series reveals that prices were indeed falling until the 1890s and then rising. Money wages, on the other hand, are rising throughout, although the trend is steeper after the turn of the century. We should also note that the Desai wage series shows a slightly higher growth rate. In the post-war period the trend of both prices and money wages is strongly

Table 8.2 Properties of the first-differenced (1D) series

Variable	OBC (1872-1913)			NBC (1951-89)		
	Mean	SD	V	Mean	SD	V
GDP	0.0285	0.0216	0.758	0.0422	0.0295	0.699
Industrial production	0.0376	0.0380	1.011	0.0450	0.0490	1.089
Employment	0.0196	0.0187	0.954	0.0130	0.0412	3.169
Employment (hours)	0.0142	0.0173	1.218	−0.0014	0.0487	−34.79
Cost of living	0.0088	0.0328	3.727	0.0295	0.0203	0.688
Cost of Living (Desai)	0.0049	0.0318	6.490	. . .	. . .	. . .
Producer prices	0.00	0.0558	n.a.	. . .	. . .	. . .
Producer prices (industrial goods)	−0.0009	0.0755	−83.9	0.0276	0.0389	1.409
Money wages (Desai)	0.0249	0.0542	2.176	0.0681	0.0286	0.420
Money wages (Bry)	0.0222	0.0411	1.851	. . .	. . .	. . .
Real wages (Desai)	0.0200	0.0527	2.635	0.0386	0.0259	0.671
Real wages (Bry)	0.0134	0.0374	2.791	. . .	. . .	. . .
Product wages (Desai)	0.0259	0.0558	2.154	0.0405	0.0361	0.891
Product wages (Bry)	0.0232	0.0526	2.260	. . .	. . .	. . .
Productivity (worker)	0.0144	0.0303	2.104	0.0320	0.0253	0.791
Productivity (hour)	0.0199	0.0322	1.618	0.0464	0.0188	0.405

Sources: See Appendix 8.1.

Notes
SD Standard deviation, V Coefficient of variation (SD/mean).

upward; both price series are growing at an average annual rate of about 3 per cent, with money wages growing even faster, at almost 7 per cent per year. With respect to the volatilities of prices and money wages the different detrending methods show virtually the same results. It is clear from looking at the standard deviations in Tables 8.2–4 that prices as well as money wages are more volatile in the old period. This is the case in absolute terms as well as relative to the volatility of industrial production (reported only in Tables 8.3–4). Desai's money wage series exhibits slightly greater volatility than the Bry data. Another difference is that the standard deviation of producer prices relative to the standard deviation of money wages is slightly higher in the OBC than in the NBC. It should be added that the old period distinguishes itself from the post-war period through the downward mobility of prices and to a lesser extent of money wages. The cost-of-living index, for example, fell in roughly one-third of the years between 1871 and 1913 but only once (in 1988) in the post-war era.

In looking at the correlation coefficients of the detrended series – summarized in Table 8.5 – differences in the cyclical behavior of prices and money wages between the two periods are even more pronounced.[15] All price series in the OBC are strongly positively correlated with

Table 8.3 Volatility of HP10 detrended series

Variable	Standard deviation (SD)		SD relative to SD of industrial production	
	OBC	NBC	OBC	NBC
GDP	0.0142	0.0143	0.568	0.518
Industrial production	0.0250	0.0276	1	1
Employment	0.0149	0.0239	0.596	0.866
Employment (hours)	0.0219	0.0305	0.876	1.105
Cost of living	0.0236	0.0131	0.944	0.475
Cost of living (Desai)	0.0226	. . .	0.904	. . .
Producer prices	0.0432	. . .	1.728	. . .
Producer prices (industrial goods)	0.0568	0.0261	2.272	0.946
Money wages (Desai)	0.0397	0.0177	1.588	0.641
Money wages (Bry)	0.0306	. . .	1.224	. . .
Real wages (Desai)	0.0338	0.0146	1.352	0.529
Real wages (Bry)	0.0240	. . .	0.960	. . .
Product wages (Desai)	0.0391	0.0201	1.564	0.728
Product wages (Bry)	0.0377	. . .	1.508	. . .
Productivity (worker)	0.0176	0.0169	0.704	0.612
Productivity (hour)	0.0174	0.0106	0.696	0.384

Sources: See Appendix 8.1.

Table 8.4 Volatility of HP400 detrended series

Variable	Standard deviation (SD)		SD relative to SD of industrial production	
	OBC	NBC	OBC	NBC
GDP	0.0231	0.0244	0.529	0.584
Industrial production	0.0437	0.0418	1	1
Employment	0.0130	0.0394	0.297	0.942
Employment (hours)	0.0262	0.0483	0.599	1.155
Cost of living	0.0340	0.0284	0.778	0.679
Cost of living (Desai)	0.0316	. . .	0.723	. . .
Producer prices	0.0587	. . .	1.343	. . .
Producer prices (industrial goods)	0.0768	0.0449	1.757	1.074
Money wages (Desai)	0.0587	0.0350	1.343	0.837
Money wages (Bry)	0.0497	. . .	1.137	. . .
Real wages (Desai)	0.0465	0.0264	1.064	0.631
Real wages (Bry)	0.0388	. . .	0.888	. . .
Product wages (Desai)	0.0531	0.0369	1.215	0.882
Product wages (Bry)	0.0521	. . .	1.192	. . .
Productivity (worker)	0.0268	0.0224	0.613	0.536
Productivity (hour)	0.0288	0.0165	0.657	0.395

Sources: See Appendix 8.1.

Table 8.5 Covariation of HP10 detrended series

Variable	1	2	3	4	5	6	7	8	9	10	11	12
					OBC (1871–1913)							
1 GDP	1											
2 Industrial production	0.79	1										
3 Employment	0.23	0.51	1									
4 Employment (hours)	0.25	0.46	0.82	1								
5 Cost of living	0.11	0.41	0.20	0.06	1							
6 Producer prices (PP)	0.26	0.61	0.62	0.36	0.78	1						
7 PP industrial goods	0.40	0.66	0.61	0.37	0.64	0.92	1					
8 Money wage	0.42	0.60	0.24	0.12	0.68	0.68	0.72	1				
9 Real wage	0.43	0.38	0.11	0.04	0.09	0.19	0.38	0.72	1			
10 Product wage	−0.15	−0.35	−0.56	−0.36	−0.24	−0.65	−0.71	−0.04	0.18	1		
11 Productivity worker	0.66	0.70	−0.22	−0.16	−0.21	−0.04	0.03	−0.04	−0.02	−0.05	1	
12 Productivity (hour)	0.71	0.78	−0.08	−0.11	−0.10	0.14	0.19	0.11	0.07	−0.15	0.97	1
					NBC (1950–89)							
1 GDP	1											
2 Industrial production	0.94	1										
3 Employment	0.78	0.79	1									
4 Employment (hours)	0.90	0.94	0.92	1								
5 Cost of living	−0.29	−0.27	−0.12	−0.29	1							
6 Producer prices (PP)	...	...	...	...	...							
7 PP industrial goods	−0.09	−0.05	0.12	−0.04	0.88	...	1					
8 Money wage	0.16	0.13	0.46	0.20	0.59	...	0.64	1				
9 Real wage	0.46	0.40	0.67	0.51	−0.19	...	−0.02	0.68	1			
10 Product wage	0.26	0.18	0.25	0.24	−0.63	...	−0.74	0.05	0.62	1		
11 Productivity worker	0.44	0.51	−0.12	0.23	−0.27	...	−0.26	−0.44	−0.29	−0.05	1	
12 Productivity (hour)	−0.14	−0.09	−0.57	−0.43	0.12	...	−0.01	−0.25	−0.42	−0.21	0.66	1

Sources: See Appendix 8.1.

industrial output. Correlation coefficients range from 0.43 for consumer prices to 0.6 for both wholesale price indexes. This is in stark contrast with the behavior of prices after the war. On the one hand, the correlation between the consumer price index and both measures of output (GDP and industrial production) is now negative, prices move countercyclically. On the other hand, the wholesale price index for industrial goods shows very little correlation with output or employment. This is indeed supportive of the hypothesis that the transition to mass production was accompanied by a change in the pricing behavior of firms. In the NBC prices are not subject to the forces of supply and demand. The introduction of mass production and mass marketing allows firms to set prices with respect to long-term strategic considerations of growth and relative market share. Short-run changes in the volume of demand can be met by adjustments in output and employment and do not force companies to vary prices as was characteristic in the era of craft technologies. Our finding of countercyclical prices in the post-war period is also confirmed by two other studies of the German business cycle. Based on quarterly data for the period 1960–89, and using the Hodrick–Prescott filter, Smeets (1992) as well as Brandner and Neusser (1992) find a negative correlation of GNP with its deflator. In fact most historical business cycle studies find strong evidence for the shift from procyclical prices in the early period to countercyclical or acyclical price behavior after World War II.[16]

Changes in the behavior of money wages are less pronounced. Before World War I money wages (only the Desai series is reported in Table 8.5) were highly positively correlated with industrial production. In the post-war period the covariation is still positive but the correlation coefficient is smaller: 0.27, compared with 0.57 in the old period. Regarding the covariation of employment and money wages, there is no indication of a changing pattern across periods.

We now turn to the cyclical characteristics of employment, output and real wages. With respect to the volatility of output across periods, different detrending methods generate different results. Whereas the Hodrick–Prescott-detrended GDP series show little change in standard deviations across time, first-difference detrending results in a higher volatility for the NBC. Industrial production is slightly more volatile in the NBC using first-differencing and the HP10 filter but shows no change in the HP400 series. Note that these results again confirm the inadequacy of the methods used in the volatility debates. To compare standard deviations across historical periods is dependent not only on the data used but also on the detrending method. Only if we look at the *relative* volatilities of employment and output can we compare historical periods.

Macroeconomists usually assume that output and employment move closely together but our analysis shows that this seems to be an appropriate assumption only for the post-war years. Only in the NBC is employment roughly as volatile as industrial production; hours worked are slightly more volatile and the employment series is slightly less so. The correlation coefficients are 0.79 for the worker and 0.94 for the hourly series. The higher correlation as well as volatility for hours worked indicate that it is easier for employers to adjust actual work time than the number of workers. In upswings employers favor overtime work to hiring additional workers and they frequently resort to short-time work arrangements in recessions rather than starting to dismiss workers. In the OBC, however, both employment series are less volatile than output, a result that is robust for all detrending methods. The two employment series are considerably less correlated with output in the OBC; the correlation coefficient of hours worked, for example, is just over 0.3 (HP10). This finding supports the Transformational Growth claim of the inflexibility of the craft production system in response to demand fluctuations. Output can be adjusted to a certain extent by varying work intensity or by reorganization of the work process. Employment, however, is sticky in the sense that work teams have to be kept together in order to have all those skills present that are necessary to assemble the product (Chapter 1 above).

The above findings, taken together, result in distinct patterns of real wage behavior over the business cycle. We will look at product real wages as well as at consumer real wages. The former are derived by using industrial wholesale prices, the latter by applying consumer prices as the deflator. The covariation of product real wages with output as well as employment is clearly negative in the early period. This is due to the fact that industrial producer prices are more volatile than money wages, i.e. in booms prices rise more than money wages and in recessions they fall more steeply. In contrast, product wages in post-war Germany move procyclically. Procyclical money wages in the presence of acyclical producer prices account for this result. The cyclical behavior of real consumer wages exhibits a different pattern. In both periods real consumer wages are procyclical but correlation coefficients tend to be higher for the NBC, especially when using the first-differenced data. The mechanisms underlying the observed procyclicality are, however, different in the two periods. In the OBC real consumer wages are procyclical because consumer prices are less volatile than money wages. Strong procyclicality in the new period, on the other hand, is due to mildly procyclical money wages in combination with countercyclical consumer prices. Another difference is that real wages are positively correlated with both output and employment in the NBC but for the early period this holds only true for the two output series. Employment as well as hours worked show little covariation with real consumer wages, with correlation coefficients ranging from 0.04 to 0.11. Differences in the cyclical behavior between real and product wages are due to the different price series used as deflator. The consumer price index for the old period is based solely on food, clothing, fuel, lighting and rent. Of these only clothing is a manufactured good. In the post-war period manufactured goods make up a much larger share of the typical consumption basket. Therefore, consumer and industrial producer prices are more closely correlated in this period compared with the old (Table 8.5).

Finally, we turn to the cyclical behavior of productivity measured as either real output per worker or per hour. Tables 8.2–4 show that both measures of productivity in manufacturing are more volatile in the OBC than in the new period. This is particularly the case for hourly productivity, with a standard deviation – absolute and relative to industrial production – that is roughly 70 per cent higher for all detrending methods. With respect to the volatility relative to employment in the OBC the different detrending methods generate ambivalent results. The standard deviation of hourly productivity is higher than the standard deviation of hours worked only when using the first difference and the HP400 filters. In the post-war period the picture is much clearer. Volatility measures for both productivity series are always smaller than employment volatility. The covariation of productivity and output in the old period is strongly positive. Note also that the first-differenced data generate a higher correlation of productivity and output. This is an indication of the very short-run nature of co-movements of the two variables because it is only the first-difference filter that still accounts for the high-frequency fluctuations. In the NBC only productivity per worker is positively correlated. In contrast, hourly productivity shows very little correlation with output using the HP10 filter (Table 8.5) and only mildly procyclical movement with first-difference detrending. Clearly, modern mass-production technology allows firms to vary output and employment without repercussions on short-run productivity.[17] In contrast, the OBC is characterized by strong short-run shifts in productivity resulting from the fact that employment is less variable than output. In boom phases output is increased by greater work intensity raising workers' productivity.[18] In recessions output is scaled back but employment remains rather stable, leading to a fall in productivity. However, this volatile environment is less conducive to long-run improvements in productivity than is the rather predictable mass production system. Consequently, average annual productivity growth rates in the period of the NBC are more than twice as high than in the OBC (Table 8.2).

The purpose of this section was to analyze the volatilities and covariation behavior of various variables in order to find evidence for the claim that business cycles have changed in character. Our findings do indeed indicate that short-run adjustments in the industrial sector are fundamentally different across the two periods under investigation. In particular, real product wages have been found to behave countercyclically in the OBC but are clearly procyclical after World War II. This and most of the stylized facts for Germany present a challenge to RBC theory. There is indeed much evidence that the OBC rather than the NBC is the closer representation of RBC models. In fact the implicit assumption of these models of perfect competition in labor and product markets presupposes an institutional setting which can be found in a craft but not in a mass-production society. First, productivity is highly procyclical and almost as volatile as output. It was mentioned above that a highly volatile productivity pattern was an essential prerequisite for generating sufficient volatility in output. Second, employment is much less volatile than output and productivity. This means that the elasticity of labor supply in response to productivity shocks can be assumed to be in the range that is suggested by micro studies of labor market behavior. In order to replicate an employment series that is as volatile as output (a stylized fact for the post-war economy) RBC models usually have to assume elasticities that are unrealistically high. The fly in the ointment, however, is that real product wages move countercyclically, a fact that is irreconcilable with RBC models, which are characterized by procyclical real wages. Until now our analysis was based solely on descriptive statistical tools without any attempts at testing our results. In the next section simple regression analysis will be employed to test whether the structural change between the two periods is indeed statistically significant for certain key relationships.

TESTING FOR STRUCTURAL CHANGE

The objective of this section is to provide statistical support for our set of stylized facts with particular attention to testing for the significance of structural change between the two periods. Neither of the specifications is designed to provide a structural model of price or wage behavior. The regressions are simply meant to measure the changes in these variables associated with the changes in output.

To test for the significance of structural change in the coefficients the following models will be estimated:

$$\ln x_t - \ln x_{t-1} = (\alpha + \alpha_{NBC}) + (\beta + \beta_{NBC})(\ln y_t - \ln y_{t-1}) + \varepsilon \tag{8.1}$$

$$\ln x_t - \ln x_{t(HP)} = \alpha + (\beta + \beta_{NBC})(\ln y_t + \ln y_{t(HP)}) + \varepsilon. \tag{8.2}$$

In specification (8.1) the variables are defined as the first differences of the logs of the series. This specification is also used in the other country studies in this volume. Specification (8.2) defines business cycle fluctuations as deviations from the Hodrick–Prescott trend.[19] Since one of the advantages of the Hodrick–Prescott filter is that it normalizes a time series around mean zero, there is no need for allowing the constant to vary across periods. In fact, as will be seen later, the constant is not significantly different from zero in all regressions using specification (8.2).[20] The dependent variable is the wholesale price index for industrial goods, the money wage or the product wage. The cyclical variable y represents an index of industrial production. The NBC coefficients are defined to be zero for the period of the OBC. The coefficient β can thus be interpreted as the coefficient for the period of the OBC. The NBC coefficients measure the change in the value of the coefficient in the new period relative to the period of the OBC. Or, in other words, their t statistics test the hypothesis that the coefficients of output deviation from trend (note that the constant is also allowed to vary when using first differences) remains the same across the two periods. The coefficients for the NBC can be derived by adding the NBC coefficients to the coefficients for the entire period; for example, the output coefficient for the period of the NBC is equal to $(\beta + \beta_{NBC})$. The following hypotheses can be derived from the theory of Transformational Growth and our preliminary findings above:

Industrial producer prices: $\beta > 0$; $\beta_{NBC} < 0$; $(\beta + \beta_{NBC}) \leq 0$

The coefficient of current output measures the change in the mark-up. In the OBC in the short run prices are determined by supply and demand. When demand increases firms are able to increase prices and when there is a slump prices have to be lowered, i.e. the mark-up varies procyclically. In contrast, mark-ups in the NBC are likely to be constant or even countercyclical as a result of competitive conditions in oligopolistic markets. See, for example, Kalecki (1968, 1971), who pointed out that firms may be reluctant to cut prices in a recession in fear of starting a price war. Similarly, during boom periods prices will be cut to deter new entry into the market.

The results reported in Table 8.6 are supportive of the proposition of structural change in the behavior of prices between the two periods. The coefficients of structural change for both detrending methods are negative and significant at the 1 per cent level. We can therefore reject the null hypothesis that the output coefficients did not change. Prices in the OBC are strongly procyclical, as is indicated by highly significant (1 per cent) and positive coefficients. In the NBC prices are much less volatile but still mildly procyclical; the magnitude of the output coefficients falls by 90 per

Table 8.6 Cyclical behavior of wholesale prices

Variable	HP10 N=83 OBC: 1871–1913 NBC: 1950–89	1D N=81 OBC: 1872–1913 NBC: 1951–89
Constant	0.0004	−0.039***
	(0.10)	(−3.45)
Constant$_{NBC}$	n.a.	0.062***
		(3.80)
Industrial production	1.311***	1.028***
	(6.02)	(4.74)
Industrial production$_{NBC}$	−1.147***	−0.926***
	(−3.73)	(−3.25)
R^2	0.415	0.355
Percentage change in output coefficient	−88	−90

Sources: See Appendix 8.1.

Notes
Numbers in parentheses are *t* statistics; significance levels: *** 1 per cent; ** 5 per cent, * 10 per cent.

cent. Overall, the regressions thus show a decrease in the association of prices and output, as hypothesized by the theory of Transformational Growth.[21]

Money wages: β, $(\beta + \beta_{NBC}) > 0$; $\beta_{NBC} < 0$

These sign expectations are clearly also compatible with the sticky wage hypothesis. There are several studies employing similar econometric tools that do confirm decreasing cyclical responsiveness of money wages to changes in aggregate demand.[22] Keynesians usually attribute nominal wage rigidity to imperfections in labor markets such as labor unions or long-term wage contracts. Again institutional change is seen not as an integral part of market relationships but rather as an imperfection inhibiting the equilibrating forces of an otherwise perfect market system. Heterodox economists like Sylos-Labini (1993), on the other hand, emphasize the role of changing labor market institutions in determining the level of wages as part of the historical evolution of the capitalist system. In much the same way as the oligopolization of industry transformed pricing decisions in product markets so did the evolution of collective bargaining between labor unions and employers' associations transform the wage-setting process. It was mentioned earlier that German labor market institutions underwent a similar transformation around the turn of the century.

Table 8.7 Cyclical behavior of money wages

Variable	HP10 N=83 OBC: 1871–1913 NBC: 1950–89		1D N=81 OBC: 1872–1913 NBC: 1951–89	
	Desai	*Bry*	*Desai*	*Bry*
Constant	0.0006 (0.22)	0.0003 (0.14)	0.008 (0.98)	−0.0005 (−0.08)
Constant$_{NBC}$	n.a	n.a	0.048*** (4.10)	0.059*** (6.49)
Industrial production	0.741*** (4.75)	0.688*** (5.68)	0.457** (2.86)	0.616*** (5.00)
Industrial production$_{NBC}$	−0.473** (−2.18)	−0.447** (−2.58)	−0.222 (−1.08)	−0.414** (−2.60)
R^2	0.390	0.435	0.467	0.566
Percentage change in output coefficient	−64	−65	−49	−67

Sources: See Appendix 8.1.

Note
See Table 8.7.

Our results – reported in Table 8.7 – confirm the hypothesis of decreased cyclical variation in money wages. Three of our four regressions show a negative and significant (5 per cent level) coefficient of structural change; the fall in the cyclical variation amounts to between 64 per cent and 67 per cent. Only the specification using the growth rates of the Desai money wage series fails to confirm the significance of change between the two periods. This finding, however, is not central to the propositions of the theory of Transformational Growth. The key relationship is the *change* in the relative behavior of money wages and prices. The Keynesian school usually assumes that prices are set by a mark-up over costs, which in turn mostly consist of money wages. Hence price stickiness is a direct result of wage stickiness. In contrast, Transformational Growth emphasizes the change in the pricing behavior of firms independent of the cyclical variation of money wages. The following product wage regressions analyze this adjustment.

Product wages: $\beta < 0$; $(\beta + \beta_{NBC}) \geq 0$, $\beta_{NBC} > 0$

The sign expectations reflect the change from a countercyclical to a procyclical real wage, as discussed above. These hypotheses are overwhelmingly supported by the data. All the coefficients of industrial output in the OBC are negative and significant at the 5 per cent or even 1 per cent

Table 8.8 Cyclical behavior of product wages

Variable	HP10 N=83 OBC: 1871–1913 NBC: 1950–89		1D N=81 OBC: 1872–1913 NBC: 1951–89	
	Desai	Bry	Desai	Bry
Constant	0.00009	−0.00007	0.038***	0.038***
	(0.03)	(−0.03)	(5.44)	(5.93)
Constant$_{NBC}$	n.a.	n.a.	n.a.	n.a.
Industrial production	−0.556***	−0.564***	−0.349**	−0.411***
	(−3.22)	(−3.55)	(−2.18)	(−2.77)
Industrial production$_{NBC}$	0.598**	0.611***	0.430**	0.477***
	(2.52)	(2.80)	(2.51)	(2.98)
R^2	0.226	0.309	0.145	0.209
Percentage change in output coefficient	107	108	123	116

Sources: See Appendix 8.1.

Note
See Table 8.7.

level. The coefficients of structural change, on the other hand, are all positive and significant at the 5 per cent or 1 per cent level. In fact the percentage change in the output coefficients from one period to the other is greater than 100 per cent for the four regressions, indicating a procyclical product wage in the post-war period. The above results confirm that the change in the cyclical behavior of product wages is due mainly to a change in the cyclical behavior of prices. It is the acyclicality of producer prices in combination with mildly procyclical money wages that accounts for (mildly) procyclical product wages in the post-war era. Mark-ups thus move countercyclically, confirming propositions made by Kalecki. In contrast, in the OBC prices were highly sensitive to aggregate demand conditions. Price adjustments were made over and above money wage costs, leading to strongly procyclical mark-ups. The changing pattern has to be explained in the context of the shift from craft to mass-production technologies and the associated change in the nature of competition.

IMPLICATIONS FOR MACRO-MODELING

Our previous analysis has been concentrated on the cyclical behavior of the industrial sector. This sector has been the most dynamic sector over much of the period that we are studying, so that it is likely to have macroeconomic implications. To substantiate the hypothesis of a shift from price to output adjustments in the industrial sector we first try to quantify the importance of price adjustments in the OBC and NBC respectively. To do this we start by dividing the price and output series for the industrial sector into upswings and downswings. For the OBC we use Spiethoff's business cycle chronology but rely on the NBER dates for the NBC. In order to abstract from trends this exercise is based on the HP10 detrended series. The results are summarized in Table 8.9. The numbers in the third and fourth columns are the peak-to-trough and trough-to-peak changes in prices or quantities in absolute terms. In column five we simply divide the price change by the sum of the price and output change and multiply that by 100. This represents the percentage share of price adjustments in the change in total monetary expenditure. In the downswing between 1882 and 1886, for example, the fall in industrial wholesale prices accounted for 90 per cent of the decline in monetary expenditure. Comparing the periods of the OBC and NBC clearly confirms the dominance of price adjustments in the earlier period. The percentage shares range from 62 per cent to 90 per cent in the OBC but account for only 0 per cent to 28 per cent in the NBC period.[23]

It therefore seems reasonable to construct two separate macro-models for the OBC and the NBC respectively in order to account for these differences. The following will simply provide a sketch of the two models.

Table 8.9 Price and output adjustments in the industrial sector

Period	Upswing/downswing (Peak/Trough)	Δ industrial wholesale prices (Δ P)	Δ industrial production (Δ X)	(ΔP/(ΔP + Δ X))*100 (%)
		OBC		
1873–79	P–T	−0.20	−0.04	83
1879–82	T–P	0.08	−0.04	n.a.[a]
1882–86	P–T	−0.09	−0.01	90
1886–90	T–P	0.10	0.06	62
1890–94	P–T	−0.15	−0.03	81
1894–1900	T–P	0.20	0.05	80
1900–02	P–T	−0.21	−0.08	72
1902–07	T–P	0.15	0.07	67
1907–09	P–T	−0.13	−0.05	72
1909–13	T–P	0.05	0.01	81
		NBC		
1951–54	P–T	−0.08	−0.04	67
1954–55	T–P	0.01	0.05	17
1955–59	P–T	0.00	−0.07	0
1959–61	T–P	0.01	0.05	17
1961–63	P–T	−0.002	−0.04	5
1963–65	T–P	0.02	0.05	28
1965–67	P–T	−0.01	−0.11	8
1967–70	T–P	−0.01	0.12	PC[b]
1970–71	P–T	0.001	−0.03	3
1971–73	T–P	−0.015	−0.03	PC[b]
1973–75	P–T	0.01	−0.11	PC[b]
1975–80	T–P	−0.04	0.10	PC[b]
1980–83	P–T	0.02	−0.06	PC[b]
1983–89	T–end of period[c]	0.006	0.05	11

Sources: For prices and output see Appendix 8.1; absolute changes were computed by using the respective HP10 detrended series. Business cycle peaks and troughs for the OBC are taken from Spiethoff (in Bry 1960) and from the NBER business cycle chronology for the NBC.

Notes
(a) The problem is that W. G. Hoffmann's index of industrial production declines although the period from 1879–82 is defined as an upswing. Lewis (1978: 79–80) points out that Hoffmann fails to account for changes in the trade statistic in 1879. The upswing clearly shows in the growth rates for metal production, minerals and railway traffic, which were 16 per cent, 12 per cent and 13 per cent respectively in 1879–80.
(b) Prices are countercyclical so that no ratio is computed.
(c) The peak for this business cycle was not reached before 1991.

A good starting point is the one-sector closed economy models presented in Taylor (1991: 42), because they represent a generic framework which allows for different closures to model different macro-adjustment mechanisms. He develops a model with mark-up pricing as well as a neoclassical version based on marginal productivity theory. The mark-up version seems to be preferable because it allows for modeling changes in income distribution as a crucial variable for adjustment. For both models we assume that workers consume all their income and that savings are a share of profit income. The OBC as well as the NBC versions are Keynesian in the sense that investment is not dependent on savings but is defined as an exogenous variable driving the system. Furthermore, the principle of effective demand is underlying both adjustment mechanisms. In its simplest form it states that after an initial change in the level of investment (ΔI) a new equilibrium will be reached when enough savings have been set aside to match the initial change. The adjusting variable in this process is thus the change in total nominal income (ΔY), which is defined as follows:

$$\Delta Y = \Delta P\, X_1 + P_0\, \Delta X = (1/s)\, \Delta I$$

Our stylized facts have confirmed that it is reasonable to assume the inflexibility of craft production in adjusting output and employment ($\Delta X = 0$). Hence output and employment can be set exogenously. Supply-side restrictions are usually associated with the availability of capital or foreign exchange in a developing country setting (Taylor 1991: 47). In neoclassical models output is assumed to be at full employment level. Here, inflexible production technologies in the pre-World War I period motivate the output/employment constraint. If output is fixed and cannot adjust to changes in the level of demand, prices will have to become endogenous. In our mark-up price setting it means that the mark-up rate will be flexible and move procyclically. In the case of a surge in desired investment, for example, prices will rise relative to a rather inflexible money wage. Consequently, this fall in real wages will reduce consumption, since we assume that savings are only taken out of profit income. Higher savings to match the initial increase in investment are "forced" through an endogenous adjustment in the distribution of income to balance savings and investment. This "forced savings" adjustment is characterized by a countercyclical real wage (as observed in the OBC) and an inverse relationship between investment and consumption, both of which are typical neoclassical macro results. Note that the sketched model arrives at these rather conventional results without making the typical neoclassical assumptions but through explicitly modeling income distribution dynamics as a result of price fluctuations.

In the period of the NBC there is no justification for an exogenously determined level of output. Mass-production technology is designed to accommodate fluctuations in sales and is usually operated at below full capacity. To capture the characteristic adjustments in the NBC, output and employment are now determined endogenously. This model is based on the Keynesian–Kaleckian proposition that the level of activity in the economy is determined by the level of effective demand. In this version

– again taking money wages as constant – prices will be constant if the mark-up factor is fixed ($\Delta P = 0$). Output and employment increase in response to a surge in investment until sufficient savings (profits) have been set aside to match investment expenditure. This multiplier adjustment, especially when combined with an accelerator mechanism, generates the strong fluctuations in output and employment that can be observed in post-World War II Germany and other advanced capitalist countries. The model could be extended by using a countercyclical flexible mark-up rule based on the work of Kalecki and Steindl in order to generate procyclical real wages.

In summary, the Transformational Growth perspective can shed a different light on the history of the debates on output v. price adjustments in macroeconomics. For example, Keynes, as Amadeo (1989) has shown, emphasized price/forced savings adjustment in the *Treatise* (1930) but identified the output multiplier adjustment as the key adjustment mechanism in the *General Theory* (1936). Similarly, for Schumpeter shifts from one circular flow to the other are driven by increases in the level of investment, which are in turn due to spurts of technological innovations. The additional demand for investment goods will drive up prices and thereby depress consumption spending; the system thus generates additional savings in response to exogenous shifts in demand by shifting income distribution away from wage earners, who are likely to save comparatively little. Hence Schumpeter assumes relatively fixed output and employment as well as countercyclical real wages. From our perspective it is interesting to note that Schumpeter wrote *The Theory of Economic Development* at the beginning of the twentieth century (German edition 1912), when the economies on the Continent still largely operated inflexible craft production technologies. The position adopted here is that both mechanisms are indeed characteristic of different historical periods. Forced savings adjustments dominate in the nineteenth century characterized by the operation of inflexible craft technologies. In contrast, the mass-production system of the post-World War II period exhibits no supply constraint, so that output adjustments serve as the equilibrating mechanism.

An admittedly crude way of testing for the above-mentioned changes in macroeconomic adjustment mechanisms is to study the relationship between consumption and investment. It is expected that consumption and investment will move closely together in the NBC period. In contrast, this positive correlation is assumed to be far smaller or even negative for the OBC period. From the above discussion we can derive the following sign expectations when regressing consumption on investment, using the specifications introduced above. ·

Investment: $\beta \le 0$; $(\beta + \beta_{NBC})$, $\beta_{NBC} > 0$

Regression analysis allowing for structural change similar to that used above yielded results partly supporting this claim (Table 8.10). When real private consumption was regressed on net investment the coefficients were positive but not significantly different from zero for the period between 1852 and 1913. Coefficients of structural change as well as coefficients for the post-World War II period were positive and significant (5 per cent level). Note, however, that the old period in these regressions extends back to 1851. Comparing the 1871–1913 period with the post-war years does not result in significant coefficients of structural change. Our attempts to relate changes in the cyclical behavior of the manufacturing sector to differences in macroeconomic behavior are therefore inconclusive. The problem seems to be that the manufacturing sector represented a much lower share of total output in the period of the OBC. Not surprisingly, correlation coefficients between industrial output and Net Social Product (NSP) are much lower in the old period than in the new (Table 8.5). Furthermore, we have seen earlier that the cyclical behavior of real consumer wages and real product wages was different in the OBC. This is clearly due to the fact that industrial workers in the nineteenth century did not consume what they produced. Or, in other words, consumer and producer prices are based on different goods baskets. Considerably more effort, therefore, has to be invested in disentangling the

Table 8.10 Relationship between consumption and investment

Variable	HP10 N=103 OBC: 1851–1913 NBC: 1950–89	1D N=101 OBC: 1852–1913 NBC: 1951–89
Constant	n.a.	0.023*** (7.5)
Constant$_{NBC}$	n.a.	0.013*** (2.84)
Net investment	0.017 (0.83)	0.01 (1.21)
Net investment$_{NBC}$	0.104** (2.1)	0.06** (2.36)
R^2	0.07	0.17
Percentage change in investment coefficient	611	600

Sources: See Appendix 8.1.

Notes
See Table 8.7.

relationship between the manufacturing sector and macro-adjustment in the pre-war period.

CONCLUSION

In general, the above results strongly support the usefulness of a historical, institution-based approach to the analysis of the cyclical nature of capitalist economies. The purpose of this chapter was to link the transformation from a craft to a mass-production economy in Germany to differences in the cyclical behavior of the industrial sector over time. There is substantial evidence that the changes in the flexibility of production had a profound impact on adjustments to fluctuations in aggregate demand. In particular, simple regression methods have found significant structural breaks in the cyclical behavior of producer prices and product wages. Our attempts to link our results for the industrial sector with the macroeconomy generated only rather suggestive support. Furthermore, our findings represent a challenge for the RBC approach to economic fluctuations. The key shortcoming of this school is its reliance on maximization exercises on the firm or household level presumed to be universal across different historical periods. In addition, it seems to be inadequate to define technology as a production function on which firms can move along in response to relative factor price shifts. Instead, the historical analysis of technological and institutional constraints has been found to be a superior (micro-) foundation for the analysis of short-run fluctuations.

Further research on two different levels will be necessary to substantiate our still rather suggestive results. First, it would be useful to investigate changes in technology and institutional structure on the micro-level. Examples of this kind of analysis are studies of the role of electrical machinery in the flexibilization of production or the structure and variability of cost under craft production for specific industries or individual firms. Second, the relationship between the industrial sector and macroeconomic adjustment in the nineteenth century could be further analyzed in a two-sector (agriculture and industry) computable general equilibrium model which would employ the appropriate closure rules. This would liberate analytical macroeconomic history from the prevailing neoclassical "straitjacket" and contribute to our further understanding of the development of capitalist systems.

APPENDIX 8.1
DATA SOURCES AND DEFINITIONS

Old business cycle (1871–1913)

The basic sources are Hoffmann (1965), Desai (1968), Bry (1960), Jacobs and Richter (1935) and Kuczynski (1959 ff.). All series are indexes with 1913=100.

GDP. Hoffman (1965): net social product.

Consumption. Hoffman (1965): real private consumption.

Investment. Hoffman (1965): real net investment, including public investment.

Industrial production. Hoffman (1965): industrial and craft production, excluding mining. Industries included are construction materials (*Steine und Erden*), metal production, metal processing, chemicals, textiles, leather and garments, timber, paper and food.

Industrial employment. Hoffman (1965): industrial and craft employment, same coverage as industrial production. Own computation: annual hours worked in industry derived from industrial employment, using Schröder's (1980) series for average weekly hours worked in industry and assuming no absenteeism.

Cost-of-living. Kuczynski (1959 ff.): consumer prices based only on food and rent. Desai (1968): consumer prices, including food, clothing, fuel, lighting (1890–) and rent.

Industrial producer prices. Jacobs and Richter (1935): wholesale prices of industrial goods, including sugar, coal, iron, non-ferrous metals, textiles, chemicals, oil and construction materials.

Money wages. Bry (1960): average *weekly* money wages in industry based on Kuczynski (1959 ff.). Industries covered are metals, textiles, timber, printing, chemicals, transportation, mining and building. The hourly series was derived by using Schröder's (1980) series for average weekly hours worked in industry. Desai (1968): average *annual* wages in industry based on the following sectors: 1871–1886, building, machinery, cotton textiles, printing, mining and steel; 1887–1913, extended coverage of twenty-seven industries. The hourly series was derived by using Schröder (1980).

New business cycle (1950–89)

The basic sources are publications of the Statistisches Bundesamt, the Council of Economic Experts and the Deutsche Bundesbank (1988). All series are indexes with 1980=100.

GDP. Statistischers Bundesamt: net domestic product.

Consumption. Statistisches Bundesamt: real private consumption.

Investment. Statistisches Bundesamt: real net investment, including public investment.

Industrial production. Council of Economic Experts: index of manufacturing production.

Industrial employment. Council of Economic Experts: index of manufacturing employment; index of hours worked in manufacturing.

Cost-of-living. Statistisches Bundesamt: consumer prices based on consumption basket of four-person, middle-income household.

Producer prices. Bundesbank and Council of Economic Experts: wholesale prices for manufacturing and mining products (excluding construction).

Money wages. Council of Economic Experts and Bundesbank: gross hourly wages in industry, including mining but excluding construction.

NOTES

1 Original contributors are Kydland and Prescott (1982) and Prescott (1986). See McCallum (1989) and Stadler (1994) for recent surveys and Mankiw (1989) for a critical discussion. The collection of essays in Cooley (1995) presents state-of-the-art RBC models.
2 See also Mankiw (1989) and Stadler (1994), who criticize RBC models on similar grounds.
3 It should be noted that Sylos-Labini (1993) proposes a theory of the changing nature of the business cycle that is also grounded in historical transformations of the institutions of capitalism. Sylos-Labini emphasizes the emergence of collective bargaining arrangements and oligopolistic competition around the turn of the century to explain these changes. The main distinction of the Transformational Growth perspective is its focus on the role of technological change, but both theories are certainly compatible.
4 In some industries a few firms dominated the market right from the start. A good example is the market for electrical products which in the 1890s was dominated already almost by two producers – Siemens and AEG – in much the same way as Westinghouse and GE dominated in the United States. Note, however, that production in the individual production units was still organized very much along craft lines (Brady 1933).
5 This point is confirmed by the following quote from the governing board of the coal cartel in 1892: "The length of the current upswing, which of course pleases us, depends in large part on the stability which all participants, not only coal mining, have brought to their pricing decisions. It is a fact proven through experience, that an upward leap in prices is followed as a rule by an even more rapid decline. A calm development of all interrelationships, including prices, promises lasting and satisfactory returns, and is preferred in any case to the short-run fluctuations which we know from the past" (quoted in Kinghorn 1995).
6 Sylos-Labini (1993) also notes that changes in the behaviour of money wages started to occur around the turn of the century in Britain and the United States. Hanes (1993) finds that money wages in the United States show less volatility, especially downwards after 1890. The change in the cyclical volatility of money wages in Germany will be analyzed later in this chapter.

7 Landes (1969: 317), writing about Britain and Germany, states: "For both countries the system of mass production was essentially the work of the famous rationalization of the 1920s."

8 "To what extent standardization has actually been carried through is shown by the fact that out of 5,424 various parts for the passenger locomotives of type IcI-H2 (tender and locomotive) there are 1,451 standard and 2,842 type parts; that is, single parts which will find application in locomotive construction, while 1,131 parts are left unstandardized" (A. Meckel, "Die deutsche Lokomotivnormierung 1918 bis 1927," *VDI Nachrichten* 43:9 (October 26, 1927), quoted in Brady 1933: 25–6).

9 See also Polster and Voy (1991) for the same point.

10 See, for example, Smeets (1992) and Brandner and Neusser (1992) for studies of the German economy. Danthine and Donaldson (1993) and Backus and Kehoe (1992) provide international comparisons.

11 It should be noted that the study by Backus and Kehoe does indeed include an empirical analysis of nineteenth-century business cycles. Some of the results – such as procyclical and highly volatile prices in the nineteenth century and rather stable or even countercyclical price fluctuations in the post-World War II period – are indeed supportive of the hypothesis advanced here.

12 There is indeed overwhelming evidence for the relatively high volatility of both prices and outputs in the inter-war period in Germany and in all other industrialized countries (Backus and Kehoe 1992; Sylos-Labini 1993; and Zarnovitz 1992).

13 See Appendix 8.1 for a more detailed description of the data used.

14 No attempt is made here to provide a technical presentation of the different filters (see, for example, Enders 1995 of Baxter and King 1994). It should be noted, however, that the Hodrick–Prescott filter allows a smoothing parameter λ to be set. The parameter is an arbitrary constant reflecting the penalty of incorporating fluctuations into the trend. It is customary to set $\lambda = 1,600$ for quarterly data (see Brandner and Neusser 1992 and Smeets 1992 on Germany). Studies using annual data most commonly use $\lambda = 10$ or 100 or 400. Increasing the value of λ acts to smooth out the trend. If $\lambda = 0$ the trend is equal to the original series and if $\lambda \rightarrow \infty$ the trend approaches a linear time trend. For the purpose of testing for the robustness of our results we use both 10 (HP10) and 400 (HP400) as our parameters.

15 Owing to space limitations only the covariations of the first-differenced and the HP10 detrended series are reported here. Baxter and King (1994) found relatively smaller correlation coefficients for the first-differenced data compared with the Hodrick–Prescott filtered series. Our results do not confirm this result; there is no systematic difference in the covariation behavior of differently detrended data. The Baxter and King result is based on the observation that the first-difference filter emphasizes the irregular component of time series by reweighting strongly toward the higher-frequency fluctuations (one to three years). This would make the filtered series less persistent and thus likely to generate smaller covariation overall. From our specific perspective, it is interesting to note that the OBC series in general tend to be less persistent than NBC data – independent of the detrending method – pointing to a greater importance of high-frequency fluctuations in the old period. High-frequency fluctuations, however, don't seem to be due to irregularities but are rather systematic in nature, as the high level of covariation indicates.

16 See, for example, the comparative studies of Backus and Kehoe (1992) and Danthine and Donaldson (1993). It is interesting to note that the only country in the latter study that exhibits a procyclical price movement in the post-war period is South Africa, the only developing country in the sample and thus the only country that is likely to still use craft technologies.

17 This view of behavior of productivity and cost under mass production also seems to dominate in the business economics literature. In a recent textbook Moschandreas (1994: 157) writes. "The evidence on short-run cost curves indicates that the average variable cost is constant over the relevant range of production. This is thought to be intentional and is considered as a rational response to the uncertainties surrounding a business. Since the firm is unlikely to know its demand with any degree of certainty, it is suggested that it makes sense for firms to organize production in a way that ensures flexibility. Therefore, firms may adopt flexible techniques capable of producing a range of output at constant variable cost."

18 Landes writes (1969: 318): "Most entrepreneurs and managers . . . relied on 'hard driving' by foremen and master workmen to get them value for their money in the short run, on the quiet effect of technological change to cut labour costs in the long." Furthermore, referring to the contractions in the 1860s and 1870s in Britain, "when wages held up better than profits," Landes notices a shift in employment strategy (p. 319): "Employers attempted to cut labour costs by increasing performance, and the question of the nature and size of the work load supplanted wages as the major issue in labour disputes."

19 Thanks to Levent Koçkesen from New York University for providing his GAUSS subroutine to perform the HP detrending.

20 Regression results using the HP400 detrended data are similar to the first-difference as well as the HP10 regressions and are not reported here.

21 These results are similar to the studies of Backus and Kehoe (1992) and Cooley and Ohanian (1992). In fact, both studies find that consumer prices defined as deviation from the HP trend are procyclical in the pre-World War I period but countercyclical in the post-war era.

22 See, for example, Hanes (1993) for a study of the United States.

23 The only exception is the downswing between 1951–54 when the fall in prices accounted for 67 per cent of the change in monetary expenditure. This can, however, be attributed to a downward adjustment from extraordinarily high price levels in the immediate post-war period and is not due to the forces of supply and demand.

ACKNOWLEDGMENTS

Thanks to all members of the "Transformational Growth" group at the New School for Social Research, especially Ed Nell and David Kucera. I would also like to acknowledge the help of Levent Koçkesen, Chris Hanes and David Backus. Special thanks to Ute Pieper for providing detailed comments on earlier versions of this chapter. The usual caveats apply.

9

TRANSFORMATIONAL
GROWTH IN JAPAN

David Kucera

One of the central ideas of Transformational Growth as developed by Edward Nell is that prices adjust less readily to changes in output in the mass-production than the pre-mass-production period. A key underlying reason for this difference is the Chandlerian notion that mass production implies mass marketing. In his book *The Visible Hand* (1977) Chandler describes the connection between mass production and mass marketing as follows:

> The new mass producers were keenly aware of the national and international markets opened up by the new transportation and communication infrastructure. The potential of that market had impelled them to adopt the mass-production machinery. However, as long as merchandising enterprises were able to sell their goods, they saw little reason to build marketing organizations of their own. Once the inadequacies of existing marketers became clear, manufacturers integrated forward into marketing.
>
> (1977: 287)

The "inadequacies" to which Chandler refers resulted "because existing marketers were unable to sell and distribute products in the volume they were produced." Mass marketing of mass-produced goods typically involves relatively long-term pricing policies, with wholesale prices set by the firms that manufacture the goods, compared with the pre-mass-production period, in which wholesale prices were typically set by independent merchants. This suggests greater independence in the mass-production period between price and output changes.[1] One of the distinctive characteristics of Japanese marketing arrangements in the post-war years is that they operate through extensive and often exclusive contracting arrangements, explicit and implicit, among groups of closely allied firms called *keiretsu*. These arrangements are referred to by one author as "vertical semi-integration" (Ito 1992: 392).

The historical development of mass-production techniques is most closely associated with manufacturing, suggesting that the changing relation of prices and output will hold most strongly for this sector. As a corollary of these changing price patterns, changes in product wages are likely to be related to changes in output in a more strongly positive manner in the new period, associated with mass production, than in the old.[2] This result is expected across a wide range of money wage responses including those observed in Japan, where changes in money wages in manufacturing vary positively with changes in manufacturing output in a broadly similar manner across periods.[3] The two main hypotheses of this chapter are, then, that domestic wholesale manufacturing prices moved more procyclically and product wages in manufacturing moved more countercyclically in the old than in the new period.

Transformational Growth attempts to take seriously the impact of institutional development on the patterns of real wages over business cycles and in this sense is distinct from studies rooted in the ahistorical assumptions of marginal productivity theory. In contrast with other studies of real wage movements over business cycles, this study decomposes the cyclical movement of product wages into the cyclical movement of its components, money wages and wholesale prices in manufacture. Such decomposition reveals that the changing cyclical pattern of product wages across old and new periods is driven by the changing cyclical pattern of prices across these periods, with the change in the product wage–output relation essentially a residual effect. In this sense the cyclical movement of product wages is removed from the realm of marginal productivity theory and optimization on the part of workers and capitalists and becomes instead an unintended consequence of prevailing production techniques and their associated marketing arrangements.

Transformational Growth argues, then, that techniques of production have a large impact on the nature of marketing arrangements and that the nature of marketing arrangements, in turn, has a large impact on the movement of manufacturing prices over business cycles. Mass marketing of mass-produced goods is generally associated with relatively stable prices, comparing the new period with the old, and there is consistent evidence that this is so for Japan. Changes across the old and new periods in the cyclical behavior not only of prices but also, by derivation, of product wages can thus be traced back to the transformation of techniques of production. It is in this sense that pre-mass-production and mass-production technologies serve as the defining characteristics of the old and new periods and that technical change serves as the prime mover in the theory of Transformational Growth.

In the econometric tests of structural change that follow, the old, pre-mass-production period spans the years from 1880 to 1939 and the new, mass-production period the years from formal independence in 1952 up to 1991. Classifying by periods can be problematic, given the typically gradual change in the defining characteristics of periods. None the less, the transition to mass-production techniques was particularly dramatic in Japan, based in large part on the rapid borrowing and diffusion of Western technologies in the early post-war years. Because of this rapid transition (and because Japan was less affected by economic instability in the inter-war years than the other advanced capitalist countries considered in this volume) the old, pre-mass-production period is defined to include the inter-war years, consistent with Japan's late industrialization.

What follows is a characterization of key issues of technical change and market development in the old and new periods. This is followed by formal hypotheses and econometric tests of structural change, with cyclical movements evaluated using logarithmic growth rates and the Hodrick–Prescott non-linear detrending filter. These tests provide consistent support for some of the central ideas of Transformational Growth, indicating that prices moved more procyclically and product wages more counter-cyclically in the old, pre-mass-production period. More than that, the tests indicate that the change in the cyclical movement of product wages across periods is driven by the change in the cyclical movement of prices.

THE OLD PERIOD

The old period begins in the 1880s and follows the transitional years of the Meiji "reconstruction," the unstable early years of the Meiji era, 1868–1911 (Allen 1972: 30). The 1880s marked the beginning of rapid economic growth in Japan. Rostow gives the 1878–1900 years as the approximate take-off period. Kuznets dates the beginning of modern economic growth at 1874–79 and Rosovsky at 1886 (Macpherson 1987: 9; cf. Yoshihara 1994: 1–2). Another purely practical reason for starting in the 1880s is that reliable data for Japan are not available prior to these years (Ohkawa 1979: 4).

From the Meiji Restoration of 1868 to the 1930s, Japanese manufacturing was predominantly made up of the textile and food industries. Macpherson (1987: 18) describes this as follows:

> Until the 1930s manufacturing output was dominated by food-stuffs such as bean paste, soy sauce and sake, and textiles, especially silk and cotton . . . . The dramatic rise in heavy industry was mainly a feature of the 1930s, associated both with industrial maturity and military requirements.

Manufacturing was commonly rural and household-based, making up one-half of a dual occupation for smallholding or tenant farmers. As of the

234

late 1930s, over one-half of farmers were part-time and were involved in by-employment in a wide range of other occupations. (Macpherson 1987: 17). These producers typically worked under contract to small regional wholesale merchants, and the wealthy traditional Japanese merchant families did not become greatly involved with industrial production (Smith 1955: 67).

Food accounted for about two-thirds of all consumption expenditure until 1920 and about half in the 1930s. In 1880 clothing accounted for about 8 per cent of consumption expenditure, increasing to 13 per cent by 1940 (Macpherson 1987: 20). Clothing and processed foods were overwhelmingly produced by households and other small-scale producers, who dominated production for the home market throughout the pre-World War II years. In his economic history of Japan, from the Meiji Restoration to World War II, Allen (1972: 89) describes these small-scale producers as follows:

> In every centre of population there were a large number of people who prepared various kinds of Japanese food and who either sold their products in little shops attached to their houses or peddled them round the neighbourhood. In the same way, *geta* (wooden footwear) were then for the most part turned out by craftsmen who sold direct to local customers; while the coloured thongs which attached the *geta* to the feet were produced by domestic workers in their spare time . . . . The very small production units which . . . remained typical of much of the weaving trade, were well adapted to serving a market composed of consumers who insisted on individuality in the design of their dress materials.

This is not to say that large-scale production was insignificant, even in the early years of the Meiji era. While silk reeling was done on a small scale and based in the countryside, cotton spinning factories were large, with hundreds of workers per factory, and were urban-based (Smith 1955: 11, Nakamura 1983: 63). None the less it was not until 1910, the mid-point of the old period, that the value added by factories consistently exceeded that added by households for manufactured goods (Ohkawa 1957: 79–80; cf. Nakamura 1983: 80, who notes that the ratio of factory to total manufacturing output exceeded one-half by 1914). As late as 1930, according to the *Report on the National Income Survey of 1930*, about one-third of net industrial income came from cottage industry, much of it based in the countryside (Nakamura 1983: 79).

It is arguable that the inter-war years, not the post-World War II years, marked the transition to heavy industry and mass production. Yoshihara, for example, identifies the 1912–36 period with the "rise of heavy industry" (1994: 8). Minami also notes that between 1920 and 1938 the predominance of light industries, including textiles, foodstuffs, ceramics and wood products, was overtaken by heavy industry, including metals, metal products, machinery and chemicals (1986: 133). More than that, there was a significant transformation of the light industries in the inter-war years. Until the 1930s textiles made up about two-thirds of manu-factured exports and employed one-fourth of industrial workers. It was during the inter-war years that there was a large shift in export content from silk to cotton textiles, implying a shift toward large-scale factory production (Yamazawa and Yamamoto 1979: 136). At the same time, a greater proportion of reeled silk and woven silk for the export market came to be produced on a large scale (Allen 1972: 118).

Though the inter-war years were indeed transitional, the most dramatic changes in terms of heavy industry occurred in the 1930s, as suggested by Macpherson above. This is most clearly shown by looking at the changing ratio of heavy industry to total industry, in terms of both employment and production. (Nakamura 1983: 180–1. Heavy industry is defined to include metals, metal products, machinery, chemicals, cement and lime; light industry is defined as the total of all other industries.) As Table 9.1 indicates, it was not until 1930 that heavy industrial production really took off and not until the mid-1930s for employment in heavy industry. It seems reasonable, on these grounds, to treat the 1880s to the 1930s as a single, fairly cohesive period.

At the same time, large-scale production is as applicable to light as to heavy industry, and there were significant changes in this regard, as noted above for the textile industry. Yet the inter-war years were marked by the development and consolidation of a dual structure, with large-scale firms predominantly producing for export and small-scale firms and households producing for the home market. It is production for the home market that is of particular relevance to this study, given that the econometric tests examine the relationship between changes in manufacturing output and *domestic* wholesale manufacturing prices. (Cf. Noda 1979: 226 regarding the

Table 9.1 Proportions of heavy industry to total industry: 1920–36

Year	Employment	Production
1920	25.4	32.8
1922	27.3	28.0
1924	26.1	26.2
1926	25.5	28.8
1928	27.1	31.6
1930	24.1	36.6
1932	26.7	39.8
1934	33.8	45.4
1936	34.8	53.6

definition of wholesale manufacturing prices.) Allen (1972: 124) describes this dual structure and its relation to the export and home markets as follows:

> [I]t must not be forgotten that a large part of the goods and services produced in Japan remained peculiar to that country. Along with the development of new industries of Western style, there continued to flourish numerous small-scale trades which provided for the special wants of the Japanese purchasers. Some indication of the importance of these has been given in the description of the textile and pottery industries. But there were many others which, unlike the textiles, had been almost completely unaffected by contact with the West – the *geta*-making trade, the house-building trade, the Japanese-style dress trade, the foodstuffs industry and many others. The development of great new industries, and the appearance of large factories in the cotton-spinning, engineering, iron and steel and pottery industries, had not meant the general disappearance of older trades or of older methods of production in them. Thus, by the twenties, every observer of Japan's industrial system was impressed by the contrast between large-scale production in one part of the economy and small-scale enterprise, often of an unfamiliar kind, in the rest . . . .

In woven silks and cotton textiles, for example, the techniques and organization of production for the home market remained essentially the same throughout the pre-World War II years, in spite of the transformations in production for export (Allen 1972: 118–20; cf. 85–6 regarding similar dual structures in the paper and brewing industries). Of the cotton textile industry, in which the first large-scale factories in Japan originated, Nakamura writes as follows: "Diversity of preferences for patterns and coloring of the narrow breadth cloth used in the home market necessitated small-scale production. It was in this market that small local producers were able to survive and prosper" (1983: 87).

The persistent demand for traditional consumption goods produced by traditional means is argued by Kuznets, Ohkawa and Rosovsky to have been beneficial to Japan's economic growth. Kuznets (1968: 404), for example, regards it as a plausible hypothesis that

> the persistence of demand for traditional products – whether agricultural, manufactured, or services – has been a source of strength in the economic growth of Japan, minimizing the adoption of far more costly Western consumer goods while increasing efficiency and utilizing established skills and supplementing labor

with relatively inexpensive adaptions of modern power and technology . . . .

The complementarity of the two halves of the dual structure is emphasized by Nakamura, who argues that large-scale manufacturers provided intermediate goods, such as thread, flour and sugar, that facilitated the growth of small-scale manufacturers. This interdependence created the conditions for balanced growth between large- and small-scale manufacturers (1983: 87).

Though a dual firm structure was re-established in the post-war years, it was of a distinctly different character. The pre-war dichotomy between large-scale manufacture for export and small-scale manufacture for the home market no longer held, as there was a dramatic Westernization of consumption in post-war Japan, with an ever larger share of domestic consumption goods produced by the largest and most technically advanced firms. As a consequence, there was a tighter connection in the post-war years between large, technically advanced firms and domestic wholesale prices in manufacture, whereas there was little such connection in the pre-war years.

The *zaibatsu* were large family-controlled conglomerates that grew rapidly in the inter-war years. In some respects their growth marked a significant turning point towards large-scale enterprise. Of the *zaibatsu* directly engaged in industrial production, the Mitsubishi and Mitsui groups were the most important. Mitsubishi was involved in heavy industrial production and Mitsui in textile and food manufacture. Both groups had exclusive buying and selling arrangements with firms within their group. Mitsubishi and Mitsui were exceptions, however, and most *zaibatsu* focused their activities on the tertiary sector and on mining. Nakamura (1983: 210–12) writes that

> the main emphasis of zaibatsu management was on mining, commerce, and financial sectors . . . . These sectors were also the origins of high zaibatsu profits and were the base from which they could exercise their tremendous power over the economy. But tertiary concentration was also the reason that zaibatsu weakened with the advance of heavy and chemical industry. It was in this way that the Japanese zaibatsu differed from the classic industrial groups of Germany.

It was Mitsui in particular that became heavily involved in the small-scale manufacture that characterized production for the home market. Mitsui supplanted the role of traditional wholesale merchants in the foodstuff and textile industries, advancing funds and giving technical advice. This did not occur, though, until the late 1920s (Allen 1972: 134–5). Thus

238

while the Mitsui *zaibatsu* stands as a significant forerunner of post-war relations among firms, its role was too little and too late to have had a sizable impact on the relation of wholesale prices and output in the manufacturing sector at large.

Nakamura disputes the commonly held view that the years just after World War I saw the rise of oligopoly, associated with the strengthening of the *zaibatsu*. Nakamura defines an oligopolistic industry as one in which capital per firm is rising and the number of firms is declining. By these measures, there was a clear overall trend towards oligopoly in only two industries over the span of years from 1914 to 1934, electric power and banking and finance. Nakamura writes that "It is mainly due to concentration in these two industries that the inter-war period had been characterized as one of monopolization" (1983: 202). In fourteen of the twenty-six industries Nakamura evaluates there was a trend towards an increased number of firms and no trend increase in capital per firm. That is, there was a trend away from oligopoly in the majority of industries in the inter-war years (1983: 200–1). Nakamura also notes that the establishment of cartels did not occur until the 1930s (1983: 202). Even taking into account the inter-war rise of the *zaibatsu*, then, it seems plausible to regard the span of years from the 1880s to the 1930s as a fairly cohesive period in Japan, antedating both mass production and "vertical semi-integration" (Ito 1992: 392).

From the point of view of Transformational Growth, the key characteristics of the old, pre-mass-production period can be summarized as follows. Until the transitional period of the 1930s, the largely decentralized nature of production and marketing and the general lack of vertical integration between production and marketing remained distinguishing characteristics of the economy. This was all the more true of those establishments producing manufactures for the home market.

THE NEW PERIOD

Nakamura notes that the World War II years are often omitted from accounts of Japanese economic development (1995: 3). The author argues that this omission neglects the beneficial legacy of wartime developments on Japan's subsequent development. It was during the war, for example, that the system of subcontracting between large parent firms and small firms was consolidated, a key element of *keiretsu* (enterprise group) arrangements. Nakamura also argues that the post-war pattern of government administrative guidance, manifested in the policies of the Ministry of International Trade and Industry (MITI) and the Bank of Japan, was also a legacy of the wartime experience (1995: 18–19). Last, the war had a

239

significant impact on the development and diffusion of new technologies. Nakamura (1995: 16–18) describes this process as follows:

> The training of engineers and workers who acquired a mastery of their technologies in these factories also directly prepared the country for postwar development. Factories that made machine guns turned to making sewing machines; optical weapons factories began turning out cameras and binoculars. In this way the facilities, technology, and skills acquired during the war exerted a tremendous influence on the subsequent direction of the economy.

As in the 1930s, heavy industry was the driving force in the Japanese economy into the 1960s (Yoshihara 1994: 19). Key among these heavy industries were chemicals, machinery, steel, shipbuilding, electrical power and coal (Peck 1976: 535, 538, Nakamura 1995: 46). Barriers to technology transfer, established in the 1930s, were removed in the post-war years, enabling Japan to obtain rapidly the best of the science-based technologies developed in the 1930s and 1940s (Yoshihara 1994: 19, Nakamura 1995: 50). Many of these particular technologies saw their first use in Japan during these early post-war years (Peck 1976: 535). Partly as a response to favorable demand conditions resulting from the Korean War, there was an increasingly large inflow of foreign technologies after the early 1950s, based largely on technology agreements with foreign firms. The number of such agreements increased from twenty-seven in 1950 to 103 in 1953, 460 in 1965 and 1,157 in 1970 (Peck 1976: 540, Nakamura 1995: 50).

One of the distinctive characteristics of Japan's economic development was its ability to succeed largely on the basis of imported technology. Among the developed countries, Japan relied to an unusual degree on learning rather than invention (Amsden 1989: 4–5). Nakamura describes the Japanese achievement in these years as follows:

> Certainly, in the 1950s and 1960s, little [technology] that is epoch-making was independently developed in Japan . . . . Japan's achievement during this period, however, was the combining of numerous imported technologies to create low-cost mass production systems . . . . This combination of synthesizing technology and heavily investing produced the facelift undergone by many industries such as steel, shipbuilding, and automobiles within the space of about ten years.
>
> (1995: 82. Cf. Kosai 1986: 113–19
> for a similar account of the rapid transition
> to mass production in the heavy industries
> during these years.)

The rapid adoption of mass-production technologies in the 1950s occurred not only in the heavy industries but in more consumer-oriented industries such as home appliances, sewing machines, cameras, watches and consumer electronics (Kosai 1986: 120, Nakamura 1995: 80). Competition on the basis of borrowed technology was made possible by the emphasis of Japanese manufacturers on cost reduction and quality control, involving continuous and often incremental improvements in the application of widely available capital goods. This emphasis was distinct from that of US producers, who placed greater emphasis on new product development (Peck 1976: 543–4).

Mass-production techniques were not only introduced rapidly in Japan but, just as important, were rapidly diffused throughout the economy. This resulted in part from MITI's administrative guidance policies. Of the steel industry, for example, Peck writes that "All Japanese steel companies had at least two liquid oxygen furnaces by 1961, only four years after the first use of the process in Japan. This quick diffusion was prompted by MITI policies" (1976: 557. Cf. 554–6 regarding MITI's similar role in the diffusion of technologies for the production of polyethylene). There were other distinctive institutions in Japan that facilitated the diffusion of new production technologies to small firms. These were the extensive subcontracting arrangements between large and small firms, small business associations, and local government research institutions (Peck 1976: 565–6, Patrick and Rohlen 1987: 346). The particularly rapid diffusion of new production techniques strengthened the ability of the Japanese economy to be competitive in the world market on the basis of borrowed technologies (Peck 1976: 582–3). The rapid borrowing and diffusion of mass-production technologies in the early post-war years also suggests the appropriateness of defining the pre-war years as the old, pre-mass-production period and the post-war years as the new, mass-production period.

During World War II the government liquidated most small businesses that were not directly connected with the production of munitions. After the war, though, the number of small businesses increased rapidly, resulting in the consolidation of a dual industrial structure analogous to that which developed in the inter-war years (Nakamura 1995: 162, 180). Patrick and Rohlen call small enterprises "the economic, political, and social heart and backbone of Japan" (1987: 331). In recent years almost one-half of manufacturing jobs have been in establishments with fewer than fifty employees, compared with about 15 per cent of manufacturing jobs in the United States (Tabb 1995: 82).

There were significant differences between the dual structures of the pre- and post-World War II years, however, differences that affect the relationships among techniques of production and changes in output and domestic wholesale prices in manufacturing. In the pre-war years, large-scale production was generally associated with the export market and small-scale production with the home market. This fairly neat dichotomy no longer held in the post-war years, during which an ever larger proportion of goods for the home market came to be produced by modern mass-production technologies. This resulted from the Westernization of consumption in the home market (which was particularly rapid after the late 1950s), the reduced reliance of Japanese producers as a whole on production for export, and the diffusion of capital-intensive mass-production technologies to small firms.

Nakamura (1995: 100, 118) describes the "abrupt Westernization of the national lifestyle" as follows:

> As consumption patterns changed in favor of Westernization, they produced the lifestyle of contemporary Japan: people eat bread and meat, acquire color television sets, refrigerators, and the full spectrum of household electrical appliances, own automobiles, enjoy their leisure, have a taste for travel, and are very fashion-conscious.

The rapid changes in consumption patterns can be measured by the percentage of households possessing mass-produced consumer goods. For televisions, washing machines and refrigerators, the percentage of households possessing these goods increased from less than 10 to more than 90 over a span of ten years, primarily from the late 1950 to the late 1960s. For automobiles, air conditioners, microwave ovens and video-cassette recorders this increase was also very rapid, though less dramatically so. There was also over the post-war years a substantial decline in *per capita* consumption of the traditional foodstuffs (miso and soy sauce, for example) that once made up a large proportion of manufacturing output (Nakamura 1995: 101). The Westernization of consumption was also reflected in the changing character of technology agreements after the late 1950s, with an increasing share of agreements related to the production of consumer-oriented goods (Peck 1976: 535, 538).

Though the bulk of exports were manufactured goods both before and after World War II, Japan's dependence on the export market was substantially less in the post-war years. In the mid-1930s exports as well as imports made up about 20 per cent of GNP. This share declined by about half in the post-war years up to the 1973 oil crisis (Nakamura 1995: 45). As regards techniques of production in small manufacturing firms, low productivity was regarded as problematic (Ackley and Ishi 1976: 175, Peck 1976: 565). There was, none the less, a significant shift towards more sophisticated and capital-intensive technologies in the post-war years, with a lesser technological gap between large and small firms than had characterized the dual structure in the pre-war years. Regarding the persistence of the dual structure in the post-war years, Nakamura writes that

The only thing that has changed is that small businesses are shifting to capital intensiveness since . . . they are no longer able to get along as before with only labor-intensive technology that relies on what had once been cheap labor, now that they are surrounded by a labor shortage and great technological progress.
(1995: 180. Cf. Kosai 1986: 149–50 and Tabb 1995: 89 for similar accounts of the technological sophistication of small and medium-size firms)

As suggested above, the diffusion of new technologies was facilitated by the extensive *keiretsu* subcontracting arrangements between large parent firms and their smaller suppliers.

There was, then, a breakdown of the pre-war dichotomy between large-scale manufacture for export using modern techniques and small-scale manufacture for the home market using traditional techniques. The significance of this change is that the relation between more modern techniques of production and domestic wholesale prices in manufacture was more direct in the post-war years, a result of the larger proportion of goods for the home market produced by such techniques.

The *zaibatsu* were dismantled as part of post-war occupation policy under the Supreme Commander for the Allied Powers. In this effort to lessen economic concentration, fifty-seven *zaibatsu* families and eighty-three holding companies were ordered to give up their holdings, which were sold to other parties (Yoshihara 1994: 124). A number of the largest *zaibatsu*, including Mitsubishi and Mitsui, evolved into some of Japan's largest post-war enterprise groups, or *keiretsu*. These enterprise groups were distinct from the *zaibatsu*, however, in that they were no longer controlled by holding companies, that companies within groups were more independent, and that their focus was more on industrial production than on finance and trade. As Kosai writes, "The breakup of the zaibatsu prepared the way for the demise of the era dominated by finance capital and for the arrival of the new industrialism" (1986: 27).

The *keiretsu* system involved a number of arrangements, including sales among companies within a group, subcontracting for parts, financing by a core *keiretsu* bank to member firms, and forward integration by manufacturers into distribution and marketing (Shimokawa 1985: 3, Kosai 1986: 121). Ito (1992: 392) describes *keiretsu* marketing arrangements as follows:

Japanese manufacturers develop exclusive distribution systems (distribution *keiretsu*). Panasonic stores, Sony stores, Toshiba stores, and others carry a wide range of electronic products, but all from one brand. This vertical semi-integration makes it difficult for new entrants, including importers, to penetrate the market.

243

Though they remained dominant in the marketing of automobiles, exclusive *keiretsu* marketing arrangements, in which retailers sold only goods from one enterprise group, were of declining importance in the 1980s for some products (such as consumer electronics), replaced to some extent by "mass sales stores" (Shimokawa 1985: 19–21). None the less, manufacturers not only set wholesale prices but commonly controlled retail and discount prices, and it is this price-setting by producers that is of decisive importance for price stability (Ito 1992: 393, 397).

Such forward integration by manufacturers into marketing created the possibility of greater independence of price and output, a possibility realized by the pricing policies of many Japanese firms. The so-called "non-cost" principle of pricing was adopted by Toyota Motors after World War II. Under this principle, Toyota attempted to maintain stable prices or to lower them in the face of increased costs and demand (Shingo 1980: 75). A large number of Japanese manufacturers practised the similar principle of pricing for market share (McMillan 1984: 208).

The Japanese government did not play a large role in the price stabilization of manufactured goods. It was not until the Economic Plan of 1965 that the government set inflation targets for the economy (McMillan 1984: 73). In the winter of 1973–74 the government established price controls for liquefied petroleum gas and kerosene and a system of administrative guidance for the prices of about sixty other commodities. Beginning in the early 1970s, however, the government pursued an expansionary monetary policy that is argued to have contributed greatly to the inflation of the time (Lincoln 1988: 38, Kosai 1993: 148). The government practised little price intervention during the oil crisis of the late 1970s.

As regards Transformational Growth, the key characteristics of the new period can be summarized as follows. The post-war years were marked by the rapid transition to mass-production techniques in manufacturing industries and forward integration into marketing to accommodate these techniques, with wholesale pricing decisions in the hands of producers rather than merchants. Along with the development of the national and of international markets, this transition created the possibility of substantially greater price stability, a possibility realized by the market-share pricing policies that were typical of Japanese manufacturing firms.

PRICES, WAGES AND OUTPUT IN THE MANUFACTURING SECTOR

For the old period this study uses data from Ohkawa and Shinohara (1979), a compilation of data from their fourteen-volume *Estimates of Long-term Economic Statistics of Japan since 1868*. The data are widely regarded as definitive and result from a decades-long project "to provide a set of data as complete and accurate as possible"[4] (1979: xiii).

The changing relation of domestic wholesale prices and product wages to output in the manufacturing sector is evaluated by ordinary least squares estimates of the following equation:

$$X_t = \alpha + \beta1(Y_t) + \beta2(Y_t * Dummy_t) + \beta3(Y_{t-1}) + \beta4(Y_{t-1} * Dummy_{t-1}) + \epsilon$$

where $X \equiv$ the logarithmic growth rate of either wholesale manufacturing prices or product wages in manufacturing; $Y \equiv$ the logarithmic growth rate of real manufacturing output; $Dummy \equiv 0$ for the old period (1880–1939) and 1 for the new (1952–91), with intervening years left out; $t \equiv$ current values; $t-1 \equiv$ values lagged one year and $\epsilon \equiv$ an error term. (The equation was also estimated by adding the dummy variable itself, allowing the intercept to vary, but coefficient estimates of the dummy variable did not prove significant in any of this study's regressions.)[5] Lagged output variables were included following Michie (1987), on the plausible assumption that prices and wages respond to changes in output with a lag. The inclusion of dummy-modified output variables enables a test of structural change across the old and new periods, for which $\beta1$ and $\beta3$ represent coefficients for the old period of current and lagged output, respectively, and $\beta2$ and $\beta4$ represent coefficients of structural change across periods for current and lagged output, respectively.

For wholesale manufacturing prices Transformational Growth hypothesizes a more strongly positive relation with output in the old period than in the new, implying that the coefficients testing structural change are negative. That is, $\beta1$ and $\beta3 > 0$; $\beta2$ and $\beta4 < 0$.

For product wages in manufacturing, transformational growth hypothesizes an inverse relation with changes in output in the old period and a positive relation in the new, implying that the coefficients testing structural change are positive. That is, $\beta1$ and $\beta3 < 0$; $\beta2$ and $\beta4 > 0$.

Table 9.2 shows results for regressions using wholesale prices as the dependent variable and Table 9.3 for regressions using product wages as the dependent variable. Beta coefficient estimates and absolute t-statistic values (in parentheses) are shown in the main body of the tables. To the right are adjusted R^2s, standard errors of the regressions, Durbin–Watson statistics, indicators of autocorrelation (ARMA) corrections (in parentheses) and degrees of freedom. To facilitate presentation, coefficient estimates of constants are not presented. Augmented Dickey–Fuller tests were run on all time series and revealed no statistically significant evidence of non-stationarity at the 1 per cent level.[6] All tables include results for two regression equations, the fully specified equation, indicated by A to the left of the tables, and the equation yielding the highest adjusted R^2, indicated by B. Statistical significance of beta estimates is indicated by an

Table 9.2 Wholesale manufacturing prices regressed on manufacturing output (based on logarithmic growth rates)

	Current output			Lagged output	
	Old period $\beta 1$	Structural change $\beta 2$		Old period $\beta 3$	Structural change $\beta 4$
A	0.147 (0.949)	−0.004 (0.021)		0.489*** (3.180)	−0.400** (2.208)
	Adjusted R^2 0.309. Standard error 0.068. Durbin–Watson statistic 1.977 (AR1, MA1). Degrees of freedom 89.				
B				0.424*** (2.763)	−0.373** (2.238)
	Adjusted R^2 0.311. Standard error 0.068. Durbin–Watson statistic 1.976 (AR1, MA1). Degrees of freedom 91.				

Notes
Old period: 1880–1939; new period: 1952–91. Asterisks indicate significance at the 10 per cent (*), 5 per cent (**) and 1 per cent (***) levels, using one-tailed tests.

Table 9.3 Product wages in manufacturing regressed on manufacturing output (based on logarithmic growth rates)

	Current output			Lagged output	
	Old period $\beta 1$	Structural change $\beta 2$		Old period $\beta 3$	Structural change $\beta 4$
A	−0.021 (0.124)	0.095 (0.466)		−0.298** (1.796)	0.458** (2.360)
	Adjusted R^2 0.164. Standard error 0.073. Durbin–Watson statistic 1.960 (AR1). Degrees of freedom 90.				
B				−0.305** (1.890)	0.480*** (2.543)
	Adjusted R^2 0.179. Standard error 0.072. Durbin–Watson statistic 1.963 (AR1). Degrees of freedom 92.				

Notes
Old period: 1880–1939; new period: 1952–91. Asterisks indicate significance at the 10 per cent (*), 5 per cent (**) and 1 per cent (***) levels, using one-tailed tests.

asterisk (*) for the 10 per cent level, two asterisks (**) for the 5 per cent level and three asterisks (***) for the 1 per cent level, using one-tailed tests. All results referred to as statistically significant are so at the 5 per cent level or better.

Consistent with the above hypotheses, row A in Table 9.2 indicates a large positive and statistically significant relation between prices and lagged output in the old period, and a negative and statistically significant estimate for the test of structural change with lagged output. Since estimates of current output are insignificant, these variables are dropped from the regression equation. Results are shown in row B of Table 9.2, revealing essentially the results, though with a higher adjusted R^2. These results are consistent with the Transformational Growth hypothesis that the relation of changes in price and output in manufacturing was more strongly positive in the old period than in the new.

Coefficients are also estimated using the above equation with the logarithmic growth rate of money wages in manufacturing as the dependent variable. The regression revealed a positive estimated relation between money wages and output in the old and new periods on both current and lagged output, with beta estimates ranging between 0.133 and 0.215 for current and lagged output in the old and new periods.[7] All estimates in the regression, though, were statistically insignificant. The significance of coefficients testing structural change was particularly weak, with t statistics of 0.276 and 0.051 for estimates of current and lagged output respectively. That is, the relation between changes in money wages and output is not significantly different across periods, based on this test of structural change.[8]

Table 9.3 shows results for regressions using product wages as the dependent variable. As suggested by the above regressions using prices and money wages as the dependent variable, row A of Table 9.3 shows a significant inverse relation between product wages and lagged output in the old period. The coefficient estimate on the test of structural change was positive and significant on lagged output. As with regressions on prices, coefficient estimates of current output are insignificant, and these variables were dropped from the equation. This yielded the results in row B of Table 9.3, which are essentially the same. The results are consistent with the Transformational Growth hypothesis that the relation of changes in product wages and output in manufacturing is inverse in the old period and more positive in the new.

Michie (1987) also examines the relation of product wages and output in Japanese manufacturing. In contrast to the above results, Michie's regressions show significant negative correlations for the years 1950 to 1982 (Michie 1987: 57–61). There are two reasons why the above results are preferable to Michie's.

First, given the price stability of manufactured goods in post-war Japan, as well as the flexible system of money wage determination, it seems improbable that anyone would hypothesize *a priori* a negative relation between product wages and output in the manufacturing sector. This alone suggests that one should be skeptical of Michie's results. (Cf. Cole 1971: 73 and McMillan 1984: 187 regarding the flexibility of money wage determination in Japan.)

Second, Michie's detrending procedure is problematic. In an effort to isolate the cyclical relation between product wages and output, Michie detrends by taking percentage deviations from five-year moving averages. The problem with abstracting from five-year moving averages is that these averages are themselves made up of trend and cyclical components, so that the technique decycles as well as detrends. As a consequence, Michie's regressions isolate the least systematic relations between product wages and output. The difference in sign observed between Michie's and the present study is not attributable to data differences or to the different span of years considered. Michie's detrending technique was used on the same data as the present study and also showed a negative though statistically insignificant relation between product wages and current and lagged output in the manufacturing sector for the years 1952 to 1991.[9] Michie's detrending technique also calls into question the more general conclusion of his book that there was no consistent pattern in the relation between product wages and output in the advanced capitalist economies in the post-war years.

The use of growth rates can result in the opposite problem from Michie's method, conflating changes resulting from trend and cycle. This potential problem was addressed by redoing the above analysis, using, instead of logarithmic growth rates, the Hodrick–Prescott non-linear detrending filter.[10]

The results are shown in Table 9.4, using wholesale prices as the dependent variable and in Table 9.5 using product wages as the dependent variable. For wholesale prices, the most significant difference using the Hodrick–Prescott filter are these: the coefficient estimate for the old period of current output is larger and statistically significant, and the coefficient estimates for the old period and for structural change with lagged output are also larger in absolute value, with the same levels of statistical significance as before. The similar results obtained from using the Hodrick–Prescott filter and logarithmic growth rates suggest their robustness.

For product wages, the differences in using the Hodrick–Prescott filter are more substantial. While coefficient estimates of lagged output for the old period and for structural change are not much smaller in absolute value, they are significant only at the 10 per cent level, not at the 5 per cent level or better, as before. Thus the Transformational Growth hypothesis regarding the changing relation of product wages and output is not as

248

Table 9.4 Wholesale manufacturing prices regressed on manufacturing output (based on Hodrick–Prescott filter)

	Current output			Lagged output	
	Old period $\beta1$	*Structural change* $\beta2$		*Old period* $\beta3$	*Structural change* $\beta4$
A	0.336** (2.175)	−0.195 (0.855)		0.650*** (4.253)	−0.526** (2.346)
		Adjusted R^2 0.454. Standard error 0.040. Durbin–Watson statistic 1.894 (MA1). Degrees of freedom 93.			
B	0.246** (2.185)			0.613*** (4.182)	−0.466** (2.202)
		Adjusted R^2 0.455. Standard error 0.040. Durbin–Watson statistic 1.858 (MA1). Degrees of freedom 94.			

Notes
Old period: 1880–1939; new period: 1952–91. Asterisks indicate significance at the 10 per cent (*), 5 per cent (**) and 1 per cent (***) levels, using one-tailed tests.

Table 9.5 Product wages in manufacturing regressed on manufacturing output (based on Hodrick–Prescott filter)

	Current output			Lagged output	
	Old period $\beta1$	*Structural change* $\beta2$		*Old period* $\beta3$	*Structural change* $\beta4$
A	−0.042 (0.218)	0.238 (0.862)		−0.290* (1.520)	0.438* (1.589)
		Adjusted R^2 0.194. Standard error 0.050. Durbin–Watson statistic 1.834 (MA1). Degrees of freedom 93.			
B				−0.279* (1.505)	0.402* (1.488)
		Adjusted R^2 0.203. Standard error 0.049. Durbin–Watson statistic 1.855 (MA1). Degrees of freedom 95.			

Notes
Old period: 1880–1939; new period: 1952–91. Asterisks indicate significance at the 10 per cent (*), 5 per cent (**) and 1 per cent (***) levels, using one-tailed tests.

consistently supported as the hypothesis regarding the changing relation of wholesale prices and output.[11]

As a final test of robustness, regressions were run allowing the variance of the error term (as well as the constant) to vary across the old and new periods. That is, regressions were run separately for the old and new periods, regressing wholesale prices and product wages on current and lagged output using both logarithmic growth rates and the Hodrick–Prescott filter. Differences across the periods were then tested with confidence intervals. The results are shown in Table 9.6. The first two columns show structural change coefficient estimates of lagged output from Tables 9.2–5, and the last two columns show implied structural change coefficient estimates, which are derived from the difference across periods of coefficient estimates of lagged output.[12]

For wholesale prices regressed on output, the implied structural change coefficient estimates in the last two columns are a fair amount larger than the structural change coefficient estimates in the first two columns and remain significant at the 5 per cent level.

For product wages regressed on output, the implied structural change coefficient estimates in the last two columns are somewhat smaller than the structural change coefficient estimates in the first two columns. The implied coefficient based on logarithmic growth rates is significant at only the 10 per cent level, though, compared with the 1 per cent level shown in the first column, using the direct test of structural change. Though it remains large and positive, the implied coefficient of structural change

Table 9.6 Wholesale manufacturing prices and product wages regressed on lagged manufacturing output

---

Wholesale prices

Structural change coefficients (from Tables 9.2 and 9.4, row B)		Implied structural change coefficients (from within period regressions)	
Log. growth rates	Hodrick–Prescott	Log. growth rates	Hodrick–Prescott
−0.373**	−0.466**	−0.568**	−0.546**

Product wages

Structural change coefficients (from Tables 9.3 and 9.5, row B)		Implied structural change coefficients (from within period regressions)	
Log. growth rates	Hodrick–Prescott	Log. growth rates	Hodrick–Prescott
0.480***	0.402*	0.414*	0.398

Note
Asterisks indicate significance at the 10 per cent (*), 5 per cent (**) and 1 per cent (***) levels, using one-tailed tests.

based on the Hodrick–Prescott filter is not significant, at even the 10 per cent level.

CONCLUSION

Two of the most central hypotheses of Transformational Growth are that wholesale manufacturing prices moved more procyclically and product wages more countercyclically in the old, pre-mass-production period than in the new, mass-production period. The econometric analyses provide consistent if not always significant support for these hypotheses. In all regressions using wholesale prices and product wages as dependent variables, the signs of all coefficient estimates of output (current and lagged) and structural change are as hypothesized. For the product wage–output relation, three of four specifications testing structural change on lagged output are significant at the 10 per cent level or better. For the wholesale price–output relation, all four specifications testing structural change on lagged output are significant at the 5 per cent level. Thus the hypothesis regarding the changing relation of wholesale prices and output is more strongly supported than that regarding the changing relation of product wages and output. This outcome is also reflected in the substantially higher adjusted R^2s for the regressions of wholesale prices on output. The results of the tests are consistent with the view that the change in the price–output relation across the old and new periods is the driving force underlying the change in the product wage–output relation across periods. It is argued that the change in the price–output relation results from the transition from pre-mass-production techniques in the old period to mass-production techniques in the new, for mass production implies mass marketing, generally associated with relatively long-term pricing policies.

The value of a theory lies in its capacity to generate interesting and testable hypotheses, and in this sense Transformational Growth reveals its promise. Just as important, Transformational Growth creates new linkages among diverse fields, integrating issues of price and wage movement over business cycles with issues of technical change and market development. By examining the macroeconomic implications of prevailing production techniques and their associated marketing arrangements, Transformational Growth provides a historical foundation with which to evaluate the cyclical pattern of real wages. Rather than being determined by optimizing behavior on the part of workers and capitalists in the face of marginal productivity of labor schedules, Transformational Growth suggests that the cyclical pattern of real wages is largely a residual effect, driven by the extent of price procyclicality.

NOTES

1 One might argue that price mark-ups were more procyclical in the pre-mass-production period, but this depends on the cyclical pattern of the unit cost–output relationship. That is, there may be a substantial difference across periods in unit cost changes with respect to output changes. The basic argument has two components, both working in the same direction. First, short-run marginal costs may well increase more with respect to output increases in the old, pre-mass-production than in the new, mass-production period, a result of the lesser flexibility of pre-mass-production technologies in the face of demand increases. Second, with greater capital intensity and thus higher proportions of fixed costs in the new period, there is a stronger tendency for unit costs to decline as output increases. For the mass-production period, this view of costs is essentially the same as that practised by manufacturing cost accountants, who generally assume constant short-run marginal costs and declining unit costs with respect to output increases, with declining unit costs a function of fixed costs spread over more units of output. (Cf. Shillinglaw 1978 regarding the contrast between cost accountants' and marginal economists' views of short-run marginal cost.) These views are reflected, for example, in cost accountants' methods of determining break-even sales levels and standard costs (estimates of unit costs at targeted levels of capacity utilization).

2 In this case, product wages are defined as money wages in manufacturing, adjusted by the domestic wholesale price index for manufactured goods. Product wages are thus real wages from the firm's point of view and are appropriate here, given the exploration of the implications of changing techniques of production for price determination.

3 If anything, there was less procyclicality of money wages in the new period, based on the Hodrick–Prescott detrending filter, strengthening the argument that the difference in the cyclical movement of product wages across periods is driven by changes in the cyclical movement of wholesale prices. See note 11 for measures of structural change for the money wage–output relation across the old and new periods, based on logarithmic growth rates and the Hodrick–Prescott detrending filter.

4 Regarding data consistency, changes in daily wages in the old period are compared with changes in hourly wages in the new. This reflects not an inconsistency in data collection but the transformation of the system of wage payment, which was predominantly on a daily basis in the old period and on a monthly basis in the new. Hourly data for the new period were derived by dividing average monthly earnings over the year by average monthly hours over the year. Comparing changes in daily and hourly wages is consistent, as long as hours worked per day in the old period did not fluctuate greatly. This seems plausible, given that employers would presumably have required a full day's work for a day's wages. For the old and new periods, earnings include irregular payments, such as bonuses. All variables were converted to index values where 1935 = 100 for the old period and 1980 = 100 for the new.

5 It should be noted that this chapter focuses on price fluctuations, not trends. Regarding the latter, domestic wholesale manufacturing prices rose more rapidly in Japan in the pre-mass-production period than in the mass-production period. From 1880 to 1939 these prices rose by an average annual rate of 2.3 per cent, compared with 1.6 per cent for the 1952 to 1991 years (based on logarithmic growth rates).

6 At the 5 per cent level for money wages, using logarithmic growth rates, though at the 1 per cent level for money wages using the Hodrick–Prescott detrending procedure, discussed below. Stationarity was tested not only for the entire 1880–1991 period but for the 1880–1939 and 1952–91 subperiods, with practically the same results.

7 With estimates for the new period being $(\beta 1 + \beta 2)$ and $(\beta 3 + \beta 4)$ for current and lagged output, respectively.

8 Using the same regression equation but detrending with the Hodrick–Prescott filter rather than logarithmic growth rates, there is more substantial evidence of structural change in the money wage–output relation, with greater procyclicality in the old period than in the new. See note 11. As noted above, this strengthens the argument that the difference in the cyclical movement of product wages across periods is driven by changes in the cyclical movement of wholesale prices.

9 In a single regression without dummy-modified variables, the beta estimate of current output was −0.067, with a t statistic of 0.458; the beta estimate of lagged output was −0.163, with a t statistic of 1.109.

10 With a smoothing parameter of 10. The data were filtered separately across the old and new periods. In their pre-filtered form the data are based on indices (with 1935 = 100 and 1980 = 100) converted to natural logarithms. See Chapter 8 for a brief discussion of the Hodrick–Prescott filter and its associated smoothing parameter.

11 Based on the Hodrick–Prescott filter rather than logarithmic growth rates, there was a greater difference across periods in the money wage–output relation, with a coefficient estimate of −0.410 and a t statistic of 1.570 for the test of structural change on current output (compared with a coefficient estimate of −0.060 and a t statistic of 0.276 based on logarithmic growth rates); and a coefficient estimate of −0.343 and a t statistic of 1.327 for the test of structural change on lagged output (compared with a coefficient estimate of 0.011 and a t statistic of 0.051 based on logarithmic growth rates). That is, when one more fully abstracts from trend effects, there is evidence that money wages were substantially (if not significantly) more procyclical in the old period than in the new.

12 Estimates of lagged output were drawn from best-specified equations, which included current output when indicated by adjusted R^2s. Actual coefficient estimates of lagged manufacturing output (followed by significance symbols as well as, in parentheses, absolute t statistic values) are as follows.

For wholesale manufacturing prices in the old period, based on logarithmic growth rates, 0.583*** (3.230) and, on Hodrick–Prescott filtering, 0.642*** (3.504).

For wholesale manufacturing prices in the new period, based on logarithmic growth rates, 0.015 (0.121) and, on Hodrick–Prescott filtering, 0.096 (1.171).

For product wages in the old period based on logarithmic growth rates, −0.271* (1.325) and, on Hodrick–Prescott filtering, −0.273 (1.243).

For product wages in the new period based on logarithmic growth rates, 0.144* (1.435) and, on Hodrick–Prescott filtering, 0.125 (0.933).

10

ARGENTINA

Transformational Growth in the absence of the new cycle

Enrique Delamonica

In this chapter a case, Argentina, which is strikingly different from those of other chapters is analyzed. Both in terms of current *per capita* income and in the development of industrial activities Argentina is not in the same league as the other countries in this book.

However, there are at least three theoretical reasons why considering such a case could be useful. First, by applying the Transformational Growth perspective to a developing country its capacity to generate new insights and interpretations can be explored and it can be shown that it is more than a (complex) statement about differences before and after World War II in OECD countries. Second, and in contrast to the other countries, Argentina has always been an "open, small" economy.[1] This means that external transactions (both in goods and in financial capital) need to be explicitly incorporated. Third, I will attempt to show that the high instability of the economy in the last decades is due mainly to the characteristics of its industrial structure and that, at the same time, this structure is not independent of the macroeconomic instability. Consequently, a set of policy implications can be derived which is broader than the traditional macroeconomic management which dominates both the academic and the policy debates.

The chapter is organized as follows. The second and third sections (pp. 256–65) look at what could be broadly classified as the "old cycle". In the third section the emergence of a craft industry at the turn of the century is briefly described. The effects it had at the macroeconomic level are looked at. In the fourth section the opposite perspective is taken: the effects of macroeconomic fluctuations (and external shocks) on the industrial structure are analyzed.

In the fifth and sixth sections a similar exercise is performed for the period beginning in the 1940s. This is the period when the import substitution industrialization (ISI) strategy takes hold. In the fifth section (see pp. 265–71) the different stages of ISI as well as its successes and limitations are explored. The industrial structure which took shape in this period is the basis for the kind of "stop–go" cycle characteristic of these decades. In the sixth section (see pp. 271–5), the "two-gap" model which describes those cycles is used to illuminate what has happened to the industrial structure during that period.

The compatibility of structuralism and Transformational Growth is evident in that both emphasize the role of the productive structure, in particular the characteristics of the industrial sector, in shaping macro-economic fluctuations. Methodologically, they both share a view in which economies are never at, or necessarily approaching, equilibrium. Their differences are mainly of emphasis, as structuralism is often applied to contemporary developing countries with recurrent balance of payment problems while Transformational Growth has mostly been used to contrast the behavior of advanced economies during different historical periods.

In this chapter the longer-term, historical view of Transformational Growth is applied to contrast the economic behavior and characteristics of Argentina during different periods. Also, rather than taking the productive structure of the economy as given in order to understand its macroeconomic behavior, an attempt will be made to link the industrial and the macroeconomic performance so that they impinge on each other. This and other lessons are summarized in the seventh and concluding section.

A few comments on method and approach are due before entering the substantive discussion of each section.

METHODOLOGICAL COMMENTS

First, in spite of the attempt to generate a model which will endogenously provide an explanation of macroeconomic fluctuations together with the evolution of the industrial structure, there are crucial points in time when exogenous shocks play a very prominent role. These shocks, however, should not be confused with the constant stream of exogenous productivity shocks used to describe fluctuations in neoclassical models. On the contrary, although they are not rare events, they are not continuous. Moreover, in the main they do not even affect the technology but the institutional, organizational and regulatory context.

Second, some of these shocks are due to sudden shifts in economic policy – devaluations, introduction/removal of price and wage controls, modifications of laws and regulations regarding the flow of financial capital, etc. In so far as these policies have an economic rationale (they are promoted by certain groups which expect to benefit from them), they could be considered endogenous to the economy. Nevertheless, it is not always analytically clear or appropriate to linearly ascribe policies to group interests and pursuing a more careful explanation would lead me to stray from the main point of the chapter.[2] Consequently, they will be treated as exogenously determined.

Finally, the argument will be presented without recourse to econometric testing because the quantity and quality of the time series data would not warrant it.

THE EMERGENCE OF CRAFT INDUSTRY

After decades of civil strife a constitutional order was set up in the 1860s and the frontier of usable land was effectively incorporated by 1880. These institutional changes opened the possibility of attracting foreign capital, mainly for the construction of railroads (see Table 10.1).

Table 10.1 Total foreign investment and railroad investment, 1885–91

Year	Foreign direct investment (1)	Railroad investment (2)	(2)*100/(1)
1885	13.5	11.5	85.2
1886	26.0	16.0	61.5
1887	106.9	37.8	35.8
1888	156.0	89.4	57.3
1889	112.8	51.9	46.0
1890	34.0	20.0	58.8
1891	5.7	5.7	100.0

Source: Di Tella and Zymelman (1973), p. 62.

Table 10.2 Growth of population, railroads and main exports, 1889–1914

Year	Population (000)	Railroads (000 km)	Exports Grain (000 tonnes)	Wool	Frozen meat
1889	3,066	6.5	389	129	12
1890–94	3,612	12.7	1,038	139	27
1895–99	4,219	15.0	1,711	211	56
1900–04	4,860	17.7	3,011	178	137
1905–09	5,803	22.2	4,825	170	239
1910–14	7,203	31.1	5,294	137	376

Source: Di Tella and Zymelman (1972), p. 25.

The railroads in turn reinforced the advantages of agriculture to become the dominant export commodity. Consequently, in a few years the country became a major international exporter of agricultural products (see Table 10.2). This is the first and fundamental characteristic of the working of the economy during the period. The influence of the connection between railroad construction and agricultural export had several consequences.

First, the industrial sector developed in the shadow of the agricultural one, which is the main generator of foreign currency. This sector had clear international comparative advantages in the traditional sense of the term. The only exportable manufactured goods were simple transformations of agricultural products: flour, frozen meat, canned meat, etc. Its volume and value were, however, substantially less significant than those of non-manufactured goods (grain, livestock, wool) in terms of both production and exports (Di Tella and Zymelman 1972).

However, although the industrial sector did not represent a substantial share of total exports, it was using the newest available technologies, which gave it an edge in international markets. This sector, nevertheless, had limited backward and forward linkages (Katz and Kosacoff 1989). It was not important in fostering growth and innovation in other sectors and reproduced a regressive distribution of income based on land rents and its distribution among a small urban elite.

Second, there was an unintended effect of the expansion of agricultural trade which fostered a particular – if limited – kind of growth. It was the creation of an urban middle class which provided goods and services to the landowners. These groups were concentrated in Buenos Aires, which was not only the political capital but also by far the most important port. Also, there emerged a budding working class (Villanueva 1972).

Third, in spite of the limited impact of agriculture-based manufactures in industry, the rise of the wealthy upper and middle classes provided the markets which allowed other sectors to spring up. Their growth represents the real transformation of the Argentine economy during this period. It was a gradual and slow process which imprinted upon industry

Table 10.3 Evolution of firm size, 1895–1935

Year	No. of firms	No. of employees	Horse-power
1895	5,700	30,000	15,000
1908	8,650	48,800	41,000
1913	14,844	99,000	269,000
1935	10,345	127,500	914,000

Source: Dorfman (1942), p. 126.

Table 10.4 Index of industrial production, 1900–30 (1950=100)

Year	Total	(a)	(b)	(c)	(d)	(e)	(f)	(g)	(h)	(i)	(j)	(k)	(l)	(m)	(n)	(o)
1900	9	17	23	3	21	27	7	7	9	–	–	16	22	3	1	–
1901	9	18	15	3	23	28	7	7	10	–	–	16	19	2	1	–
1902	10	17	18	3	24	27	7	5	10	–	–	18	30	3	1	–
1903	11	18	32	3	28	27	12	5	11	–	–	19	29	3	1	–
1904	12	18	33	4	31	29	16	7	11	–	–	21	38	4	1	–
1905	14	19	22	4	34	61	14	10	13	–	–	24	40	5	1	–
1906	15	19	26	4	29	44	17	16	19	–	–	24	56	6	1	–
1907	16	22	32	4	33	56	18	17	15	–	–	24	67	6	1	–
1908	17	24	44	4	35	56	16	17	17	–	–	29	61	6	2	–
1909	17	23	37	4	36	56	13	22	21	–	–	31	50	7	2	–
1910	21	28	37	5	36	67	26	27	20	–	–	30	89	10	3	–
1911	22	34	32	5	35	66	24	29	24	–	–	34	89	11	2	–
1912	21	31	44	5	40	56	20	32	22	–	–	36	77	11	3	–
1913	22	31	43	7	45	57	32	34	29	–	–	38	66	12	4	–
1914	20	32	39	7	39	39	23	25	25	–	–	38	64	10	5	–
1915	18	28	60	8	48	31	15	20	28	–	–	45	24	7	5	–
1916	19	30	49	3	43	30	44	28	31	–	–	44	31	8	3	–
1917	19	33	42	11	38	27	23	28	24	–	–	43	25	8	4	–
1918	22	39	72	14	43	30	37	26	30	–	1	53	26	6	2	–
1919	23	39	51	13	51	34	30	42	30	–	1	55	26	9	6	–
1920	24	37	51	10	52	46	52	42	29	–	1	48	37	12	10	–
1921	25	42	40	12	49	49	54	45	29	–	1	48	47	10	10	–
1922	28	45	56	12	50	57	67	55	32	2	1	54	41	12	14	–
1923	33	53	69	11	56	72	54	68	43	3	1	64	56	16	10	–
1924	34	56	41	15	58	72	74	70	37	4	1	68	62	23	15	–
1925	37	63	53	12	60	69	42	89	43	4	1	76	70	26	20	–
1926	37	59	51	15	64	64	45	88	46	10	1	75	52	29	18	1
1927	39	60	52	13	70	70	45	92	47	14	2	75	58	37	25	1
1928	43	58	71	17	75	78	68	108	49	17	3	76	75	42	33	1
1929	46	59	70	13	75	88	98	108	55	26	4	66	83	43	37	1
1930	45	59	68	22	70	82	70	109	48	29	4	65	84	35	44	3

Source: Diaz Alejandro (1970), pp. 449–50.

Notes
(a) Foodstuffs and beverages. (b) Tobacco. (c) Textiles. (d) Clothing. (e) Wood products. (f) Paper and cardboard. (g) Printing and publishing. (h) Chemicals. (i) Petroleum refining. (j) Rubber products. (k) Leather products. (l) Stone, glass and ceramics. (m) Metals (excluding machinery). (n) Vehicles and machinery (excluding electrical). (o) Electrical machinery and appliances.

a characteristic present even today: the duality between export and local market specialization (Schvarzer 1996).

Fourth, the mainspring of local industrial activity is related to the introduction of the railroads, as a substantial part of non-agricultural manufacturing was concentrated in the production of small parts for the locomotives and similar products. Also, most importantly, technological and entrepreneurial knowledge was transferred from this to other

Table 10.5 Production of vehicles and machinery (excluding electrical), 1935

Location	No. of firms	Number of employees Total	Number of employees Production	Value of production
Shipyards	82	2,039	1,888	8.446
Railroad shops	70	20,242	18,454	69.431
Trolley shops	13	1,010	930	2.255
Body shops	82	3,378	3,176	55.611
Spare parts	2,963	10,977	10,198	35.668
Carriages	1,051	2,682	2,607	9.476

Source: Government of Argentina, Industrial census, 1935.

Note
Value of Production is in million of National Pesos.

manufacturing sectors (such as paper products and printing, basic chemicals, etc.) (Katz and Kosacoff 1989).

A fifth important characteristic of the industrial development of the period is that the average number of employees per firm only grew from five to six between 1895 and 1908, it had increased to less than seven by 1914 (see Table 10.3). As this occurred while some large factories were established (in particular in meat processing) it is probably accurate to say that for most sectors the optimum size remained fairly constant for a long period of time.

This means that growth occurred mainly by the creation of new units rather than the expansion of existing ones (see Table 10.3). Thus firms could not gain in efficiency through economies of scale. They reproduced the craft-like methods and did not enjoy a high level of innovation. Moreover, on top of the creation of new units producing the same goods, many new activities and products were slowly incorporated into the range of local output (see Table 10.4).

Sixth, it is important to dwell on the relatively slight importance of machine tools during the period. As late as 1935 most of the production under the heading Vehicles and Machinery was actually devoted to repairing imported machinery, and producing parts and small engines (see Table 10.5).[3] This illustrates that during this crucial period – and in contradistinction to the other economies analyzed in this book – no local capital goods sector was established. Although a full exploration of this important topic cannot be pursued here, two complementary hypotheses could be presented. First, there was an insufficient group of firms demanding these goods such as to warrant the emergence of local producers. Second, although some immigrants and local workers were very skilled and innovative there were not enough of them to create an innovative network or community (Thomson, 1991).[4]

259

Nevertheless, industrial output was not the most significant component of output, especially in the early years. Agricultural output continued to expand, if at a slower pace or after a decline, as the cultivated frontier expanded. Still, for the years for which information is available, the overall level of industrial output did not decline, except in 1912 and the World War I years (see Table 10.4).[5] Moreover, as mentioned, the composition of industrial output altered significantly as the output of new products, and the rising living standards of the middle class, required greater diversity of production.[6]

In particular, as is shown in Table 10.6, the rural sector, although growing in absolute terms, slowly declined in importance during the first three decades of the century. Nevertheless, by the late 1930s it still represented close to a third of total output. Most of the decline was made up by the growth of the manufacturing, services, and transport sectors. It is also interesting to note that both personal and government services remained relatively constant throughout this period.[7]

This has theoretical significance on two accounts. First, the small share of industry in total output was not enough to "determine" the characteristics of the macroeconomic cycles of the period (cf. Chapter 8). As is observed in the following section, there were several peaks and troughs

Table 10.6 Structure of GDP, 1900–29

Sector	Share of GDP (%)					
	By sub-sector			By sector		
	1900–04	1910–14	1925–29	1900–04	1910–14	1925–29
Agriculture	15.8	14.8	14.9			
Livestock	17.2	10.2	10.6			
Fisheries	0.2	0.2	0.2			
Subtotal: rural				33.3	25.2	25.7
Mining	0.2	0.3	0.4			
Manufacturing	13.8	15.6	17.7			
Construction	6.6	10.8	6.5			
Subtotal: industry				20.6	26.7	24.6
Commerce	19.0	21.7	21.3			
Transport	3.7	5.6	7.2			
Communications	0.3	0.5	0.7			
Other utilities	0.2	0.4	0.7			
Housing	6.8	5.6	4.8			
Finance	1.5	1.7	2.0			
Personal services	9.1	7.4	7.5			
Government services	5.5	5.3	5.5			
Subtotal: services				46.1	48.1	49.7
Total	100.0	100.0	100.0	100.0	100.0	100.0

Source: Diaz Alejandro (1970).

during the period but, as was mentioned above, no similar behavior is observed in industrial output. From a Transformational Growth perspective this means that the "old" cycle was not exactly determined by the technological and institutional characteristics of small industrial firms but by the conditions affecting agricultural exports and the concomitant external financial flows.

Second, the growth trend of the economy shows a characteristic highlighted by Transformational Growth models: growth is not steady in a class economy (Nell 1992). In this case, as the economy grew, the share of different sectors (industry, agriculture), the weight of different sectors within industry, and the social composition of population were fundamentally altered. This was partly a result of the internal dynamics of industrial expansion as well as the result of the specific conditions which were promoting aggregate growth. These are explored in the next section.

MACROECONOMIC CYCLES BEFORE 1929

The previous section has shown that most of the output of the industrial sector was not very mechanized and depended heavily on imported raw materials. Furthermore, it competed against imported goods. This resulted in its market share being increased during periods of foreign currency shortage (external crisis). This was, also, the period when its inputs became costlier.

This shows that the external sector plays a fundamental role in the explanation of both the industrial structure and the macroeconomic fluctuations of the economy. The focus will now be on the effect of the latter on the former.

First, exports were the most important element of (autonomous) aggregate demand. These exports, moreover, were specifically agricultural products. This sector prospered not only because of the natural resources abundant in the country but also because of the nature of political organization, which perpetuated a particular kind of land ownership and favored foreign direct investment. These elements helped to define a macroeconomic context which reproduced the prevailing economic organization. As will be seen shortly, though, this system based on agricultural expansion could not be maintained indefinitely.

Second, the foreign direct investment was a fundamental element of external influence. It was directed to a few critical sectors (mainly the infrastructure to facilitate the export of agricultural products), shaping the productive structure of the economy, as discussed in the previous section (in particular the role of railroad construction).

One clear result of this influence is the commercial importance of the port of Buenos Aires, even to this day. It was the center on which all railroads converged because of its favorable position to export goods. Thus a process of regional economic concentration was set in motion. Producers built factories in or around Buenos Aires because it was the main market, and it was the main market because all the producers were located there. Between 1895 and 1914, according to the industrial census, between 50 per cent and 60 per cent of all factories were in Buenos Aires and the surrounding area. The industrial census of 1914 reports that over 50 per cent of invested capital, employment and power generation were installed in this area. Over 80 per cent of textile and chemical products, over 75 per cent of printed matter, and almost 50 per cent of processed foods had their origin in this area as well.[8]

Third, throughout this period the cycles are determined by external events: movements in the terms of trade, the volume of agricultural output (and concomitantly exports), and balance of payment crises (a combination of the previous two elements and the behavior of international capital flows). Nine short term cycles can be identified during this period. 1876–85, 1885–92, 1902–08, 1908–14, 1914–17, 1917–22, 1922–26 and 1926–33 (Di Tella and Zymelman 1972).

Fourth, although the evidence is scant, it seems that prices and wages fluctuated more significantly than output and employment. This is to be expected in a craft economy,[9] the reason why it also applies to an agriculture based one can be simply clarified. As in a craft economy there are many producers who cannot control the price of their output. In an agricultural economy this is exacerbated by climatic factors, which affect supply and the market price. Moreover, in the case of Argentina, it is not just the price of products in the local market which is relevant but international prices as well. Also, as in the case of the craft-based shop, the possibility of adjusting employment to changing demand and priceconditions is limited by the prevailing "technology"[10] in the agricultural sector. Consequently, because of the preponderance of agriculture and the characteristics of the emerging industry as described in the previous section, behavior similar to the old cycle is to be expected.

Several elements characterize the cycles in Argentina during this period. To start with, most of these cycles represent a slow-down in the expansion of output, especially of the manufacturing sector, rather than a decline. Poor harvests led to a reduced inflow of resources which, if coupled with liquidity problems in the rest of the world (European capital markets), forced a reduction in the rate of growth of the economy and consequently of industrial output.

Moreover, prices, and to a lesser extent wages, fluctuated considerably during this period within a short cycle. This is particularly the case with the terms of trade (see Table 10.7).

Also, employment did not fluctuate as much as prices did. This is the issue which presents the most difficulties in terms of obtaining reliable

ARGENTINA

Table 10.7 Terms of trade, 1885–1902 (1900=100)

Year	Export prices	Import prices	Terms of trade
1885	103	92	112
1886	87	87	100
1887	106	89	119
1888	118	93	127
1889	137	96	143
1890	102	97	105
1891	–	91	–
1892	110	87	126
1893	81	86	94
1894	71	81	88
1895	68	79	86
1896	74	80	93
1897	87	80	109
1898	87	82	106
1899	95	86	110
1900	100	100	100
1901	99	87	114
1902	107	86	124

Source: Di Tella and Zymelman (1972), pp. 228 and 246.

Table 10.8 Immigration flows, 1885–1902 (000)

Year	Immigrants	Emigrants	Net balance
1885	109	15	94
1886	93	14	79
1887	121	14	107
1888	156	17	139
1889	261	41	220
1890	110	80	30
1891	52	82	−30
1892	73	44	29
1893	84	49	35
1894	81	41	40
1895	81	37	44
1896	135	46	89
1897	105	57	48
1898	95	53	42
1899	111	62	49
1900	106	55	51
1901	126	80	46
1902	96	79	17

Source: Di Tella and Zymelman (1972), pp. 229 and 235.

data. However, a proxy can be found for the earlier periods by looking at immigration data (see Table 10.8). It can be observed that the country absorbed large numbers of immigrants in all the years except 1891.[11] Although it could be argued that net immigration moved cyclically, it does not mean that employment did. Closer inspection of the data reveals that in years when output declined or slowed down not as many new immigrants found jobs and consequently many left the country.[12] Still, for every year except 1891[13] job creation outpaced natural population growth plus immigration. This implies that although the rate of creation of jobs may have varied, employment rates did not vary as much.

Moreover, for later periods there is information on the average hours worked (see Table 10.9). These declined steadily and slowly between 1914 and 1934. The important point is that the decline occurred both in good and in bad periods. This is further evidence for the stability of the number of employees per firm.

Finally, another element to consider is that the trend underlying these cycles is one of unbounded expansion. Fertile land was available and an active immigration policy was implemented to attract European settlers. Thus agricultural output increased in absolute terms and an ever larger economic surplus was generated. It is within this expanding context that the slow changes took place.

Moreover, and contrary to the experience in the United States, Germany or Canada, successive governments maintained a strict *laissez-faire* policy and never attempted to introduce tariffs in order to foster local industry. Hence, the piecemeal pace of industrial expansion and lack of backward linkages.

Of course, as mentioned above, land was not unlimited and already by the time of World War I strains could be felt as agricultural expansion gave way to a more stable level of production. Nevertheless, no major changes or crises occurred for a few years.

When the effects of the international financial crisis of 1929 hit the country,[14] they were coupled with the exhaustion of the expansion of the agricultural frontier.[15] At that time the internal and external conditions

Table 10.9 Weekly hours worked in Buenos Aires, 1914–39

Year(s)	Average No. of hours worked during a week
1914	53.6
1915–19	53.4
1920–24	49.5
1925–29	49.3
1930–34	47.5

Source: Diaz Alejandro (1970), p. 43.

were such that it was impossible to maintain the traditional growth pattern. This period marks the beginning of import substitution industrialization. Its characteristics are discussed in the next sections.

THE RISE AND STAGNATION OF ISI

Although many policy interventions (foreign exchange controls, the creation of a central bank, abandoning the gold standard, etc.) were important in fostering industrial growth, they were not intended to do so. Rather they were responses to the balance of payments difficulties (Llach 1984). It is only after 1945 that a conscious effort to promote the development of local industry is pursued. The main differences between these two subperiods are related to the treatment of foreign direct investment.

During the first subperiod, and as a response to the crisis, import duties were raised and a dual exchange rate was introduced to prevent a drain on reserves. However, traditional exports were promoted as well as the traditional inflow of foreign capital. In the second subperiod the situation was quite different, as many foreign firms were nationalized (in particular infrastructure firms which enjoyed "natural" monopolies like electricity and railroads). Also, the State took up the production of several crucial inputs (e.g. steel). Thus markets were not only protected from external competition, the role of foreign firms was minimized and foreign investment was discouraged. After a brief boom, the economy started to stagnate. This resulted from the dual constraint of balance of payment restrictions and saturation of the local market.

Local firms which lacked the capacity either to innovate or to expand their production into more complex goods rapidly caught up with the lagged unsatisfied demand generated by the wartime restrictions but were not able to embark on a long-run expansion path. After almost twenty years of import substitution the distribution of employees by firm size was roughly the same as it had been in 1935, showing the failure up to that point in terms of generating a dynamic industrial sector.[16] Moreover, the subperiod is characterized by increasing balance of payments problems as traditional exports were stagnant and imports continued to rise in order to maintain industrial output (Katz and Kosacoff 1989; Kuerzinger 1988).

A third subperiod began in the late 1950s when, again, the rules affecting foreign direct investment were radically changed. This is the most interesting subperiod to analyze, owing to the contrast between local firms and the subsidiaries of multinational enterprises. The latter introduced mass-production methods. These firms rapidly dominated the sectors they entered. Some local producers also assimilated their production and organizational methods, albeit with modifications and usually on a smaller scale. However, this crude generalization is not enough to capture the differences between the two sectors or to do justice to the complex evolution of industry in the last four decades.

This subperiod is characterized by firms which were substantially smaller than their counterparts in the industrial countries. This applies both to local and to international firms. Also, the range of goods produced by their plants was wider than in the industrialized countries, showing difficulty in specialization. Both of these characteristics led to firms not being able to capture economies of scale. Their costs were considerably higher than the costs of similar firms abroad. Given the level of protection they enjoyed, this did not represent a problem.

Further, the internal market structure was highly concentrated and oligopolistic. Especially so in industries with high participation by foreign firms. During this period two clearly distinct industrial subsectors emerged. One, dominated by foreign-based firms, was modern and highly concentrated. It produced durable consumption goods and some intermediate goods. The second group, producing mainly non-durable consumption goods, was more traditional and less concentrated (Gerchunoff and Llach 1975; Katz and Kosacoff, 1989).

Foreign firms accounted for 30 per cent of total production in 1973. However, their distribution by sector was not homogeneous. In the highly concentrated and dynamic sectors (such as machinery and chemical products) they represented almost half of total production (see Table 10.10). It was also the case that most of the production was due to firms whose majoritarian control was foreign-based (i.e. even when they joined local firms they kept more than half of the shares) and their production was mainly geared towards the local market (see Table 10.10).

Downward price rigidity was dominant in the industrial sector. High market concentration and protection from foreign competition allowed this. Stable prices which prevent reductions in current and future revenues are crucial to develop and execute investment plans in the presence of the high investment needed by the modern sector (Nell 1992). However, as will be discussed in the next section, the emergence of inflation later in the period, and the concomitant variability of relative prices depressed investment levels as firms' pricing policies became less reliable, i.e. nominal rigidity did not prevent real reductions in their prices and revenues.

The foreign firms also played an important role in terms of diffusing technologies and organizational structures to local firms. New production processes, quality control and subcontracting practices were introduced.[17] Also, foreign firms had to adapt their practices to the local circumstances – availability of raw materials, workers' and consumers' characteristics, etc. (Katz 1993). This two-way learning fostered substantial productivity increases which, by the early 1970s, resulted in increasing industrial exports. Thus, while exports of industrial manufactures[18] were almost nil in 1960 and amounted to U$ 100 million in 1969, they were close

Table 10.10 Indicators of the presence of transnational corporations in the mid-1970s

Distribution	% of transnationals' production	% of total output
By type of product		
Metal products, machines and vehicles		45.5
Chemical products		42.2
Basic metallurgy		30.5
Other		14.4
Total		30.4
By kind of good		
Non-durable consumption	21.2	23.0
Intermediate	44.1	30.0
Durable consumption	26.0	38.8
Capital	8.7	34.4
Total	100.0	30.4
By firm size		
Fewer than fifty employees	1.7	4.0
Between 51 and 100 employees	3.9	11.7
Between 101 and 300 employees	19.7	29.1
Over 300 employees	74.9	49.6
Total	100.0	30.4
By market concentration		
High	66.9	45.0
Medium	19.2	18.2
Low	10.8	15.9
Other	3.1	22.9
Total	100.0	30.4
By control of the firm		
Less than 20 %	7.6	
Between 20.1 and 50 %	11.4	
Over 50.1 %	81.0	
Total	100.0	
By sales destination[a]		
Internal market	84.6	
United States	0.7	
Other countries	14.7	
Total	100.0	

Source: Kosacoff (1992).

Note
(a) Only for American firms.

Table 10.11 Share of traditional and industrial exports, 1970–85

Year	Primary products	Agricultural manufactures	Industrial manufactures	Unclassified
1970	38.5	49.5	11.5	1
1975	48.5	29.5	21	1
1980	40	37	22	1
1985	44	31	18	5

Source: Government of Argentina, Boletin Comercio Exterior, Nos 11 and 31.

Table 10.12 Structure of GDP, 1927–65

Sector	Share of GDP (%)	
	1927/29	1963/65
Agriculture, livestock, and fisheries	27.4	17.1
Oil and mining	0.3	1.5
Manufacturing	23.6	33.7
Construction	4.2	3.6
Electricity and other utilities	0.5	1.8
Transport	5.5	6.5
Communications	0.8	0.9
Commerce	23.5	16.9
Financial services	1.4	2.0
Housing services	2.1	2.2
Government services	4.5	6.8
Other services	6.2	7.1
Total	100.0	100.0

Source: Diaz Alejandro (1970).

to U$ 900 million in 1974. This amounted to over 20 per cent of total exports (see Table 10.11).

At this point it would be interesting to take a longer-term view of the aggregate structure of total production. This is done in Tables 10.12–13. Table 10.12 illustrates the declining importance of the rural sector. Its share in total output declined dramatically between the late 1920s and the early 1960s. Almost all the share given up by this sector was taken up by manufacturing, which became the most important sector in the economy. It is also important to note that, although commerce declined, housing and other services[19] remained at their 1920s level, while financial and government services increased sharply (especially the latter).

In Table 10.13 the rise, stagnation and fall of the dynamic industrial sector based on metallurgy, machinery and vehicle production is illustrated in terms of the information in subsequent industrial censuses. These were

Table 10.13 Main industrial activities, 1935–85

Year	Food, beverages and tobacco	Textiles	Metal products, machines and vehicles	Oil refining and pharmaceuticals
Share of industrial production				
1935	43	20	10	..
1946	35	28	10	..
1954	23	23	20	..
1964	30	16	21	9
1974	27	13	24	8
1985	24	13	21	13[a]
Share of industrial employment				
1935	28	23	17	n.a.
1946	25	25	19	n.a.
1954	20	23	25	n.a.
1964	22	22	30	n.a.
1974	21	16	30	n.a.
1985	26	15	26	n.a.
Share of industrial establishments				
1935	30	16	20	n.a.
1946	25	20	25	n.a.
1954	17	20	30	n.a.
1964	21	21	30	n.a.
1974	22	15	24	n.a.
1985	26	11	25	n.a.

Source: Government of Argentina, Industrial census, 1935, 1946, 1954, 1964, 1974, 1985.

Notes
.. Close to 0. (a) Refers only to oil refining. By 1985 basic plastics and basic chemical substances had replaced pharmaceutical goods from the top three products in the chemical industry.

commissioned roughly at ten-year intervals. The evolution of the number of firms, of employees and of the value of production in three main industrial subsectors – agricultural manufactures (which includes food, beverages and tobacco), textiles (which includes leather products) and metal products (which includes machinery and vehicles) are presented in Table 10.13.

It can be observed that up to the mid-1970s textiles and agricultural manufactures suffered a secular decline. Their place was taken up by the production of metal products. However, since then they have tended to recover (in particular in terms of employment on establishments) as metal products and machines started to decline. Oil and refineries, however, have become more important in terms of production, although they are more concentrated and less labor-intensive.

Moreover, it can also be observed that up to the mid-1950s the

Table 10.14 Distribution of total output, 1970–87

	Share of GDP (%)		
Sector	1970	1980	1987
Agriculture	13.2	12.5	14.7
Mining	2.3	2.5	2.5
Industry	27.0	24.6	23.6
Construction	6.5	6.5	3.7
Transportation and communication	11.3	10.6	11.5
Electricity, gas, and water	2.3	3.5	4.9
Commerce	15.2	16.2	14.5
Financial and insurance services	7.6	8.9	8.0
Other services	14.6	14.6	16.5
Total	100.0	100.0	100.0

Source: Kosacoff and Azpiazu (1989).

industrial structure was very much as it had been in the 1930s and earlier. Expansion took place primarily through the creation of new establishments. Although this trend was reversed during the 1960s, a fully modern mass-production industry never took hold in the country. This is explained by the concentration of foreign investment in a few sectors, the size of the local market, and the capacity of some local firms to exploit their knowledge of local circumstances to remain competitive. Subsequently the importance of the modernizing sector declined while agricultural manufactures seemed to recover. This occurred during a general retrenchment of industrial output as whole. As can be seen from Table 10.14 the share of industrial production in total output is approaching its share in the 1920s (slightly above 20 per cent).

All these characteristics are related to two theoretical points. First, this industrial structure provides the basis for the "stylized facts" of many structuralist models, i.e. models where industrial output depends on foreign inputs. In these models increases in output negatively affect the external accounts and solving or preventing a balance of payments crisis requires a slowdown or contraction of internal demand. This model is further discussed in the next section.

Second, these characteristics were not static. They had important dynamic elements which were transforming the industrial structure and the macroeconomic behavior of the economy. Not only were industrial exports rising (which could have resulted in a lessening foreign exchange constraint) but also, as the industrial sector developed, so did the distributional conflicts between workers and employers, between industry and agriculture (which was indirectly financing industrial subsidies) and within industry.[20] This set of distributional conflicts underlies all the other inflationary pressures.

Both these elements affected the macroeconomic behavior of the economy. This in turn plays a fundamental role in trying to fully appreciate how the changes depicted in Tables 10.13–14 came about. It is necessary, then, to look at the effects of macroeconomic developments on industry.

THE EFFECTS OF GAPS CYCLES ON INDUSTRY

The typical cycle throughout this period can be briefly summarized as follows. Internal demand and industrial output go up, leading to a reduction of exports (being primarily wage goods) and to an increase in imports (intermediate goods for industry). The combination of these two movements leads to a balance of payments crisis in the absence of capital inflows. Adjustment is necessary and takes the form of a combination of devaluation and contractionary fiscal and monetary policies.

The devaluation increases the price of agricultural goods relative to industrial goods. The real wage is reduced and income is shifted to agricultural producers, who are wealthier and save a higher proportion of their income. As a result, aggregate demand for industrial goods declines, reinforcing the contractionary effect of the fiscal and monetary policies.[21]

The depressed level of demand induces a reduction in investment. The lower industrial output also results in lower imports. At the same time the reduction in real wages leads to higher exports. The cycle is ready to start again.[22]

In this context inflation was a constant feature of the economy. For many years it remained at high, but unsteady, levels. These were a result of the distributional conflicts and downwardly rigid prices discussed above, on one hand and the effect of income share changes occurring through the cycle just described, on the other hand [23]. In order to cope with this high inflation level several indexation mechanisms were introduced into many types of contracts.[24] This resulted in inflation showing a high inertial component. Thus, when adjustments in relative prices were required to conform to the new conditions of the economy,[25] indexation played the role of a defense mechanism to prevent falls in real income. As a consequence, inflation crept up, becoming ever higher. Several attempts at controlling it with a wide variety of macroeconomic policy instruments failed to subdue it for long stretches of time (Heyman 1986).[26]

This is a relatively well known cycle and it applies to the stylized facts of many semi-industrialized countries. The interesting points to make, from a Transformational Growth perspective, are several.

First, this cycle shows as much variability in output as it does in (relative) prices. Although this may seem contradictory to the hypothesis of the "old" and the "new" trade cycle at first glance, further thought shows it is not contradictory at all. The premise of the "old" and "new" cycle – as clearly exemplified in Chapters 8, 9, and 11 on Germany, Japan, and Canada – is that the post-war period has been characterized by modern mass production plants.

However, the previous section has illustrated that this is not at all the case with Argentinian industrial plants. Consequently the "new" cycle in Argentina does not take place. What seems to be observed is a combination of the "old" cycle with *only some elements* of the "new" one. Correspondingly, economic instability is heightened in the case of semi-peripheral countries as the price instability of the "old" cycle is retained – notice that in the case of Argentina agriculture, especially agricultural exports, remains an important feature of the economic structure – and is combined with the quantity instability of the "new" cycle.

Second, there is a more direct effect of macroeconomic instability on industry. Incapacity to plan ahead because of inflation results in decreased investment (which further causes output to stagnate) and reduces incentives to innovate (which leads productivity to stagnate). This does not mean that investment and technological change did not occur – the previous section shows otherwise – only that they followed a pattern much closer to the one expected in an "old" cycle in industrialized countries, i.e. innovations were local and unsystematic. They affected only the innovative firm and had very small spill-over effects.

Third, and related to the previous point, the uncertainty about relative prices due to market instability induced firms to rely on in-house provision of machinery and technical supply. This increased costs and reduced the rate of innovation for the firm *vis-à-vis* external competitors but it enhanced the likelihood of survival against other local producers within a protected market. Moreover, it also meant that many of the innovations had limited applicability outside their particular market (whether they were process innovations resulting from particular problems in terms of local characteristics of inputs or product innovations geared toward local requirements). This feature, however, was not entirely negative, as it allowed several firms to export goods (or machinery, or know-how) to other countries (especially in Latin America) with similar market characteristics (see Table 10.11).[27]

Fourth, and highlighting the role of institutional factors linking macroeconomic behavior with the industrial structure, it must be observed that a capital market which would allow savings to be channeled to productive investment never fully developed during this period. This was partly the result of foreign direct investment, which did not require a local capital market to finance its operations, and the small scale of local producers, who did not need large funds and could raise what they did need on their own. High relative price instability and high inflation variability also undermined the possibility of developing a well functioning financial market.

Fifth, foreign capital and capital flows played a fundamental role shaping the macroeconomic conditions as well as the industrial structure. This influence was felt at different levels. A more detailed look at the sequence of events is needed to fully appreciate this.

As was discussed above, in the period starting with the late 1950s foreign direct investment played a prominent role in introducing technological and organizational innovations. This investment was attracted by the conditions of the local market. i.e. a large suppressed demand from the previous period, a large sector of relatively affluent consumers, guarantees in terms of market protection and transfer of benefits to headquarters, etc. However, after the internal market has become saturated, and inflation started to creep up and become more volatile, these advantages disappeared.[28] Arguably, given the industrial export figures presented in the previous section for the mid-1970s, an export-led strategy could have been pursued.[29] However, economic policy took a completely different route.

The application of monetarist policies presented the possibility of substantial profits for financial capital.[30] These, of course, were only short-term. The country relied on foreign capital flows, which, because of their speculative characteristics, had only a short-term horizon. As this occurred in the mid and late 1970s when international lending conditions were favorable to developing countries it seemed that the external constraint was not binding (Canitrot 1993). However, once the conditions compared with the rest of the world were not as favorable, a massive capital outflow ensued.

By then, nevertheless, in roughly half a decade the industrial system had changed radically in response to the (perverse) incentives built into the monetarist balance of payments policies implemented to control the inflation rate. The policies were based on the belief that by lowering tariffs, promoting external borrowing and gradually approaching a fixed exchange rate not only would inflation conform to the international rate but also local industrial productivity would be enhanced.[31] The results, however, were very different. The price divergence between tradable and non-tradable goods widened as internal prices continued to increase. This led to a loss of competitiveness which reinforced by the consequent overvaluation of the local currency[32] and lower tariffs led to an inflow of imported goods. For example, automobile production declined from 240,000 units in 1975 to 172,000 in 1981, tractor production in the same period declined from 18,000 to 1,500 and machine tools from 15,000 to 4,400.[33]

Both local and foreign direct investment declined dramatically as a result of these macroeconomic policies.[34] Partly from the lack of an internal savings to investment transfer mechanism this led to a reduced investment rate. Two effects resulted from this. On the one hand the "technological transfer" from abroad declined and the internal "learning by doing" derived from expanded production slowed down too.

Moreover, a financial crisis occurred in 1981 just a few months before the Mexican default which triggered the Debt Crisis.[35] From then on the rest of the decade was characterized by increased economic instability. This affected the State's capacity to pursue a proactive macroeconomic policy. Different attempts, more or less successful, were made at stabilizing the economy and generating the necessary commercial surplus to service the debt. Sooner or later they all failed. As these problems absorbed most of the government's attention, little was done to foster, guide or revive the industrial sector.[36]

Also, starting in the mid-1970s, increased dollarization of the economy was observed. For several years the US dollar had been used as a unit of account and American means of payment for major transactions (real estate, automobiles, large capital goods, etc.). However, with the increased instability more firms and households turned to it for savings as a strategy to protect themselves from inflation. Also, because of the fundamental role of intermediate goods in internal production, the exchange rate became a key relative price affecting the local price level.[37] This meant that when the government had to face the new conditions of the 1980s and needed to make external debt payments a third restriction was added to the working of the "two-gap model", the transfer of assets owned by private agents (dollars) to the government.[38]

This had an effect not only on real wages (as was expected and widely analyzed) but also on industrial competitiveness. Soya oil, seamless tubes and other manufactured goods with little value added joined agricultural products as the commodities in which the country could specialize at the expense of vehicles or machine tools. The former are more competitive than the latter in a context of exchange rate and real wage fluctuations because of the relatively low labor – and imported raw materials – intensity. The technologies of these "raw material processing industries" are less complex than that of the mechanical engineering sector and thus require less R&D effort and uncertain investments. Thus the many years of macroeconomic instability drove the country to a more traditional specialization based on static comparative advantage rather than a dynamic industrial development path (Katz and Kosacoff 1989, Kosacoff 1993a).

In this section some of the connections between well known structuralist models have been integrated to the ideas of Transformational Growth. In particular, both approaches stress the importance of the characteristics of the productive sector in influencing macroeconomic outcomes. Moreover, this productive structure does not remain constant as the economy grows. It is changing both because of its own internal dynamics and because macroeconomic fluctuations and instability affect investment and R&D decisions through various channels.[39]

Also, fluctuating relative prices, investment and growth affect institutions and organizational features both at the firm and at the aggregate level. These, in turn, help to determine the characteristics of the cycle too. Finally, these institutional and organizational characteristics also depend on conditions in external markets and the specific ways in which the economy is linked with them. These elements, too, enter into the determination of the cycle.[40]

CONCLUSION AND LESSONS

Several features described above correspond closely with Transformational Growth models. First, the structure of the economy cannot be assumed to remain the same as the economy grows. In this case this seems to be the result of exogenous policy shocks which alter the incentives structure. However, these policy shocks are the result of successive attempts at correcting some feature of the economy. This characteristic would change from crisis to crisis (it could be inflation, foreign exchange constraints, etc.) but it would always be a sign of the instability resulting from the distributional conflicts among sectors due to the characteristics of the industrial structure and macroeconomic constraints.

It would be easy, and mistaken, to interpret these policy changes as completely exogenous policy shocks. There is no need to model the specific interventions to realize that, for the four main changes discussed in this chapter (the early 1930s, the mid-1940s, the late 1950s and the mid-1970s) sooner or later there was going to be a fundamental change in economic structure. The country was following an unstable growth path which had to be changed.[41] The instability was directly related to the inherent unsteadiness of growth. One of the main differences between Argentina (and other similar developing countries) and developed countries is that not enough mechanisms to counterbalance this unsteadiness were in place. This was partly the result of the "incomplete" industrial transformation but it was also due to the institutional framework and the links with the international economy.

Within this context, nevertheless, two clearly distinct periods may be found. During the first one the industrial sector is emerging and the main elements of the business cycles are related to the behavior of the external sector, i.e. agricultural production: in particular, the terms of trade and the availability of foreign credit.

In the second period, as the industrial sector gains relevance, the new cycle results from a combination of internal and external elements. The "newer" cycle – to distinguish it from the new cycle discussed in the other chapters for developed economies – depends on the specific links between local industry and foreign-based companies; wages, inter-industry and agriculture–industry distributional conflicts; the export (agricultural) sector; and the external accounts.

The "newer" cycle, then, is affected not only by the technological characteristics of industrial production but also by institutional mechanisms such as widespread indexation, the lack of a well developed stock market, the need of the government to obtain foreign exchange to service the external debt, etc. All these elements proved influential in shaping the context in which industrial firms had to develop. It should be noticed that the role of the external sector, although transformed, did not disappear in the "newer" cycle even during the period of import-substituting industrialization.

Consequently, a circular process whereby the microeconomic base underlying the unstable macroeconomic fluctuations was transformed and this transformation led to changes in macroeconomic behavior which further affected the path of industrial development is described. This transformation was also due to innovations and adaptations of industrial firms to the specific characteristics of the local markets.

The "newer" cycle, moreover, cannot be considered as a virtuous circle of growth or simply as a misguided attempt at creating an industry in a country without comparative advantages (leading to a vicious circle). Some elements of this cycle proved that, even under difficult circumstances and increasing instability, a competitive industrial sector capable of generating export earnings was emerging. However, because of internal market limitations, insufficient institutional and State support, and severe distributional conflicts a modern mass-production industrial sector enjoying robust backward and forward linkages never fully took hold in the country.

Thus this "newer" cycle exhibits some characteristics of the old cycle (relatively weak and unsystematic innovation, nominal fluctuations) in conjunction with some of the new cycle (output fluctuations, wage indexation). As successive governments tried to deal with the most "visible" of these problems – which over the last two decades were inflation and debt payments – they paid less attention to the problems of the industrial sector and the connections between industrial growth and macroeconomic performance.

In so far as the discussion in this chapter is accurate this lack of policies expressly directed towards bolstering industrial exports or industrial competitiveness was detrimental to growth and worsened the distributional conflicts underlying the inflationary process. Also, it means that current and future policies which fail to look at these issues will have little chance of succeeding and permanently stabilizing the economy.

In particular, the currently fashionable policies aimed at privatizing State enterprises, liberalizing international trade and capital movements, and dismantling the trade unions would, at best, result in an economic context similar to the old cycle. That is, a situation where a few reap most of the benefits from exporting goods with little value added, requiring few workers and lacking the intersectoral linkages to foster a dynamic industrial sector. At worst, they could leave the country impoverished, at the mercy of exogenous changes in the terms of trade and in interest rates, with an industry decimated, and with a State unable to implement any kind of macroeconomic management or industrial development policies.

NOTES

1 Of the other countries discussed in this book only Canada during the earlier period would come close to sharing these characteristics. In later periods, however, these economies followed very different paths.
2 A good starting point for such analysis is O'Donnell (1978), where economic actors pursue different political objectives along the business cycles, see also Acuña (1993).
3 In the other sectors production was also concentrated on technologically simple goods. For instance, the breakdown for the chemical sector shows that most of the output consisted of household cleaners and soap.
4 The contrast with Canada in this regard is particularly interesting, as it is clear that in terms of market size there was not much difference between the two countries (thus weakening the first hypothesis). Nevertheless, the close links with the US economy (not only in terms of geography but also culturally and linguistically) allowed Canadian innovators to participate in the same area as US ones.
5 This could be paradoxical, as the war years are usually interpreted as the first substantial impetus for local industry which did not have to face international competition (Dorfman 1992).
6 The theoretical underpinning of this kind of process is discussed in Chapter 1 and 2 above and in Nell (1992).
7 As was mentioned in the second section (pp. 256–61), the basic information needed to compile long series on output does not exist. This is the reason why the structure of GDP is presented in three separate tables in this chapter. Strictly speaking, the figures in the three tables are not comparable. Nevertheless, taken as whole, they convey a sense of the major trends in the sectoral distribution of total output. Moreover, there are other estimates which yield different shares but similar trends (see Diaz Alejandro 1970).
8 Even today more than half of industrial production takes place in this region (Wolf 1991).
9 See Chapter 2 and 4 above.
10 The importance of cattle in total output must be kept in mind at this point. On the lack of scope for input flexibility in agricultural production as an incentive to technological change and mechanization see David (1975). For a contrast between the institutional and marketing differences between the case described by David and the situation in Argentina see Flichman (1978).
11 It should be remembered that the worst external crisis of the whole period occurred in 1890.
12 It must be noted that a large proportion of those counted as immigrants and emigrants were actually migrant workers who left and returned to the country repeatedly.

13 It must be pointed out that this was in the aftermath of the 1890 crisis.

14 The value of international transcactions declined by 60 per cent between 1929 and 1932 as the sharp reduction in prices, particularly of the agricultural goods exported by Argentina, was compounded by the decline in the quantum of trade; see Landes (1969) and Lewis (1949).

15 Most of the territory was available to European settlers from the 1880s. This allowed the expansion of rural activities (mainly raising sheep and cattle). This expansion continued until all the most fertile land was taken up, in the mid-1910s. By the late 1920s even "poor" land had been taken up.

16 Diaz Alejandro (1970: 504).

17 It is worth noticing that although advertisement departments and agencies were created, mass marketing did not take place as in the United States. Big department stores were rare and supermarket chains did not exist, except for a consumer cooperative which was geographically limited. Mail order purchases were unheard of and only in the last few years have telephone purchases been introduced (mainly for imported goods). The importance of mass merchandising as a prerequisite of mass production is highlighted by Chandler (1990).

18 The term "industrial manufactures" is commonly used when discussing industrial exports in Argentina in order to differentiate them from agricultural manufactures. Industrial manufactures are those based on industrial inputs and agricultural manufactures are based on primary-sector inputs. More details may be found in Bisang and Kosacoff (1993).

19 Other services includes personal services.

20 The argiculture-industrial relative price instability is discussed by Olivera (1964) and Canavese (1982), the wage–price dichotomy is highlighted by Canitrot (1975, 1981), and within industry price conflict is mentioned by Kosacoff (1992). Most of these authors, especially Canitrot, also include an exchange rate adjustment problem in the price dynamics. I return to some of these problems below.

21 Diaz Alejandro (1963); Krugman and Taylor (1978).

22 Chenery and Bruno (1962); Braun and Joy (1968).

23 Some readers may be puzzled by the fact that monetary factors are not included in this list. Neither are they explicitly discussed in the rest of the chapter. This is so for two reasons. On the one hand exploring the connections between Transformational Growth and monetary mechanisms would lead me astray of the main theme of this chapter (a useful approach to these issues can be found in Delaplace and Nell 1996). On the other hand, and following a long tradition of structuralist economists (and others), I will accept that monetary factors are not the cause of inflation but that money is endogenous.

24 Especially wage contracts; see Frenkel (1986).

25 Not all these realignments of relative prices were due to the evolving structure of the economy. Some were the result of external variables like the terms of international trade or interest rates.

26 Of course, the sequence of macroeconomic policy decisions affected the industrial sector. Details are given later in this section.

27 More details on these exports may be found in Katz (1974), Katz and Kosacoff (1983), Ablin and Katz (1985) and Ablin et al. (1985).

28 Especially as the combination of periods of high inflation followed by stabilization policies created serious distortions in the real exchange rate.

29 This would have required at least selective assistance from the State which

would have facilitated a transition from ISI to an export-led strategy similar to the one witnessed in the East Asian NICs. Although this is not the place to analyze why this did not happen, good analyses and comparisons are presented in Deyo (1987), Amsden (1989), Haggard (1990), Wade (1990), Evans (1995) and the collection edited by Gereffi and Wyman (1990). It should also be pointed out that, at roughly the same time as these changes were going on internally, international markets were changing, and the electronics industry was becoming the more dynamic sector in which local producers had little experience.

30 See Schvarzer (1983).

31 These policies and their consequences are well documented in Kasacoff (1983), Fernandez (1979), Canitrot (1981) and Sourrouille (1981).

32 As the government steadfastly refused to alter the pace or proportion of its ever smaller devaluations in spite of actual inflation being consistently above the government's target.

33 See Katz and Kosacoff (1989); Kosacoff (1993b).

34 During the late 1970s many foreign firms actually left the country for good (e.g. General Motors, Chrysler, Citroen, Peugeot, Olivetti, etc.). Kosacoff and Bezchinsky (1993).

35 The crisis had particularly negative consequences because due to the lack of a well developed financial market may firms had taken up the role of credit providers. These firms were doubly hit and a radical process of business concentration took place (Damill and Fanelli 1988; Damill *et al.* 1988).

36 This is slightly exaggerated. However, the few efforts (especially tax rebates to decentralize industrial production) were relatively small in proportion to total industrial output and grossly ineffective. Their main result was to allow a few local corporations to enrich themselves. See Azpiazu *et al.* (1986); Gatto *et al.* (1988); Azpiazu and Basualdo (1989); Acevedo *et al.* (1990).

37 These processes are well described in Canitrot (1983) and Rozenwurcel (1985).

38 See Bacha (1990); Fanelli *et al.* (1987); Fanelli and Chisari (1989).

39 Frenkel and Fanelli (1995) also identify many of these mechanisms, although their emphasis is different.

40 A very important factor is income distribution. Since the mid-1970s, when industrial output and employment started to decline and inflation accelerated, income distribution became increasingly unequal. The share of the top earners increased at the expense not only of the lower end of the income distribution but also of the middle classes. Thus increasing inequality was accompanied by a rise in poverty (Beccaria 1993).

41 And it was bound to change by one set of policies or another.

11

CANADA AND ARGENTINA

A comparison

Thomas F. Phillips

In terms of Transformational Growth, the comparison of Argentina and Canada in the OBC and NBC is very revealing. In the OBC, both were predominantly agricultural economies with small craft-based manufacturing. By the end of World War II Canada had moved ahead of Argentina and their paths continued to diverge through the NBC. There are many aspects that could be considered in analyzing the differences between Canada and Argentina in the NBC, but, as Carlos Diaz-Alejandro (1970: 30) aptly put it, "Canada benefited from her proximity to the US and her special association with Great Britain." The close association with Great Britain had a tremendous impact on Canada's development in the OBC (particularly on its social and political institutions) but the country's proximity and close trading ties with the United States had a great impact on it in the NBC.

The first indications of the substantial differences that emerge in the NBC came in the late OBC (see pp. 142–8 above). By the late OBC it was clear that the Canadian economy had begun the transition from a rural to a manufacturing economy. At least this was true of southern Ontario. Policies had been put in place to encourage the establishment of manufacturing establishments in Canada. Tariffs were one method of protecting infant Canadian producers, but they did more to encourage US producers to open Canadian branch plants than to protect Canadian producers. Canadian policy also encouraged foreign-owned manufacturers to locate in Canada to take advantage of Canada's preferential access to the Commonwealth, and Canadian patent law afforded US patent holders protection only if they had Canadian-based facilities. Such policy clearly indicates Canada's intention of developing an industrial manufacturing base.

In stark contrast to Canada, Argentina did not look so favourably upon manufacturing. "It is the nearly unanimous opinion of students of Argentine economic history that before 1930 public policy was either indifferent or hostile to the expansion of manufacturing, unless it was directly related to exports of goods of rural origin" (Diaz-Alejandro 1970: 217). The differences in approach to the importance of manufacturing may be the greatest factor contributing to the differences between Canada and Argentina in the NBC.

Clear as it is that Canada, shortly after the turn of the century, was moving from craft-based manufacturing to the concentration of production in fewer, mass-production establishments, it is equally clear that, even at the beginning of the NBC, Argentina had not made the transition to mass production. Diaz-Alejandro (1970: 243) points out that "after 1943 it [industrial growth] gave rise to an abnormally large number of small establishments of doubtful long-run efficiency." Even in the period after World War II, new Argentine manufacturing establishments were very small – typically six employees (ibid.). In the same period Canadian manufacturing was characterized by relatively few large firms, with many more employees (see pp. 142–3).

In Chapter 10 it was argued that manufacturing in Argentina in the NBC shows clear indications of being much more like optimally sized craft-based establishments that were found in the OBC of the modern mass-production economies. It is not surprising, then, to find Argentina having stylized facts in the NBC much like Canada's (and its own) in the OBC.

With Canada clearly having the advantage of being geographically close to the United States,[1] policy to encourage US manufacturers to locate in Canada (and to bring with them their mass-production technology) made it possible for Canada to develop a manufacturing sector that was able to achieve substantial economies of scale.[2] In many instances United States technology was adapted to the scale necessary to make it productive in the Canadian setting.[3] Although technological adaptation was important, it was also necessary to use policy to enable potential economies of scale to be realized.

The most striking example of policy used to achieve economies of scale in Canadian manufacturing came with the Auto Pact of 1964. The Auto Pact provided for free trade in automobiles and automobile parts between Canada and the US. Although there were restrictions that would ensure that production would still take place in Canada,[4] the Pact enabled both US and Canadian plants to have larger production runs and therefore achieve greater economies of scale. This had a tremendous impact on Canadian production, since the industry had not, before the Pact, been able to achieve the scale necessary to produce efficiently. With the pact, Canadian exports to the US increased substantially, productivity gains were realized, car workers' wages rose and a general boost to the Canadian economy was achieved. This is the most prominent example of the technological and institutional links between Canada and the US that have enabled Canada to take advantage of its proximity to American markets. Trade with the US continues to form a substantial proportion of Canada's GDP and the two countries' trading relationship remains the largest in the world.

With trade with the US forming such a large proportion of Canada's GDP, and given the fact that the Canadian economy is only about one tenth the size of the US economy, it is not difficult to argue that Canada is a small open economy. The case is even easier to make for the Argentinian economy. With these two economies both being small open economies, why are they so different in the NBC? It is assumed that there is little or no influence by small economies on the price of traded goods. Although they participate in export and import markets, their relatively small quantities will not affect price. Therefore small open economies can, in Neoclassical terms, be considered "price-takers." But, comparing Canada and Argentina in the NBC, there is more price stability in Canada than in Argentina. Argentinian prices in the NBC appear to behave much more like other countries' prices in the OBC. This difference can, in part,[5] be attributed to the technological nature of production and the trading relations between the two countries.

In domestic production in the NBC, Canada is dominated by mass production. For Transformational Growth, this means that the technological nature of production leads to more stable prices. There is clear evidence of this for Canada and several other modern industrial economies presented in this volume. Canada's close trading relations make it subject to the nature of the pricing mechanism in the US. Since the US has the stable prices typical of the mass-production economies of the NBC, and the technological nature of production (and therefore pricing) in Canada is like that of the US, it is not surprising to find price behaviour in Canada and in the US much the same, even though Canada is a small open economy. On the other hand, in the NBC, Argentina was dominated by small manufacturing establishments that were much more like the craft-based establishments of the OBC in other countries. Also, Argentina's trading links with the US are not as strong as Canada's, but its links with other Latin American countries are much greater. Since Latin American countries are more like Argentina, and likely exhibit many of the stylized facts (such as small unit manufacturing and price variability) of Argentina, it is not surprising to find Argentina showing more price volatility in the NBC than the mass-production economies. Even though Canada and Argentina are both small open economies, the domestic nature of production and the nature of production among their trading partners makes for very different stylized facts in the NBC.

NOTES

1 For an interesting discussion of the importance of geography to international trade see Krugman (1991).
2 Although the scale tended to be smaller than for US producers, Canadian producers did produce for more than just the Canadian market. Goods produced in Canada were often exported to the United States and the Commonwealth.
3 For a thorough discussion of this see Wylie (1989).
4 The Auto Pact was a very restricted version of free trade. For instance, Canada was assured that as many cars would be produced in Canada as were sold in Canada. This enabled manufacturers to have longer production runs in both Canada and the United States, and therefore to achieve greater economies of scale in both Canada and the United States.
5 Price instability, as pointed out in Chapter 10 can also be attributed to international financial difficulties, e.g. the balance of payments and devaluation.

Part IV

IMPLICATIONS FOR ECONOMIC ANALYSIS

12

ON TRANSFORMATIONAL
GROWTH

Edward J. Nell interviewed by Steve Pressman

Pressman. One of the main problems facing not just the United States but also most developed economies throughout the world has been a slow-down in "long-term growth." It is well known that growth rates of productivity and of GDP *per capita* during the 1970s and 1980s were not as great as during the 1950s and 1960s. You have called your explanation for these changes "Transformational Growth." Could you explain briefly what Transformational Growth is all about, and then tell us how the notion of Transformational Growth can be used to explain the growth slowdown of the past quarter-century?

Nell. To explain Transformational Growth we have to go back earlier, to the pre-1914 economy. This was the era of "craft-based" factories, as opposed to Transformational Growth. Craft-based production rests on a work team functioning closely together as a unit. Morale is important, and the team has to pull together. Everyone has to be in place and on the ball for any production to take place. Hence the system does not allow for lay-offs. In slack times the work force will clean up, repair equipment, paint the building or whatever. In boom times, work will be speeded up to the maximum. Thus output is varied by varying productivity rather than employment; lay-offs and rehiring are rare (Nell, in Thomson, 1993).

By contrast, under mass production – continuous throughput – productivity is to a great extent built into the equipment. The pace of work is set by the speed of the assembly line. Tasks are simpler and more repetitive. The division of labor, of course, is also characteristic of craft work, but "division of labor is limited by the extent of the market," so it proceeds much further under Transformational Growth. To vary output, employment will be varied, keeping productivity more closely constant. Productivity will vary somewhat, procyclically, due to overhead labor.

These two different ways of organizing production lead to different cost structures for business and, as a result, different reaction patterns by business to exogenous changes, especially to changes in autonomous demand. In short, markets adjust differently. For craft-based factory production the market adjusts in ways that are more or less adequately documented by marginalist microeconomics of the Marshallian sort. With mass production, adjustment depends on the multiplier (and the accelerator), and is described by Keynesian/Kaleckian macroeconomics.

Transformational Growth is the study of how the processes and problems generated by the normal operation of the market, when production is organized according to one dominant format, lead to technological innovations which transform that format into another, thus changing the structure of human efforts and costs and leading, therefore, to a new and different pattern of normal business responses, and so to a new pattern of adjustment (Nell, 1988: 1992).

Now, with this background, we can look at the 1970s and 1980s. In this era the mass-production economy is drawing to an end. Many of the markets for major consumer durables in the advanced centuries appear to have become saturated, in the sense that they are now growing more slowly than the average of all industries. Investment likewise has slowed down, as has productivity growth. In a very broad sense, not much more can be squeezed out of mass production. A new technological format is called for. One is waiting in the wings, something that might be called the "information economy", but we don't know much about it yet. One thing that perhaps can be seen is that the structure of the economy is changing again. Another is that the mix of labour required is going to be very different. In the meantime, however, investors have to be cautious: there's not much point in investing heavily in old methods and old products if they are going to be displaced, but it's dangerous to move too quickly into unexplored territory. The result is a kind of stalemate. No one will invest in the old because it's about to become obsolete; but no one wants to be first with the new because it's untried.

Pressman. What can be done to end this stalemate?

Nell. What may be required is a massive absorption of risk by governments, as we did in moving all sorts of industries to mass production during the Second World War.

Pressman. Let us turn to some alternative explanations of the phenomenon of slow economic growth. The main explanation coming out of traditional economic theory derives from the Solow growth model. Do you regard a Solow growth model as a failure and if so why?

Nell. Yes. It's not only a failure but a distraction. It's an intellectual failure for reasons explored in the capital controversies (Laibman and Nell 1977, reprinted in Nell 1992). But its major impact has been to distract attention from the real issues. It has focused the intellectual efforts of economists in directions that are wrong in three ways. First of all, it has focused our attention largely on steady states, and that, I think, is a major mistake. No actual economies ever grow steadily. Secondly, it has focused our attention on an approach to growth which emphasizes a choice of techniques. Whether or not the neoclassical production function is a useful device in some contexts, it embodies the notion of choosing techniques under the influence of market forces. Both the critics and the supporters of this method have concentrated their attention on the question of how techniques are chosen, on whether or not the capital intensity of techniques varies inversely with the rate of profit. The neo-Ricardian critics have developed very elaborate critical discussions of the choice of technique, which are just as beside the point as the approach of the neoclassicals. Techniques grow and develop; they are not "chosen." And thirdly, the Solow model is in an important sense a supply-side model. That is to say, most of its conclusions arise from the structure of the production function and the marginal productivity conditions which determine the distribution of income and many other aspects of the economy, and shifts in the production function, which are taken to represent technical progress, likewise are treated solely from the supply side. This seems to me a terrible mistake in that, arguably, capitalism is fundamentally demand-driven. Thus the Solow model has diverted our attention from examining three features that must be considered central to a realistic account of growth: persistent structural changes; persistent biased technical progress; and the influence of long-term and growing demand pressures (Nell 1992: ch. 10).

Pressman. When you were speaking about the problems with the Solow model, one point that you made was that growth involves demand-side factors to a greater extent than supply-side factors. How do you see demand-side factors coming in to play in the development of a more adequate theory of long-term growth?

Nell. Well, this is a complicated question. I feel that our treatment of demand has suffered very badly from too great a reliance on Keynes for our approach to macroeconomic demand. Keynes was wonderful, and Keynes was right about lots of things, but Keynes was also sixty years ago and maybe we should have made a little bit of progress by now. In particular, Keynes provided us with a short-run theory of aggregate demand. A long-run theory of aggregate demand was supposedly supplied by Harrod and Domar. A little bit of reflection, however, should immediately show that this is not the case. Take a very simple derivation of the warranted growth path. On the one side we have capacity output. This is determined by the capital stock, times its social average marginal productivity – to employ the rather long phrase that Domar used. On the other side we have the level of investment times the multiplier. You put those together and we derive the warranted rate of growth that we call s/v. This is not a theory of the growth of demand; rather, it is the momentary level of the rate of growth that balances the current level of demand with the current level of capacity. It is, in fact, a static conception.

If we wish to develop a growth theory based on demand, we need a theory of the growth of demand – that is to say, a theory of the growth of markets. There is no such theory in economics. Of course, there is Rosa Luxembourg; there are some Marxian studies; there are one or two other things here and there; there are a lot of Engel curves; there are various notions of the changing structure of the economy and explanations as to how this would generate demand. But there is no systematic theory of the growth of demand. Therefore there is no systematic demand-side theory of the growth of capitalism. This seems to me a very serious shortcoming. It affects among other things our discussion of the distribution of income and the class structure of the economy. One of the most notable features of the emergence of modern industrial capitalism in the nineteenth century (following the stories of people like Alfred Chandler) is the concurrent development of large-scale continuous throughput production with the emergence of a new class of professionals, a new middle class. Not a middle class of proprietors but a middle class of managers. Recognizing and explaining such developments in class structure is one aspect of a theory of the growth of demand.

Pressman. So what you're saying is that right now one of the most important things missing in economics is a theory of long-term demand that relates demand changes to structural economic changes?

Nell. Yes. That is a central element in an interconnected set of missing theoretical links. The structure of the economy is going to respond to changing demand pressures, and, in doing so, it is going to generate further changes in demand pressures. The changing structure of the economy is something which has been addressed chiefly by development economists. There was a famous set of papers by Taylor and Chenery, for example, in the late 1960s which explored many of these issues. There is likewise the work of Walter Hoffmann. Economic historians have discussed the change of sectoral composition, and have put this together with the changing class and income group composition. But these relationships have not been handled by economic theorists, and the economic historians haven't dealt with them very effectively, as far as understanding the role of market pressures in bringing about these changes. But, it seems to me, this is what we need to do in developing a theory of growth. An adequate theory of growth must show the transformation of the economy as a result of the systematic pressures that develop within the market mechanisms of the economy – which, of course, sometimes generate countervailing pressures, and sometimes further pressures in the same direction. This theory must then be expanded to include the role of the State. To develop an adequate theory of the State, we surely have to show the relationship of the State to the market pressures that are generated during the process of growth.

For example, pre-1914 total State expenditure, including transfers, in relation to GDP ranged between 5 per cent and 10 per cent in Europe and North America. The development of mass production, creating large factories and concentrating the labor force, while industrializing agriculture, dramatically changed the role of government, shifting on to it many responsibilities formerly carried by the family and the local community. By the end of the Second World War State spending in relation to GDP had risen to around 30 per cent, and it continued to rise, reaching 40–50 per cent and even higher by the mid-1980s. The decline of employment in agriculture, the rise first in manufacturing and then in services, the changing composition of services, and the rise in government spending are among the best documented and most persistent features of the development of the modern economy. The steady-state approach, based on timeless rational choices – particularly where rational choice is thought to determine a choice of technique – is radically at variance with the problems of growth as they are posed for us by economic history (Nell 1988: Chs 6–7).

Pressman. It's somewhat understandable that traditional mainstream neoclassical economic theory would ignore the issues of Transformational Growth that you've just described. But on the other hand it is rather surprising that those strands of economic theory that have been critical of neoclassical orthodoxy have not taken steps forward in this direction. Do you have any explanation as to why, for example, the neo-Ricardians and the post-Keynesians have ignored these important issues of long-run growth and structural change?

Nell. Well, it may seem hard to explain intellectually, but perhaps it's not so hard from a sociological perspective. Research develops under the influence of argument and through competition for positions. It develops under pressures that are generated in the academy and in the publishing world, in the world of journals and above all in arguments with colleagues. For example, the neo-Ricardian approach has been very deeply embedded in the capital controversy. This is an important controversy, and in my opinion the neo-Ricardians have had the better of it. The arguments have explored important deficiencies in the neoclassical approach, and have led to a better understanding of what that approach can and cannot do. But as far as explaining the world, that controversy leads to a dead end. Neither side has paid any attention to the history of technology. The neo-Ricardian critique of neoclassical theory is deliberately constructed by accepting the ground that the neoclassicals have staked out: the framework of rational choice among a pre-existing set of techniques. Yet, in reality, there is no pre-existing set of techniques; the coefficients cannot be known for certain until a technique has been put into use and "learning by doing" has taken place. Besides, techniques are not "rationally chosen." There are many lines of argument which can be used to show the defects of "rational choice" models, and Martin Hollis's elaborate constructions of

291

rational choice leading to radically irrational results are undoubtedly among the most compelling.

But I don't think that arguments about rationality are what is most relevant here. The problem for economists is to understand the working of a production system governed by markets, and how it develops over time. For this, we should look to the history of technology and institutions. We should study the way techniques have emerged, the way they have grown, the kinds of pressures they respond to, the way they develop through practice, and the way techniques displace one another. When we do this we find that the development of technology is deeply intertwined with the development of institutions, and both are influenced by the way the market mechanisms work. I say "mechanisms," deliberately using the plural, because I do not want to try to (inadequately) describe markets in terms of one general overarching theory of "the market." There are many kinds of market and they interact. An adequate understanding of macroeconomics depends on understanding the many different kinds of market and how they interact.

To return to the question. I think that the neo-Ricardian approach has failed to deliver because it never developed itself on an independent footing. It has too closely mimicked the structure of neoclassical theory and has therefore distanced itself from the historical development of capitalism, which is surely what it was originally intended to explain.

Pressman. Are there any positive connections between Transformational Growth and neo-Ricardian economics, or is there anything that neo-Ricardian economics can contribute to the development of a theory of Transformational Growth?

Nell. Speaking very generally, neo-Ricardian economics should provide the foundation of the theory of Transformational Growth. We need a representation of the economy that shows its input–output structure. We need a representation of the economy that classifies the connections in that structure, as the basic–non-basic distinction does. We need a theory of the relationship between rate of profit, prices, and real wages. The surplus approach, broadly speaking, as Garegnani calls it, is the right foundation.

However, the neo-Ricardian studies in the choice of technique seem to me to be a neoclassically inspired deviation from a realistic approach. Those studies are not very useful. I am also skeptical of attempts to extend the neo-Ricardian approach to reconstruct Keynesian theory according to "the long-run method." This strikes me as quite wrong. Keynesian theories are short-run theories and should be understood in that way. Moreover, once we have left the world of the family firm and craft-based technology, we have entered a world in which technological change is driven by competition and market mechanisms and takes place through investment. In addition, once investment is in place, it brings further innovation and technological changes in its wake, through learning, and this leads to all kinds of unexpected effects on the profits of corporations. In this world, it does not seem to me that we can plausibly talk of movement towards a long-period position. In every short run there will be significant competition-driven technological innovation which will render some capital obsolete and will unpredictably increase productivity in other areas. It still remains true that competition will tend to lead to the formation of a rate of profit; capital, especially financial capital, including depreciation funds, will always seek the highest rate of return. This is important in understanding the rate of interest. But you can't say that this will tend to lead to the formation of a particular level of profit rate, because innovations will be changing the coefficients from each short period to the next. Nor can "long-period prices" be determined on a "best practice" basis, since the same competitive processes that might tend to make the rate of profit uniform will also tend to change the best-practice coefficients from one short period to another (Nell, in Dymski and Pollin 1994).

Thus, while the notion of a long-period position may perhaps make sense in the world of family firms and craft-based technologies, it doesn't really make sense in a Keynesian world, where we have Keynesian investment, Keynesian uncertainty, modern corporations, multiplier and accelerator mechanisms, and competitively driven innovation. Some neo-Ricardians try to rule out uncertainty and "abstract" from innovation, but such work cannot help in understanding Keynes and is useless to the theory of Transformational Growth.

This doesn't mean, however, that the Sraffian equations have no meaning in a realistic approach to the modern world. On the contrary, once we drop both the "best practice" interpretation and the "long-period" method, it seems to me that they give us an indispensable picture of the essential relationships of the system, and they are able to do this because the bulk of the economy changes only slowly, i.e. no faster than the rate of gross investment. There are rapid changes at the margin brought about by investment, but in fact the concept of vintage capital provides a correct and useful vision of the modern economy. You have layers and layers of vintages, and the whole shifts rather slowly. So, if we think of the coefficients of a Sraffa model as representing average coefficients rather than best-practice coefficients, these average coefficients tell us what the interrelations of the economy are. The Sraffa equations provide a picture of basic wage–profit–price connections, capable of being studied empirically as Leontief and Ochoa have done. They reveal the structure of the economy, and reveal it as a slowly changing structure. But the neo-Ricardian interpretation is flawed (Nell, in Dymski and Pollin 1994).

Pressman. What about the post-Keynesian school? Why have they failed to develop a theory of the growth of demand?

Nell. The post-Keynesian school, I think, has tied itself a little too closely to Keynes. The Keynesian project – at least, Keynes's project – was to provide a set of economic ideas that would help to explain the breakdown of the 1930s. He thought that those ideas could be extended to the business cycle, and that they might possibly also extend to a theory of growth. But he didn't develop a theory of growth, although, of course, he said things about the economic possibilities for our grandchildren and also, in his lecture on demographics, he had interesting things to say about the processes of growth, but they didn't amount to a theoretical construction.

To a large extent, the major concern of the post-Keynesians has been to defend and protect the central insights of Keynes and Kalecki from neoclassical critics and revisionists. I think they are absolutely right to do this. Their approach is sound, but because of the defensiveness it hasn't led to much development of Keynes's ideas. So their situation has been similar to that of the neo-Ricardians, but with an important difference. The neo-Ricardians have been engaged in a conflict with the neoclassicals on the neoclassicals' ground, which they are attacking; the post-Keynesians have been engaged in a conflict with the neoclassicals on Keynes's ground, which they are defending.

The problem is that Keynes's ground is essentially short-run, and the development of a theory of the growth of demand, connecting the growth of demand with the changing structure of the economy, has not been part of the post-Keynesian vision. This is not to say that it is inconsistent with the post-Keynesian vision. Far from it; it seems to be a perfectly natural development of that vision. Minsky, in developing the theory of financial fragility, has tried to put some building blocks in place – although, if you were to ask me what theory there is of financial fragility behind the very well coined phrase, I would have to admit I don't really know. There are some clever insights and a lot of remarks, but "theory" is putting it a little bit too strongly. Nevertheless, it's a step in the right direction. Many more should be taken (see Deleplace and Nell 1994).

Pressman. Do you see any possibilities that the new Keynesian school of economics might lead to some theoretical advances that relate demand to structural or transformational economic change?

Nell. Many of the "new Keynesian" models are designed to explore the significance of imperfections, or of limited rationality, or problems of asymmetrical information, or how limited information can create difficulties for markets. For example, Stiglitz has developed models that involve rationing credit, in which Keynesian results (for example, unemployment and under-used capacity) can be reached, although all agents optimize. Efficiency wage models, which partly rest on employers not having adequate information about workers and their real skills, provide another example. And, of course, there are also many different kinds of models of sticky prices. These models are supposed to give us good reasons for wage and price stickiness in conditions where firms and households are making rational choices governed by their utility functions or otherwise engaging in maximizing behavior. Of course, if prices and/or wages are sticky, we can expect Keynesian-type results. The development of these models has become a major cottage industry in modern economics.

One problem with this approach is that we should expect to find imperfections and asymmetrical information to be more prominent in an economy that is relatively backward technologically. The more difficult travel is, the more difficult communication is, the more problematical information is, the harder it is to check up, the more likely the market adjustment will be impeded. By contrast, today you punch into a computer system, find out someone's social security number, crack into a couple of data banks and you can find out practically everything there is to know about them. Imperfections in communication and the flow of data are easy to overcome. In the nineteenth century this was not possible. But today, if you have a desktop Macintosh, or use Windows, you can publish all your manuals as fast as you like. Then you can fax them to everybody. In this situation your "menu costs" are negligible. In the nineteenth century, by contrast, you had to print a new Sears catalog and deliver it to the farm on horseback.

We should, then, expect to find that the things which the new Keynesians worry about were much more serious problems in the nineteenth century. But in what I have called the conditions of "the old trade cycle" prices were flexible; that is to say, they flexed up and down. We even find money wages flexing down a little bit, although not by very much. In the post-Second World War era, however, you almost never find prices or money wages flexing downward. In the nineteenth century real wages moved inversely to employment, as traditional theory implies. But after the Second World War real wages are largely procyclical. So the bizarre feature of the new Keynesian models is that they provide a better explanation of the stickiness of money wages and prices in the very period in which they were flexible!

This historical perspective helps to drive home the importance of understanding the structural changes in the economy and developing a theory of these changes. It helps us to see and understand why markets work differently in different eras, and under different conditions. The way to understand how markets work is through the patterns that we find in the time series of the major market variables. We find one pattern of relationships in the old trade cycle, roughly 1870 to 1914. We find a systematically different pattern in the time series relations between the various variables in the 1945 to 1990 period. This is the kind of thing we should be looking at, and I think the explanation of these differences lies in the interrelated development of technology and institutions.

Pressman. From what you have said about Transformational Growth and the limits of neoclassical growth theory it would seem that one of the keys to developing an adequate theory of long-term economic growth is to develop a theory of economic institutions and how institutions change over time. Do you think that economics should take such an institutionalist direction? And do you think that the institutionalists offer an avenue for the development of a theory of the long-term growth of demand?

Nell. Yes I think that's right, as long as by "institutionalists" you mean people like Dewey and Commons and Veblen. If you mean the modern institutionalists – for example, Richard Langlois and friends – I don't think they have an awful lot to offer. Again, they have adopted too much of the neoclassical framework, the framework of rational choice, which, as I have said, is not rational and offers no choice. (It's not rational because the framework leads to paradoxes, and it offers no choice because the real problems of choice are all predetermined by assumption in the preference set.) I don't think much can be done by adopting that framework, and so I am not hopeful along these lines. But yes, I think that understanding institutions is crucial to understanding growth – indeed, to understanding markets.

Let me give you an example. In the late nineteenth century the methods of mass production are developed. This begins with scientific advance and the practical application of science, which, in turn, leads to the emergence of new professions – for example, engineering. To see the effect on markets requires that we examine the new cost structure facing business. Changing the cost structure also changes the risks that businesses face. It changes not only the quantitative risks but also the quality of risk and the kinds of things that are at risk. It means that business institutions will react differently to different kinds of exogenous developments, or "shocks," as they are often called in conventional economics. What we see is the emergence of a new institution from the business firm that existed in the earlier part of the nineteenth century. From a firm that was largely a family affair the modern corporation develops. It takes over half a century to develop and spread, but we can observe its beginnings in the nineteenth century. Here we have interrelated developments: a new technology, the changing cost structure; the growth of a new institution; a changing class structure; and, of course, a changing sectoral composition of output and a changing sectoral composition of the labor force. To relate these interacting patterns – economic time series and market data, institutional developments, the workings of markets and market pressures – is the kind of work that is needed. To call this "institutional" is perfectly acceptable to me. But it should be understood that such an approach incorporates many of the things that macroeconomists and growth economists normally do. But it does them with a wider awareness, and specifically by drawing on the ideas, the techniques, and the approach of historians.

Pressman. How would this analysis of the development of a new institution – for example, the modern corporation – relate to issues of long-term growth?

Nell. First of all, the development of the corporation gives economics a new "agent." The family firm is subjected to a certain set of pressures and it has a certain pattern of decision-making. I don't want to uncritically accept the conventional economic analysis of the firm, the theory as you would find it in a microeconomic textbook, because it is too closely based on the notion of simple rational choice and, of course, scarcity pricing. But if we put some of these concerns aside for the moment it seems to me that the picture presented is perhaps not altogether wrong. The firm tries to achieve an optimal size, both in the short run and in the long run. It makes its decisions on prices and outputs with an eye to the informational signals it is receiving from its market environment, and then it tries to establish itself at such-and-such a size. Much of this story can and should be accepted as an account of firms operating with craft technologies.

In contrast, the modern corporation does not try to achieve an optimal size. The modern corporation reinvests and grows. If anything, it is looking for an optimal growth path. However, the modern corporation is not quite so easily represented as a unitary decision-maker. The family firm, especially in a patriarchal family structure, can rather plausibly be represented as a unitary decision-maker. The corporation, on the other hand, has three main sectors: finance, production and marketing. It is not so easy to regard this trinity as having a single focus, or a single target, or a single decision-maker. The board, indeed, makes decisions, but the board makes decisions in a process of political compromise, and, anyway, in practice, it may not be the board that makes decisions. It depends on what the actual structure of power within the institution is. Sometimes it will be the board, but sometimes it will be the senior management, and the board will simply be a rubber stamp. Sometimes there may be no single center of power: decisions may be made through a fluctuating set of compromises. To understand the working of this institution is to apply, at least from time to time, a political framework of analysis. However, this political framework of analysis must be situated in an economic environment, an environment of costs and demands. These costs and demands will be critical, because if decisions are not made properly the firm will go bankrupt, while if they are made well the firm's profit will grow, perhaps increasing its market share. Although there are political elements in this, there are also very conventional economic elements. It is the interaction of the two which needs to be studied without the imposition of an arbitrary framework, the kind that is often imposed by the assumptions that there is a single objective function, a single set of constraints and a single program to be maximized.

Pressman. How do you see this analysis of the changing institutional structure of the business firm leading to an explanation of long-term economic growth, and specifically an explanation for the slowdown of growth in the United States and other developed economies throughout the world?

Nell. Let me postpone the second half of that for a moment and take up the issue of the changing nature of the firm and economic growth. We were talking about the emergence of the modern corporation from the family firm, a development that took place in the late nineteenth century and early twentieth century. This transformation requires some careful scrutiny, because if we look at the time series for the business cycle and for the changing structure of the economy in the nineteenth century, and compare it with later periods, we find some really very striking differences. In the late nineteenth century we find a very similar pattern of statistical time series behavior in the United States, the United Kingdom, Canada and Germany. We find that prices generally tend to move downward until the period just before the First World War. We find that money wages are rather steady; they don't fluctuate much, although they do fluctuate in both directions, and over time they rise slightly. We find that manufacturing prices fluctuate both up and down; they're flexible in both directions. Manufacturing prices are not, however, as flexible on the whole as raw material prices, except in Germany, where we have Bismarck's supports for agricultural prices. Thus we find that raw material prices are more flexible in both directions than manufacturing prices, which are more flexible in both directions than money wages, which only occasionally fall and tend to be level or slightly rising. Interestingly, we find that fluctuations in employment are restrained; the fluctuations in employment may be even smaller than during the post-Second World War period.

This sounds a little bit like Christina Roemer, but the point is quite different. Fluctuations in output are more considerable than fluctuations in employment, but fluctuations in output are highly correlated in the short run with fluctuations in productivity. Productivity fluctuates a lot in the short run, and fluctuates more than employment. It is this that gives rise to the fluctuations in output. Now when we look at this pattern we find that these statistical series in relation to each other provide a rather distinctive pattern, and in fact it's quite a famous pattern. Marshall called attention to it in connection with the 1870s in England, and it is the pattern associated with marginal productivity theory: real wages inversely related to employment and output. Hicks suggested a very simple explanation for this. What happens is that changes in demand drive prices up initially, lowering the real wage and making it worth while to disrupt work crews and routine by introducing additional workers (Nell 1994).

Pressman. What about the long run? Do changes in demand drive prices up over a longer period of time?

Nell. In the nineteenth century prices fell over the long run. Rising productivity and competition forced them down. But, in the short run, prices varied with demand, because output could be varied only with difficulty. Productivity could be increased in the short run by working more intensively, but this is a temporary response and it can't last. Therefore, when demand increases permanently, employment will have to be increased. But to increase employment means to add workers to a labor force that has to work together. That is to say, you have to reorganize work crews. You are not simply adding people to an assembly line, you are adding them to a group of skilled workers who have to cooperate. This requires disrupting the normal flow of work in order to reorganize. It is therefore expensive. Thus a rise in prices is necessary to pay for the disruption and the reorganization of the labor process. Hence we find the inverse relationship between real wages and employment. It is a consequence, on the one hand, of demand pressures and, the other hand, of the nature of the labor process, that is to say, technology and the organization of labor that exists in the conditions of the family firm and in what I have called craft-based factories. Once the reorganization is complete, and production has expanded, prices may very well fall below their earlier level, or continue to wind down, if economies of scale are eventually realized. Hence the long-run downward trend of prices.

Pressman. How does this relationship between demand and prices change with the introduction of the modern corporation?

Nell. The rise of the modern corporation based on mass-production technology changes a number of economic relationships. First of all, continuous throughput makes it possible to greatly speed up work, and, because work is carried out in a way that does not require all labor crews to work together all the time, it makes it possible to shut down and start up production, and to lay off and rehire workers in a relatively simple and not very costly manner. It makes it possible, in short, to adjust employment and output to demand. Hence we would expect to find that the variation of productivity with output in the short run was much less after the introduction of mass production. This is not to suggest that the correlation of productivity and output in the long run would be affected by the changing nature of the firm. This is a different matter and the connections have come to be known as Kaldor's Laws. But the relationship between output and productivity in the short run is different. Quarterly data, half-yearly, and yearly data show a very strong correlation in the nineteenth century where we have such data, which is only industry by industry. We would expect to find after the introduction of mass production that prices were very much less sensitive to demand, particularly manufacturing prices. We would expect prices not to fall, because, when demand falls, employment and output will be reduced, so there will be no necessity to dump and force prices down, while costs will be adjusted by laying workers off. So, with mass production, lay-offs will develop as an institutionalized practice. When workers are laid off there is either an implicit or an explicit promise to rehire them. So we would expect the adjustment process here to be significantly different from the adjustment process in the nineteenth century.

Pressman. Are the two adjustment processes in fact different?

Nell. We do find that the time series are different. Prices in the post-Second World War period rise, almost without exception, in all advanced countries. We find very few down-trends in prices. We find money wages rising faster than prices, in marked contrast to the relationship before the First World War. Productivity gains, in other words, accrue through the more rapid increase of money wages than of prices. In contrast, during the pre-First World War period we find money wages tending to be steady and prices falling. Productivity gains are transmitted to the economy through falling prices in the pre-First World War period. In the post-Second World War period they're transmitted by the more rapid rise of money wages, a different kind of mechanism – a point Sylos-Labini has stressed. As a result of this different mechanism we would expect to find output and employment quite flexible in response to demand. With prices relatively stable in the short run, we would also expect to find a multiplier, and perhaps a multiplier–accelerator, process. We see this most clearly in the inter-war period, because in the inter-war period there is no attempt to stabilize the economy through countercyclical government spending or other countercyclical measures. Hence there were very large fluctuations. In the post-Second World War period these fluctuations are dampened by countercyclical measures. But we still find that employment and output are more flexible, in both directions, than prices, which are flexible only upwards.

Pressman. Does this help to account for the prevalence of inflation in the post-Second World War era?

Nell. In the advanced countries, moderate inflation has been a consequence of the way the price mechanism has distributed the gains from rising productivity. When productivity rose, the money wages of the production workers, the workers on the lines, would rise in proportion. That is the effect of collective bargaining. But these increases disrupt relative status positions, so the wages and salaries of other kinds of workers or workers in other sectors would have to rise too, to keep pace. If auto and steel workers earned more as their productivity rose, teachers and lawyers and doctors – to say nothing of business executives – had to maintain their relative social standing, so their earnings would have to rise more or less in step. (A similar point was made by Baumol and Bowen about the performing arts.) But this implies that costs will rise. So prices rise and a wage–price spiral is established.

Transformational Growth suggests another mechanism. Even when mass production has become dominant, some sectors and industries retain characteristics of the craft system. In particular, agriculture and primary production tend to have inflexible employment and to produce goods which, after a point, are expensive to stockpile and have to be dumped. Their prices are therefore flexible. Another industry which retained strong craft characteristics (for different reasons) is machine tools, and there again prices tend to be demand-sensitive.

In each case, when demand falls, prices will tend to drift down – even, on occasion, to collapse. Conversely when demand rises, prices in these sectors will rise. Price flexibility reflects difficulties in adjusting, hence the effect depends not only on the size of the movement but also on its speed. These price changes will be transmitted as cost increases to all the other sectors: raw materials and primary products enter production at the beginning; while machine tools affect the cost of investment and hence influence future prices.

Prior to the First World War this flexibility would cut in both directions. But not any more. The price-flexible industries supply the dominant mass-production sector, which adapts its level of output to demand. Prices rise when demand is strong, and large quantities of raw materials are needed. The price increase is therefore weighted heavily, and has a substantial impact on other sectors. When demand is weak, prices will be low, but their impact will be weak, because the quantity is low. Similarly for machine tools: when demand is strong, investment will be large, and the high prices will have a strong impact; but when demand is weak prices will decline. However, the impact will be small, because little investment will be undertaken. Hence price increases will always be weighted more heavily than price declines, and the effect of fluctuations will be to impart an upward bias to prices (Nell 1994).

Once we understand that moderate inflation results from the way the system works, it should be clear that most anti-inflationary policy is misguided.

Pressman. Let's try to carry this analysis up to the 1970s, 1980s and 1990s. You talked about a change of the business enterprise from family-owned firm to a large modern corporation that operates as Galbraith describes in *The New Industrial State.* But the modern corporation itself has undergone important changes in a number of ways over the past quarter-century. In the United States there has been a decline in manufacturing and a similar decline in the use of mass-production manufacturing processes. Likewise the firm is no longer a national firm but is really a global firm which is producing all over the world. How does this changing nature of the corporation affect the relationships between demand, prices, productivity and employment?

Nell. These recent changes in the corporation are important, but hard to analyze, because we are at the beginning of the process. Hegel says somewhere that the owl of Minerva takes wing only at dusk. So it's easier to see the shape of the mass-production economy now, at the end of its life, and as it's beginning to change into the information economy, than it is to see the real shape of the emerging economy based on information technologies and global production. However, I think that some things are clear. One is that there is a changing cost structure and that the changes are very considerable. Fixed costs are important in the mass-production economy, but such fixed costs are embodied in capital equipment. In the information economy we find a lot of invisible sunk costs. They show up in the contractual obligations of firms. These costs were incurred in the process of research and development. So there's nothing tangible like a factory or set of buildings that correspond to them. This is one change. Another change is that variable costs appear to be shrinking, very remarkably. Variable costs are quite important in mass production; it appears they're not so important in the cost structure of the global multinational corporation. The importance of information and of managerial and technical skills (that is, the skills of highly trained Ph.D. engineers, computer specialists, software developers and managers) is clearly very significant in the global arrangements of firms. Moreover, the multi-division structure of the large corporation may be giving way to a more fragmented structure that is less hierarchical and based more on contacts and franchising than on command from above. The image is of a network, rather than a hierarchy; a spider web rather than a pyramid. These developments mean greater flexibility in moving capital around the globe, and also greater flexibility in moving highly skilled, high-paid managerial and entrepreneurial labor from country to country. The position of the working-class labor force, however, is much less flexible. Such labor is much less mobile, and, of course, local government structures and even national government structures are at the mercy of those who can pull up stakes and leave for better climates. Government is experiencing much greater difficulty in controlling macroeconomic processes and in regulating microeconomic issues and disputes. Part of the economic malaise that we're facing at present surely comes from the inability of government to keep pace.

Pressman. Do you see this relative increase in the ability of capital to cross national boundaries, especially in comparison with the relative immobility of laborers, and governments as contributing to the slowdown of economic growth and the slowdown in productivity growth that we have experienced recently?

Nell. Yes, if you mean national growth and national productivity. The problems of government in the face of the changing nature of capital have been quite significant. As capital's mobility has increased, and as the nature of technology has changed, capital has been very anxious to remove regulations and restrictions in order to take advantage of the new possibilities. Therefore, it has put considerable political pressure on governments to remove regulations and has tried to limit government control, government investment and government domination of economic decisions. It has weakened or undermined the instruments of government control.

Pressman. And its greater mobility has given it greater power over governments as well?

Nell. That's right.

Pressman. So it's not just a desire, it's also an ability, to pick up and move elsewhere that is giving the business firm greater clout relative to State, local and national governments. What are the ramifications of this with respect to the theory of Transformational Growth?

Nell. An important result of the business and conservative assault on government – Reagan and Thatcher – has been a slowing down of the rate of growth of government expenditures, and that has had a very predictable multiplier effect on the macroeconomy, leading to stagnation and, through the effects of Kaldor's laws, to the slowing down of the growth of productivity. Besides the Kaldor's laws phenomenon there is also the problem posed by the complementarity of infrastructure investment and private productivity. Private investment, arguably, is complementary to public investment. Larger public investment engenders larger private investment. This point – the exact opposite of "crowding out" – deserves more attention than it has received. The decay of infrastructure, which is notable in the United States but also exists in other advanced capitalist economies (though perhaps not to the same extent), has led to a decline in the rate of growth of productivity and probably also to a decline in investment. So I would suggest that the slowdown in investment is related to the impact of the changing nature of capital on government.

There is another aspect to the slowdown, however. Many of the major markets of advanced capitalism have reached temporary saturation points, saturation points that are determined by the distribution of income. All those Americans who could afford a second car, at a certain point, had one. All those Americans who could afford a second television set had one. If we look at the rate of the growth of expenditure on consumer durables, we find that it slows down around the beginning of the 1970s. This slowdown is significant. We also find that an important support for consumer spending, and therefore for investment in the expansion consumer goods production, disappears in the 1970s, or rather shrinks to insignificance. This is the GI Bill of Rights. The GI Bill of Rights gave a whole generation of Americans the possibility of founding a family and carrying it right through the entire life cycle. The true life-cycle theory of consumption is not the one appearing in the textbooks but would describe the life cycle guaranteed by government through the GI Bill. You could go to college or get vocational training, take out a mortgage, have medical insurance, have a pension and have guaranteed medical care for you and your family all your life, if you were a GI. There were about 12 million Second World War GIs, followed by Korean War GIs and then all who went through the draft. All would have families, and businesses could plan to supply their needs, knowing these families had the government behind them.

This was not the case, however, after Vietnam. The same package of benefits was not extended. The elimination of the draft meant that benefits and coverage were both much more restricted. The universal GI bill of the 1950s and early 1960s came to an end, and the new generations growing up in the 1970s and 1980s had no such benefit. Therefore, their consumption plans were not underwritten by government, and the expansion of consumption couldn't be as reliably foreseen. One important consequence of this for the business firm was that investment could not be planned on the same basis as earlier. The removal of this government guarantee underlying the growth of consumption for a high proportion of the population introduced an element of uncertainty, and an element of variability into consumption which hadn't existed in the early post-Second World War period. These government guarantees imparted greater stability to consumption, helped to generate a higher growth of consumption, and helped to generate greater business confidence and therefore more investment. Again, this is a topic that hasn't been adequately explored, but it is a natural topic, which the theory of Transformational Growth suggests.

Pressman. You've mentioned growing market saturation, and the emergence of the information technologies as factors contributing to a general slowdown. Do you think this explains why unemployment seems to be getting worse?

Nell. There are long-term and short-term reasons for the increase in unemployment in the advanced economies. We've discussed the long-term reasons; the short-term, of course, include the worsening of the business cycle, a development that is itself a long-term phenomenon. But besides these factors there are two important policy issues, which in a way are related to Transformational Growth. The first is the conservative attack on Keynesian expansionist policy – the triumph of austerity. There can be little doubt that simultaneous austerity in the Reagan–Bush United States, in Thatcher's Britain and in Kohl's Germany has contributed strongly to stagnation. And deregulation has weakened the ability of governments to carry out policy. The second is the nearly universal trend to cut back on State spending. Very few countries have actually succeeded in cutting back the State, but most have slowed its growth. And this contributes to stagnation.

Perhaps we should ask why the conservative tide is rising in most of the leading nations of the advanced world at nearly the same time? Maybe the conservative flood was just an accident. Or it might be argued that Keynesian policies had failed. But we should consider the possibility that conservative regimes have come to power in order to accomplish new tasks, needed for the development of a new stage of capitalism.

Earlier we discussed the growing internationalization of capital and the correlative need, from the business point of view, to limit the ability of States to regulate or control these movements. Another reason to limit regulation is the need to experiment with new technologies and to develop markets for the resulting new product lines. Regulation and concern for worker and public safety can hinder innovation and inhibit product development. Rightly, we may say, when the products (e.g. biotech) are potentially dangerous on a massive scale. But from the point of view of companies in a competitive race these dangers are too distant and too speculative to matter, especially when compared with the immediate threat of being beaten in the scramble for the pot of gold.

But Transformational Growth suggests another, strategic reason for the conservative surge at this time. The major field for capitalist development since the nineteenth century has been the industrialization and marketing of goods and services formerly performed by the household and extended family, abetted by local craftsmanship. Home preserves have been replaced by canning, home births by hospitals, home crafts by furniture, sewing and tailoring by department stores, home cooking by fast foods. Whatever your great-grandmother did around the house, the chances are it's now an industry. And what your great-grandmother or other members of the family could not do, local craftsmen and shopkeepers did: carriage-making, harness-making, blacksmith work, the local doctor and druggist, and they likewise have been replaced by mass production and mass marketing.

But this process has more or less come to an end. There is little or nothing left to transform; all the traditional functions of the household have been commodified, industrialized and marketed on a mass scale, from the maternity care industry, hospital births, children's foods, clothing, toys, school aids, home furnishings, right on through home appliances and automobiles to old age nursing homes, caskets and funerals. What new fields are there to be taken over and transformed?

If the household is largely exhausted as a source of opportunities, it might pay to look elsewhere, and a prime candidate appears to be the State. The activities of the State can be taken over, privatized, commodified and marketed, exactly as the activities of the household were. Of course there are differences; most of the activities of the State are services, and, moreover, services of a collective nature. Education, criminal justice, the postal service, telephones and mass media all have important public dimensions which may be lost or underplayed when these are carried on for private profit. But, on the other hand, private capital can provide these services and can do so at a profit in a competitive atmosphere. If the horizon for capital investment appears to be shrinking, privatizing the activities of the State may seem a good bet, all the more so since the State, not wishing to see these activities go unperformed in the event of bankruptcy, can be persuaded to assume the risks!

As might be expected, privatization has generated problems. Critics have charged that it has contributed to stagnation and cutbacks in employment, and has led to deteriorating services while generally raising costs. These charges may well be true, but they are beside the point here. Privatization is important because it is part of a general revamping of the relationship between capital, labor, consumers and the State. The trends suggest momentous changes, which can only be sketched here. Needless to say, any such sketch must be very speculative. Capital is becoming institutionalized, meaning that it is less and less under the control of families or individuals, and more and more embodied in institutions. As an example, "ownership" has become a form of finance, and managerial control, in turn, a consequence of financial control. Labor is becoming less important and more easily replaceable in production as information technology takes over skills and makes possible far more detailed control and supervision. Management is also less important and more replaceable. Seniority counts for less. Hierarchy is less appropriate as the mode of organization, at least in some areas. Many corporations are reforming themselves, sometimes under great pressure, as at IBM. The aim is to slim down, to become more flexible, to be able to shift operations quickly in response to opportunities and to become more mobile in the world market. Long-established connections with communities or with consumers count for less. Capital no longer needs or wants, or can afford, a close relationship with government or the community; nor can it afford to be indebted to its workers, no matter how long or loyal their service. To put it succinctly, capital is shedding commitments to labor and to communities throughout the advanced world.

I'd like to take this thought a step further, but I have to admit that the idea is still undeveloped. What is it for a person to be "included" in the economy? Clearly you are part of the economy if you own capital or property. You are likewise included if you possess an entitlement, a pension, a disability claim, or whatever, and, of course, if you have a job, although some jobs are more tenuous than others. If you were a laid-off union member in the 1950s you would have been called back in order of seniority. You have a recognized claim. If you have a public sector job, after a certain time, you have enough seniority that you can't be fired. But many jobs carry no security. A worker is part of the system only while actually holding such a job. If you lose it, you are on the periphery. Some kinds of qualifications may be sufficient to include a person: being a product of certain school systems; having a degree from a top university, or one in a crucial subject; or a professional qualification, passing the bar or medical exams; or, in the old days, membership in certain clubs. Without going into it further, what I'm suggesting could be put this way: "membership" in the economy is becoming more exclusive. Standards are tightening. More people are being expelled to the periphery, where they will have to survive in "informal" economies, until they are needed, if ever.

Pressman. Throughout this interview you've made a number of negative comments about neoclassical economic theory and also about various unorthodox schools of economic thought. I would like to try to close on a more positive note. How would you like to see economic theory develop so that it adequately addresses the issues that you have raised here?

Nell. Economic theory needs a greater awareness of history. Economic theory is supposed to tell us how markets work, what goods are produced, and how, for whom, and at what prices and profits, just as the textbooks say. But this doesn't happen in the same way at all times in all places. Technologies are different, calling for different kinds of skills and organizations, which, in turn, create different cost structures. Different cost structures are associated with different patterns of risk, and therefore of market responses. Markets have different characteristic patterns of adjustment, based on the underlying technologies and institutions. Faced with this sort of claim, the conventional wisdom responds that there is nevertheless a core of rational behavior: maximizing subject to constraints, the behavior of "rational economic man," which is the same everywhere, any time. As a descriptive proposition this turns out to be an idea that cannot be made coherent – that was the point of Hollis and Nell (1975). Nevertheless there is a role for maximizing theory, but it is not descriptive.

Descriptive theory has to be based on exploring and modelling the actual institutions of the economy in each era, to show how they work and interconnect. This means learning history and also doing "fieldwork" in something like the sense in which anthropologists use the term. That is, we have to understand the day-to-day working rules and procedures of our banks, markets, hiring and promotion systems and corporate boardrooms. Modern economics does much less of this than it should, partly because so many practitioners don't regard it as necessary or even useful; instead it is assumed that, whatever workers or managers or housewives seem to be doing, we know that they are maximizing subject to constraints. As a research strategy this amounts to betting that one can learn something new from a tautology.

This institutional and historical approach offers some surprising insights. For example, conventional textbook micro-theory "partial equilibrium" can rather plausibly be understood as an account of the adjustment process of markets in a world of family firms operating craft technologies, or running small craft-based factories using steam or water power. The corresponding macro-theory is based on price adjustments, so that, when demand falls, prices fall and real wages rise (Nell 1992: ch. 16).

According to this perspective, utility theory should be understood as Marshall sometimes seems to have meant it, as a theory describing how a representative consumer feels about, and will react to, progressive deviations from a settled position. Preferences should not be considered to range over all possible options. Rather, the question at issue is how to react to small changes in various directions from the present, settled, long-run position. This is likewise the question at issue in marginal productivity theory: what change in the real wage will be needed to compensate for an increase or decrease in employment, given that such a change will disrupt the organization of work? On an economy-wide basis, a change in overall employment will disrupt the use of land and fixed resources, requiring changes in methods of production. The new methods will be less productive, otherwise they would have been in use earlier. At a given rate of profit, therefore, in order for employment to increase, the real wage will have to decline. Marginalist theory, then, should be understood as a theory of adjustment.

By contrast, Keynesian economics is the theory of the mass-production economy that emerged in full dress after World War II. It is likewise a theory of adjustment. Technology had developed so that output could be readily adjusted to sales, through variations in employment, while keeping the productivity of line workers constant. This resulted in a multiplier–accelerator adjustment process, which magnified fluctuations and destabilized the system. In the absence of government intervention and/or a large public sector with built-in stabilizers, the system produced wide swings, as happened in the inter-war period.

General equilibrium theory, on the other hand, as a grand choice of bundles of goods and methods of production, from among all possible combinations, has to be rejected as misconceived. Not only does it face internal technical difficulties (the problems of instability and multiple equilibria) but it is also unable to accommodate the concept of capital and a general rate of profit. In addition, the project is all wrong. Early utility theorists were looking for rules that would tell us how to move in the best direction, starting from a given position. They were looking for the best local move. General equilibrium theory tries to determine a global optimum, which presumes that abstract agents, occupying no present position and having no commitments, obligations or other social characteristics, can rank all possibilities.

The textbook idea of a "grand neoclassical synthesis," promoted over the years by Samuelson, Modigliani, and Patinkin, is clearly misconceived, judged from this perspective. The neoclassical labor market and production function cannot be combined with the IS–LM system, Pigou effects or no, because they are each the economics of a different era and reflect different and incompatible assumptions about the underlying technology and organization of the business world.

Finally, models of market adjustment should not simply be thought of as alternatives. The point of Transformational Growth is that market processes set up incentives that lead to technical progress, which in turn leads to institutional development. And this all reacts back on the way markets work. The market adjustment process in the craft-based economy sets up incentives to technological and organizational change. Price fluctuations are costly when employment is fixed, or difficult to change, and output is variable largely through varying productivity. Firms will look for innovations that will help them increase the flexibility of their operations. These innovations will lead, in turn, to changes in organization. In short, the operation of markets in the craft-based system set up incentives that led to the innovations that changed the system into one based on mass-production.

Pressman. You mentioned that there was a role for maximizing models in all this, although not a descriptive one. What do you mean by that?

Nell. Any serious market analysis depends on the assumption of gain-seeking behavior. Market agents are looking for the best deals they can get. If you like, that is a kind of maximizing behavior. But it does not implausibly assume detailed preference functions, or knowledge that can't be had because it doesn't exist. The Transformational Growth approach steers us away from any such global assumptions. Instead it considers the points where market adjustments impose costs that could be relieved. It looks for signals as to the places and directions where innovation would be helpful.

In this regard certain kinds of quasi-engineering maximizing models are extremely helpful. Operations research models of many kinds can be used to find the key blockages and cost constraints: scheduling, linear programming, queueing theory, network and critical path analyses are all designed to pick out the features of the current technology or organization in which improvements would make the greatest difference. Most of these models have duals in which some kind of shadow prices are generated. These prices indicate the gain that would be provided by the unit-shifting of a constraint. However, it should be noted that this is not descriptive, and is not a market analysis. It is a management/engineering analysis of what ought to be done in order to improve current operations. In this context, it seems to me, "scarcity" theorizing comes into its own. Of course, many neoclassical textbook models are too abstract to be much practical help, but they do present the general principles. However, if they are presented as descriptive, only confusion can result (Hollis and Nell 1975).

Pressman. From all that you have said it is clear that Transformational Growth is a kind of dynamic theory. What does this dynamic theory tell us about the directions in which economics should move?

Nell. My sense is that the future of economic theory will lie primarily in developing various kinds of dynamic models. Of course, we need good structural models, which show the interdependence of industries, sectors, classes of income recipients and consumers. But this kind of model-building is fairly well developed already. What is more interesting, and less well understood, is how such structures work in the market, whether they are stable or unstable according to various definitions in various circumstances, and how they change in response to the many internal and external pressures impinging on them.

Transformational Growth aims to revive the "grand dynamics" of the classics, as well as to draw on the many kinds of mathematical dynamic theory now being developed. In this regard it suggests some very large and disturbing questions. One concerns the prevalence of "negative dynamics," or vicious circles, in many aspects of political economy today. For example, government has been caught offguard by economic processes which call for strong government regulation. The effect has been to injure the public, which becomes disaffected with government. Public disaffection further weakens government, leading to further injury, and so to still further disaffection. The political process, expressing the public's attitude, moves away from a solution.

But perhaps the most serious issue concerns the market itself. The market has been the organizing institution of economic behavior for the past five centuries or more. The conventional wisdom tells us that markets allocate scarce resources efficiently. This is surely fanciful. But markets do help resolve disputes over distribution which might otherwise end in violence. It is unlikely that such resolutions are "optimal," but they are likely to be better than civil war. More important – and this, I think, is their true function – markets generate incentives to technical progress. This is the message of Transformational Growth: markets don't allocate scarce resources, they generate pressures and provide the means to innovate. That is what they have been doing the past five centuries, and the result has been an almost unimaginable transformation of the world. There have been costs to this process, but in general it has led to higher and higher standards of living for those in the forefront of the development. This may be changing now. It may be that "negative externalities" are growing faster than productivity plus positive externalities. If this is so, then market-generated technical progress will make us worse-off, so much so that the gainers would not be able to compensate the losers. (Not that they would be likely to try!) Another way of putting this is to say that, under such conditions, the incentives to technological innovation can no longer be left to the market. But these same pressures are undermining the ability of governments to regulate and control economic processes.

This is not a cheerful picture, but it may well be a realistic one. Transformational Growth draws on classical foundations, and classical economics was known as the "dismal science"!

13

CONCLUSION

Edward J. Nell

Joan Robinson posed the opposition, "history *v.* equilibrium". Our investigations have shown the importance of history in economics: the economy – in particular, the system of market adjustment – does not *function* the same way in different periods. In our earlier period we find evidence of a price mechanism that is moderately stabilizing, so long as the fluctuations are not too extreme. But in the second period there is little or no evidence of this price mechanism. Instead we find a quantity adjustment process which is highly volatile, and possibly unstable. Equilibrium, then, may be a useful hypothesis in the earlier period; it is less likely to be useful in the second. Moreover, the institutions are different: the way labor is remunerated is different, and the incentives governing employment are also different. As a result the labor market adjusts differently. Further, the firms, the institutions making decisions, are constituted differently. Family firms and modern corporations have different social foundations, and behave differently in the market. Family firms tend to find their optimal size and remain there; corporations retain earnings and reinvest them to grow with the growth of their markets. Family firms are slow to introduce new technologies; corporations support R & D, and re-tool and upgrade their product lines regularly. Government plays a different role in the two periods; over-simplifying, it is the nightwatchman in the first, the manager of the Welfare State in the second. And the implications of the differences for many debates within contemporary economics are substantial.

This has an important implication for the history of thought in economics. In the natural sciences theories are, broadly speaking, true or false. That is, they are accepted as true, until falsified, at which time they must be improved or rejected in favor of a better theory. The Bohr model of the atom, at first, appeared to be a good theory, and, indeed, it was an advance over what had gone before. But as science learned more about the atom its flaws became evident, and it was seen to be incorrect, eventually to be superseded by quantum theory. But atoms did not at one time work according to the principles embodied in the Bohr model, and then, at a later time, change their practices so as to work according to quantum mechanics. A proposed law of physics, if true at all, will be true for all times and places – allowing for specific exceptions. But markets are historical institutions, and like all institutions they develop and change. A theory describing how markets work – a set of principles of economics – can therefore correctly describe one period and not another. It can be true in one era or set of circumstances and not in another.

EFFECTS OF THE CHANGE FROM CRAFT TO MASS PRODUCTION

We have seen that the shift from a craft-based to a mass-production economy had ramifications across the entire spectrum of economic and economic-related activities. But it is not just that the changes were extensive, nor that they were systematic. The point to be emphasized here is that these changes led to a different pattern of market adjustment. They resulted in a system that worked on different principles.

Changes in technology

The shift to mass production entailed a change in the scale and scope of technology, to use Chandler's phrase in a slightly different sense. Production took place on a far larger scale, but not only in terms of the space occupied by a single unit of production, or the volume of materials processes at a single time. It also vastly extended the time horizon over which production and marketing were planned, and it likewise extended the scope of production and marketing over the social and geographical scale. No longer was production primarily local, devoted to a market that the producers knew directly. Commodities were routinely produced for anonymous buyers, for geographical regions unknown and social or ethnic groups unfamiliar to the suppliers.

It also extended the control by business management over output and labor, and also over a variety of external circumstances. In the case of output, for example, we have seen that processes of mass production could be adapted to the needs of the market, so that output could be expanded or cut back readily. In the case of labor, because work was the exercise of skills, craft workers controlled many aspects of the pace, timing and intensity of production, and in many respects determined the quality of work as well. Mass production embodied skills in the machinery, and set the pace of work by adjusting the speed of the production line, while the time and motion engineers established the timing of operations. This removed most remaining control over work from the workers, and put it firmly in the hands of management.

But the greater control also extended to many external circumstances. The new technologies increasingly freed production – even in agriculture – from dependence on weather. Refrigeration allowed for longer storage and for shipping greater distances. Heating and cooling systems improved warehousing and chemical pest controls safeguarded inventory. Communications became faster and more reliable. Natural disasters could be controlled or offset, to some extent at least – as with fires and floods – or their consequences managed, as with the development of insurance.

As we have seen the result was a change in the character of costs, with fixed capital costs growing, while current costs shifted from being largely fixed to become increasingly variable. As the time horizon expanded, the character of risk changed, from predominantly short-term price risk to longer-term risks of technological obsolescence, leading to developments in financial instruments. As scale and scope increased, and time horizons lengthened, the possible externalities, positive and negative, also expanded, calling for regulation in the public interest, so leading to a greater role for government.

Family firms and modern corporations

Many firms were owned and operated, wholly or partially, by families in the earlier period. By contrast there were fewer such firms in the later, and they tended to come under pressure to change. But the concept of the "family firm" should not be confined to the firm that is owned and operated by a single family. It is rather that the firm is owned by *families* and is operated by workers and managers who have a *family relationship* with the firm. Workers receive a wage designed to support and raise a family. Moreover the firm considers workers with seniority to be part of the firm's own metaphorical "family". Managers, likewise, are part of the "team", and their wives, for example, are expected to comport themselves appropriately in local society. Many of these characteristics continue on in the modern corporation, which, however, increasingly comes to be owned, not by families, but by institutions, including other corporations.

Family firms established themselves at an optimal size, and tended to operate at that level. So the system would grow by mobilizing savings and investing them in newly created firms. Corporations, however, exhibit a different pattern of behavior; they retain and reinvest profits to grow, branching out in new directions when their markets become saturated. Family firms can reasonably be modeled as unitary decision-makers. This is less plausible in the case of corporations, where the interests of the finance, marketing and production divisions – not to mention multiple products – have to be reconciled.

Households: from production to consumption

In the craft economy the household was an important producing unit, as well as the chief means of bringing up, socializing and training the next generation of workers and managers or owners. Households would buy raw materials or partly finished products – lumber, dry goods – and produce finished goods – furniture or dresses. These functions have been removed from it, and are now served by the market. Canning has replaced home preserves, mass produced clothing home dress-making, pharmaceuticals have supplanted home remedies, fast food and prepackaged groceries have taken over home cooking – and the list goes on. From baby food to nursing homes, activities formerly carried out in the household have become staples of the modern market place. The household, no longer a scene of production, has been reduced to the place of leisure-time consumption.

In the craft era the household was the center of education; the skills and trade secrets of the fathers were passed on to the sons, the domestic lore of the mothers to the daughters. No longer; in the era of mass production the pace of technological change is too great. The skills and secrets of the fathers and the mothers are both largely outmoded by the time the children enter the adult world. To prepare them for the labor market they have to undergo formal education; a large part of socialization has shifted from the household to the schools of the state.

Preferences arise from lifestyles; goods are desired or preferred to other goods because of the ways in which they contribute to lifestyles. But lifestyles change as technology and institutions develop; preferences therefore cannot be considered among the "givens." Moreover in a competitive system, higher social position can be earned. Households will compete to rise in social rank.

The labor market

Basically labor markets are demand-driven in both periods. That is, the level of employment depends fundamentally on the level and composition of demand. Unemployment emerges for two reasons. First, ("Marxian" unemployment), there may not be enough capital or land to employ the available labor, given the prevailing technology. Second, (Keynesian unemployment), the productive facilities that exist may not be operating at full capacity.

This contrasts sharply with mainstream thinking, in which labor is considered a scarce resource, allocated efficiently by the market in response to its price relative to other inputs. If labor is unemployed, it cannot be scarce. If it is not scarce, its price must be zero. Hence if the wage is positive labor must be fully employed – even if there appear to be people out of work.[1] Treating such people as *voluntarily* unemployed does not explain how families without property or other non-wage income can survive; nor do proponents of such an approach consider the importance of employment in the competitive effort to rise in the world.

Demand pressures work through very different channels in the two periods. In the first period demand impacts chiefly on prices, leading to a variation in the real wage in the opposite direction. As we have seen, when employment is comparatively inflexible, and household spending is dependent on wages, this leads to a change in consumption in the opposite direction to the inital change in aggregate demand. Thus, if investment falls, consumption will rise, and vice versa. Since the real wage has risen, employment will have fallen, but in a lesser proportion. The implication is that aggregate demand, overall, will have changed in *composition* but not very much in level. In the OBC the level of employment depends on the composition of aggregate demand. Workers are thrown out of work *en masse* in this period only when there has been a *breakdown* in the system, leading firms to shut down, very often followed by bankruptcy and re-organization.

By contrast, in the NBC the level of employment depends on the *level* of aggregate demand. There is no price mechanism at work; the multiplier–accelerator relationship implies that a change in one component of aggregate demand will bring in its wake changes in the same direction in other components. The lay-off system is developed in this period, in which workers are routinely laid off and re-hired, according to a formula based on seniority. Fluctuating unemployment, then, is part of the normal working of the system.

Prices and demand

Long-run or normal prices in a capitalist economy can be expressed by "normal cost" equations: the price of one unit equals its wage cost plus the input costs plus the profit. Breaking this down shows the coefficients of the various inputs into each process, each multiplied by the amounts employed and by its price, aggregated to get total input cost. This figure will be multiplied by the gross rate of profit – the net rate plus the rate of depreciation – and then combined with the labor inputs times the wage rate. This results in the familiar "Sraffian" or classical matrix expression for prices and the rate of profit, given the wage.

This equation shows how the basic planning or benchmark prices, set at the time when investment projects are decided, interact with each other and the rate of profits, but it does not tell us how firms settle on the prices they will actually charge in changing conditions, nor do the coefficients tell us how the system of production operates. To arrive at an account of how firms vary their prices in actual conditions it is necessary to know more about the technology. In particular, we have considered two idealized systems: an "artisan" economy and an "industrial" economy. Each can be considered a complete economy, capitalist, described by the classical equations and capable of growth. But, as we have seen, the behavior of costs and prices and the pattern of growth will be different.[2] Moreover, the basic "normal" price equation will have to be interpreted differently.

In the craft economy long-run prices are independent of demand (apart from indirect influences in cases of joint production and land, where changes in demand may call for switching techniques). Long-run craft prices depend on technological coefficients and on the level of real wages, and, of course, on the relative degree of competition in the various sectors. In strongly competitive conditions, capital will shift in response to differentials in profit rates, tending to establish a uniform rate. Long-run prices are set at the same time investments are planned, and function thereafter as benchmarks or guidelines. But short-run prices under a fixed employment system reflect current market conditions: that is, the balance of current supply and demand. They are highly volatile precisely because costs, and to a lesser extent output, are inflexible.

In the mass production economy, however, while prices are also set in the course of planning investment and are independent of the level of current demand, they are not independent of the growth of demand. Indeed, the rate of growth of demand is fundamental in the sense that prices have to be set to cover the costs of the investment necessary to construct the capacity to service the new demand, by the firms presently in any given industry. ("Entry" is chiefly a phenomenon in new industries, and will be associated with variations or improvements of a new product.) This will lead to price equations that are almost identical to those describing the craft system. Interestingly, however, the balance of current supply and demand has little or no impact on prices; market prices tend to stay near the benchmark levels, and variations in demand chiefly affect output and employment. This is due partly to the fact that output and employment are variable, but it also reflects the shift in the nature of competition, from a concern with prices to a race for new technology (Eichner 1976; Wood 1978; Nell 1992, Ch. 17; Nell 1997).

In short the Classical equations showing the structural links between wages, prices and profits, apply to both the craft and mass production economies, though the equations must be interpreted differently. But pricing behavior in the two systems is markedly different. Marshallian models of supply and demand provide a reasonable account of price adjustment in the craft economy; but the modern corporation prices according to a markup which will be set in accordance with its investment plans.

CONCLUSION

Inflation

In the OBC, in the cases studied here, there was no inflation. Inflation occurred during the US Civil War, and in Europe, earlier during the Napoleonic Wars. But during the normal peacetime years of the Nineteenth century, prices actually tended to drift slightly down. Overall, prices both rose and fell – as indeed they had to for the price mechanism to work. By contrast, low-level inflation was endemic during the post-war era. Prices rose at least a little in virtually every year in virtually every advanced country. It has to be accepted that inflation had become part of the normal operation of the system. It was not, as most mainstream thinking continues to believe, a symptom of malfunctioning markets, or of social disease, or of mismanagement of economic policy. Inflation had become built into the system, and variation in the rate of inflation was part of the mechanism of adjustment.

For inflation was normally "non-neutral", that is, it had real effects. Two are especially important. First, higher inflation tended to reduce the real rate of interest, hence tended to provide a stimulus. Lower inflation raised the real rate of interest. Second, wage and price inflation rarely proceeded at the same rate. On the contrary, sometimes price inflation exceeded wage inflation, and sometimes it fell short. In the first case, other things being equal, profits would rise relative to wages, in the second they would fall. So inflation performed the function of making small adjustments in distribution.

Inflation probably contributed to the generally strong performance of the economy in the first half of the NBC, for it systematically lowered the real interest rate, and helped to keep it below the growth rate of GNP.

Rationality and methods of analysis

Two pillars of traditional methodology are called into question by the analysis here. First, the approach we have followed does not rest on "rational choice", or "microfoundations", nor does it in any way need such foundations. The method employed here has been to develop and study "stylized facts", facts which portray the basic and essential working of the economic systems under study, looking at those systems from many different perspectives, so that the way they work can be seen from many angles at the same time. These facts are then modeled in simple ways, to bring out the dynamic processes of adjustment. Of course agents are supposed to do their jobs in the best way possible; they are "economically motivated". Indeed, if they are acting in the market, it is their *responsibility* to get the best bargains possible.

But that does not imply that they will act in terms of a "rational choice" model, in which all possible courses of action are set out and compared, with the best global choice determined. Quite the contrary; such behavior would be contrary to both the principle of the division of labor, and that of comparative advantage. Jobs are defined according to the division of labor; no job should require, for example, the simultaneous exercise of two different skills. Comparative advantage tells us that agents should be appointed to do the jobs for which they are relatively best suited. So a production manager should manage production, which means hiring and supervising workers, organizing and overseeing the throughput of materials and the operation of equipment, and maintaining the system in proper condition. This is quite different from the job of a consultant, which is to lay out all the *other* possible ways of organizing the system of production, cataloging their benefits and drawbacks, and suggesting ways of improving or replacing the present system. These are two very different kinds of work, requiring very different skills. Nor are the decisions reached necessarily compatible – the production managers may regard the suggestions of the consultants as untested and airy-fairy, while the latter, in turn, may regard the managers as stuck in the mud. Yet the textbook theory of the firm, taking a "rational choice" approach to the selection of the method of production (a necessary condition for properly defining marginal products), telescopes these two jobs, and assumes that the management of the firm encompasses both, without conflict, in one single decision.

A model, in short, should correctly describe the institutions that exist and show how they interact, on the assumption that agents do their jobs properly. Such agents will be economically motivated; they will do their jobs to the best of their abilities, given the resources at their disposal, or alternatively, they will meet the standards required, as cheaply as possible. But they will not do what they are not qualified to do, namely seek a global optimum.

The second pillar of orthodox method is the so-called "long-run method", common to the classics and the early neoclassical economists. It can claim to be the appropriate analytical approach for studying the changing configurations of economic variables in the craft economy. The classical procedure was to determine the prices and rate of profit, on the basis of a historically given real wage; then to establish the level of capacity that corresponded to the level of demand. The result would be the system's "fully adjusted" position, which could then be compared to similar positions with different configurations of the basic parameters (Garegnani, in Eatwell and Milgate 1983). (Of course, a neoclassical analysis would determine the prices and outputs together, rather than separately, and the real wage would be determined by supply and demand. But the neoclassical analysis, say, of Wicksell, was based firmly on the long-run method.)

This approach, however, is not well suited to the study of the mass production economy. First, there is no reason to restrict output to a particular level. Since it is easily variable, it may settle on a path, a particular pattern of motion, rather than a level, even in the short run. The analysis would therefore have to be explicitly dynamic. Second, the final resting point may itself depend on the pattern of movement towards rest: the equilibrium may be "path-dependent". Certain paths, for example, may induce more or different technical progress, or may lead to more pressure on fixed resources, than others (Robinson 1980, Ch. 7). Third, since technical progress, in regard both to products and processes, is a regular and endogenous feature of the system, equilibrium configurations are bound to be very short-lived, if they exist at all. It is more appropriate to identify the trends, noting, however, that technical progress need not be uniform across sectors, so relative costs may be changing. Appreciation of these points undoubtedly contributed to movement, by Keynesians and neoclassicals alike, away from the long-run method and in favor of "temporary equilibrium", often treating growth paths as successions of temporary equilibria.[3]

Nevertheless, there will still be comparatively stable benchmark prices which will have to be determined, and which will reflect the planned prices at the time of the investment decisions that created the presently existing capital structure. These prices will be expressed by the same classical equations used in the long-run approach, adjusted for "vintages," but the interpretation will be different (which will explain the comparative stability in the face of continuous change). The "long-run" classical equations are defined on the basis of the "best practice" coefficients, since the resulting values are the ones towards which competitive pressures are forcing the system. But this overestimates the actual size of the surplus, and therefore the rate of profit. It would also imply continuous and often large price changes. Under mass production technical change is continuous, and firms are constantly rebuilding or renovating plant and equipment; the purpose of the equations is to exhibit the benchmark values and determine the size, composition and distribution of the surplus. Competitive pressures are not able to enforce any tendencies since, even as they begin to act in a particular direction, new technical innovations will open up new opportunities. Moreover, the new improvements will be in the renovated or new equipment of existing producers; it will not be in the hands of new firms, eager to put older firms out of business. Under mass production the growth of the market is supplied by the expansion of the firms already serving the market, so they will set prices on the basis of their average, rather than their best practice, coefficients of production. The average, of course, changes much more slowly, and actual prices (as shown in inter-industry studies) are quite stable over time and remain close to direct plus indirect labor costs (Ochoa 1984).

So, different theories will apply in different historical periods – prior to

World War I a sensible approach would be a theory of adjustment via a weakly stabilizing price mechanism, periodically upset by (partly endogenous) financial and monetary disturbances. But after World War II adjustment takes place through the multiplier–accelerator (broadly defined) and the financial system tends to be weakly stabilizing in the short run, but to become more fragile over the long. More importantly, the role of Government is radically different. On the other hand, both of these are Capitalist – so we need a theory of the basic institutional *structure* of Capitalism, the relations between prices, wages and profits, growth, consumption and sectoral size. This theory must show how these relationships can be reproduced over time, from period to period. And of course, it must allow for the fact that reproduction will lead to changes – there will be innovations and the market will act as a selector.

SOME IMPLICATIONS FOR CURRENT DEBATES

As between the two eras, the pattern of the cycle is different, the structure of the economy has changed, and the State has developed from a night-watchman to the guarantor of welfare. Given both different institutions and different patterns of wage, price, output and productivity movements, it might seem unlikely, on the face of it, that the same models would apply to both. Yet most contemporary discussions disregard such differences and appear to be predicated on the belief that the basic explanatory models should be universal, implying that the market mechanism, apart from imperfections, would be the same in the two periods. Different results will be the consequence of institutions, interventions or imperfections, rather than different market mechanisms.[4]

Contemporary mainstream schools of thought

First, consider two schools of thought that stress "microfoundations", and hold that macro phenomena are to be explained by theories of rational choice under constraints, where these constraints may include various kinds of imperfections, and interference by government or other institutions, and where rationality itself may be limited. In each case we will see that the way markets and the cycle have developed is the opposite of what might have been expected from the theory.

The new Keynesians

Keynesian theory was developed at the beginning of the second period, in which output adjustment is comparatively rapid while price fluctuations are slight. But Keynesian theory is not consistent with full neoclassical equilibrium. To justify Keynesian theory, while still accepting the basic premisses of the neoclassical approach, "new Keynesians" have proposed a variety of mechanisms that purport to explain why real or nominal prices and/or wages are rigid. Being rigid, prices do not adjust to clear the corresponding markets, and this failure is then shown to result in Keynesian consequences.

Many ingenious suggestions have been offered: nominal wages may be rigid because actual or implicit labor contracts are cast in nominal terms (Gordon 1990). Such contracts, however, are often clearly sub-optimal; moreover, if prices are flexible, they imply a countercyclical movement of the real wage. Recent work has instead focused on rigidities in nominal prices, attributed to "menu costs" (Mankiw 1990). Such nominal rigidities may interact with real rigidities – it may cost more to change prices than the expected gain, because of difficulties in disseminating information. Real wages may be sticky because of fears that a variable, market-driven real wage will result in productivity losses (The "efficiency" wage, first noted by Adam Smith (Michl 1992)). Or there may be "coordination failures," resulting from the resistance of firms to lowering prices. In such cases there may be multiple positions of "normal" output. Capital and labor markets may fail to adjust readily because of asymmetric information and/or risk aversion (Greenwald and Stiglitz 1989). Similarly, small effects may be magnified, because of risk aversion. Firms may take decisions in these circumstances in the light of "near rationality", rather than full rationality (Akerlof and Yellen 1985b). That is, they may decide it is not worth the trouble to recalculate continually (Greenwald and Stiglitz 1989, Mankiw 1990, Gordon 1990).

Broadly speaking, the "new Keynesians" focus on one or another realistic aspect of market interaction, which would be ruled out by assumption in a world of "perfect markets," and then develop models of maximizing behavior showing how such "imperfections" prevent prices and/or wages from adjusting to clear the relevant markets. There is thus no single dominant explanation for Keynesian' results; rather there is a whole class of possible explanations, each applicable to appropriate circumstances.[5]

Almost without exception, however, the imperfections cited in these models were more serious in the period of the old trade cycle, when prices and money wages were flexible, than in the post-war era, when they were not. The costs of changing prices, for example, were greater when printing costs were larger, mail was slower and faxes were non-existent. Asymmetric information must have been more serious before the existence of data banks and computers. Informational problems must have been greater in the days before telecommunications. (If information costs were not greater then, it would not have been worth while to invent and introduce the new methods of communication.) Insider–outsider relations must have been more important before the development of standardized tools and equipment, for then training had to be done on the job, and workers had to learn to cooperate together under unique circumstances. No shop would be exactly like any other. And so on . . . The conditions that the New Keynesians have identified as causing prices to fail to adjust were more prominent in the period when prices *did* adjust.

In the same way, the claim that small "shocks" can have large effects, either because of the risk aversion of firms (Greenwald and Stiglitz 1989), or because of limited rationality and real rigidities, (Mankiw 1990, Akerlof and Yellin 1985b), also appears likely to be truer of the older period, in which, in fact, prices and wages, both nominal and real, were relatively more flexible. Surely risk aversion would be greater when uncertainty was greater, communications poorer and information harder to come by. Full rationality would be less likely under these conditions, there would be more "frictions" and the real costs of each would be larger, since adjustment would be slower.

In short, while the new Keynesian approach directs attention to important aspects of markets, it cannot explain the change from relatively flexible money prices and wages, with an inverse relationship between real wages and employment, to downwardly inflexible, upwardly drifting nominal wages and prices, exhibiting a mildly procyclical real wage–employment pattern.

The new classicals

New classicals consider that the price mechanism works to bring about market clearing in all sectors, impeded only by market imperfections or government interference. The latter works only when market agents do not expect it, or during the time it takes for them to learn how to adapt their behavior to compensate. Since market imperfections prevent optimality, it will pay those in suboptimal positions to remove the imperfections, and it will be in no one's long run interest to preserve them – the gains from a change would outweigh the losses, so the losers could be compensated. Hence over time imperfections will be eliminated. We should expect, therefore to see market processes improve their operation over time; market clearing and market adjustments should be more efficient as time goes on (Hoover 1988).

Price flexibility appears only in the first period, at a time when market imperfections must be considered more serious than later. Communications were less developed, transportation was slower and more costly, credit was more difficult to check, and calculation was harder and slower. Yet in this period, in spite of the imperfections, the price mechanism appeared to play a role, and the real wage behaved in accordance with marginal productivity theory. But it is only in this period that we see evidence in time series statistics of the price mechanism at work. Market adjustment through prices and market clearing is less in evidence as time passes.

(Of course, the market did not always clear in the early period, but crises and periods of unemployment went with *falling*, never with stable or rising prices and money wages, as happened later.)

"Rational expectations," at least when combined with market-clearing, imply results that also fit the earlier period better, although the formation of such expectations makes sense only in the later. It is relatively plausible to assume rational expectations in the modern period, when firms have computers, modern telecommunications and, access to extensive data banks, and employ trained statisticians and econnomists – although it must also be assumed that agents know what the relevant variables are, something economists cannot agree on! But having "rational expectations," as the phrase is usually understood, does not make much sense in an era of family firms, little education, pencil and paper calculation, poor communications – and when economic theory was so little developed that it would not have been possible to identify the relevant variables in many situations. Yet it is in the earlier era that we see evidence of price movements that suggest a tendency towards market clearing, and where market adjustments appear to accord with marginal productivity theory.

Contemporary alternative schools

Next consider two groups that explain macro-phenomena by reference to institutions, including competition, the economic and technological structure and the conditions of the world.[6] Both are therefore much closer to the perspective suggested here, but both nevertheless overlook important historical changes in the economy and, as a result, place unwarranted emphasis on certain aspects of market behavior.

The post-Keynesians

Rather than adapt Keynes to neoclassical micro-foundations, post-Keynesians have sought to defend and develop Keynesian thinking, building foundations on a realistic account of institutions (Davidson 1994). Lexicographical and need-based theories of household choice, together with mark-up accounts of corporate pricing, provide an appropriate setting for the theory of effective demand (Nell 1992; Lavoie 1992, Eichner 1989). Labor markets respond chiefly to demand pressures (Nell 1988; Lavoie 1992). Money is seen as adapting endogenously to demand. (Moore 1988) Financial institutions are treated as simply another form of profit-seeking firm responding to market incentives. (Minsky 1986). Uncertainty is ubiquitous, and money and monetary contracts are seen as institutions designed to provide a way of managing practical affairs in the face of our inability to predict the future (Davidson 1994). Uncertainty is so pervasive that the economy cannot be expected to gravitate towards equilibrium; as Keynes remarked, "Equilibrium is blither". Not all post-Keynesians agree; Davidson (1994) holds that the concept may be useful at times for organizing our thoughts. But many post-Keynesians would argue that it can play no practical role, and should be replaced with the study of dynamics. Investment, in particular, will be volatile, and through the multiplier this will cause fluctuations throughout the economy. These will be exacerbated by financial markets, in which instability is endemic, since financial fragility tends to grow during boom periods (Minsky 1986). Conflicting claims during booms give rise to built-in inflation, which is not corrected during the slump, since money wages are not flexible downwards (Lavoie 1992).

Uncertainty, however, must have been much more serious and pervasive in the economic conditions prior to World War I. Communications were poorer, data bases were less developed, calculation was slower, and the basic economic relationships were less understood.[7] There was far less control over the natural environment, and methods of storage and preservation were still backward. Yet in this period talk of equilibrium was not altogether blither; the economy had built-in stabilizing influences. Conflicts, especially class conflict, were more intense and less civilized in this period; but there was no inflation at all. Prior to World War I financial and real crises were strongly linked. Each, it seemed, was capable of precipitating the other, and certainly each exacerbated the other. But in the post-war world, for the developed economies, the linkage is much weaker. A financial crisis, as in 1987, may do no significant harm to the real economy. A serious recession, as in the early 1990s, may do no harm to the stock and bond markets. The characteristics of the post-war world cannot be adequately understood in terms of post-Keynesian uncertainty and its effects on financial markets. (This does not imply criticism of other aspects of post-Keynesian thinking).

The neo-Ricardians

Taking its cue from Sraffa (1960) neo-Ricardian theory builds on given technology, given the size and composition of output and a given real wage. From these givens the set of relative prices that will support a uniform rate of profit in a "long-period position" can be found (Garegnani 1976). Alternative real wages will be associated with different rates of profit and prices; the wage–profit rate tradeoff can be defined, and its properties examined. Choices of technique can be analyzed. A devastating critique of the marginal productivity theory of distribution follows from this, while Walrasian general equilibrium theory can be shown to be characteristically overdetermined, or unable to accommodate a uniform rate of profit (Pasinetti 1977, 1981). The "dual" consumption–growth rate tradeoff can be examined in relation to the relative sizes of sectors. Paths of steady growth can be examined, and the effect of alternative wages or techniques explored (Kurz 1991).

The neo-Ricardian method is to compare alternative "long-period positions." The economy is assumed to gravitate towards those positions, or revolve around them. Actual positions of the economy will not normally, perhaps never, be fully adjusted long-period positions. The latter refers to a *theoretical ideal*. But although an ideal, they are considered to be the goal towards which the economy is moving, under the pressure of competitive forces. Capital will be shifted about until prices and industry sizes are correct. (This same perspective is taken by many who work in the newly developing fields of non-linear dynamic analysis and chaos theory.)

But in the modern era technological change is regular and widespread; it *results* from economic activity – from "learning by doing," and from organized research and development. Innovation is a part of competitive investment strategy. The coefficients are changing continually, and investment plans are subject to constant revision. Movement towards a long-period position – or, for that matter, in any direction – is quite likely to change the data on which that position is based. The positions towards which the system tends are path-dependent.

In addition, for many purposes neo-Ricardian theory takes the size and composition of output as given; but in the modern era the composition of output, and the structure of the economy generally, are continually changing.

Moreover, in the modern world market forces are often destabilizing, which means that there is no process of gravitation. Even if a long-period position could be defined, the forces of competition would not direct the economy towards it.

By contrast, in the era of craft-based production, it may well have made sense to approach the economy on the assumption that at any time it was tending towards a long-period position. Technological change was irregular; firms distributed profits, and entrepreneurs borrowed them to invest. Market forces were stabilizing. Processes of structural change were slower. Under these conditions the "long-period method" could provide insights. But it is not an appropriate method for studying the post-war economies of mass production.[8] (This does not imply that the neo-Ricardian equations cannot be used to study mass production; they can, but the interpretation must be different, cf. Nell 1997)

Finally, consider the implications of this approach for a recent debate over the amplitude of business cycles.[9]

Cyclical amplitudes

In a different vein a dispute has arisen over the relative amplitude of fluctuations prior to World War I compared to after World War II. Christina Romer (1986, 1987) has argued, in a series of papers, that the fluctuations in unemployment (and in output) in the pre-World War I economy have been overstated. Her argument begins with a critique of Lebergott, on whose painstaking work most estimates rely. She notes that he had to interpolate extensively to construct his series, but argues that in doing so, he relied on assumptions that magnified the actual fluctuations. She advances similar objections to Kuznets' series. Her recalculations reduce the fluctuations considerably (though they are still greater than those of the post-war era); but her methodology requires assuming that relationships, such as Okun's law, which characterize the post-war economy, also apply to the pre-World War I economy. This is unlikely; moreover she ignores the extensive contemporary commentaries on economic events which Lebergott, especially, used to corroborate his work. (Sheffrin 1989) Other writers, e.g. Balke and Gordon 1989; Altman, 1992, re-examining the question, find much larger differences than she did. Taylor, in Gordon 1986, found that wages and prices were more flexible in the earlier period, but that fluctuations were also more severe. But if pre-World War I fluctuations turn out to be smaller than hitherto believed, the distinctive patterns outlined above will only be enhanced.

From the perspective suggested here, then, the debate over business cycle volatility is on the wrong track. The issue appears to be whether post-World War II Keynesian policies helped to stabilize the economy, with Keynesian supporters arguing that such policies made a difference, while critics hold that little or no benefit is evident.[10] The method has been to compare the amplitude of post-War fluctuations with those of an era in which there was no government intervention, i.e the period prior to World War I. But the character of the cycle in the two periods is not comparable – prices, wages and employment behaved differently. So did money and interest. And the size and nature of government spending differed dramatically. Focussing on the amplitude of fluctuations in employment and output simply misses the more significant changes, which occur, for example, in the relations between the fluctuations in prices, wages and employment. Instead of comparing the time-series of a variable from one period directly with that from the other, more would be revealed by comparing the patterns made by the relationships between the time-series variables in one period, with the patterns revealed among those relationships in the other.

CONCLUSION

FINAL THOUGHTS

A review of "stylized facts" reveals dramatic differences between periods, as regards both the structure and institutions of the economy and the way markets work. A plausible explanation for the changes can be found in the development of technology, as it evolved from what can be termed "craft-based factory production" to mass production. The reason is that this change affects the nature of costs, turning fixed current costs into variable costs, which, in turn, affects the way markets adjust.

In the earlier period markets adjusted through stabilizing price and real wage changes, where real wages and employment varied inversely. But these stabilizing movements were often upset by unstable financial markets, resulting in noticeable volatility. By contrast, in the later period, the market mechanism, working through output and employment adjustments, is unstable, and wages tend to move directly with employment and output. Financial markets, although also tending to instability, no longer so directly destabilize the system. Floors and ceilings help to prevent excessive fluctuation, but a larger and more active government holds the key to stabilizing the economy's behavior. There may be an endogenous cyclical mechanism, but the cycles are damped and controlled. The volatility in the two periods is roughly comparable, but the factors shaping it are quite different. Clearly there is work to be done studying the changing character of the monetary system and financial markets, and this will have to be complemented by a study of the development of government, both as regards its sheer size, and in respect of its altered "Agenda", to use Keynes's term.

Between the two periods considered here lie the inter-war years. In this period mass production had not yet developed fully, and governments had not learned to cope with the evolving instability of markets. From the perspective suggested here we should expect this period to be the most unstable of all, as indeed it was. The implication for applied economic analysis is that no "micro-foundations" for "macro" are possible or relevant. "Micro" concerns adjustment through flexible prices and applies to the earlier period – and to developing countries with a large sector of craft-based production – while "macro" applies to mass production economies. Each describes a distinct pattern of adjustment and neither is more fundamental than the other.

NOTES

1 This is an important foundation of the view that there cannot "rationally" be involuntary unemployment in equilibrium. What appears to be unemployment, therefore, must be due to a preference for leisure over work, or to difficulties

in conducting a search for a suitable job. In the first case, of course, people would classify themselves as "out of the labor force," rather than unemployed, when asked, and would not register as job-seekers. In the second, we should expect the level of vacancies to match the level of unemployment, which is typically not the case.

2 Leijonhufvud, 1986, presents a similar account of the development of factory work.

3 See the *Mini-Symposium on the Long-Period Method* in the *Review of Political Economy*, Vol. 8, no 4, Oct. 1996, especially Nell, "Transformational Growth and the Long-Period Method".

4 New Keynesians, for example, try to explain the emergence of Keynesian relationships by appealing to imperfections, asymmetric information, risk aversion, and institutional factors. When sufficiently pronounced these can be shown to create price and/or wage rigidity, leading to Keynesian-type relationships. Yet all of these were more strongly present in the earlier period, when the economy still appeared to exhibit neoclassical features. Technological innovations have surely improved communications, transportation, data banks, information processing, the calculation and analysis of risk, and have created more institutional awareness, if not flexibility. The historical record is exactly the reverse of what the New Keynesian approach would lead one to expect. The same can also be shown to apply to aspects of Post-Keynesian, New Classical and Neo-Ricardian thought.

5 "The challenge is to choose between the myriad of ways in which markets can be imperfect, and to decide on the central questions and puzzles to be explained." (Greenwald and Stiglitz 1989, p. 25)

6 It is not implied that these models eschew maximizing behavior; on the contrary, virtually all draw on some form of maximizing, or profit-seeking behavior, under some circumstances. But both the goals and the means are shaped by the institutions and social conditions. What both deny is that there could exist an abstract individual with well-ordered preferences, endowments, etc., able to act in a similarly abstract market. Agents in the market, if persons, are themselves *products* of training and education. That is how they acquired their skills and knowledge. Agents which are institutions – corporations – have to be modeled as institutions, since such agents typically make decisions in different ways than individuals.

7 At least two senses of "uncertainty" can usefully be distinguished – "natural uncertainty" meaning that the world is non-ergodic and that in general the future cannot be predicted from study of the past, and "market uncertainty" which arises from the fact that agents do not know each other's intentions, and/or how the various strategies will work out when played. Neither can be reduced to calculable risk. Davidson, for example, stresses the former; Graziani, Nell and Cartelier the latter. The former is compatible with endogenous stability, the latter is not.

8 This does not imply that the Sraffa equations and related models (Von Neumann, Morishima, Pasinetti) are inapplicable; only that they cannot be applied by way of the "long-period approach." But if the coefficients are interpreted as weighted averages of the vintages in use (rather than as "best-practice") the equations will exhibit a picture of the position of the economy at a particular moment. This will change only slowly, as the capital stock changes, and it represents the starting point of dynamic adjustment processes. (Nell 1997)

9 Another recent business cycle discussion also warrants mention. It is now clear that in the post-war period production is more variable than sales. Firms build up inventory during booms and run it down during recessions. But this is at odds with the traditional microeconomic view that holding inventory will help to *smooth* production, and also provide buffer stocks. If marginal costs are rising, as the traditional theory of supply assumes, then firms should reduce it in booms and produce for stock in slumps. From our perspective the latter pattern of behavior is appropriate to craft economies and the former to mass production. (A. Blinder and L. Maccini survey the issues in *The Journal of Economic Perspectives*, Winter 1991; see also Szostak, 1995, pp. 92–3).

10 Since the late 1970s Western governments have adopted austerity policies, and have tried to cut back on the growth of state expenditure. These efforts have tended to slow growth and raise unemployment. In addition, world trade has grown faster than world output, without a corresponding development of credit to ease balance of payments problems. Keynesians tend to argue that many of the economic difficulties of the last two decades stem from mistaken policies. However, the perspective here would suggest looking at developments in technology as well. Are new technologies leading to changes in patterns of cost, and in methods of organizing production? If so – and surely they are – what effects are they having on the responsiveness of markets to policy?

REFERENCES

Ablin, E., and J. Katz. 1985. *De la industria incipiente a la exportación de tecnología. La experiencia Argentina en le venta intrernacional de plantas industriales y obras de ingeniería.* Buenos Aires: CEPAL/Eudeba.

Ablin, E., F. Gatto, J. Katz, B. Kosacoff and D. Soiffer. 1985. *Internacionalización de empresas y tecnología de origen argentino.* Buenos Aires: CEPAL/Eudeba.

Abraham, K.G., and J.C. Haltiwanger. 1995. "Real Wages and the Business Cycle." *Journal of Economic Literature.* 33. 1215–64.

Acevedo, M.E.B., and M. Khavise. 1990. *Quién es quién? Los dueños del poder económico (Argentina 1973–1987).* Buenos Aires: Editora 12.

Ackley, G., and H. Ishi. 1976. "Fiscal, Monetary, and Related Policies" in H. Patrick and H. Rosovsky (eds) *Asia's New Giant: How the Japanese Economy Works,* Washington, DC: Brookings Institution.

Acuña, C. 1993. "Business Interests, Dictatorship, and Democracy in Argentina." Mimeo. Buenos Aires: CEDES.

Aftalion, A. 1913. *Les Crises périodiques de surproduction.* 2 vols. Paris: Riviere.

Aircraft Industries Association of America. 1946. "Aircraft Manufacturing in the United States" in R.M. Cleveland and F.P. Graham (eds) *The Aviation Annual of 1946.* Garden City: Doubleday.

Akerlof, G., and J. Yellin. 1985a. "Can Small Deviations from Rationality make Significant Differences to Economic Equilibrium?" *American Economic Review.* 75. 708–21.

Akerlof, G., and J. Yellin 1985b. "A Near-Rational Model of the Business Cycle with Wage and Price Inertia." *Quarterly Journal of Economics.* Supplement 100. 823–38.

Alchian, A. 1950. "Uncertainty, Evolution and Economic Theory." *Journal of Political Economy.* 58. 211–21.

Aldrich, N. 1892. *Wholesale Prices, Wages and Transportation.* Washington, DC: US Government Printing Office.

Allen, G. 1972. *A Short Economic History of Modern Japan, 1867–1937.* Revised edition. London: Allen & Unwin.

Altman, M. 1987. "A Revision of Canadian Economic Growth, 1870-1910." *Canadian Journal of Economics.* 20. 86–113.

Altman, M. 1992. "Business Cycle Volatility in Developed Market Economies, 1870–1986: Revisions and Conclusions." *Eastern Economic Journal.* 18 (3). 259–75.

REFERENCES

Amadeo, E. 1989. *Keynes's Principle of Effective Demand.* Aldershot: Edward Elgar.

Amsden, A. 1989. *Asia's Next Giant: South Korea and Late Industrialization.* Oxford: Oxford University Press.

Anderson, R.A. 1983. *A Look at Lockheed.* Princeton: Princeton University Press.

Andic, S., and J. Veverka. 1963/64. "The Growth of Government Expenditure in Germany since the Unification." *Finanzarchiv.* 23(2). 169–278.

Andrews, P.W.S. 1949a. *Manufacturing Business.* London: Macmillan.

Andrews, P.W.S. 1949b. "A reconsideration of the theory of the individual business." *Oxford Economic Papers.* 1. 54–89.

Andrews, P.W.S. 1964. *On Competition in Economic Theory.* London: Macmillan.

Argyrous, G. 1990. "Investment and the Capitalist Dynamic: The US in World War II." *Journal of Australian Political Economy.* 20. 36–55.

Argyrous, G. 1992. "Investment, Demand and Technological Change: Transformational Growth and the State in America During World War II." Unpublished Ph.D. dissertation. New School for Social Research, New York.

Arthur, W.B. 1989. "Competing Technologies, Increasing Returns, and Lock-in by Historical Small Events." *Economic Journal.* 99. 116–31.

Aschauer, D. 1990. *Public Investment and Private Sector Growth.* Washington, DC: Economic Policy Institute.

Asimakopulos, A. 1988. *Investment, Employment and Income Distribution.* Oxford: Polity Press.

Asimakopulos, A. 1991. *Keynes's General Theory and Accumulation.* Cambridge: Cambridge University Press.

Azpiazu, D. and E. Basualdo. 1989. *Cara y contracar de los grupos económicos, estado y promoción en la industria argentina.* Buenos Aires: Cántaro Editores.

Azpiazu, D., E. Basualdo and M. Khavise. 1986. *El nuevo poder económico en la Argentina de los años 80.* Buenos Aires: Legasa.

Bacha, E. 1990. "A Three-gap Model of Foreign Transfers and the GDP Growth Rate in Developing Countries." *Journal of Development Economics.* 32. 279–96.

Backus, D.K., and P.J. Kehoe. 1992. "International Evidence on the Historical Properties of Business Cycles." *American Economic Review.* 82. 864–88.

Bain, J.S. 1956. *Barriers to new Competition.* Cambridge, MA: Harvard University Press.

Bain, J.S. 1968. *Industrial Organization.* New York: Wiley.

Baldwin, R. 1971. "Determinants of the Commodity Structure of US Trade." *American Economic Review.* 61. 126–45.

Baldwin, R. 1988. "Hysteresis in Import Prices: The Beachhead Effect." *American Economic Review* 78. 773–85.

Balke, N.S., and R.J. Gordon. 1989. "The Estimation of Prewar Gross National Product: Methodology and New Evidence. *Journal of Political Economy.* 97. 38–92.

Bank of Japan. 1965, 1974, 1983, 1991. *Economic Statistics Annual,* Tokyo.

Baran, P., and Sweezy, P. 1966. *Monopoly Capital.* New York: Monthly Review Press.

Baranzini, M., and G.C. Harcourt. 1993. *The Dynamics of the Wealth of Nations.* London: Macmillan.

Barger, H. 1955. *Distribution's Place in the American Economy.* Princeton: Princeton University Press.

Barnes, R.M. 1952. *Motion and Time Studies.* Sixth edition. New York: Wiley.

Baron, S. 1962. *Brewed in America.* Boston, MA: Little Brown.

Basalla, G. 1988. *The Evolution of Technology.* Cambridge: Cambridge University Press.

Baumol, W.J. 1958. "On the theory of oligopoly." *Economica.* 25. 187–98.

Baumol, W.J. (1962) "On the theory of expansion of the firm." *American Economic Review.* 52. 1078–87.

Baxter, M., and R.G. King. 1994. "Measuring Business Cycles: Approximate Band-pass Filters for Economic Time Series." Mimeo. University of Virginia.

Beccaria, L. 1993. "Estancamiento y distribución del ingreso" in A. Minujín (ed.) *Desigualdad y exclusión. Desafíos para la política social en la Argentina de fin de siglo.* Buenos Aires: UNICEF/Losada.

Bell, S. 1918. "Fixed Costs and Market Price." *Quarterly Journal of Economics* 32. 507–24.

Berle, A.A. and G.C. Means. 1932. *The Modern Corporation and Private Property.* New York: Macmillan.

Bernstein, R.J. 1978. *The Restructuring of Social and Political Theory.* Philadelphia: University of Pennsylvania Press.

Bhaduri, A. 1996. "Implications of Globalization for Macroeconomic Theory and Policy." Manuscript.

Bharadwaj, K. 1989. *Themes in Value and Distribution: Classical Theory Reappraised.* London: Unwin Hyman.

Bharadwaj, K., and B. Schefold (eds). 1990. *Essays on Piero Sraffa: Critical Perspectives on the Revival of Classical Theory.* London: Unwin Hyman.

Bhaskar, R. 1993. *Reclaiming Reality.* London: Verso.

Bisang, R., and B. Kosacoff. 1993. "Las exportaciones industriales en una economia en transformacion: las sorpresas del caso argentino" in B. Kosacoff (ed.) *El desafío de la productividad. La industria argentina en transformacion.* Buenos Aires: Alianza Editoria.

Blackall, F.S. 1953. *Price Control in the Machine Tool Industry.* New York: American Enterprise Association.

Blackwell, R., J. Chatha and E.J. Nell. 1993. *Economics as Worldly Philosophy.* New York: St Martin's Press.

Blair, J.M. 1971. *Economic Concentration.* New York: Harcourt Brace Jovanovich.

Blair, J.M. 1975. "Inflation in the United States: A Short-run Target Return Model." in *The Roots of Inflation.* G. C. Means *et al.* (eds). New York: Franklin. 33–67.

Blanchard, O.J., and S. Fischer. 1989. *Lectures on Macroeconomics.* Cambridge, MA: MIT Press.

Bloomfield, A.I. 1959. *Monetary Policy under the International Gold Standard, 1880–1914.* New York: Federal Reserve Bank of New York.

Boehm-Bawerk, E. 1975 [1914]. *Macht oder ökonomisches Gesetz.* Darmstadt: Wissenschaftliche Buchgesellschaft.

Boggio, L. 1990. "The Dynamic Stability of Production Prices: A Synthetic Discussion." *Political Economy:* Special Issue.

Bollinger, L.L., and T. Lilley. 1943. *Financial Position of the Aircraft Industry,* Bureau of Business Research, Graduate School of Business Administration. Cambridge, MA: Harvard University Press.

Borchardt, K. 1976. "Germany 1700–1914." in T. Cipolla (ed.) *The Emergence of*

Industrial Societies. Fontana Economic History of Europe 4. Brighton: Harvester Press.

Borchardt, K. 1991. *Perspectives on Modern German Economic History and Policy.* Cambridge, UK: Cambridge University Press.

Bordo, M.D. 1981. "The Classical Gold Standard: Some Lessons for Today." *Federal Reserve Bank of St. Louis Review.* 63. 2–18.

Boulding, K.E. 1952. "Implications for General Economics of More Realistic Theories of the Firm." *American Economic Review* (Papers and proceedings). 42. 35–44.

Bowen, H., E. Leamer and L. Sveikauskas. 1987. "Multicountry, Multifactor Tests of the Factor Abundance Theory." *American Economic Review.* 7. 791–809.

Bowles, S., and M. Gintis. 1977. "The Marxian Theory of Value and Heterogeneous Labour: A Critique and Reformulation." *Cambridge Journal of Economics.* 1 (2). 173–92.

Boyer, R. 1988. "Technical Change and the Theory of 'Regulation'" in G. Dosi, C. Freeman, R. Nelson, G. Silverberg and L. Soete (eds) *Technical Change and Economic Theory.* London and New York: Pinter Publishers.

Boyer, R. 1990. *The Regulation School: A Critical Introduction.* New York: Columbia University Press.

Brady, R. 1933 [1974]. *The Rationalization Movement in German Industry.* New York: Howard Fertig.

Brady, D.S. 1966. "Price Deflators for Final Product Estimates in Output, Employment and Productivity in the United States after 1800." *Studies in Income and Wealth.* 30. 92–104.

Brandel, F. 1979. *The Structures of Everyday Life.* New York: Harper & Row.

Brandner, P., and K. Neusser. 1992. "Business Cycles in Open Economies: Stylized Facts for Austria and Germany." *Weltwirtschaftliches Archiv.* 128(1). 67–86.

Braun, H. -J. 1990. *The German Economy in the Twentieth Century.* London and New York: Routledge.

Braun O., and L. Joy. 1968. "A Model of Stagnation: A Case Study of the Argentine Economy." *Economic Journal.* 78. 868–87.

Brenner, R., and M. Glick. 1991. "The Regulation Approach: Theory and History." *New Left Review.* 188. 45–119.

Broehl, W.G. 1959. *Precision Valley: The Machine Tool Companies of Springfield, Vermont.* Englewood Cliffs, NJ: Prentice-Hall.

Bronfenbrenner, M. (ed.) 1969. *Is the Business Cycle Obsolete?* New York: Wiley-Interscience.

Brunner, K., and A.H. Meltzer. 1977. *Stabilization of the Domestic and International Economy.* Carnegie Conference on Public Policy 5. Amsterdam: North-Holland.

Bry, G. 1960. *Wages in Germany 1871–1945.* Princeton: Princeton University Press.

Bryant, R.C. *et al.* (eds) 1988. *Empirical Macroeconomics for Interdependent Economies.* Washington, DC: Brookings Institution.

Bryant Woods, G. 1946. *The Aircraft Manufacturing Industry.* New York: White Weld.

Buchanan, R.A. 1994. *The Power of the Machine.* New York: Penguin.

Bukharin, N. 1930. *Empirialism and World Economy.* London: Martin Lawrence.

Bureau of Economic Analysis. 1987. "GNP: An Overview of Source Data and Estimating Methods." *Methodology Paper Series.* Mp-4.

REFERENCES

Bureau of Labor Statistics, United States. 1991. *Employment, Hours and Earnings, US, 1909–90*. Washington: US Department of Labor. Bulletin 2370.

Bureau of Labor Statistics, United States. 1931. *Index Numbers of Estimates in Output, Employment and Productivity in the United States after 1800*. Studies in Income and Wealth 30.

Burns, A.F. 1954. *The Frontiers of Economic Knowledge*. Princeton: Princeton University Press for NBER.

Burns, A.F., and Mitchell, W.C. 1946. *Measuring Business Cycles*. New York: National Bureau of Economic Research.

Burns, A.R. 1927. *Money and Monetary Policy in Early Times*. New York: Knopf.

Cain, L.P. 1986. "N.R. Lamoreaux: The Great Merger Movement in American Business." Review. *Business History Review*. 60. 132–4.

Cairncross, A.K. 1989. "In Praise of Economic History." *Economic History Review*. 42. 173–85.

Caldwell, B. 1991. "Clarifying Popper." *Journal of Economic Literature*. 29. 1–33.

Calomiris, C.W., and C. Hanes. 1994. "Historical Macroeconomics and American Macroeconomic History." NBER Working Paper 4935.

Canavese, A. 1982. "The Structuralist Explanation in the Theory of Inflation." *World Development*. 14. 523–9.

Canitrot, A. 1975. "La experiencia populista de redistribución de ingresos." *Desarrollo Económico*. 15 (59), 331–51.

Canitrot, A. 1981. "Teoría y práctica del liberalismo. Política antiinflacionaria y apertura económica, 1976–1981." *Desarrollo Económico*. 21 (82). 131–89.

Canitrot, A. 1983. "El salario real y la restricción externa de la economía". *Desarrollo Económico*. 23 (91). 423–7.

Canitrot, A. 1993. "The Exchange Rate as an Instrument of Trade Policy." UNCTAD Discussion Paper 71. Geneva.

Canova, F. 1991. *Detrending and Business Cycle Facts*. Badia Fiesolana: European University Institute.

Carus-Wilson, E.M. 1952. "The Woollen Industry." Reprinted in Economic History Society (ed.) *Essays in Economic History*. London: Arnold.

Carus-Wilson, E.M. 1954a. "An Industrial Revolution of the Thirteenth Century." in Economic History Society (ed.) *Essays in Economic History*. London: Arnold.

Carus-Wilson, E.M. 1954b. "Evidences of Industrial Growth on some Fifteenth Century Manors" in Economic History Society (ed.) *Essays in Economic History*. London: Arnold.

Caskey, J., and S. Fazzari. 1992. "Rising Debt in the Private Sector: A Cause for Concern?" in D. Papadimitriou (ed.) *Profits, Deficits and Instability*. London: Macmillan. 202–18.

Chamberlin, E. 1933. *The Theory of Monopolistic Competition*. Cambridge, MA: Harvard University Press.

Chandler, A.D. 1977. *The Visible Hand: The Managerial Revolution in American Business*. Cambridge, MA: Belknap Press.

Chandler, A.D. 1990. *Scale and Scope: The Dynamics of Industrial Capitalism* Cambridge, MA: Belknap Press.

Chenery, H., and M. Bruno. 1962. "Development Alternatives in an Open Economy: The Case of Israel." *Economic Journal*. 79–103.

REFERENCES

Chenery, H.B., and L. Taylor. 1968 "Development Patterns among Countries and over Time." *Review of Economics and Statistics*. 50. 391–416.

Chick, V. 1983. *Macroeconomics after Keynes*. Oxford: Philip Allan.

Christiano, L., and M. Eichenbaum. 1989. "Current Real-Business-Cycle Theories and Aggregate Labor Market Fluctuations." *American Economic Review*. 79. 733–48.

Clark, J.B. 1899. *Distribution of Wealth*. New York and London: Macmillan.

Clark, J.M. 1923. *Studies in the Economics of Overhead Costs*. Chicago: University of Chicago Press.

Clemence, R. 1950. *Readings in Economic Analysis II: Prices and Production*. Cambridge, MA: Addison-Wesley.

Cleveland, R.M., and F.P. Graham (eds). 1945. "Aviation Manufacturing Today in America." *Aviation Annual of 1945*. 75–89.

Coase, R. 1937. "The Nature of the Firm." *Economica*. 4. 386–405.

Coase, R. 1960. "The Problem of Social Cost". *Journal of Law and Economics*. 3. 1–44.

Cole, R. 1971. *Japanese Blue Collar: The Changing Tradition*. Berkeley, CA: University of California Press.

Commons, J.R. 1968. *Legal Foundations of Capitalism*. Madison, WI: University of Wisconsin Press.

Cooley, T. (ed.) 1995. *Frontiers in Business Cycle Research*. Princeton: Princeton University Press.

Cooley, T.F., and L.E. Ohanian. 1992. "The Cyclical Behavior of Prices." *Journal of Monetary Economics*. 28. 25–60.

Costabile, L., and R.E. Rowthorn. 1985. "Malthus's Theory of Wages and Growth." *Economic Journal*. 95. 418–35.

Council of Economic Experts, Germany. Various years. *Sachverständigenratsgutachten*. Stuttgart: Metzler-Poeschel.

Coutts, K., W. Godley, and W. Nordhaus. 1978. *Industrial Pricing in the United Kingdom*. Cambridge: Cambridge University Press.

Crafts, N.F.R. 1987. "Cliometrics, 1971-1986: A Survey." *Journal of Applied Econometrics*. 2. 68–86.

Crafts, N.F.R., and T.C. Mills. 1994. "Trends in Real Wages in Britain, 1750–1913." *Explorations in Economic History*. 31. 341–50.

Crafts, N.F.R., S.J. Leybourne and T.C. Mills. 1990. "Measurement of Trend Growth in European Industrial Output before 1914: Methodological Issues and New Estimates." *Explorations in Economic History*. 27. 442–67.

Craven, W.F., and J.L. Cate. 1955. *The Army Air Forces in World War II: Men and Planes*. Chicago: University of Chicago Press.

Cunningham, W.G. 1951. *The Aircraft Industry: A Study in Industrial Location*. Los Angeles: Morrison.

Cyert, R.M., and J.G. March. 1963. *A Behavioral Theory of the Firm*. Englewood Cliffs, NJ: Prentice-Hall.

Damill, M. and J. Fanelli. 1988. "Decisiones de cartera y transferencia de riqueza en un período de inestabilidad macroeconómica." Buenos Aires: Documento CEDES.

Damill, M., J. Fanelli, R. Frenkel and G. Rozenwurcel. 1988. "Las relaciones financieras en la economía argentina." Buenos Aires: Documento CEDES.

Danthine, J.-P., and J.B. Donaldson. 1993. "Methodological and Empirical Issues in Real Business Cycle Theory." *European Economic Review*. 37 (1). 1–35.

REFERENCES

Danthine, J.-P., and J.B. Donaldson. 1995. "Non-Walrasian Economies" in T. F. Cooley (ed.) *Frontiers in Business Cycle Research*, Princetown, NJ: Princeton University Press.

David, P. 1975. *Technical Choice, Innovation, and Economic Growth*. Cambridge: Cambridge University Press.

Davidson, D. 1984. "Reality without Reference" in his *Inquiries into Truth and Interpretation*. Oxford: Oxford University Press.

Davidson, P. 1978. *Money and the Real World*. Second edition. London: Macmillan.

Davidson, P. 1994. *Post-Keynesian Macroeconomic Theory*. Brookfield, MA: Edward Elgar.

Davis, H.G. 1945. *Public Policy in Postwar Aviation*. US Senate, 79th Congress, 1st Session, Document 56, Washington, DC: US Government Printing Office.

Davis, L. 1966. "The Capital Markets and Industrial Concentration: The US and UK, a Comparative Study." *Economic History Review*. 19. 255–72.

Davis, L. 1986. "N.R. Lamoreaux: The Great Merger Movement in American Business." Review. *American Historical Review*. 91. 477–8.

Day, J.S. 1956. *Subcontracting in the Airframe Industry*. Norwood, MA: Plimpton.

Dean, J., and T.O. Yntema. 1936. *Statistical Determination of Costs with Special Reference to Marginal Costs*. Chicago: University of Chicago Press.

Deaton, A. 1992. *Understanding Consumption*. Oxford: Clarendon Press.

Deleplace, G., and E.J. Nell (eds). 1996. *Money in Motion: The Circulation and Post-Keynesian Approaches*. London: Macmillan.

Denison, E. 1962. *The Sources of Economic Growth in the US*. New York: Committee for Economic Development.

Denison, E. 1985. *Trends in American Economic Growth 1929–82*. Washington, DC: Brookings Institution.

Desai, A. 1968. *Real Wages in Germany, 1871–1913*. Oxford: Clarendon Press.

Deutsche Bundesbank. 1988. *Währung und Wirtschaft in Deutschland*. Frankfurt am Main: Knapp.

Deyo, F. (ed.). 1987. *The Political Economy of the New Asian Industrialism*. Ithaca, NY: Cornell University Press.

Di Tella, G., and M. Zymelman. 1972. *Las etapas del desarrollo económico argentino*. Buenos Aires: Eudeba.

Di Tella, G., and M. Zymelman. 1973. *Los ciclos económicos argentinos*. Buenos Aires: Paidos.

Diamantopoulos, A., and B. Mathews. 1995. *Making Pricing Decisions: A Study of Managerial Practice*. London: Chapman & Hall.

Diaz Alejandro, C. 1963. "A Note on the Impact of Devaluation and the Redistributive Effect." *Journal of Political Economy*. 577–80.

Diaz Alejandro, C. 1970. *Essays on the Economic History of the Argentine Republic*. New Haven: Yale University Press.

DiFilippo, A. 1986. *Military Spending and Industrial Decline: A Study of the American Machine Tool Industry*. New York: Greenwood.

Dobb, M. 1973. *Theories of Value and Distribution since Adam Smith*. Cambridge: Cambridge University Press.

Domar, E. 1957. *Essays in the Theory of Economic Growth*. New York: Oxford University Press.

Dorfman, A. 1942. *Evolución industrial Argentina*. Buenos Aires: Losada.

338

REFERENCES

Dorfman, A. 1983. *Cincuenta años de industrialización en la Argentina, 1930–1980. Desarrollo y perspectivas.* Buenos Aires: Ediciones Solar.

Dorfman, A. 1992. "La industrialización argentina en una sociedad en cambio." *Realidad Economica.* 112. 69–160.

Dornbusch, R. 1987. "Exchange Rates and Prices." *American Economic Review.* 77. 93–106.

Dornbusch, R., and S. Fischer. 1990. *Macroeconomics.* fifth edition. New York: McGraw-Hill.

Dosi, G. 1988. "Sources, Procedures and Microeconomic Effects of Innovation." *Journal of Economic Literature.* 36. 1126–71.

Dosi, G., C. Freeman, R. Nelson, R. Silverman and L. Soete (eds). 1988. *Technical Change and Economic Theory.* London: Pinter.

Douglas, P.H. 1930. *Real Wages in the United States.* Boston, MA: Houghton Mifflin.

Dresdner Bank. 1988. *Statistische Reihen.* Frankfurt.

Du Boff, R.B. 1992. "Toward a New Macroeconomic History" in W. Milberg (ed.) *The Megacorp and Macrodynamics: Essays in Honour of Alfred Eichner.* Armonk, NY: Sharpe.

Dumenil, G., and D. Levy. 1987. "The Dynamics of Competition: A Restoration of the Classical Analysis." *Cambridge Journal of Economics.* 11 (2). 133–64.

Dumenil, G., and D. Levy. 1990a. "Stability in Capitalism: Are Long-term Positions the Problem?" Special Issue. *Convergence to Long-period Positions. Political Economy. Studies in the surplus Approach*, Vol. 6, numbers 1–2. [Hereafter: *Political Economy: Special Issue.*]

Dumenil, G., and D. Levy. 1990b. "Convergence to Long-period Positions: An Addendum." *Political Economy.* Special Issue.

Dumke, R.H. 1992. "The Future of Cliometric History – a European View." *Scandinavian Economic History Review.* 15 (3). 3–28.

Dunlop, J.T. 1938. "The Movement of Real and Money Wage Rates." *Economic Journal.* xlviii. 413–34.

Dusenberry, J. 1958. *Business Cycles and Economic Growth.* New York: McGraw-Hill.

Dutt, A.K. (ed.). 1994. *New Directions in Analytical Political Economy.* Aldershot: Edward Elgar.

Dutt, A.K., and E.J. Amadeo. 1990. *Keynes's Third Alternative.* Aldershot: Edward Elgar.

Dymski, G., and R. Pollin. 1994. *New Perspectives in Monetary Macroeconomics.* Ann Arbor: University of Michigan Press.

Eastman, W. 1968. *The History of the Linseed Oil Industry in the United States.* Minneapolis: Danison.

Eaton Manufacturing Company. 1948. *A Chronicle of the Aviation Industry in America, 1903–1947.* Cleveland.

Eatwell, J., and M. Milgate (eds). 1983. *Keynes's Economics and the Theory of Value and Distribution.* New York: Oxford University Press.

Edger, W.W. 1906. "Trade Combinations in Canada." *Journal of Political Economy.* 14. 427–34.

Edwards, R. 1979. *Contested Terrain: The Transformation of the Workplace in the Tweintieth Century.* New York: Basic Books.

REFERENCES

Eggertsson, T. 1990. *Economic Behavior and Institutions*. Cambridge, MA: Cambridge University Press.

Ehrbar, H., and M. Glick. 1988a. "Micro Advancement toward Long-term Equilibrium." *Journal of Economic Theory*. 53 (2). 369–95.

Ehrbar, H., and M. Glick. 1988b. "Structural Change in Profit Rate Differentials: The Post-World War II US Economy." *Boston Review of Economic Issues*. 10 (22). 81–102.

Eichengreen, B. 1985. *The Gold Standard in Theory and History*. New York and London: Methuen.

Eichengreen, B. 1987. "Macroeconomics and History." in A. J. Field (ed.) *The Future of Economic History*. Boston, MA: Kluwer-Nijhoff.

Eichner, A.S. 1969. *The Emergence of Oligopoly: Sugar Refining as a Case Study*. Baltimore: Johns Hopkins University Press.

Eichner, A. 1976. *The Megacorp and Oligopoly*. New York: Cambridge University Press.

Eichner, A. 1987. *The Macrodynamics of Advanced Market Economies*. Armonk, NY: Sharpe.

Eiteman, W. J. 1945. "The Equilibrium of the Firm in Multi-Process Industries." *Quarterly Journal of Economics*. LIX. 280–6.

Elberton Smith, R. 1959. *The Army and Economic Mobilization. The United States Army in World War II: The War Department*. Washington, DC: US Government Printing Office.

Enders, W. 1995. *Applied Econometric Time Series*. New York: Wiley.

Enke, S. 1951. "A Distinction between Chamberlin and Robinson." *American Economic Review*. 61. 566–78.

Evans, M. 1969. *Macroeconomics: Theory, Forecasting and Control*. New York: Harper & Row.

Evans, P. 1995. *Embedded Autonomy*. Princeton: Princeton University Press.

Fair, R.C. 1984. *Specification, Estimation, and Analysis of Macroeconometric Models*. Cambridge, MA: Harvard University Press.

Fama, E. 1980. "Banking in the Theory of Finance." *Journal of Monetary Economics*. 6. 39–57.

Fanelli, J., and O. Chisari. 1989. "Restricciones al crecimiento y distribución del ingreso: el caso argentino." Buenos Aires: Documento CEDES.

Fanelli, J., and R. Frenkel. 1995. "Micro–macro Interaction in Economic Development." *UNCTAD Review*. 1–55.

Fanelli, J., R. Frenkel and C. Winograd. 1987. *Argentina*. Stabilization and Adjustment Policies and Programmes Country Study 12. Helsinski: WIDER.

Federal Reserve, Board of Governors of. 1986. *Industrial Production*. Washington, DC.: Federal Reserve.

Feinstein, C. 1972. *National Income, Expenditure and Output of the United Kingdom, 1855–1965*. Cambridge: Cambridge University Press.

Fell, J.E. 1979. *Ores to Metals*. Lincoln, NB: University of Nebraska Press.

Feyerabend, P. 1975. *Against Method*. London: Verso.

Field, A.J. 1987. "The Future of Economic History" in A. J. Field (ed.) *The Future of Economic History*. Boston, MA: Kluwer-Nijhoff Publishing.

Fischer, D.H. 1996. *The Great Wave: Price Revolutions and the Rhythm of History*. New York: Oxford University Press.

Fischer, W. 1976. "Bergbau, Industrie, Handwerk" in H. Aubin and W. Zorn (eds), *Handbuch der deutschen Wirtschafts- und Sozialgeschichte*. Stuttgart: Klett-Cotta.

Flaschel, P. 1987. "Classical and Neoclassical Competitive Adjustment Processes." *Manchester School*. 55. 13–37.

Flichman, G. 1978. *Notas sobre el desarrollo agropecuario en la región pampeana argentina (o por que Pergamino no es Iowa)*. Buenos Aires: Estudios CEDES.

Florence, P.S. 1953. *The Logic of British and American Industry*. London: Routledge.

Fogel, R.W., and G.R. Elton (1983) *Which Road to the Past? Two Views of Economic History* New Haven. CT: Yale University Press.

Fogel, R.W., and S.L. Engerman (1974) *Time on the Cross. Economics of American Negro Slavery*. Boston, MA: Little Brown.

Freedman, D., R. Pisani, R. Purves and A. Adhikari. 1991. *Statistics*. New York: Norton.

Freeman, C. 1994. "Economics of Technical Change." *Cambridge Journal of Economics*. 18. 463–514.

Frenkel, R. and Fanelli, J.M. 1995. "Micro-Macro Interaction in Economic Development". UNCTAD Review. 95: 129–54.

Frenkel, R. 1986. "Salarios e inflación en America Latina." *Desarrollo Económico*. 25 (100). 587–622.

Freudenthal, E.E. 1968. "The Aviation Business in the 1930s" in G.R. Simonson, (ed.) *The History of the American Aircraft Industry*. Cambridge, MA: MIT Press.

Freyberg, T. von. 1989. *Industrielle Rationalisierung in der Weimarer Republik*. Frankfurt and New York: Campus Verlag.

Frickey, E. 1947. *Production in the United States*. Cambridge, MA: Harvard University Press.

Friedman, B.M. 1986. "Money, Credit and Interest Rates in the Business Cycle" in R.J. Gordon (ed.) The American Business Cycle. Chicago: University of Chicago Press. 395–458.

Friedman, M. 1953. *Essays in Positive Economics* Chicago: University of Chicago Press

Friedman, M., and A.J. Schwartz. 1982. *Monetary Trends in the United States and the United Kingdom: Their Relations to Income, Prices and Interest Rates 1867 to 1975*. Chicago: University of Chicago Press.

Gallman, R.E. 1966. "Gross National Product in the United States, 1834–1909." *Studies in Income and Wealth*. 30. 3–75

Gandolfo, E. 1983. *Economic Dynamics: Methods and Models*. New York: North-Holland.

Garegnani, P. 1976. "On a Change in the Notion of Equilibrium in Recent Work on Capital Theory" in M. Brown, K. Sato, and P. Zarembka, *Essays in Modern Capital Theory*. Amsterdam: North-Holland. Reprinted in J. Eatwell and M. Milgate (eds). *Keynes's Economics and the Theory of Value and Distribution*, New York: Oxford University Press. 1983.

Garegnani, P. 1983. "Notes on Consumption, Investment and Effective Demand" and "Reply to Joan Robinson" in Eatwell and Milgate (eds).

Gatto, F., G. Gutman, and G. Yoguel. 1988. *Restructuración industrial en la Argentina y sus efectos regionales*. Doc. No. 14. Buenos Aires: CEPAL-CFI.

REFERENCES

Gemmel, N. 1993. *The Growth of the Public Sector: Theories and International Evidence.* London: Edward Elgar.

Georgescu-Roegen, N. 1971. *The Entrophy Law and the Economic Process.* Cambridge, MA: Harvard University Press.

Gerchunoff, P., and J. Llach. 1975. "Capitalismo industrial, desarrollo asociado y distribución del ingreso entre los dos gobiernos peronistas 1950–1972." *Desarrollo Económico.* 15 (5). 3–54.

Gereffi, G., and D. Wyman (eds) 1990. *Manufacturing Miracles: Paths of Industrialization in Latin America and East Asia.* Princeton: Princeton University Press.

Gilboy, E. 1967. "Demand as a Factor in the Industrial Revolution" in R.M. Hartwell (ed.) *The Causes of the Industrial Revolution in England.* London: Methuen.

Glastetter, W., G. Högemann and R. Marquardt. 1991. *Die wirtschaftliche Entwicklung in der Bundesrepublik Deutschland 1950–1989.* Frankfurt: Campus Verlag.

Godfrey, E. 1918. "Canada" in John Koren (ed.) *The History of Statistics: Their Development and Progress in Many Countries.* New York: Macmillan.

Goldfeld, S.M. 1976. "The Case of the Missing Money." *Brookings Papers on Economic Activity.* Washington, DC: Brookings Institution. 683–730.

Goodwin, R. 1966. "A Growth Cycle" in C. H. Feinstein (ed.) *Socialism, Capitalism and Economic Growth.* Cambridge: Cambridge University Press

Gordon, R.J. 1969. "$45 billion of US Private Investment has been Mislaid." *American Economic Review.* 59. 221–38.

Gordon, R.J. 1983. "A Century of Evidence on Wage and Price Stickiness in the United States, the United Kingdom, and Japan." in J. Tobin (ed.) *Macroeconomics, Prices and Quantities.* Oxford: Blackwell. 185–234.

Gordon, R.J. (ed.). 1986. *The American Business Cycle: Continuity and Change.* Chicago: University of Chicago Press.

Gordon, R.J. 1990. "What is New Keynesian Economics?" *Journal of Economic Literature.* 28 (3). 1115–71.

Government of Argentina. Various years. *Boletin Comercio Exterior.* Buenos Aires.

Government of Argentina. Various years. *Industrial Census.* Buenos Aires.

Granger, C. 1977. "Comment." *Journal of the American Statistical Association.* 72. 22–4.

Greene, W.H. 1993. *Econometric Analysis.* Second edition. New York: Macmillan.

Greenwald, B.C., and J. Stiglitz. 1989. "Toward a Theory of Rigidities." NBER Working Paper 2938.

Griliches, Z. 1986. "Economic Data Issues" in Zvi Griliches and Michael Intriligator (eds) *Handbook of Econometrics* III. Amsterdam: North-Holland.

Haggard, S. 1990. *Pathways from the Periphery: The Politics of Growth in the Newly Industrializing Countries.* Ithaca, NY: Cornell University Press.

Hahn, F. 1973. *On the Notion of Equilibrium in Economics: An Inaugural Lecture.* Cambridge: Cambridge University Press.

Halevi, J., D. Laibman and E.J. Nell (eds). 1992. *Beyond the Steady State.* London: Macmillan.

Hall, R. 1982. "Explorations in the Gold Standard and Related Policies for Stabilizing the Dollar" in R. Hall (ed.) *Inflation: Causes and Effects.* Chicago: University of Chicago Press. 111–22.

Hall, R.L., and C.J. Hitch. 1939. "Price Theory and Business Behavior." *Oxford Economic Papers*, 2. 15–24.

Hanes, C. 1992. "Comparable Indices of Wholesale Prices and Manufacturing Wage Rates in the United States, 1865–1914." *Research in Economic History.* 14. 269–92.

Hanes, C. 1993. "The Development of Nominal Wage Rigidity in the late Nineteenth Century." *American Economic Review.* 83. 732–56.

Hanes, C. 1995a. "Consistent Wholesale Price Series for the United States, 1860–1990." University of Pennsylvania, Department of Economics. Mimeo.

Hanes, C. 1995b. "Changes in the Cyclical Behavior of Real Wage Rates, 1870–1990." Working paper. University of Pennsylvania, Department of Economics.

Hansen, A. 1948. *Monetary Theory and Fiscal Policy.* New York: McGraw-Hill.

Harcourt, G. 1995. *Capitalism, Socialism and Post-Keynesianism.* Aldershot: Edward Elgar.

Harcourt, G., and P. Kenyon. 1976. "Price Theory and the Investment Decision." *Kyklos.* 29. 449–77.

Hargreaves-Heap, S. 1989. *New Keynesian Economics.* Aldershot: Edward Elgar.

Hawke, G.R. 1993. "Getting your Hands Dirty: Economic History and Policy Advice" in G.D. Snooks (ed.) *Historical Analysis in Economics.* New York: Routledge.

Hayek, F. 1932. *Monetary Theory and the Trade Cycle* trans. N. Kaldor and H. Croome. New York: Harcourt Brace.

Hayek, F. 1941. *The Pure Theory of Capital.* London: Routledge.

Herman, E.S. 1981. *Corporate Control, Corporate Power.* Cambridge: Cambridge University Press.

Heyman, D. 1986. *Tres ensayos sobre inflación y políticas de estabilización.* Buenos Aires: CEPAL.

Hicks, J.R. 1939. *Value and Capital.* Oxford: Clarendon Press.

Hicks, J.R. 1950. *A Contribution to the Theory of the Trade Cycle.* Oxford: Oxford University Press.

Hicks, J.R. 1963. *The Theory of Wages.* Second edition London: Macmillan

Hicks, J.R. 1965. *Capital and Growth.* Oxford: Clarendon Press.

Hicks, J.R. 1967. *Critical Essays in Monetary Theory.* Oxford: Clarendon Press.

Hicks, J.R. 1989. *A Market Theory of Money* London: Macmillan.

Hirsch, F., and H. Goldthorpe. 1978. *The Political Economy of Inflation.* Oxford: Martin Robertson.

Hirschman, A. 1959. *The Strategy of Economic Development.* New Haven: Yale University Press.

Hoffman, W.G. 1958. *The Growth of Industrial Economies.* Manchester: Manchester University Press.

Hoffman, W.G. 1965. *British Industry 1700–1950.* Oxford: Blackwell.

Hoffmann, W.G. *et al.* 1965. *Das Wachstum der deutschen Wirtschaft seit Mitte des 19. Jahrhunderts.* Berlin, Heidelberg and New York: Springer Verlag.

Holley, I.B. 1964. *Buying Aircraft: Materiel Procurement for the Army Air Forces.* The United States Army in World War II: Special Studies. Washington: US Government Printing Office.

Hollis, M. 1995. *Philosophy of Social Science.* Cambridge: Cambridge University Press.

Hollis, M., and E.J. Nell. 1975. *Rational Economic Man.* Cambridge: Cambridge University Press.

REFERENCES

Homer, S., and R. Sylla. 1991. *A History of Interest Rates*. Third edition. New Brunswick, NJ: Rutgers University Press.

Hoover, K.D. 1990. *The New Classical Macroeconomics*. Oxford: Blackwell.

Horsman, G. 1988. *Inflation in the Twentieth Century*. New York: St Martin's Press.

Hotchkiss, G. 1943. "Modification Centres: An American Military Innovation." *Aviation*. 20. 134–6.

Hounshell, D. 1984. *From the American System to Mass Production. The Development of Manufacturing Technology in the US*. Baltimore: Johns Hopkins University Press.

Howell, D. 1993. "Stages of Technical Advance, Industrial Segmentation and Employment" in R. Blackwell, J. Chatha and E. J. Nell (eds) *Economics as Worldly Philosophy*. New York: St Martin's Press. 75-106.

Hughes, T.P. 1983. *Networks of Power: Electrification of Western Society, 1880–1930*. Baltimore and London: Johns Hopkins University Press.

Hunter, L.C. 1979. *A History of Industrial Power in the US, 1780–1930* I *Waterpower*. Charlottesville: University of Virginia Press.

Hunter, L.C. 1985. *A History of Industrial Power in the US, 1780–1930* II *Steam Power*. Charlottesville: University of Virginia Press.

Hunter, L.C. 1991. *A History of Industrial Power in the US, 1780–1930*. III *The Transmission of Power*. Cambridge, MA: MIT Press.

Imperial Bureau of Statistics. 1919. "The Official Statistics of Japan." *Quarterly Publications of the American Statistical Association*. 16. 339–46.

Ito, T. 1992. *The Japanese Economy*. Cambridge, MA: MIT Press.

Jacobs, A., and H. Richter. 1935. *Die Großhandelspreise in Deutschland von 1792 bis 1934*. Berlin: Institut für Konjunkturforschung.

James, J.A. 1984. "The Use of General Equilibrium Analysis in Economic History." *Explorations in Economic History*. 21. 231–53.

Janeway, E. 1951. *Struggle for Survival: A Chronicle of Economic Mobilization in World War II*. New Haven: Yale University Press.

Japan Ministry of Labour. 1952–1991. *Yearbook of Labour Statistics*. Tokyo.

Jennihsen, H.F. 1967. *Gewinnmaximierung und Rentabilitätsmaximierung als Ziel erwerbswirtschaftlich orientierter Unternehmungen und die Erreichung dieses Zieles durch optimalen Einsatz des Eigenkapitals*. University of Cologne.

Jones, E. 1920. "Is Competition in Industry Ruinous?" *Quarterly Journal of Economics*. 34. 473–519.

Jones, J.H. 1951. *Fifty Billion Dollars*. New York: Macmillan.

Kaldor, N. 1940. "A Model of the Trade Cycle." *Economic Journal*. 5. 78–89.

Kaldor, N. 1950. "The Economic Aspects of Advertising." *Review of Economic Studies*. 18. 1–27.

Kaldor, N. 1956. "Alternative Theories of Distribution." *Review of Economic Studies*. 23. 83–100.

Kaldor, N. 1970. "The New Monetarism". *Lloyd's Bank Review*. (October).

Kaldor, N. 1982. *The Scourge of Monetarism*. New York: Oxford University Press.

Kaldor, N. 1985. *Economics without Equilibrium*. Armonk, NY: Sharpe.

Kalecki, M. 1955. *Economic Dynamics*. London: Allen & Unwin.

Kalecki, M. 1971. *Selected Essays on the Dynamics of the Capitalist Economy*. Cambridge: Cambridge University Press.

Kalecki, M. 1990. *The Collected Works of Michal Kalecki*. J. Osiatinski (ed.). Oxford: Clarendon Press.

Katz, J. 1974. *Importación de tecnología, aprendizaje e industrialización dependiente*. Mexico City: Fondo de Cultura Economica.

Katz, J. 1993. "Organización industrial, competitividad internacional y política pública" in B. Kosacoff (ed.) *El desafío de la productividad. La industria argentina en transformación*. Buenos Aires: Alianza Editorial.

Katz, J., and B. Kosacoff. 1983. "Multinationals from Argentina" in S. Lall (ed.) *The New Multinationals. The Spread of Third World Enterprises*. New York: Wiley.

Katz, J., and B. Kosacoff. 1989. *El proceso de industrialización en Argentina. Evolución, retroceso y prospectiva*. Buenos Aires: CEAL/CEPAL.

Kennedy, P. 1992. *A Guide to Econometrics*. Third edition. Cambridge, MA: MIT Press.

Keynes J.M. 1930. *Treatise on Money*. London: Macmillan.

Keynes J.M. 1936. *The General Theory of Employment, Interest and Money*. London: Macmillan.

Keynes, J.M. 1939. "Relative Movements of Real Wages and Output." *Economic Journal*. 49. 34–51.

Keynes J.M. *The Collected Works of John Maynard Keynes*. D. Moddridge (ed.). Vol. 13, 1972; Vol. 14, 1973.

Kindleberger, C.P. 1978. *Manias, Panics and Crashes: A History of Financial Crises*. New York: Basic Books.

Kinghorn, J.R. 1995. "Kartells and Cartel Theory: Evidence from Early Twentieth Century German Coal, Iron, and Steel Industries." Mimeo. Washington University, St Louis.

Kipers, R.F. 1949. *Manufacturing Analysis*. New York: McGraw-Hill.

Kitson, M., and J. Michie. 1995. "Trade and Growth: A Historical Perspective" in J. Michie and J.G. Smith (eds) *Managing the Global Economy*. Oxford: Oxford University Press.

Knauth, O. 1956. *Business Practices, Trade Position and Competition*. New York: Columbia University Press.

Koopmans, T. 1953. *Three Essays on the State of Economic Science*. New Haven: Blackwell.

Kosacoff, B. 1993a. "La industria argentina: un proceso de reestructuración desarticualda" in B. Kosacoff (ed.) *El desafío de la productividad. La industria argentina en transformación*. Buenos Aires: Alianza Editorial.

Kosacoff, B. 1993b. "Industrial Development in Argentina: Transformation and Structural Changes." Working paper. Buenos Aires: ECLAC.

Kosacoff, B., and D. Azpiazu. 1989. *La industria argentina: desarrollo y cambios estructurales*. Buenos Aires: CEPAL/Centro Editor de America Latina.

Kosacoff, B., and G. Bezchinsky. 1993. "De la sustitución de importaciones a la globalización. Las empresas transnacionales en la industria argentina" in B. Kosacoff (ed.) *El desafío de la productividad. La industria argentina en transformación*. Buenos Aires: Alianza Editorial.

Kosai, Y. 1986. *The Era of High-speed Growth: Notes on the Postwar Japanese Economy*. Tokyo: University of Tokyo Press.

Kosai, Y. 1993. "Anti-inflation Policy: Japan." in H. Fukui *et al.* (eds) *The Politics of Economic Change in Postwar Japan and West Germany* 1 Macroeconomic Conditions and Policy Responses. New York: St Martin's Press.

Kotz, D.M., T. McDonough and M. Reich (eds). 1994. *Social Structures of*

Accumulation: The Political Economy of Growth and Crisis. Cambridge: Cambridge University Press.

Kozul-Wright, R. 1995. "Transnational Corporations and the Nation State" in J. Michie and J. G. Smith (eds) *Managing the Global Economy.* Oxford: Oxford University Press. 135–71.

Kregel, J. (ed.). 1983. *Distribution, Effective Demand and International Economic Relations.* London: Macmillan.

Krugman, P. (1991) *Geography and Trade*, Cambridge, MA: MIT Press.

Krugman, P., and M. Obsfeld. 1994. *International Economics.* Third edition. New York: Harper Collins.

Krugman, P., and L. Taylor. 1978. "Contractionary Effects of Devaluation." *Journal of International Economics.* 8. 445–56.

Kubin, I. 1990. "Market Prices and Natural Prices: A Model with a Value Effectual Demand". *Political Economy.* Special Issue.

Kuczynski, J. 1959– . *Die Lage der Arbeiter unter dem Kapitalismus.* Thirty-eight volumes. Berlin.

Kuerzinger, E. 1988. *Argentina: Blocked Development.* Occasional Papers of the German Development Institute 94. Berlin.

Kurdas, C. 1993. "A Classical Perspective on Investment: Exegesis of Behavioral Assumptions" in Nell. 1993c. 335–55.

Kurdas, C. 1994. *Theories of Technical Change and Investment.* New York: St Martin's Press.

Kurihara, K. 1957. *Post-Keynesian Economics.* New Brunswick. NJ: Rutgers University Press.

Kurz, H. 1991. "Technological Change, Growth and Distribution: A Steady-state Approach to Unsteady Growth on Kaldorian Lines." in E. J. Nell and W. Semmler (eds) *Nicholas Kalder and Mainstream Economics.* London: Macmillan 421–48.

Kurz, H., and N. Salvadori. 1995. *The Theory of Production.* Cambridge: Cambridge Unviersity Press.

Kuznets, S. 1946. *National Product since 1869.* New York: National Bureau of Economic Research.

Kuznets, S. 1961. *Capital in the American Economy: Its Formation and Financing.* New York: National Bureau of Economic Research.

Kuznets, S. 1968. "Notes on Japan's Economic Growth" in L. Klein and K. Ohkawa (eds) *Economic Growth: The Japanese Experience since the Meiji Era.* Homewood, IL: Irwin.

Kuznets, S. 1972. *Quantitave Economic Research: Trends and Problems.* New York: Columbia University Press.

Kydland, F., and E.C. Prescott. 1982. "Time to Build and Aggregate Fluctuations." *Econometrica.* 50 (6). 50–70.

Kydland, F., and E.C. Prescott. 1986. "Introduction." *Federal Reserve Bank of Minneapolis Review.* 10 (4). 1–4.

Lacey, M.J., and M. Farmer. 1993. "Social Investigation, Social Knowledge, and the State: an Introduction" in their *The State and Social Investigation in Britain and the Unitied States.* Washington, DC: Woodrow Wilson Center Press. 1–21.

Laibman, D., and E.J. Nell. 1977. "Reswitching, Wicksell Effects, and the Neoclassical Production Function." *American Economic Review.* 63. 100–13.

Lakatos, I. 1970. "Falsification and the Methodology of Scientific Research Programmes" in I. Lakatos and A. Musgrave (eds) *Criticism and the Growth of Knowledge*. Cambridge: Cambridge University Press.

Lakatos, I. 1978. "The Methodology of Scientific Research Programmes" in J. Worral and G. Currie (eds) *Philosophical Papers* 1. Cambridge: Cambridge University Press.

Lamoreaux, N.R. 1985. *The Great Merger Movement in American Business, 1895–1904*. New York and Cambridge: Cambridge University Press.

Lancaster, K. 1966. "A New Approach to Consumer Theory." *Journal of Political Economy*. 74. 132–57.

Lancaster, K. 1979. *Variety, Equity and Efficiency*. New York: Columbia University Press.

Landes, D. 1969. *The Unbound Prometheus: Technological Change and Industrial Development in Western Europe from 1750 to the Present*. Cambridge: Cambridge University Press.

Lavoie, M. 1992. *Foundations of Post-Keynesian Analysis*. Aldershot: Edward Elgar.

Lazonick, W. 1991. *Business Organization and the Myth of the Market Economy*. Cambridge: Cambridge University Press.

Leacy, F.H. (ed.). 1983. *Historical Statistics of Canada*. Second edition. Toronto: Statistics Canada.

Lee, F.S., and W.J. Samuels (eds). 1992. *The Heterodox Economics of Gardiner C. Means: A Collection*. Armonk, NY: Sharpe.

Leijonhufvud, A. 1985. "Capitalism and the Factory System" in R. Langloys (ed.) *Economics as a Process: Essays in the New Industrial Economics*. Cambridge: Cambridge University Press.

Leontief, W. 1951. *Structure of the American Economy*. New York: Oxford University Press.

Leontief, W. 1953. "Domestic Production and Foreign Trade: The American Capital Position Re-examined." *Proceedings of the American Philosophical Society*. 97. 331–49.

Leontief, W. 1966. *Input–Output Analysis*. New York: Oxford University Press.

Lester, R. 1946. "Shortcomings of Marginal Analysis for Wage–Employment Problems." *American Economic Review*. 35. 63–82.

Lester, R. 1947. "Marginalism, Minimum Wages, and Labor Markets." *American Economic Review*. 36. 135–48.

Lewis, W.A. 1949. *Economic Survey, 1919–1939*. London: Allen & Unwin.

Lewis, W.A. 1978. *Growth and Fluctuations, 1870–1913*. London: Allen & Unwin.

Lilley, T., P. Hunt, J.K. Butters, F.F. Gilmore and P.F. Lawler 1946. *Problems of Accelerating Aircraft Production during World War II*. Cambridge, MA: Harvard University Press.

Lincoln, E. 1988. *Japan: Facing Economic Maturity*. Washington, DC: Brookings Institution.

Livesay, H.C. 1975. *Andrew Carnegie and the Rise of Big Business*. Boston: Little Brown.

Llach, J. 1984. *La Argentina que no fue*. Buenos Aires: Ediciones del IDES.

Long, C. 1960. *Wages and Earnings in the United States, 1860–1890*. Princeton: Princeton University Press.

Lowe, A. 1965. *On Economic Knowledge*. Armonk, NY: Sharpe.

Lowe, A. 1976. *The Path of Economic Growth*. Cambridge: Cambridge University Press.

Lowe, P. 1970. *The Study of Production*. London: Macmillan.

Lucas, R. 1977. "Understanding Business Cycles" in K. Brunner and A. H. Meltzer (eds) *Stabilization of the Domestic and International Economy*. Amsterdam: North-Holland.

Lucas, R. 1987. *Models of Businesss Cycles*. London: Blackwell.

Lynn, R.A. 1968. "Unit volume as a goal for pricing." *Journal of Marketing*. 32. 34–9.

Machlup, F. 1946. "Marginal Analysis and Empirical Research." *American Economic Review*. 35. 519–54.

Machlup, F. 1947. "Rejoinder to an Antimarginalist." *American Economic Review*. 36. 148–54.

Macpherson, W.J. 1987. *The Economic Development of Japan, 1868–1941*. Basingstoke: Macmillan.

Maddison, A. 1982. *Phases of Capitalist Development*. New York: Oxford University Press.

Maddison, A. 1984. "Origins and Impacts of the Welfare State." *Banca Nazional del Lavoro*. 15. 55–87.

Maddison, A. 1992. *Dynamic Forces in Capitalist Development*. Oxford: Oxford University Press.

Madrick, J. 1995. *The End of Affluence*. New York: Random House.

Majewski, R. 1996. "Elasticity to Effective Demand and the Institutions of Exchange". New School for Social Research, unpublished Ph.D. dissertation.

Mankiw, N.G. 1989. "Real Business Cycles: A New Keynesian Perspective." *Journal of Economic Perspectives*. 3 (3). 79–90.

Mankiw, N.G. 1990. "A Quick Refresher Course in Macroeconomics." *Journal of Economic Literature*. 28. 1645–60.

Mankiw, N.G., and D. Romer (eds). 1991. *New Keynesian Economics* 1–2. Cambridge, MA: MIT Press.

Mansfield, E. 1978. *Monopoly Power and Economic Performance*. New York: Norton.

Mantoux, E. 1928. *The Industrial Revolution in the Eighteenth Century*. London: Cape.

Marglin, S., and J. Schor. 1990. *The Golden Age of Capitalism*. Oxford: Clarendon Press.

Marris, R.L. 1963. "A Model of the Managerial Enterprise" in M. Gilbert (ed.) *The Modern Business Enterprise*. Harmondsworth: Penguin. 211–37.

Marshall, A. 1961 [1895]. *Principles of Economics* Ninth(Variorum) Edition. London: Macmillan.

Marx, K. 1967. *Capital*. Three volumes. New York: International Publishers.

Maschke, E. 1969. "Outline of the History of German Cartels from 1873 to 1914" in Crouzet *et al.* (eds) *Essays in European Economic History, 1789-1914*. New York: St Martin's Press.

Matthews, R.C.O. 1959. *The Trade Cycle*. Cambridge: Cambridge University Press.

Mayer, T. 1993. *Truth v. Precision*. Edward Elgar.

McCallum, B.T. 1989. "Real Business Cycle Models" in R. J. Barro (ed.) *Modern Business Cycle Theory*. Cambridge, MA: Harvard University Press.

McCloskey, D. 1985. *The Rhetoric of Economics*. Madison: University of Wisconsin Press.

McMillan, C. 1984. *The Japanese Industrial System*. New York: Walter de Gruyter.

REFERENCES

Means, G.C. 1962. *Pricing Power and the Public Interest: A Study Based on Steel*. New York: Harper.

Means, G.C. 1975. "Simultaneous Inflation and Unemployment: A Challenge to Theory and Policy" in G.C. Means *et al.* (eds.) *The Roots of Inflation*. New York: Franklin. 1–31.

Michie, J. 1987. *Wages in the Business Cycle*. London: Pinter.

Michie, J., and J.G. Smith. 1995. *Managing the Global Economy*. Oxford: Oxford University Press.

Michl, T. 1992. "Why is the Rate of Profit still so Low?" in D. Papadimitriou (ed.) *Profits, Deficits and Instability*, London: Macmillan. 40–59.

Mill, J.S. 1848 [1987] *Principles of Political Economy* III. Fairfield, NJ: Augustus Kelley.

Mills, T. 1990. *Time Series Techniques for Economists*. Cambridge: Cambridge University Press.

Minami, R. 1986. *The Economic Development of Japan: A Quantitative Study*. New York: St Martin's Press.

Minsky, H. 1975. *John Maynard Keynes*. New York: Columbia University Press.

Minsky, H. 1986. *Stabilizing an Unstable Economy*. New Haven: Yale University Press.

Mirowski, P. 1992. *What could Replication mean in Econometrics?* Mimeo. University of Notre Dame.

Mirowski, P. (ed.). 1994. *Natural Images in Economic Thought*. Cambridge: Cambridge University Press.

Mishkin, F. 1981. "The Real Interest Rate: An Empirical Investigation." *Carnegie–Rochester Conference Series on Public Policy*. 15. 151–200.

Mishkin, F. 1992. *Money, Banking and Financial Markets*. Third edition. New York: Harper Collins.

Mitchell, B.R. 1976. *European Historical Statistics, 1750–1970*. New York: Columbia University Press.

Mitchell, B.R. 1988. *British Historical Statistics*. Cambridge. Cambridge University Press.

Mitchell, B.R. 1992. *International Historical Statistics*. Cambridge: Cambridge University Press.

Mitchell, W.C. 1951. *What Happens during Business Cycles?* New York: National Bureau of Economic Research.

Modley, R., and T.S. Cawley. 1956. *Aviation Facts and Figures*. Washington, DC: Lincoln Press.

Moore, B.J. 1988. *Horizontalists and Verticalists: The Macroeconomics of Credit Money*. Cambridge: Cambridge University Press.

Moore, G.H. and J.P. Cullity. 1988. "Trends and Cycles in Productivity, Unit Costs, and Prices: An International Perspective" in G.H. Moore (ed.) *Business Cycles, Inflation and Forecasting*. Second edition. Cambridge: Cambridge University Press.

Moschandreas, A. 1994. *Business Economics*. London: Routledge.

Mowery, D.C., and N. Rosenberg. 1982. "Technical Change in the Commercial Aircraft Industry, 1925–1975" in N. Rosenberg (ed.) *Inside the Black Box: Technology and Economics*. Cambridge: Cambridge University Press.

Musgrave, R.A. 1969. *Fiscal Systems*. New Haven: Princeton University Press.

REFERENCES

Nakamura, T. 1983. *Economic Growth in Prewar Japan.* New Haven: Yale University Press.

Nakamura, T. 1995. *The Postwar Japanese Economy: Its Development and Structure, 1937–1994.* Second edition. Tokyo: University of Tokyo Press.

Nash, G.D. 1990. *World War II and the West.* Lincoln, NB: University of Nebraska Press.

National Industrial Conference Board. 1931. *Rationalization of German Industry.* New York.

Nayyar, D. 1995. "Globalization: The Past in our Present." Presidential address to the Indian Economic Association. New Dehli.

Nell, E.J. 1980. *Growth, Profits and Property.* Cambridge: Cambridge University Press.

Nell, E.J. 1988. *Prosperity and Public Spending.* Boston, MA: Unwin Hyman.

Nell, E.J. 1992. *Transformational Growth and Effective Demand.* London: Macmillan; New York: New York University Press.

Nell, E.J. 1993. "Transformational Growth and Learning: Developing Craft Technology into Scientific Mass Production." in R. Thomson (ed.) *Learning and Technical Change.* London: Macmillan.

Nell, E.J. 1994. "Minsky, Keynes and Sraffa: Investment and the Long Period" in G. Dymski and R. Pollin (eds) *New Perspectives in Monetary Macroeconomics.* Ann Arbor: University of Michigan Press.

Nell, E.J. 1996. "Wicksell after Sraffa" in Mongiovi and Petri (eds)

Nell, E.J. 1997. *Keynes after Sraffa: The General Theory of Transformational Growth.* New York: Cambridge University Press.

Nell, E.J., and T.F. Phillips. 1995. "Transformational Growth and the Business Cycle". *Eastern Economic Journal.* 21 (2). 125–42.

Nell, E.J., and W. Semmler (eds). 1991. *Nicholas Kaldor and Mainstream Economics.* London: Macmillan.

Nelson, C.R., and C.I. Plosser. 1982. "Trends and Random Walks in Macroeconomic Time Series: Some Evidence and Implications." *Journal of Monetary Economics.* 10. 139–62.

Nelson, D. 1949. *Arsenal of Democracy.* New York: De Capo.

Nelson, R. 1959. *Merger Movements in American Industry, 1895–1956.* Princeton: Princeton University Press.

Nelson, R and S. Winter. 1982. *An Evolutionary Theory of Economic Change.* Cambridge, MA: Belknap Press.

Nickell, S.J. 1978. *The Investment Decisions of Firms.* Cambridge: Cambridge University Press.

Nield, R.R. 1963. "Pricing and Employment in the Trade Cycle: A Study of British Manufacturing Industry." Occasional Paper 21. Washington, DC: National Institute of Economic and Social Research.

Noda, T. 1979. "Prices" in K. Ohkawa and M. Shinohara (eds) *Patterns of Japanese Economic Development: A Quantitative Appraisal.* New Haven: Yale University Press.

North, D.C. 1991. *Institutions, Institutional Change and Economic Performance.* Cambridge, MA: Cambridge University Press.

North, D.C. 1993. "What do we Mean by Rationality?" *Public Choice.* 77. 159–63.

REFERENCES

North, D.C., and R.P. Thomas. 1973. *The Rise of the Western World: A New Economic History*. Cambridge: Cambridge University Press.

Nurske, R. 1953. *Problems of Capital Formation in Underdeveloped Countries*. Oxford: Oxford University Press.

Ochoa, E. 1984. "Labor Values and Prices of Production." Unpublished Ph.D. dissertation. New School for Social Research, New York.

O'Donnell, G. 1978. "State and Alliances in Argentina, 1956–1976." *Journal of Development Studies*. 12. 3–33.

Ohkawa, K. 1957. *The Growth Rate of the Japanese Economy since 1878*. Tokyo: Kinokuniya.

Ohkawa, K. 1979. "Aggregate Growth and Product Allocation" in K. Ohkawa and M. Shinohara (eds) *Patterns of Japanese Economic Development: A Quantitative Appraisal*. New Haven: Yale University Press.

Ohkawa, K., and M. Shinohara (eds). 1979. *Patterns of Japanese Economic Development: A Quantitative Appraisal*. New Haven: Yale University Press.

Okun, A. 1981. *Prices and Quantities*. Washington, DC: Bookings Institution.

Olivera, J. 1964. "On Structural Inflation and Latin American 'Structuralism'." *Oxford Economic Papers*. 16. 321–332.

Olsen, D.E. 1973. "Utility and profit maximization by an owner-manager." *Southern Economic Journal*. 39. 389–95.

Organization for Economic Cooperation and Development. 1994. *Economic Survey*. Paris: OECD.

Osiatynski, J. 1990. *The Collected Works of Michal Kalecki 1 Capitalism: Business Cycles and Full Employment*. Oxford: Clarendon Press.

Ott, A.E. 1979. *Grundzüge der Preistheorie*. Göettingen: Vandenhoeck & Ruprecht.

Pacey, A. 1976. *The Maze of Ingenuity: Ideas and Idealism in the Development of Technology*. Cambridge, MA: MIT Press.

Papadimitriou, D. (ed.). 1992. *Profits, Deficits and Instability*. London: Macmillan.

Pasinetti, L. 1981. *Structural Change and Economic Growth: A Theoretical Essay on the Dynamics of the Wealth of Nations*. Cambridge: Cambridge University Press.

Pasinetti, L. 1975. *Growth and Income Distribution*. Cambridge: Cambridge University Press.

Pasinetti, L. 1977. *Lectures on the Theory of Production*. New York: Columbia University Press.

Pasinetti, L. 1960. "A Mathematical Formulation of the Ricardian System." *Review of Economic Studies*. 27. 78–98.

Patinkin, D. 1947. "Multiple-plant Firms, Cartels, and Imperfect Competition." *Quarterly Journal of Economics*. 61. 173-205.

Patinkin, D. 1965. *Money, Interest and Prices*. Second edition. New York: Harper & Row.

Patrick, H., and T. Rohlen. 1987. "Small-scale Family Enterprises" in K. Yamamura and Y. Yasuba (eds) *The Political Economy of Japan 1 The Domestic Transformation*. Stanford: Stanford University Press.

Peacock, A.T., and J. Wiseman. 1961. *The Growth of Public Expenditure in the United Kingdom*. Princeton: Princeton University Press.

Peck, M. 1976. "Technology" in H. Patrick and H. Rosovsky (eds) *Asia's New Giant: How the Japanese Economy Works*. Washington, DC: Brookings Institution.

351

REFERENCES

Pedersen, J. and O. Pedersen. 1938. *An Analysis of Price Behaviour.* London: Oxford University Press.

Penrose, E. 1954. *A Theory of the Growth of the Firm.* Oxford: Blackwell.

Penrose, E. 1974. *The Large International Firm.* London: Oxford University Press.

Perez, C. 1983. "Structural Change and Assimilation of New Technologies in Economic Social Systems." *Futures.* 12. 357–75.

Perez, C. 1985. "Microelectronics, Long Waves and World Structural Change: New Perspectives for Developing Economies." *World Development.* 13 (3). 441–63.

Peukert, H. 1995. "Das Handlungsparadigma in der Nationalökonomie". Unpublished Habilitation, Department of Economics, University of Frankfurt.

Phelps Brown, H., and S. Hopkins. 1981. *A Perspective of Wages and Prices.* London: Methuen.

Pickering, J.F. 1971. "The Prices and Incomes Board and Private Sector Prices: A Survey." *Economic Journal.* 81. 225–41.

Pierce, D.A. 1975. "On Trend and Autocorrelation", *Communications in Statistics.* 4. 163–75.

Pigou, A.C. 1927. *Industrial Fluctuations.* London: Macmillan. Reprinted New York: Augustus Kelley.

Pigou, A.C. 1944. *Employment and Equilibrium.* London: Macmillan.

Pindyck, R.S., and D.L. Rubinfeld. 1991. *Econometric Models and Economic Forecasts.* Third edition. McGraw-Hill.

Polanyi, K. 1944. *The Great Transformation: The Political and Economic Origins of our Time.* Boston: Beacon Press.

Polster, W., and K. Voy. 1991. "Von der politischen Regulierung zur Selbstregulierung der Märkte. Die Entwicklung von Wirtschafts – und Ordnungspolitik in der Bundesrepublik" in K. Voy *et al.* (eds) *Marktwirtschaft und politische Regulierung.* Marburg: Metropolis.

Portes, A., M. Castells and L Benton. 1989. *The Informal Economy: Studies in Advanced and Less Developed Countries.* Baltimore: Johns Hopkins University Press.

Prescott, E.C. 1986. "Theory ahead of Business Cycle Measurement." *Federal Reserve Bank of Minneapolis Review.* 10 (4). 9–22.

Rae, J.B. 1968. *Climb to Greatness.* Cambridge, MA: MIT Press.

Ricardo, D. 1951. *On the Principles of Political Economy and Taxation.* P. Sraffa (ed.). Cambridge: Cambridge University Press.

Rich, G. 1988. *The Cross of Gold: Money and the Canadian Business Cycle.* Ottawa: Carlton University Press.

Ritter, G.A., and K. Tenfelde. 1992. *Arbeiter im deutschen Kaiserreich 1871 bis 1914.* Bonn: Dietz Verlag.

Robbins, L. 1930. "The Conception of Stationary Equilibrium." *Economic Journal.* 40. 194–214.

Robbins, L. 1935. *An Essay on the Nature and Significance of Economic Science.* Second edition. London: Macmillan.

Robertson, D. 1931. "Wage Grumbles" in his *Economic Fragments.* P.S. King & Son Ltd. 42–57.

Robertson, D. 1957. *Lectures on Economic Principles.* London: Fontana.

Robertson, D. 1962. *Money.* Chicago: University of Chicago Press.

REFERENCES

Robinson, E.A.G. 1931. *The Structure of Competitive Industry.* Cambridge: Cambridge University Press.

Robinson, J. 1962. *Essays in the Theory of Economic Growth.* London: Macmillan.

Robinson, J. 1980. *Collected Economic Papers* 5. Cambridge, MA: MIT Press.

Rockoff, H., and G.M. Walton. 1991. *History of the American Economy.* San Diego: Harcourt Brace Jovanovich.

Rodriguez, C. 1979. "El plan argentino de estabilización del 20 de Diciembre." Mimeo. Buenos Aires: CEMA.

Romer, C. 1986a. "New Estimates of Prewar Gross National Product and Unemployment." *Journal of Economic History.* 46 (2). 341–52.

Romer, C. 1986b. "Is the Stabilization of the Postwar Economy a Figment of the Data?" *American Economic Review.* 76. 314–39.

Romer, C. 1989. "The Prewar Business Cycle Reconsidered: New Estimates of Gross National Product, 1869–1908." *Journal of Political Economy.* 97 (1). 1–37.

Romer, C. 1994. "The End of Economic History?" *Journal of Economic Education.* 25 (1). 49–66.

Rorty, R. 1991. *Objectivity, Relativism and Truth.* Cambridge: Cambridge University Press.

Rosenberg, A. 1992. *Economics: Mathematical Politics or Science of Diminishing Returns.* Chicago: University of Chicago Press.

Rosenberg, A. 1994. "Does Evolutionary Theory give Inspiration to Economics?" in P. Mirowski (ed.) *Natural Images in Economic Thought.* Cambridge: Cambridge University Press. 384–407.

Rostow, W.W. 1990a. *The Stages of Economic Growth.* Third edition. Cambridge: Cambridge University Press.

Rostow, W.W. 1990b. *Theories of Economic Growth from David Hume to the Present.* New York: Oxford University Press.

Rotemberg, J.J., and M. Woodford. 1995. "Dynamic General Equilibrium Models with Imperfectly Competitive Product Markets" in T. F. Cooley (ed.) *Frontiers in Business Cycle Research,* Princeton: Princeton University Press.

Rozenwurcel, G. 1985. "La restricción externa antes y después de la deuda." Buenos Aires: Documento CEDES.

Rymes, T.K. (ed.). 1989. *Keynes's Lectures, 1932–35: Notes of a Representative Student.* Ann Arbor: University of Michigan Press.

Sabel, C. 1982. *Work and Politics.* Cambridge: Cambridge University Press.

Samuelson, P. 1989. "Revisionist Findings on Sraffa" in K. Bharadwaj and B. Schefold (eds). *Essays on Piero Sraffa.* London: Routledge.

Samuelson, P., and W. Nordhaus. 1990. *Economics.* Thirteenth edition. New York: McGraw-Hill.

Sargent, T. 1987. *Macroeconomic Theory.* Second edition. New York: Academic Press.

Sayers, R. 1957. *Central Banking after Bagehot.* London: Oxford University Press.

Schabas, M. 1995. "Parmenides and the Cliometricians" in D. Little (ed.) *The Reliability of Economic Models.* Dordrecht and Boston, MA: Kluwer.

Schelling, T. 1960. *Strategy of Conflict.* Cambridge, MA: Harvard University Press.

Scherer, F.M. 1971. *Industrial Market Structure and Economic Performance.* Chicago: Rand McNally.

353

REFERENCES

Schoeffler, S. 1955. *The Failures of Economics: A Diagnostic Study.* Cambridge, MA: Harvard University Press.
Schroeder, W. H. 1980. "Die Entwicklung der Arbeitszeit im sekundären Sektor in Deutschland 1871 bis 1913." *Technikgeschichte.* 47 (3). 252–302.
Schumpeter, J. 1934. *The Theory of Economic Development.* New York: Harper.
Schumpeter, J. 1942. *Capitalism, Socialism and Democracy.* New York: Harper.
Schvarzer, J. 1983. *José Martínez de Hoz: la lógica política de la política económica.* Buenos Aires: CISEA.
Schvarzer, J. 1989. *Bunge y Born. Crecimiento y diversificación de un grupo económico.* Buenos Aires: CISEA/GEL.
Schvarzer, J. 1996. *La industria que supimos conseguir. Una historia político-social de la industria argentina.* Buenos Aires: Planeta.
Schwert, G.W. 1987. "Effects of Model Specification on Tests for Unit Roots in Macroeconomic Data." *Journal of Monetary Economics.* 20. 75–103.
Semmler, W., and R. Franke. 1996. "The Financial–Real Interaction, and Investment in the Business Cycle: Theories and Empirical Evidence" in G. Deleplace and E.J. Nell (eds) *Money in Motion,* London: Macmillan. 606–34.
Sheffrin, S.M. 1989. *The Making of Economic Policy.* Oxford: Blackwell.
Shepherd, W.G. 1989. "On the Nature of Monopoly" in S. Bowles *et al.* (eds) *Unconventional Wisdom.* Boston, MA: Houghton Mifflin. 161–87.
Shillinglaw, G. 1978. "Economic Concepts in Cost Accounting" in S. Davidson and R. Weil (eds) *Handbook of Cost Accounting.* New York: McGraw-Hill.
Shimokawa, K. 1985. "Japan's *Keiretsu* System: The Case of the Automobile Industry." *Japanese Economic Studies.* 13(4). 3–31.
Shingo, S. 1980. *A Study of the Toyota Production System from an Industrial Engineering Viewpoint.* Cambridge, MA: Productivity Press.
Simonson, G.R. 1960. "The Demand for Aircraft and the Aircraft Industry, 1907–1958." *Journal of Economic History.* 20 (3). 361–82.
Simonson, G.R. (ed.) 1968. *The History of the American Aircraft Industry.* Cambridge, MA: MIT Press.
Skidelsky, R. 1992. *John Maynard Keynes* 1–2. New York: Viking.
Sloan, A.P. 1972. *My Years with General Motors.* New York: Doubleday.
Smeets, H.-D. 1992. "'Stylized Facts' zum Konjunkturverlauf in der Bundesrepublik Deutschland." *Jahrbuch für Nationalökonomie und Statistik.* 210 (5-6). 512–32.
Smith, A. 1961 [1776]. *An Inquiry into the Nature and Causes of the Wealth of Nations.* Cannan edition. London: Methuen.
Smith, T. 1955. *Political Change and Industrial Development in Japan: Government Enterprise, 1868–1880.* Stanford: Stanford University Press.
Snyder, C. 1924. "New Measures in the Equation of Exchange." *American Economic Review.* 14. 698–713.
Solomou, S. 1987. *Phases and Economic Growth, 1850–1973: Kondratieff Waves and Kuznets Swings.* Cambridge: Cambridge University Press.
Solon, G., R. Barsky, and J.A. Parker. 1994. "Measuring the Cyclicality of Real Wages: How Important is Composition Bias?" *Quarterly Journal of Economics.* 109. 1–25.
Sombart, W. 1929. "Economic Theory and Economic History." *Economic History Review.* 2 (1). 1–19.
Sorenson, C.E. 1956. *My Forty Years with Ford.* New York: Norton.

REFERENCES

Sourrouille, J., B. Kosacoff and J. Lucangeli. 1985. *Transnacionalización y política económica en la Argentina*. Buenos Aires: Centro Editor de America Latina.

Spaventa, L. 1970. "Rate of Profit, Rate of Growth, and Capital Intensity in a Simple Production Model." *Oxford Economic Papers*. 22. 129–47.

Spiethoff, A. 1955 [1925]. *Die wirtschaftlichen Wechsellagen. Aufschwung, Krise, Stockung*. Tübingen.

Spree, R. 1978. *Wachstumstrends und Konjunkturzyklen in der deutschen Wirtschaft 1820 bis 1913*. Göttingen: Vandenhoeck & Ruprecht.

Sraffa, P. 1926. "The Laws of Returns under Competitive Conditions." *Economic Journal*. 36. 535–50.

Sraffa, P. 1960. *Production of Commodities by Means of Commodities*. Cambridge: Cambridge University Press.

Stadler, G. 1994. "Real Business Cycles." *Journal of Economic Literature*. XXXII. 1750–83.

Statistisches Bundesamt. 1991. *Volkswirtschaftliche Gesamtrechnungen 1950–1990. Revidierte Ergebnisse*. Stuttgart: Metzler-Poeschel.

Steedman, I. 1977. *Marx after Sraffa*. London: Verso.

Steindl, J. 1976. *Maturity and Stagnation in American Capitalism*. New York: Monthly Review Press.

Stigler, G. 1951. "The Division of Labor is Limited by the Extent of the Market." *Journal of Political Economy*. 59 (3). 185–93.

Stigler, G. 1968. "The Dominant Firm and the Inverted Umbrella" in his *The Organization of Industry*. Homewood, IL: Irwin. 108–12.

Stolper, G. 1967. *The German Economy: 1870 to the Present*. New York: Harcourt.

Stone, L. 1981. "History and the Social Sciences" in his *The Past and the Present*. Boston, MA: Routledge.

Stoughton, B. 1949. *History of the Tools Division, War Production Board*. New York: McGraw-Hill.

Sutcliffe, R.B. 1971. *Industry and Underdevelopment*. London: Addison-Wesley.

Sylos-Labini, P. 1969. *Oligopoly and Technical Progress*. Cambridge, MA: Harvard University Press.

Sylos-Labini, P. 1984. *The Forces of Economic Growth and Decline*. Cambridge, MA: MIT Press.

Sylos-Labini, P. 1989. "Changes in the Character of the so-called Business Cycle." *Atlantic Economic Journal*. 19 (3), pp. 1–14.

Sylos-Labini, P. 1993. *Economic Growth and Business Cycles*. Aldershot: Edward Elgar.

Szostak. R. 1994. *Technological Innovation and the Great Depression*. Chicago: Westview Press.

Tabb, W. 1995. *The Postwar Japanese System: Cultural Economy and Economic Transformation*. New York: Oxford University Press.

Targetti. F. 1989. *Nicholas Kaldor*. Oxford: Oxford University Press.

Tarshis, L. 1939. "Changes in Real and Money Wages." *Economic Journal*. XLIX. 150–4.

Taylor, F.W. 1911. *The Principles of Scientific Management*. New York: Harper.

Taylor, J.B. 1986. "Improvements in Macroeconomic Stability: The Role of Wages and Prices" in R.J. Gordon (ed.) *The American Business Cycle*. Chicago: University of Chicago Press. 639–79.

REFERENCES

Taylor, L. 1991. *Income Distribution, Inflation and Growth: Lectures on Structuralist Macroeconomics.* Cambridge, MA: MIT Press.

Thomas, M. 1987. "General Equilibrium Models and Research in Economic History" in A.J. Fields (ed.) *The Future of Economic History,* Boston, MA: Kluwer-Nijhoff.

Thomson, R. 1993. "Economic Forms of Technological Change" in R. Thomson (ed.) *Learning and Technical Change.* New York: St Martin's Press.

Tichy, G. 1994. *Konjunktur. Stilisierte Fakten, Theorie, Prognose.* Berlin: Springer Verlag.

Tirole, J. 1988. *The Theory of Industrial Organization.* Cambridge, MA: MIT Press.

Tobin, J. 1980. *Asset Accumulation and Economic Activity.* Chicago: University of Chicago Press.

Tobin, J. (ed.). 1983. *Macroeconomics, Prices and Quantities.* Oxford: Blackwell.

Tylecote, A. 1991. *The Long Wave in the World Economy.* London: Routledge.

US Department of Commerce. 1966. *Long Term Economic Growth 1860–1965.* Washington, DC: US Department of Commerce.

US Senate, Special Committee to Investigate the National Defence Program. 1941–48. *Hearings* and *Reports.* Washington, DC: US Government Printing Office.

Urquhart, M.C. 1965. *Historical Statistics of Canada.* London: Macmillan.

Urquhart, M.C. 1986. "New Estimates of Gross National Product, Canada, 1870–1926: Some Implications for Canadian Development" in S.L. Engerman and R.E. Gallman (eds) *Long-term Factors in American Economic Growth.* NBER Studies in Income and Wealth 51. Chicago: University of Chicago Press.

Vatter, H.G. 1985. *The US Economy in World War II.* New York: Columbia University Press.

Veblen, T. 1964 [1923]. *Absentee Ownership.* New York: Huebsch.

Vilar, P. 1969. *A History of Gold and Money, 1450–1920.* London: New Left Books.

Villanueva, J. 1972. "El origen de la industrialización argentina." *Desarrollo Economico.* 15 (59). 451–76.

Viner, J. 1958. *The Long Run and the Short.* Glencoe, IL: Free Press.

Wade, R. 1990. *Governing the Market.* Princeton: Princeton University Press.

Wagner, A. 1883. *Finanzwissenschaft* Second edition. 1890. Leipzig. Translated and reprinted in R.A. Musgrave and A.T. Peacock (eds). *Classics in the Theory of Public Finance* London: Macmillan, 1958.

Wagoner, H.D. 1968. *The US Machine Tool Industry from 1900 to 1950.* Cambridge, MA: MIT Press.

Waldrop, M. 1992. *Complexity: The Emerging Science at the Edge of Order and Chaos.* New York: Simon & Schuster.

Walras, L. 1926. *Elements of Pure Economics* or *The Theory of Social Wealth.* Ed. W. Jaffe, London: Allen & Unwin, 1954.

Walsh, V., and H. Gram. 1980. *Classical and Neoclassical Theories of General Equilibrium.* Oxford: Oxford University Press.

Warren, G.F., and F.H. Pearson. 1933. *Prices.* New York: Wiley.

Weber, M. 1949. "Critical Studies in the Logic of the Cultural Sciences" in E.A. Shils and H.A. Finch (eds) *Max Weber on the Methodology of the Social Sciences.* Glencoe, IL: Free Press. 113-63.

REFERENCES

Weintraub, S. 1978. *Capitalism's Inflation and Unemployment Crises*. Reading, MA: Addison-Wesley.

Weintraub, S., and H. Habibagahi. 1971. "Keynes and the Quantity Theory Elasticities." *Nebraska Journal of Economics and Business*. Reprinted in *Keynes, Keynesians and Monetarists*. Philadelphia: University of Pennsylvania Press 1978. 61–75.

Weisberg, D. 1967. *Guild Structure and Political Allegiance in Early Achaemenid Mesopotamia*. New Haven: Yale University Press.

Wells, P. 1960. "Keynes' Aggregate Supply Function: A Suggested Interpretation", *Economic Journal*. 70. 377–98.

White, G.T. 1980. *Billions for Defence*. University, AL: University of Alabama Press.

Wicksell, K. 1898. *Interest and Prices*. Trans. R.F. Kahn, 1936. London: Macmillan.

Wicksell, K. 1935. *Lectures on Political Economy* 1–2. Trans. E. Classen ed. Lionel Robbins. New York: Macmillan.

Wicksell, K. 1958. *Selected Papers on Economic Theory*. London: Allen & Unwin.

Wiggins, D. 1980. *Sameness and Substance*. Oxford: Blackwell.

Williamson, J.G. 1995. "The Evolution of Global Labor Markets since 1830: Background Evidence and Hypotheses." *Explorations in Economic History*. 32. 141–96.

Williamson, O.E. 1964. *The Economics of Discretionary Behavior: Managerial Objectives in the Theory of the Firm*. Englewood Cliffs, NJ: Prentice-Hall.

Williamson, O.E. 1980. "The Organization of Work: A Comparative Institutional Assessment." *Journal of Economic Behavior and Organization*. 1. 5–38.

Wilson, T., and P.W.S. Andrews. 1951. *Oxford Studies in the Price Mechanism*. Oxford: Clarendon Press.

Wolf, C. 1991. *La reestructuración industrial reciente en Argentina*. Buenos Aires: CONICET.

Wolfson, M. 1987. "Science and History: Economics and Thermodynamics." Paper presented at the fourteenth History of Economics meeting, Boston, MA.

Wood, A. 1978. *A Theory of Profit*. Cambridge: Cambridge University Press.

Woods, J.E. 1978. *Mathematical Economics*. New York: Longman.

Wray, L.R. 1990. *Endogenous Money*. Aldershot: Edward Elgar.

Wylie, P.J. (1989) "Technological Adaptation in Canadian Manufacturing, 1900–29," *Journal of Economic History* 49: 569–91.

Yamazawa, I., and Y. Yamamoto. 1979. "Trade and Balance of Payments" in K. Ohkawa and M. Shinohara (eds) *Patterns of Japanese Economic Development: A Quantitative Appraisal*. New Haven: Yale University Press.

Yoshihara, K. 1994. *Japanese Economic Development*. Third edition. Oxford: Oxford University Press.

Zarnowitz, V. 1985. "Recent Work on Business Cycles in Historical Perspective: A Review of Theories and Evidence." *Journal of Economic Literature*. 23. 523–80.

Zarnowitz, V. 1986. "Major Changes in Cyclical Behavior" in R.J. Gordon (ed.) *The American Business Cycle*, Chicgo: University of Chicago Press. 529-82.

Zarnowitz, V. 1992. *Business Cycles: Theory, History, Indicators, and Forecasting*. Chicago: University of Chicago Press.

INDEX

absorption, exports and (Canada) 151–2
accelerator 4; multiplier-accelerator mechanism 23–4, 142, 225, 288, 293, 300, 308, 317
Ackley, G. 242
administered prices 114–19
Aftalion, A. 43
aggregate demand 21, 27, 29–30, 34, 201–2, 227, 271, 289, 317
aggregate employment, market adjustment and 25–40
agriculture 301; Argentina 257, 261, 262, 264, 271, 272
Agriculture Department (Canada) 76
Air Material Planning Council 96
Aircraft Industries Association of America 88, 91–2, 95, 96
aircraft industry (USA) 80, 87–109
Aircraft Production Board 98
Aircraft War Production Council 88, 91
Akerlof, G. 323–4
Alchian, A. 116
Aldrich Report (1892) 195
Allen, G. 234, 235, 236–7, 238
Altman, M. 135–6, 141, 147–8, 154, 328
Amadeo, E. 225
American Economic Review 81, 163, 166, 172, 173
Amsden, A. 240
analysis methods, rationality and 319–22
Andic, S. 204
Andrews, P. W. S. 116
Argentina: Canada and (comparison)

280–2; economic behavior/characteristics 81, 254–77
Argyrous, George 9, 97
ARMA corrections 245
artisan system 8, 9, 11–13, 318
associations (Canada) 143–4
augmented Dickey–Fuller test 179, 245
Auto Pact (1964) 281
automobile industry (USA) 93–4, 97–103
average-cost rule 170–1, 173
average variable cost 182
Azipiazu, D. 270

Backus, D. K. 66, 135, 210
Bain, J. S. 116, 117–18, 126
balance of payments (Argentina) 255, 262, 265, 270, 271, 273
Balke, N. S. 75, 135, 137, 193–4, 196, 328
Bank of Japan 239
banking system 44
bankruptcies 33, 139, 149
Barnes, R. M. 15, 38
Baron, S. 119
BASF 208
batch production 9, 19, 140
Baumol, W. J. 116, 301
Baxter, M. 77, 211
Bayer 208
behavioral theory 116
Bell, S. 124
Berle, A. A. 114, 117
Blair, J. M. 115, 126–7
Blanchard, O. J. 48–9
Boehm-Bawerk, E. 116
Bohr model 313–14
Bollinger, L. L. 90